Praise for *The Last Castle*

"This is fantastic stuff . . ."

—*The Atlanta Journal-Constitution*

"It's about celebrity culture, wealth disparity, the remarkable charity and foresight of a few wealthy people, the urge to create and maintain a family legacy and, in its darker moments, the ever-present potential for personal tragedy. It's grounded in Kiernan's years of globe-trotting research and yet also immediately relevant to the topics that clog social media in 2017."

—*Asheville Citizen-Times*

"Intriguing . . . With plenty of famous characters sprinkled throughout, there is enough action and history to keep readers engaged and eager to turn the pages . . . Kiernan fans and those new to her work are sure to devour this latest volume."

—*Library Journal*

"*The Last Castle* is Edith Wharton's *The Age of Innocence* sprung to life . . . Biltmore is an ideal vessel for an exploration of our worship of affluence and social cachet, and more importantly, the American myth of classlessness. *The Last Castle* plumbs these themes and history with subtle insight and élan."

—*Knoxville News Sentinel*

"*The Last Castle* gripped me from the very first page. With a historian's keen insight and a poet's gift for language, Denise Kiernan depicts life at Biltmore with such skill, I felt like I was there through it all: weddings, divorces, elaborate (and slightly bizarre) balls, financial glory, financial ruin, murder, suicide, natural disasters, betrayals, love, loss, despair, and triumph. The story of George and Edith Vanderbilt's remarkable lives will stay with me for a long time to come."

—KAREN ABBOTT, *New York Times* bestselling author of
Liar, Temptress, Soldier, Spy

"For those who couldn't get enough of *Downton Abbey, The Last Castle* might satisfy that desire to peer into the lives of wealthy members of the reigning elite."

—Bookreporter.com

"If you inherited billions, how would you spend it? Don't bother building America's largest and most lavish home. It's already been done in the Blue Ridge Mountains of North Carolina, where more than a million visitors a year stroll the grounds of Biltmore Estate. Yet only in the pages of Denise Kiernan's *The Last Castle* will they come to know George Vanderbilt, the bookish heir who began Biltmore in his twenties, and his determined widow, Edith, who kept it alive as a working estate and a time capsule of the Gilded Age. In the pages of *The Last Castle*, Kiernan serves up a true tale of American excess, generosity, and perseverance."

—BILL DEDMAN, *New York Times* bestselling author of
*Empty Mansions: The Mysterious Life of Huguette Clark
and the Spending of a Great American Fortune*

"A story that brings the glitz and glamour of the British royal family to American soil . . . Reigning royalty of the Gilded Age, Edith and George Vanderbilt and their lifetime of financial excess, ruins, scandal, and perseverance come alive on these pages."

—RealSimple.com

"This is as much a story about the creation of Biltmore House as it is a window into what it was like to be an American at the turn of the twentieth century. Kiernan makes Edith and George Vanderbilt, among the wealthiest Americans at the time, feel like living, breathing human beings navigating life's obstacles in this magnificent book. And she tells the story of how one fiercely devoted woman was able to save the home her husband loved."

—KATE ANDERSEN BROWER, author of *First Women:
The Grace and Power of America's Modern First Ladies* and
The Residence: Inside the Private World of the White House

"The rich have secrets. In her well-researched and captivating book, Denise Kiernan tells the fascinating story of how a phenomenally wealthy Vanderbilt scion transformed a rural North Carolina town by building the ultimate rich man's folly and reveals the eccentricities, heartaches, and even money problems of these Social Register denizens and their friends and employees."

—MERYL GORDON, author of *Bunny Mellon: The Life of an American Style Legend*

"The many diverting detours Kiernan takes make the book enticing for even those who will never set foot on Biltmore grounds."

—*Booklist*

"This is a timely and timeless American story of wealth and the responsibility and opportunity it carries. In Kiernan's hands, this mashup of *Downton Abbey*–like extravagance set amid the 'rugged mountain simplicity' of Appalachia reads like a Southern fairy tale—Brothers Grimm meets *Gone with the Wind*. A passionately researched family saga of death and divorce, suicide and sickness, fortunes gained and lost, spanning two World Wars and set at the crux of the Gilded Age yielding to the modern era, *The Last Castle* is ultimately a story of fortitude and survival. A stunning and important achievement."

—NEAL THOMPSON, author of *A Curious Man: The Strange and Brilliant Life of Robert "Believe It or Not!" Ripley*

"A story that is both intimate and sweeping."

—*Raleigh News & Observer*

"Evokes the grandeur of Biltmore."

—*Shelf Awareness for Readers*

"Denise Kiernan's book offers an entertaining and meticulously researched glimpse into faded grandeur . . . *The Last Castle* will appeal to audiences who delighted in *Downton Abbey* and who look forward to its creator Julian Fellowes's new series—aptly titled *The Gilded Age*."

—*The Weekly Standard*

THE
LAST CASTLE

THE EPIC STORY OF
LOVE, LOSS, AND AMERICAN ROYALTY
IN THE NATION'S LARGEST HOME

DENISE KIERNAN

ATRIA PAPERBACK

New York   London   Toronto   Sydney   New Delhi

ATRIA
PAPERBACK

An Imprint of Simon & Schuster, Inc.
1230 Avenue of the Americas
New York, NY 10020

This Atria Paperback edition October 2019
Previously published in 2017 by Touchstone, an imprint of Simon & Schuster, Inc.

ATRIA PAPERBACK and colophon are registered trademarks of Simon & Schuster, Inc.

For information about special discounts for bulk purchases,
please contact Simon & Schuster Special Sales at 1-866-506-1949
or business@simonandschuster.com.

The Simon & Schuster Speakers Bureau can bring authors to your live event.
For more information or to book an event, contact the Simon & Schuster Speakers Bureau
at 866-248-3049 or visit our website at www.simonspeakers.com.

Interior design by Erich Hobbing
The cover image is used with permission of The Biltmore Company, Asheville, N.C.
Architectural drawings of Richard Morris Hunt, Prints & Photographs Division,
Library of Congress, Washington, D.C.

Manufactured in the United States of America

15   16   17   18   19   20

The Library of Congress has cataloged the hardcover edition as follows:
Names: Kiernan, Denise. author.
Title: The last castle : the epic story of love, loss, and American royalty
in the nation's largest home / Denise Kiernan.
Description: First Touchstone hardcover edition. | New York : Touchstone,
2017. | Includes bibliographical references.
Identifiers: LCCN 2017015229 (print) | LCCN 2017017046 (ebook) |
ISBN 9781476794068 (eBook) | ISBN 9781476794044 (hardcover) |
ISBN9781476794051 (pbk.)
Subjects: LCSH: Biltmore Estate (Asheville, N.C.)—History. | Vanderbilt,
Edith Stuyvesant Dresser, 1873–1958. | Vanderbilt, George Washington, 1862–1914.
Classification: LCC F264.A8 (ebook) | LCC F264.A8 K54 2017 (print) |
DDC 975.6/88—dc23
LC record available at https://lccn.loc.gov/2017015229

ISBN 978-1-4767-9404-4
ISBN 978-1-4767-9405-1 (pbk)
ISBN 978-1-4767-9406-8 (ebook)

For Joe

CONTENTS

THE
LAST CASTLE

1

A Winter's Tale

That was the year she started spending her winters in New York again.

Edith Dresser was fifteen years old when her grandmother, Susan Elizabeth Fish LeRoy, decided that she and the Dresser children would leave their Rhode Island home for the Christmas season. The year was 1888. Seasonal migrations from Newport to New York were common among their privileged set, and the allure of the great city on the Hudson still drew their grandmother into its predictably casted embrace. Grandmother was a woman at ease in the world of drawing rooms and calling cards, one who appreciated both the ritualistic behaviors and increased social diversions that New York could be counted on to provide. "New Amsterdam"—as Manhattan had once been known—had been home to their family's Dutch ancestors. Now Grandmother, in turn, had become all that constituted home and family to Edith, her three sisters, and brother.

Grandmother had arranged to rent a house at 2 Gramercy Square, a very respectable—if not ultra-fashionable—address for the family. Its next-door twin, 1 Gramercy, had been the last home of the noted surgeon and professor Dr. Valentine Mott. Mott had helped establish the short-lived Rutgers Medical College in lower Manhattan, and gained attention as the chair of surgery at both the University Medical College of NYU and Columbia's College of Physicians and Surgeons. More salaciously, he earned some notoriety as a disruptor of all that was good and pure in the world of medical instruction when he promoted the idea of using human cadavers to instruct up-and-coming clinicians. His good works and surgical brilliance kept his reputation intact, even though the good doctor was known to have disguised himself as a laborer and visited graveyards to retrieve recently unearthed teaching aids.

Around the corner on the south side of Gramercy Square, at No. 16, was the brand-new Players Club, which was opening that winter. The building had been purchased by the actor Edwin Booth, who could currently be seen as Brutus in a production of *Julius Caesar*. Twenty-three years earlier, Booth had announced his retirement following his deranged brother John Wilkes Booth's assassination of President Abraham Lincoln. Distraught over his brother's actions, Edwin penned an open letter to "the People of the United States," which was published in several newspapers:

"For the future alas," he wrote. "I shall struggle on in my retirement bearing a heavy heart, an oppressed memory and a wounded name—dreadful burdens—to my too welcome grave."

However, he curtailed his retirement to a nine-month hiatus from the limelight, returning to the stage—and welcome audiences—in 1866 as Hamlet, a role he continued to reprise. The newly founded Players Club would house an impressive library of theater history, as well as collections of paintings and autographs. Booth wrote a friend that he wanted the club to "be a place where actors are away from the glamour of the theatre," and that thespians should spend more time mingling with minds that "influence the world." To that end, founding members of the club included author Mark Twain and the celebrated Union Army general William Tecumseh Sherman.

2 Gramercy Square, where young Edith and her family would be staying, was the home of the Pinchot family—businessman James Wallace Pinchot; his wife, Mary Jane Eno Pinchot; and their children, Gifford, Amos, and Antoinette. The Pinchot family had recently completed the building of a new Milford, Pennsylvania, home that had been designed by the noted New York City architect Richard Morris Hunt and subsequently dubbed "Grey Towers." The Pin-

chots' oldest son, Gifford, was away studying at Yale, and Edith and her sisters knew "Nettie" Pinchot from dancing class in Newport. The four-story brick house was Italianate in style, with cast-iron railings gracing its small balconies and floor-to-ceiling parlor windows. Edith's brother, Daniel—who went by his middle name "LeRoy"— was in his final year at Columbia, which meant that he would again be living under the same roof as his sisters. Susan, the oldest, was now twenty-four, and two years older than LeRoy. Natalie was nineteen and Pauline, the baby, was still just twelve. The family would be together, nestled in this house across from the gated park.

From outside those parlor windows looking in, one might have seen four young ladies and one young man living the kind of gleaming nineteenth-century life envied by scores of less fortunate citizens of the time. A closer inspection of their lives, however, revealed signs of difficulty and strain, like scuff marks hidden beneath the smooth veneer of a freshly polished parlor floor. They were five siblings, separated in age by twelve years; joined, as so many other families of the time were, by tragic loss.

■ ■ ■

Edith's parents had met at West Point, New York, where her father was a cadet and her mother, Susan Fish LeRoy, was staying nearby with her family at the Rose Hotel. After George Warren Dresser graduated from the United States Military Academy and posted at Fort Adams outside Susan's home of Newport, he pursued his love. It was not an easy road.

The Fish-LeRoy family was exceptionally well known in New York circles where names carried the weight of history and bore the shackles of expected romantic pairings. First, middle, last, and family names were shuffled around from generation to generation— perpetually recombining DNA of societal rank—so that they would always be a part of one's title, ensuring that even the smallest link to storied heritage was immediately evident upon one's first introduction. Fish . . . LeRoy . . . King . . . Schermerhorn . . . Stuyvesant.

Edith's mother had bestowed upon Edith a middle name taken from the surname of their ancestor, the famed Dutch governor Peter Stuyvesant. It would serve Edith in future times when money could not.

Edith's father was a congenial, accomplished, and educated man with an honorable if humbler background than that of her mother. George Warren Dresser was of New England stock, educated at Andover, and hailing from a line of teachers, farmers, and lawyers. Edith's grandfather Daniel LeRoy did not consider him an appropriate match for Edith's mother and objected vocally and often to George and Susan's union. But her mother's older sister, Aunty Mary King—who herself had made a predictably wealthy yet loveless match—stood firmly on the Dresser side of love. Aunty King welcomed George into her home in Newport, where he was free to call on her sister. Hearts won out. In April 1863 at Calvary Church in New York, a line of groomsmen in uniform stood proudly by as George Warren Dresser married Susan Fish LeRoy. Then George headed south to war along with classmates, volunteers, and countless immigrants just arrived from places like Ireland and Germany.

George rose from a second lieutenancy in the Fourth Artillery to major before the war ended. Along the way he fought in the Battle of Bull Run and commanded a company out of Chattanooga, Tennessee, where he played a vital part in securing federal supply lines against Confederate attack. Once the war ended, George's accolades mattered little to Edith's grandfather, who insisted his son-in-law resign from the military and give his daughter the opportunity to live a life more worthy of her bloodline.

George consented and began a career in civil engineering. He made friends easily, and acted as editor of the trade publication *American Gas Light Journal*. He had bright dark eyes, a barrel physique, and wore his hair parted down the middle with just the suggestion of a wave on each side. The lower half of his face was wreathed in the friendly muttonchops popularized by Civil War general Ambrose Burnside. George welcomed all into his home—

the children of friends, army comrades, gas workers. Edith's mother was more soft-spoken, attentive to her children, skilled with a needle and thread, and purposely eschewed much of the life laid out for her. She loved her George dearly.

Of any residences in New York or Newport, the one perhaps most deeply etched in the minds of the Dresser children was the house at 35 University Place. The salon on the front of the three-story home provided young Edith and her sisters a view through a French window of Manhattan life outside. Sitting among the brocade surroundings they watched the horse-drawn streetcars passing by. The sisters competed to see who could most quickly identify the car numbers as the vehicles made their way north in the direction of Times Square, hauled by a few of the hundreds of thousands of horses that powered the city's transportation, baptizing its streets with their urine and fertilizing whatever weeds managed to sprout between pavers with their manure.

In the back of the house, a glass conservatory overlooked the yard. From this vantage point, young Edith, all gangly legs and long, bone-straight hair, could keep an eye on her nineteen turtles. She watched as they basked happily within their shells in a warm spot, dove deep under the soil and brush to hibernate for the winter, and erupted from the earth for another season in the sun. Edith shared a room on the second floor with her two older sisters. It had one row of beds with a small conservatory outside that normally remained empty, save for the time Edith was quarantined there during a whooping cough episode. The servants' quarters were in the basement, where the children found an excellent roller-skating surface and there was always a soft perch for young Pauline atop warm, folded clothes.

It was a busy home, its halls reverberating with the broken English of French servants, the laughter of children, and the rumblings of adults at backgammon or immersed in conversation in the red library. Edith's brother, LeRoy, entertained friends in his domain on the third floor. George and Susan had visitors as well, even if the calendar of social events that regulated their world held little appeal for Edith's mother, who preferred to stay at home close to her children. Sunday evening suppers were for stewed oysters and roast chicken, often set upon a red tablecloth in the dining room. On Sunday, supper was eaten early—a high tea, as it was then called— and on those evenings Edith's father went to serve as a vestryman at Trinity Church's St. John's Chapel on Vesey Street. It took several transfers to arrive there by horsecar, but once in the hallowed space, the children watched as their father passed the collection plate among the pews.

In January 1883, the Hazelton Brothers piano factory across the street at 34–36 University Place erupted in flame. Servants and parents bundled the family's possessions into balls of sheets away from windows before the glass panes burst from the waves of heat emanating from the burning building. Once the flames subsided the Dressers were fortunate that their home survived relatively unscathed. Yet they did not avoid all tragedy.

Edith's mother had become ill during a recent trip to Europe. Her condition was worsening, and it prevented her from presenting Edith's sister Susan, then eighteen, to society. Luckily, her mother's friend Mrs. John Jacob Astor stepped in to help Susan along—a lovely gesture by a formidable doyenne of society. Still, months of increasing silence fell over the once lively household. Spring came and Edith's sister Pauline moved into the bedroom with her older sisters. Nurses arrived. Adults demanded quiet. Doors shut the inevitable from Edith's view.

One morning that April, the doors and windows of her mother's room were opened. The lifeless shell that was Edith's mother remained for the time being. Mourners and friends came and went. Edith went with Mrs. Woodworth, a family friend, to the clothiers Arnold Constable, where she was fitted for an appropriate outfit of black crepe to wear to her mother's service at Trinity. Edith's sister Susan fainted at the church.

Edith and her family could see that George's health was also waning. Still mourning her mother, Edith was faced with losing her father as well. Knowing the children would soon be orphaned, Edith's Aunty King offered to take Natalie to live with her. George begged his sister-in-law to keep the children together once he was gone, and Aunty King was soon called upon to keep her word. Edith's father died a little over a month after his wife. His funeral was held on a day best befitting his honorable career in the military—Decoration Day. Edith's parents were interred beside each other in the Newport cemetery. Edith was not yet ten years old.

Shortly after, Edith and her siblings went to Newport for what would turn out to be a lengthy stay. Her grandmother and that same, stern grandfather, the man who had frowned on his daughter's marriage to a New England army officer, took the children in. Daniel LeRoy was already eighty-five years of age, and Edith's grandmother was seventy-eight. The following year, 1884, he built a two-story addition onto the old red house at 206 Bellevue Avenue in Newport to accommodate his younger family members.

Grandfather passed away in 1885 at the age of eighty-seven, just two years after Edith's parents, his mind having departed well in advance of his body. Now, in 1888, Grandmother was bringing the Dresser brood back to New York. As another winter in the city ended, spring brought the emergence of shoots from age-old trunks, no one knowing which branches might cross and when, bending to the will of the wind.

■ ■ ■

That was also the year that another, more prominent, Manhattan resident had grown tired of New York winters and decided to make a change.

In 1888, George Washington Vanderbilt was twenty-five years old. As the youngest child of William Henry Vanderbilt and grandson of the infamously cutthroat tycoon Cornelius "Commodore" Vanderbilt, George may have wanted for nothing financially, but that hardly meant his life was void of all expectation. Quite the contrary. To be a son of the Vanderbilt dynasty was to have your every move, dalliance, chance encounter, and passing venture watched and analyzed, whether via opera glasses across the expanse of the Metropolitan Opera or by eager eyes scanning the society pages of the newspapers.

His grandfather Cornelius Vanderbilt had known much simpler times. Born in 1794, Cornelius had grown up on a farm on Staten Island, where the Vanderbilt family—or van der Bilt or van Derbilt, depending on who was signing their name—had lived for more than a century. His ancestors had seen Dutch rule pass to the English and then, finally, the birth of the American colonies. Through all the changing of guards and flags, many of the family continued to dwell within a world of their home country's language and religion. Though their farms expanded and the number of Vanderbilts multiplied, work remained arduous and compensation scant. Uneducated in the traditional sense, and lacking in the most common of courtesies, young Cornelius was a diligent worker. Whatever he lacked in finishing he made up for in grit and ambition. As the most popular version of the story goes, during Cornelius's youth, his mother, Phebe, offered him $100 to clear some acreage on the family land. Once the task was completed, Cornelius used those earnings to buy what the Native Americans in the region called a *piragua*. This "perry auger," a ramshackle boat, gave Cornelius access to the waters surrounding Staten Island, the same waters connecting their small island community to the nearby mecca of industry: Manhattan.

Thus Cornelius's New York Harbor ferry service was born, and his nickname—"Commodore"—soon followed. As his business grew, so did rumors of his ruthless dealings. The Commodore outworked and undercut competitors, making no friends but scads of money along the way. His ferries developed into steamship lines, which eventually gave way to railroad investments in the New York and Harlem, and New York and Hudson, lines. The Commodore possessed both a fondness and knack for manipulating railroad stocks, which helped him further stuff his rapidly expanding coffers. In 1867, he began construction on St. John's Freight Terminal, designed by architect John Butler Snook, on the site of St. John's Park near Trinity Church in lower Manhattan. The Hudson Street side of the freight terminal featured a not-so-subtle 150-foot-long bronze frieze featuring images from the Commodore's life, including his steam yacht, *North Star*, and various tools of the marine trade. In the midst of this sculptural scene was the man himself, regal and proud, a master of water and rail.

The Commodore finally consolidated his accumulating rail lines and created the New York Central railroad which, by 1870, would carry more than seven million passengers and a million tons of freight into the city. In 1871, the Commodore opened the immensely unpopular Grand Central Depot, again designed by Snook. Fronting East Forty-Second Street, the structure covered 5 acres and was disliked—and perhaps envied—by many who passed by or through its doors. To gain control of the acreage he needed, the Commodore used tactics such as "seizure rights"—pertaining to railroad law—to run off those unwilling to sell. The area around the mammoth structure was clogged with trains, and lives had been lost crossing the maze of tracks. But as with much of what the Commodore did, the depot was huge, unlike anything else that existed. The scrappy young waterman-turned-rail-magnate's riches eventually surpassed those of Manhattan's reigning multimillionaire, William Backhouse Astor Sr., son of fur trader and real estate mogul John Jacob Astor, America's first multimillionaire. The Vanderbilt name, once perhaps associated with farmers and river rats, was now synonymous with wealth and power.

The Commodore had fathered thirteen children, the oldest of whom was George's father, William Henry. George's mother, Maria Louisa Kissam, had met his father while William was still a young clerk in the banking house of Drew, Robinson & Company. (Partner Daniel Drew was one of the Commodore's business rivals.) The Commodore was as brusque and harsh with his children as he was with any businessman who dared cross his train tracks or ferry routes, and he routinely called his son William a "blatherskite," a fool. When

William's health faltered, the Commodore gave his son a small family farm to run in New Dorp, Staten Island. William soon increased his initial 70 acres to 350, and respectable earnings followed. The Commodore took notice, giving William more attention and responsibility. William then took the Staten Island Railroad from insolvency to profitability. Every challenge the Commodore put to him, William met and then some. As the Commodore grew older and weaker, his respect for William deepened and strengthened. When the Commodore died in January 1877, he left the bulk of his massive fortune to his son and George's father, William Henry Vanderbilt.

Though the notoriously hard-nosed and impossible to impress Commodore eventually recognized William's abilities to run the family business, he likely would never have imagined that his primary heir's accomplishments would so quickly dwarf his own. Within six years, the blatherskite had more than doubled his inheritance of about $90 million. William Vanderbilt's income in 1883 was estimated at more than $10 million—and income was not taxed at the time. George's father had an estimated net worth of $194 million and an estate exceeding $200 million. George's parents, who once had not enough money to furnish their small house on Staten Island, soon amassed the greatest fortune in America, very possibly in the world.

George's family home was a resplendent brownstone at 640 Fifth Avenue. Finished in 1881, the "Triple Palace," as it was known, took up the entire block of Fifth Avenue between Fifty-First and Fifty-Second Streets on the West Side. The so-called palace was actually two conjoined town houses comprising three distinct addresses and residences. George and his parents occupied the southern structure. A one-story vestibule connected this to the northern structure, which was divided in two and occupied by George's older sisters and their families. Emily, who had married William Douglas Sloane, lived at 642 Fifth Avenue, and Margaret, who had married Elliott Fitch Shepard, had an entrance at 2 West Fifty-Second Street.

The west side of Fifth Avenue was dominated by the Vanderbilts.

George's brother Frederick and his wife, Louise, lived at 459 Fifth Avenue, William Henry Vanderbilt's home prior to the construction of the Triple Palace. Another brother, William "Willie K." and his wife, Alva, lived at 660 Fifth Avenue in a house known as the Petit Chateau de Blois. George's father built 680 and 684 Fifth Avenue for George's sisters Lila and Florence, and their husbands William Seward Webb and Hamilton McKown Twombly, respectively. George's oldest brother, Cornelius II or "Corneil," who had been living in the heart of New York society at Fifth Avenue and Thirty-Second Street, moved uptown to join the rest of the clan, building a mansion at 1 West Fifty-Seventh Street that would become the largest private home in the history of Manhattan. This encampment of Vanderbilt homes was located farther north than the homes of most moneyed New York families twenty blocks south. Before William Henry Vanderbilt broke ground on the Triple Palace, the lot was the domain of a vegetable gardener who occasionally dealt in ice and cattle. Now the area was a much desired neighborhood referred to as Vanderbilt Row (or, depending on one's view of the family, the less patrician "Alley").

Unlike his older brothers, George had no interest in his family's railroad business. Cornelius II was chairman of the New York Central railroad and taught Sunday school at St. Bartholomew's, where the Vanderbilt family attended services. Willie K. was second vice president of the New York Central and chairman of the board of the Lake Shore and "Nickel Plate" (New York, Chicago, and St. Louis) lines. Frederick was director of the West Shore and Canada Southern lines.

In contrast, George enjoyed other pursuits available to members of their class. George's father had amassed a tremendous collection of paintings, sculpture, and books, and George had delighted in all of them since he was young. While his father may have enjoyed spending leisure time driving his sleek, trotting mares Maud S. and Aldine along fashionable stretches like the Gentlemen's Driving Park in Morrisania or along Harlem Lane, George was content to spend hours, if not days, in the parlors and sitting rooms of 640 Fifth Avenue, reading and studying. He had grown up devout in his faith and for a time thought he might pursue a calling in the Episcopal church. A priest perhaps. Diary entries from when George was thirteen years old reveal him to be a penitent, thoughtful young man: "I read my Bible this morning and began Isaiah and I think that was what made me feel so happy through the day. . . . I have been reading a book this afternoon from which I ought to learn a very useful lesson of truth and gaining control over my temper, but I can do nothing without God's help because if I rely on my own resolution I am sure to fail. . . . I don't think I have spent today as I should have done. I have trusted too much in my own ability and not enough in Jesus."

At a young age, George began diligently recording all of his expenses, down to the penny. He also detailed all the literary and academic titles he consumed in a series of notebooks titled "Books I Have Read." His fondness of the written word was well known, and he had been invited to become a founding member of the bibliophilic Grolier Club. He could often be found with his head of dark hair bowed over a tome penned in another language. He was said to be fluent in eight of them.

In 1888, three years after his father died, George, the youngest and only unmarried child of William and Maria, continued to live at 640 with his mother. The home would pass to him upon her death, along with "lots and stables" on Madison Avenue, furnishings, and "chattels and carriages." William Henry Vanderbilt left eight surviving children. (Another son, Allen, had died at the age of twelve, four years before George was born.) The bulk of his fortune and business went to George's oldest brothers Corneil—nineteen years George's senior—and Willie K. The remainder was divided between George, the youngest child, and his five older siblings: Frederick, Margaret, Emily, Florence, and Lila (Eliza).

There was more than enough wealth to go around. George had already received more than $1 million in stocks and bonds when his grandfather, the Commodore, died. That was now worth closer to

$2 million. His father gifted him another million in cash, as well as the title to the family estate, "Homestead," on Staten Island, when he turned twenty-one. And now, upon his father's death, George received $5 million in cash and the *interest* from a separate $5 million trust. (He could not access the capital.) This brought the sum of George's monies to be in the neighborhood of $12 to $13 million by the age of twenty-three, with an annual income of about $520,000.

What to do with such a sum when one had not lifted a finger to earn it? This was the enviable dilemma of many in George's class. During the latter half of the nineteenth century, the answer to that question was often presented in mortar and limestone, friezes and tapestries. It was de rigueur for a man of George's station and family name to have a summer "cottage" somewhere like Newport, or perhaps the Berkshires, to construct something lavish and lasting, a structure both opulent and memorable.

That could have been how George decided to make his mark. A year earlier, he had purchased a property in Bar Harbor, but the Maine winter held little enticement. No, George craved something other. Few, frankly, would have anticipated that young George would eventually land so far, at the very least geographically speaking, from the fold.

■ ■ ■

The train pulled into the station at a small crossroads known to some as Asheville Junction, to others as Best. The station, post office, and handful of structures were named for W. J. Best, a Boston railroad magnate who had headed up the Western North Carolina Railroad in 1880 and was credited with bringing rail service to this mountain town in North Carolina. In 1888, three years after his father's death, George had come South. After a near daylong journey from Manhattan—a long ride no matter how tufted the seats in George's private railcar—a few more miles by carriage remained. George, whose persistent bachelorhood and bursting bank accounts made him quite the New York society catch, was traveling with the most significant female in his life—his mother.

George's mother, Maria, was now in her sixty-seventh year, and agreed with her son's desire to seek out a winter climate milder than that of New York. No matter how luxurious, the walls of their city mansion were unable to keep the chill at bay. George was slight and possessed a healthy fear of tuberculosis. He was viewed by members of the society press as weak, ill, or lacking that robust manner many men of means born to a family of industry might seem to possess. But then, George was no man of industry. He was a scholar.

Mother and son stayed at the Battery Park Hotel, a grand, shingled structure perched high above Asheville, yet still dwarfed in turn by the imposing colossus of nature looming on the landscape beyond. The peaks of the Blue Ridge and the Smoky Mountains adopted varying shades of that indigo hue, each ridge growing lighter as it receded behind its neighbors, until they faded into a wash of pale-gray azure grazing the sky, cloudy wisps clinging to their slopes. The beautiful and bewitching smokiness emanated from the trees themselves—the lungs of the slopes—exhaling emissions often in the form of a blue haze of isoprene. The Battery Park had views to spare, its own house orchestra, and wide, awning-topped verandas.

Asheville was growing rapidly due in great part to the area's well established reputation as a resort and sanitarium destination. In this part of the country, those who could afford the views and the springs might be healed of everything from tropical diseases to mental distress by cures as exotically enticing as "electric bitters" and as ordinary as plain old air inhaled in the usual manner on plain old porches.

George was not the first person of means to consider a more permanent foothold in the Land of the Sky. Charlestonians had begun coming to Asheville and nearby Flat Rock from the Low Country of South Carolina at least a century earlier, building spectacular summer homes there. Milder, breezier summers lured the highest of the well born to abandon their palmettos, magnolias, and fashionable shops for a life 2,200 feet above their sweltering sea-level homes. They followed in the footsteps of decades of river explorers, holler settlers, game hunters, timber cutters, and French speakers. The Cherokee preceded all of them, calling the area Shaconage, "place of the blue smoke." The Cherokee, in turn, had myths about those who had preceded them, like the great mound builders and Judaculla, the Great Slant-Eyed Giant, who controlled thunder and rain and leaped and bounded from boulder to stream, leaving his footprints etched in the ancient stones. These aged mountains had seen more than a billion years of life in all its forms. Now many well-heeled visitors and the doctors who cared for them believed the mountain air could heal lungs ailing from tuberculosis or the suffocating by-products of the industrial age. They came, they spent, they built "breathing porches" and marveled at the freshness of a timeless resource that was free to all, but for which they were happy to pay dearly.

George's mother was still struggling with the lingering effects of a bout of malaria, so she sought treatment as well as peace and quiet while away from New York. In Asheville, she was cared for by Dr. Samuel Westray Battle, a physician well known to the area and its Northern visitors. George left his mother to relax and breathe deep the curative atmosphere while he took in the exquisite vistas the hotel offered, or hired a horse to ride out for a closer look at lands farther afield.

That's when he saw her. Pisgah.

George found her to be simply stunning. Standing proud among her neighbors, nestled in the crook of their slopes, the peak beckoned him with her silent grace. She had seen much in her time here, and age had perhaps rendered her softer, but she retained a stature and elegance that captivated George.

"And Moses went up from the plains of Moab unto the mountain of Nebo, to the top of Pisgah, that is over against Jericho...."

If Moses viewed the Promised Land from atop Pisgah, then so did this dreamer from a faraway northern island see promise in this ancient mount on the other side of the world from its biblical namesake. Promise for the kind of life he believed he wanted, for his vision. Was this the promised land, then? These peaks and valleys dotting the banks of the French Broad River? If so, then this heavenly kingdom was fit to house a castle.

That June George bought his first 661 parcels. His initial play was to buy land as secretly as a Vanderbilt could, cleverly purchasing tracts in a piecemeal fashion through purchasing agents who included Edward Burnett, an agriculturist; and Charles McNamee, a lawyer with the firm Davis, Worth and McNamee in New York. Why let the cat out of the carpetbag and run up prices? The acres began to add up. Asheville, though not a stranger to outside seasonal visitors, was still a small town. Rumors about land being snapped up and who was doing the snapping seeped into the press. It wasn't long before the man behind the money was revealed. When George's name made it into print, citizens began to wonder what this "young Croesus" intended to do with the quickly accumulating tracts.

Despite that scrutiny, the mountain town must have seemed a refuge for the quiet young man. Here is where he would build his country home. Here is where he would make his mark, far from the rocky shore of Newport, where straw boaters and candy-striped umbrellas dotted a tired scene he knew all too well. Here, in southern Appalachia, the land of Highland Scots and mountain laurel, regal Pisgah would stand as his anchor, and estates of time past and castles beyond the sea would soon serve as his muses. The altitude had his head swimming in visions of what might be.

While the land was all-important, those fields and mountains, streams and slopes, banks and burrows were merely a canvas upon which his vision would be painted. Every stroke of stonemasonry, every line drawn of maples, they all mattered. To bring this vision to life he needed a team that would see this world as a whole, an integrated destination, a place with a life and a pulse all its own. George was in a position to employ the greatest creative minds of the time to help him shape his vision, and bring it down to the earth he believed had so much promise.

He could also afford it.

2

A Lady of
the Long Man Rising

Frederick Law Olmsted was not impressed.

He rode alongside George over the south slopes of Lone Pine Mountain. The wiry-framed, twenty-six-year-old George straddled his horse and let his brooding eyes roam over his recent purchases, which now amounted to around 2,000 acres. Next to him, astride his own mount, sat the sixty-six-year-old burly, bushy-bearded Olmsted.

George's aim that day was to show Olmsted the spot that had captivated him. George knew that to make the most of the enchanting long-range vistas, and bring into sharper focus those nearby visual delights, he would need the best landscape architect available. He would need, in fact, the father of that very body of study: Olmsted. Olmsted and his former partner, Calvert Vaux, had already designed the most dynamic city parks of the day, including Central Park in Manhattan and Prospect Park in Brooklyn.

Now in North Carolina, Olmsted saw land that had been horribly overworked. Part of his lackluster response to the view before him stemmed from the fact that he knew this region of the United States well. Years earlier, Olmsted had traveled throughout the South as a journalist and landscape designer, and in 1856 he published *A Journey in the Seaboard Slave States: With Remarks on Their Economy*. He had spent a rewarding month exploring the North Carolina forests, a month Olmsted had not wished to end. He knew the expanses that lay just beyond the view upon which he now looked: forests rich in biodiversity. But right here, now, Olmsted did not see the appeal of the land upon which George hoped to site his new home.

"It is in itself (i.e. regardless of its outlooks) a generally poor and vagabondish region," he wrote a friend. There were "potentialities in parts of it, especially its little valleys, of which we can make something. Knowing that within fifty miles there was grand local scenery and almost the finest deciduous forest in the world, I was at my first visit greatly disappointed with its apparent barrenness and the miserable character of its woods."

Olmsted listened as George—forty years his junior—recalled his recent visit to Asheville and how he found the air "mild and invigorating." One day while out and about, he explained to Olmsted, he had come to this spot and thought it the perfect place for a home. There was a potential downside, which the young man confessed to Olmsted. "I saw that if I built upon [this site] I should not have pleasant neighbors," Olmsted recalled George saying, "so I sent Mr. McNamee down here to buy some of them out, and step by step, without any very definite end in view, I have acquired about 2,000 acres." Now, with increasing numbers of parcels under his financial belt, George wanted to know what Olmsted thought. Had George made what amounted, so far, to a 2,000-acre mistake? The pair sat on their horses, looking across the French Broad River valley toward regal Mount Pisgah. Olmsted took in the "good distant outlook." That was something grand. If what George wanted was good air, good climate, and a nice long view, then, *no*. Olmsted thought no mistake had been made.

The soil, however, was a different matter. The woods were a disaster. At every turn, land had been "skinned by poor white farmers," Olmsted wrote, and "great patches of cleared land [were] occupied by negroes." Decades of felling trees, selling lumber, and immediately chopping again meant the most desirable and stout trees had already found their way to home construction or to market, leaving only the "runts" behind to eke out an existence among their few towering neighbors.

Olmsted wondered what, besides a house, might be done with all this land. George suggested a park. Olmsted, no stranger to finding order amid natural chaos, didn't see that as the best option. This was no place for a giant park. However, what if their approach to this vast land were more European than American? A *managed* forest. A game preserve. Even some timber crops. Such practices, long used among the nobles of Europe, might actually prove to be a good business for George, Olmsted thought. "It would be of great value to the country to have a thoroughly well organized and systematically conducted attempt in forestry made on a large scale."

If young George wanted a park, he could have a small "pleasure ground and garden," as Olmsted put it, near the house, with acreage to spare. What land remained could remain a forest. Plant the barren fields and care for the decimated woods. Install an arboretum. This could be a sound course of action that would not only heal the troubled earth but might pay dividends down the line as well.

George took in his trusted adviser's thoughts on the matter and sat with the information for a few months. Then he was ready.

■ ■ ■

The covered wagon that stopped in front of the Tribune Building on Printing House Square in lower Manhattan did not go unnoticed, not even in this city of ongoing clamor, one punctuated by the clip-clop of trotters, the jangle of reins, and the scrape of tattered shoes along cobblestones. The area was the hub of the newspaper business, and the Tribune Building was home to the paper of the same name and the offices of Richard Morris Hunt, the architect who had designed the Tribune's magnificent clock tower which loomed over the square. Several men removed a model from the wagon. This was not an unusual sight in and of itself, but this particular creation was conspicuously large, grand enough in its size and elaborate enough in its detail to crook many a neck. Those watching estimated it might be as large as five feet in length by another three feet in width, yet it did not appear to be a model of a hotel or other institution, but rather the model of a house. The men disappeared into the building, but not before the entire affair was spotted by a newspaper reporter.

Hunt was no stranger to grand undertakings, no dilettante in the realm of Gilded Age extravagance, and his reputation was known far beyond US shores. He was the first American to enroll in and graduate from the École des Beaux-Arts in Paris. His studies there enabled him to work on the renovations of that city's Louvre Museum. Back in the United States, he eventually cofounded the American Institute of Architects, and his eye would influence many of the most evocative and enduring structures of the time, from private homes to urban designs: The pedestal of the Statue of Liberty. The great hall of the Metropolitan Museum of Art. The plan for Columbia University. He was an incomparable talent who practiced his art at a time when numerous patrons were lining up to pay top dollar for it. He had created some of the most elaborate and admired homes on the East Coast. If architectural excess were a religion, Hunt was surely its patron saint, placing the most ornate of roofs over the heads of the city's elite from cradle to crypt.

The Gilded Age was approaching its zenith. Mark Twain had skewered—and named—this age of excess in 1873 in a novel he coauthored with his neighbor Charles Dudley Warner, titled *The Gilded Age: A Tale of Today*. It was a bizarrely sumptuous, fascinatingly gaudy time. Those who summered in Italianate retreats lining the rocky shores of Newport, or entertained in French-inspired châteaus on Fifth Avenue, comprised the upper echelon of society known as the Four Hundred. This arbitrary number was believed to be an estimate of the number of persons that could comfortably fit into Mrs. Caroline "Lina" Astor's ballroom. Ward McAllister, self-asserted tastemaker, Astor family aficionado, and society clocker extraordinaire, published this so-called list of the wealthiest of the wealthy (which actually came in a few dozen shy of that illustrious number).

No matter who made whose guest book, *the* Mrs. Astor remained the reigning queen of gilded New York society, with little patience for those she considered nouveau riche industrialists, or moneyed Midwesterners and Southerners seeking to make a name for themselves in post–Civil War New York. This meant she had little time for the Vanderbilt family, having found the Commodore too newly wealthy and boorish to be endured. But if there was one way to sharpen an elbow to insert yourself into this club it was to keep on building. The rich sought to conquer one another on battlefields of architectural grandeur. Society fought wars in ballrooms and twinkling parlors, wielding the most haute of designers and decor as their weapons of choice, Italian marble beneath their feet. The carnival of spending knew no limits. The haves one-upped one another with "cottages" of tens of thousands of square feet, their interiors adorned with precious art and furnishings from abroad, all the trappings essential to life among this select strata of society.

Hunt had worked with George's sister-in-law Alva, who suspected that the bigger and better the house and the grander the fetes hosted therein, the faster the barrier to the upper ranks of Lina's list would crumble like a day-old tea scone. Hunt had designed the Petit Chateau for Alva and her husband, George's brother Willie K., a spectacular home which *Architectural Digest* called "pleasant in the color and treatment of its stone." If nothing else, the look of the house had been a welcoming—or startling, depending on the eye— contrast to the "brown stone" so prevalent in New York City. Indiana limestone had been Hunt's facade of choice for the Petit Chateau, so their house gleamed like the beacon of a grand French Renaissance lighthouse amid a coffee-colored sea. Alva wanted to make sure Hunt incorporated acorns in the decorative scheme of the new abode. She believed in the power of motifs and sigils and thought that if the Vanderbilts, possessing recently acquired wealth and no noble lineage, were ever to be fully embraced by New York society— indeed, if she were to rise to the top of it—the Vanderbilt name needed to be outfitted with all the trappings of ancient wealth. Seals. Crests. Symbols.

In March 1883, not long after the home was finished, Alva opened the house by hosting a grand dress ball. The event was at once a visual delight celebrating Hunt's masterpiece and parade of unfettered costumed excess. The *New York Times* covered the event as though it were a presidential inauguration, dutifully describing costumes, guests, and every quadrille danced, from the "Hobby-Horse" to the "Mother Goose." Alva dressed as a Venetian princess, her husband as the Duke of Guise. The architect Hunt came as the Florentine painter Cimabue. George's brother Cornelius Vanderbilt II arrived as Louis XVI with his wife, Alice, adorned in glowing sartorial homage to the recent dawn of electric light. Guests came as the bejeweled incarnations of hornets, monks, goddesses, nursery-rhyme characters, royals, sheiks, Native Americans, harlequins, and saints. There was, too, a cat costume, disturbingly fashioned from actual cats. The woman's skirt was made of cat tails, the bodice "rows of white cats' heads and the head-dress was a stiffened white cat's skin, the head over the forehead of the wearer and the tail pendant behind." To complete the look? A blue ribbon inscribed with the word "Puss." George's name was not mentioned in the extensive list of guests in attendance. Alva's frenemies the Astors attended, which alone raised eyebrows and made the newspapers.

These excesses were often denigrated in the press as much as they were ballyhooed. This age was not gilded for all, and more striking than the exuberant spending of the time was its contrast to the lives of the masses at the other end of that lopsided financial scale. While the haves sought more extreme ways of spending what seemed to be limitless sums of money—a pool of wealth naïvely believed to spring from an endless fount of riches—day laborers might hope to make two or three dollars a day. Many ordinary citizens lived on top of one another in tenements in lower Manhattan, while blocks north, affluent households might allocate thousands of dollars to a single evening's dinner and dancing. The fascination with how this section of society lived entwined with a wonder at how they could live with themselves when so many others subsisted on so very little.

The real showpiece the night of Alva Vanderbilt's ball was Hunt's work. As architects benefited from the patronage of returning clients, so did Hunt enjoy counting the Vanderbilts among his most frequent customers, as Fifth Avenue's Vanderbuilding continued apace. However, the outsize model spotted outside the Tribune Building was not destined for a chunk of Manhattan real estate. All Hunt would tell the reporter was that it was a "château in the French Renaissance style that was to be built on Mr. Vanderbilt's plantation down in North Carolina." He had no other information to offer. Too many details had yet to be decided upon.

Hunt and Olmsted were obvious choices to oversee George's venture. Though he may have preferred quiet moments among books and bindings to quadrilles and social climbing, George's tastes had nevertheless been honed in the finest homes of America and Europe. George had worked with Hunt on renovations at his parents' home at 640 Fifth and on the Jackson Square library at Thirteenth Street near Eighth Avenue, which George gifted to the Free Circulating Library of New York, forerunner to the city's public library system. Both Hunt and Olmsted were working with George on the Vanderbilt family mausoleum on Staten Island, a project which George had taken over from his father. George's keen instincts regarding aesthetics and design may have been born among the artistic treasures in his father's New York home, but they were being sharpened much farther south. The North Carolina house could be only a tiny part of the evolving plan. The mountainous setting lent as much to the future home's personality as its design. The place seemed to cry out for formal gardens yielding to the wilds beyond, long-range views, and inviting footpaths.

Olmsted had applied his genius for capturing the unique natural aspects of any place, rural or urban, to private homes, college campuses, parks, parkways, and more. As Olmsted and Vaux tamed the vast wilds of upper Manhattan to create Central Park in the 1850s and early '60s, Hunt would follow, flanking that public space with works for private and public clients. Olmsted and Hunt were both already famous, they were both already well off, they were both as sought after as they could be, and they had schedules that reflected their demand. Now together, these titans of design, one working in limestone and steel, the other in perennials and arboreal flourishes, would come together to build a home unlike any ever seen this side of the Atlantic. The venture would prove to be one of their largest, their most challenging and, for both men, one of their last.

■ ■ ■

With the Vanderbilt-Olmsted-Hunt trio in place, work began in earnest in 1889. The three men made plans and revised them, then made them once again. Meanwhile, George made more land purchases with an eye toward doubling those first 2,000 acres within the first year. In January 1889, the press estimated the Vanderbilt family wealth at $274 million. George's estimated share of that monstrous sum was in the neighborhood of $15 million. He would need it.

That summer, George set sail for England and Europe with Hunt and his wife, Catharine, in search of inspiration—and to do some shopping. Hunt pushed bravely through his latest bout of gout, and the travels began. The group planned to travel to English manors and French châteaus, taking in varying architectural styles. George would examine exteriors and accompanying gardens, considering which might be best suited not only for the southern Appalachian setting but also for the lifestyle he had begun to envision for himself, his guests and, most important, his mother. George had a growing notion to create a working farm, with a village to support the estate where workers, employees, and others might live. He was also coming around to the idea, planted by Olmsted, of making a commitment to scientific and sustainable forestry, a concept foreign to Americans at the time.

The group went first to England, where George and Hunt visited the Rothschilds' Waddesdon Manor—the site for many a "Saturday to Monday" fete. (The term "weekend," though long in existence, was foreign to many for whom a workweek had never existed.) The traveling companions admired Elizabethan gardens near Hatfield House, lunched with Lord Sackville in Sevenoaks in Kent. The offerings of a particular Oriental rug warehouse in England must have struck the right aesthetic chord. While there, George purchased three hundred rugs, and later in the trip jaunted over to Brussels in search of tapestries. Measurements of purchases were dutifully recorded for Hunt.

Afterward, the group headed to Paris, where they visited with George's brother Willie K. and his wife Alva, who also demanded Hunt's attentions as they were embarking on yet another construction project, a home called Marble House on Bellevue Avenue in Newport. Then the entire group was off to Chantilly. The Loire Valley offered numerous architectural delights, and Château de Blois, Chenonceau, and Chambord held particular allure. This was the style George sought, and this was the style that Hunt, a celebrated student of the École des Beaux-Arts, knew as well as anyone in the Western world.

Hunt had a fatherly affection for George; and Hunt's wife, Catharine, marveled at young Vanderbilt, whom she found "insatiable in his desire to see beautiful interiors and pictures." She noted that George delighted any time a particular gallery paled in comparison or size to the expanding designs Hunt planned for George's own spaces. Knowing of his passion for Napoleonic treasures, Catharine wanted to buy George something to add to his collection, and was able to locate a *petite breloque* which Napoleon had gifted to, as Catharine put it, "a complacent lady." One of the most remarkable pieces in George's possession had been given to him by railroad financier James McHenry as a gift on George's twenty-first birthday. That treasure was a chess set owned by Napoleon, which had helped him pass the hours during his six-year exile on the remote island of St. Helena off the coast of Africa. The chess pieces were carved of nineteenth-century Chinese ivory, and came with a gaming table of acacia, ivory, walnut, ebony, and brass. When the diminutive general died in 1821, doctors performed an autopsy. According to legend, Napoleon's heart had been placed upon the gaming table now in George's Fifth Avenue residence.

Heading home at the end of a successful voyage, George was eager to return to the land of the Blue Ridge. Hunt and Olmsted, too, were increasingly captivated by that overused, underappreciated, strangely magical land, upon which they would leave a legendary mark.

■　■　■

That July, Olmsted wrote George an extensive overview of what was needed to move forward. First and foremost, more roads were needed to transport materials, the amount of which was unfathomable. Also, it would be a good idea to renovate a farmhouse where Olmsted and others might stay, as hotels were a bit too far away from the estate for repeated travel. Olmsted instructed lawyer and purchasing agent Charles McNamee—now having taken on the role of estate manager—to construct and prepare Olmsted's observation platforms. These would allow Olmsted to see everything from above, as near a bird's-eye view as was available to a mere man. They would be placed at various locations around the site. Olmsted would use them to judge appropriate heights for windows, loggias, and terraces, and also to survey meandering paths through gardens, judging elevations for natural, as well as architectural, elements. As Olmsted updated George on progress—and in some cases, lack thereof—during that first summer of 1889, the pages stacked up quickly.

Stakes marking the site of the home had been pounded into the earth. The hilltop to the east would be cut to improve views from the house. The water supply had to be considered, and a reservoir that would take advantage of nearby springs was an option. There were generations of "campers, squatters and transient settlers" on the grounds, as well as old sawmills whose cutting days were long past. Olmsted further assessed the damage that had been done to the area through the constant removal of the best trees. Remnants of specimens that were no good for the lumber market had been carted off to heat cold cabins, build lean-tos, or to be exchanged for food in town.

Cherries, tulips, and black walnut trees that had once graced the landscape had been toppled and snatched up by cabinetmakers. Black birches made their way to bedstead crafters. Durable, rot-resistant locust made excellent fence posting; dogwoods headed to the woodcutter's block. Truly, this was a craftsman's land, and evidence of that history could be seen in the detritus left littering the forest floor. If you wanted chestnuts, only stumps were available. Oaks—much harder to fell and mill—dominated what remained. Olmsted longed to spot a fine silvery linden, which he knew to grow in this area. Both the hand of man and the ravages of fire had taken their toll. Corn and tobacco farming had done their part as well to sap the soil of nutrients. In the wake of the earth's rape, scrub pines meekly followed. Workers would need to painstakingly remove thin, weak saplings; amend the soil; and give the chestnuts, tupelos, beeches, and birches the opportunity to regain their footing once more.

To that end, Olmsted believed a nursery should be established. Gathering plants locally could be done at around 10 cents per plant. He laid out roads for servicing the building site and transportation, but was fixed on an Approach Road, which would carry George and his guests to the house. Olmsted wanted it "wild and secluded," as though visitors were in the "remote depths of a natural forest." No long-range views, no open spaces. But then, upon reaching the house itself, a revelation: The court. The house. The sky. The peaks and slopes beyond.

What had started for Olmsted with a tinge of disappointment—albeit lingering—about the estate's immediate setting had morphed into passion as the site began to impress him with its tremendous potential. "These are hints of the capabilities of the Estate," Olmsted wrote, adding that he thought George's home could be on par with the great estates in England and Europe.

"Where would there be anything to compare with it? You would have people crossing the Atlantic to see it."

George and Hunt were in Asheville that fall to go over the current state of plans with McNamee. There had been debates between Olmsted and Hunt about various items, including the terraces. Olmsted suggested walled courts and windbreaks to the north, so oncoming carriages wouldn't feel too harsh a wind as they made their way up to the house. Stables might be located there. The siting of the house was critical if the views—the true value of the site—were to be maximized. Hunt's concern was scale. Though George had bought a considerable amount of land, his initial views on the size of the home were modest. Early plans—including one referred to as the "Old Colonial House for G. W. Vanderbilt"—were on the order of 6,500 square feet. But as land increased and plans developed, so did the house, its size beginning to compete with the smoke-laden ridges beyond. By November 1889, the house plan was fixed.

■ ■ ■

Olmsted had also written George that the spot needed a name. McNamee had been searching for a name with some sort of "Indian heritage" but had had no luck. Olmsted wanted a name of significance—nothing of "punning, sarcasm or ridicule." He thought it should be "sonorous; should fall trippingly from the tongue . . ." He did not think "French Broad," a salute to the river that was in many ways the spine of the estate, would work. Olmsted did not think McNamee knew the "Indian" name of the French Broad River or else he would have proposed it. There were, in fact, several: The Cherokee had called the river Agiqua or "Long Man," with sections of the waters named according to their personality, such as Tahkeyostee, meaning "where they race," or tributaries called "chattering children." These were unknown to more recent arrivals to the area. Olmsted suggested George try to come up with a "concocted English name," one that used all the usual ingredients—location, river, forest—and combined them in a kind of titular recipe. He suggested "Broadwood" as a possibility. By the following spring, George had it. It would harken not to the native peoples, nor to anything so entirely anglophilic. It would take its inspiration from the Dutch land of George's own ancestry.

One of George's earliest ancestors to come to America, Jan Aartsen van der Bilt, had arrived in New Netherland from the old Netherlands in the mid-1600s. He eventually purchased a "bouwerie" (bowery or farm) in the Flatbush area of Long Island. Jan likely came from Bildt in the area of Friesland, Holland. George started with "Bilt" when devising his estate's name, chose the name "Bilton," and placed orders with the stationer. In early 1890, the *Daily Citizen* proclaimed that George had "named the baby." However, the US Post Office did not approve, stating that the name was too similar to Bolton, North Carolina. Finally, in the literal and figurative end, the English naming conceit did come into play, with the suffix "moor." This word referred to a kind of large open expanse that, while rolling and romantic in appearance, was nevertheless—and perhaps George was giving a nod to Olmsted's complaints about his ever-depleted soil—infertile. English and Dutch converged, as they had centuries before on the island of Manhattan, and the estate was named Biltmore.

George also planned to change the name of the tracts of land that comprised the small crossroads and rail station of Best. Town, train station, and post office would bear the name of the estate with which they were now associated.

Not everyone was thrilled.

"The change is a petty exhibition of pure snobbery," one citizen wrote to the local paper in March, when the name was announced. "Geo. Vanderbilt owns Biltmore. Geo. Vanderbilt is a rich man. Hence let's call Asheville Junction after him. Next we shall have a Biltmore hotel, Biltmore park, Biltmore street, Biltmore block, Biltmore sheep, cows, ducks, cloth, and (last as usual) the Biltmore bustle. Mr. Vanderbilt is a thoroughly welcome addition to North Carolina and Asheville, but really we could spare Biltmore as the name of a public railway station."

Signed: "Anti-Biltmore."

Another wrote that the very sound of the name offended the musical sensibilities of the people of North Carolina. It was fine if George wanted part of his name in the title of his home, and clearly

"Vanderbilt-more" wouldn't work. "Biltmore was the only resource left him," the letter continued, "unless he would be willing to call his estate 'Van-ity.'" Not everyone was miffed, though. At least one gentleman claimed to be pleased, writing that "this was probably the last of W. J. Best in this state."

As spring turned to summer in that first full year of construction, the site was transformed as building, blasting, and buying continued. There were two significant arrivals at the site. First was the completion of the rail spur from the main line of the Western North Carolina Railroad to the house—from Biltmore Station to Biltmore House. Three or so miles of track cost in the neighborhood of $80,000. On May 29 a Baldwin locomotive named *Ronda* chugged toward the house, running south along the esplanade then parallel to the house's growing facade, with George and the Hunts on board. Another engine aptly named Biltmore was soon added to the three-mile track. The rail spur transported workers, materials, and visitors straight from the station into the chaotic heart of the work site, the area that would become the esplanade in front of the château. It was not a perfect operation. The trains jumped their tracks five times within the first six months.

As the project progressed, so grew the intrigue. A New York *Sun* reporter traveling through North Carolina stopped by that spring to see what he could of this developing site south of Asheville and report it back to gossip-hungry readers up North. The reporter described George's abode-to-be as a "palace," and included in the feature sketches of the carefully chosen vistas, log cabins dotting the landscape, and one spot captioned "Mr Vanderbilt's Fishing Stream."

The *Sun* reporter noted that Asheville, too, was growing. Among the population of nearly 12,000 people, the *Sun* estimated that 2,000 of those residents were of the "northern" variety. Property assessments in town were estimated at $4,393,234. In stark contrast, 1880 figures were 2,610 in population and less than $1 million in property value. There seemed an element of pleasant surprise in the journalist's prose as he noted that citizens in this rural resort region enjoyed electric rail transport, electric lighting, grade schools for both white and black students, sixteen churches, two female colleges, two male academies, two daily papers, and more, modern marvels all, set against the backdrop of the mountains. Asheville and its environs were "no place for a poor man," the paper declared. "The booms of the West are as naught in comparison with the boom among the Great Smokies."

Hotels, a growing tourist industry, the lumber business, health spas—all combined to augment Asheville's rapid growth. Nevertheless, Biltmore remained a focus in the press. "George Vanderbilt appears to have set the other millionaires a pretty rad pace," the *Asheville Democrat* stated that summer, calling the town "a gilt-edged health resort."

"Every stranger in Asheville runs the risk of being mistaken for a millionaire in disguise," continued the article, noting the recent stay of Standard Oil's John D. Rockefeller at the Battery Park Hotel. The Kenilworth Inn—which counted George as an investor— commenced construction later in the year. In addition to luxury, ads promised 360-degree mountain views, a sky parlor that offered a peek at trains crossing the Swannanoa Gap, and a view of the Vanderbilt estate.

George continued buying, hotels continued rising, and land prices followed suit. Early on, Olmsted had hoped the young man might still be able to move forward with purchasing at "market rather than Vanderbilt prices." In some cases yes, others not. Reported prices for lots varied. The Brookshire farm, near the junction on the Swannanoa River, was sold by its namesake to McNamee for $10,500. The option on the 86-acre Hilliard farm, about four miles south of town, was a good get: asking price $22,000. The Patton farm cost $87,500. S. H. Reed sold a reported 28 acres to George for more than $1,000 per acre. Around the same time, another 42 acres sold for just $10,000.

"How many more hills and valleys and mountain slopes will yet be purchased by the ambitious young bachelor it is impossible to say," the *Sun* reported, adding that even the parcels of land George was presently buying had gone for as much as $1,250 or more an acre now, when the same lands would have gone for a fraction of that sum before the big buyout began. The way things were going, the local press predicted, George would soon be the "largest as well as the wealthiest land-owner in the State," and posited that "Vanderbilt may even yet own the famous mountain peaks of western North Carolina, if he keeps on buying up the mountains at the present rate." There were holdouts. Charles C. Collins, a farmer and former slave, had a property of about 6 acres on the eastern edge of George's lands and was content to live there. His refusal to sell fed the rumor mill with tales of George cutting off the man's water supply and erecting a wall around his property. None of which were true.

Local photographer T. H. Lindsey documented the landscape and views around the growing Vanderbilt holdings a few miles south of Asheville proper. According to the local paper, Lindsey would encapsulate the sights of those who "pitched their tepees along the sparkling streams that intersperse this woodland dream in days long since; before the tranquil sweetness of this favored land was disturbed by the grating sounds of the pioneer's machete . . ." His photographs captured the unceasing progress of the estate, while preserving the memory of what once was.

The crossroads formerly known as Best began to slowly evolve into what would be the village of Biltmore. Temporary wooden housing was built in the village for workers. Specialty tradesmen—stonemasons, for example—traveled down to Asheville from points north and beyond to lend their skills to the elaborately designed château. The temporary homes would eventually be torn down to make way for a more permanent, intricately designed village. The spring of 1890 also saw the dedication of the new Shiloh AME church for the black community. George had bought the original church and its 1-acre parcel of land the previous year and delivered on his promise to build the congregants a newer, better church, complete with pews, stained-glass windows, and a bell. The pastor wrote McNamee with "heartfelt thanks," adding, "We pray that you and Mr. Vanderbilt may live long to do good in our community."

Hundreds of men had been hired to clear the areas immediately surrounding the house site in order to make way for the estate's more formal gardens. The arrival of water at the esplanade on July 17 was another crucial construction step. The supply ran down from Busbee Mountain, some 266 feet above the esplanade. The Asheville Woodworking Company soon started business, as well as Biltmore Brick and Tile Works, independent firms getting a boost from the massive project. The latter benefited from North Carolina soil that was ripe with clay. A tram would eventually convey that clay from the estate lands to the brick works where it was fashioned into 25,000 to 30,000 bricks a day, sometimes more, which were then transported back to the construction site. "No flaws, cracks, bats or clinkers," Biltmore Brick's ads proclaimed. The majority of the crews rode to work on open freight cars, while the more patrician of the laborers—the stone carvers, for example—rode in passenger cars. Stonecutters might make $3.50 per day; cabinetmakers, $2.25 to $2.75; labor foremen, $1.60 per day; laborers, $1.00; and the office boys who ferried documents back and forth all day received 35 cents.

One day there would be a large, lush green lawn with a grand fountain in front of the home. But for the time being, the esplanade was the nerve center of construction. As clearing, planting, slope blasting, and foundation construction continued, the esplanade filled with a vast array of work sheds, tools, stone, brick, timber, tracks, and wagons and the horses to pull them. The burgeoning site was a symphony of progress and sweat. Booming blasts of dynamite, like Judaculla come out to play and stamp along the slopes of Lone Pine Mountain, drove the construction opus. The chime-like clinking and clanging of metal hammers striking anvils combined with the percussive thuds of a carpenter's axe against wood. There was the jangle of pulleys, the plunking of pipes, and, rising above it, a chorus of voices barking orders, howling warnings, laughing, arguing. Beneath it all was the tympanic rumble of the Baldwin locomotive as it entered the makeshift yard. The smell of tar and sawdust and the sweat of tired mountain men pierced the clear Appalachian air. Visitors took in the sight of sheds and saws and shops, while tin lunch pails caught the midday sun as they hung from saplings and swayed in the breeze. The work played out against the muddy, impressionist canvas of terra-cotta and clay, with streaks of gleaming white limestone coming through in train cars. At times, hovering above it all in one of his observation towers, was maestro Olmsted.

Both he and Hunt continued traveling and working on numerous projects for other clients, including George. George had purchased the Gouverneur Morris Ogden house in Bar Harbor for a tidy $200,000 and renamed it Point d'Acadie. Olmsted was tending to those grounds as well. As of 1890, both Hunt and Olmsted assumed key roles in the upcoming 1893 World's Columbian Exposition in Chicago. One of Hunt's responsibilities was to design the Administration Building for the expo. Olmsted's challenge was to transform the land and water that would provide the backdrop for the world's greatest technological and artistic endeavors. In their absence from Asheville, the pair employed trusted individuals to act in their stead and execute their plans. For Hunt, those men included Yorkshire-born supervising architect Richard Sharp Smith; and Hunt's son, Richard "Dick" Howland Hunt. For Olmsted, it was chief engineer W. A. Thompson; nurseryman Chauncey Beadle; and James Gall, who had worked as foreman with Olmsted during the Central Park construction. Olmsted had managed to entice the man to North Carolina in 1888. He described the site to Gall as being three miles from "a summer and winter pleasure resort, largely northern in nature," and enthused that the area was considered to be the healthiest on the continent. "It is for that reason," Olmsted wrote, "under good advice Mr. V pitches upon it as a residence for himself and his mother; both being a little delicate."

Beadle was a Canadian botanist with a mind-boggling command of agriculture that had been enhanced even more by time spent studying at the Ontario Agricultural College, and Cornell University in New York State. He was tasked with developing the estate's nursery. Edward Burnett, an agricultural consultant who had worked with the Vanderbilt family on farms at New Dorp and elsewhere, oversaw various agricultural developments. Charles McNamee, now residing in North Carolina, remained George's right-hand man.

Olmsted's travels for commissions took him to Atlanta, among other places where he also had large projects under way: Colorado and California. Richmond. Montgomery. Nashville. Olmsted often felt as though he needed more assistants, but there simply were not enough men in the nation with the right kind of experience. One might be a plantsman, but have little experience with design or extensive education in botany. A trained designer might not know the first thing about—or care for—plants. Travel was wearing on the elderly Olmsted, the very "jar of the cars" an irritant. In late 1890, he was "under the care of an old fashioned Southern doctor who dosed me excessively with calomel, quinine, whiskey and opium." His challenges were mammoth, from the decimated woods in Asheville to the swamplike land that was destined to be the site for the exposition on the Windy City shores.

Toward the end of the year, the Station Inn opened. The papers bragged that the dining establishment would be managed by a gentleman arriving from New York's renowned eatery Delmonico's, and that the kitchen would be the domain of a French chef. Visitors to Asheville not lucky enough to receive an invitation to George's new place would still have a town to entertain them, mountainsides to wander, breathing porches on which to inhale healing mountain air, or grand hotel parlors in which to puff on cigars. The chosen few who did secure invitations to stay at Biltmore, the latest and greatest of any Vanderbilt home—or any home, for that matter—ever built in this country would have need of Asheville's services as well. That is, if the home were ever finished and managed to live up to its growing hype.

The small city had long played host to consumptives and drovers, transplanted knickerbockers and snake oil salesmen. The Land of the Sky had seen them all come and go. But this slight young millionaire was one traveler who looked as though he might stay awhile.

3

Rhapsody in Mauve

These roses told your poet that they grew
But to burn incense to my Lady Sue:
These pensive violets softly murmured, that
They tired and died for love of Lady Nat;
And when I asked these valley-lilies why
They came, they whispered, "Edith," and looked shy.
And I believed them, for, i'-faith, I know,
Horr'round those names the flowers of fancy grow.

Christmas, 1890

Edith and her sisters had their share of admirers, such as the unknown suitor who penned this poem on stationery from the University Club on Madison Square and addressed it to "The Misses Dresser" at 3 West Thirty-Eighth Street in New York City. It was there, in the William R. Travers house, that the Dresser sisters and their grandmother were staying this particular winter. The home was the latest in a succession of winter homes for the young women, and a notable improvement over the dank Turnbull house at 5 West Sixteenth Street, where they had stayed the year before along with a collection of bugs. The Travers house offered better ventilation, an enormous dining room which extended over the back yard, and no noticeable roommates of the insect variety.

As their Newport–New York cycle of habitation had continued, there had been some familial changes. Edith's older brother, Daniel, had graduated Columbia and married a young woman named Emma Burnham. The ceremony had taken place the prior November at St. Luke's in Mattewan, New York. Edith's older sister Natalie stood as maid of honor, dressed neatly in white corded silk, and carrying yellow chrysanthemums. Edith was now just shy of her eighteenth birthday, and the tall, lanky physique of her youth had evolved into a more refined, proportioned, and statuesque carriage. From her grandmother there was much to learn, including impeccable posture and irreproachable manners. Grandmother read and sewed; embroidery was always near at hand. She also entertained missionaries whose lives, passions, and selfless natures set examples for Edith and her sisters.

During her various tenures in Newport, Edith had attended Mrs. Gilliat's School until it closed, followed by a procession of private tutors. For one winter, Henri Francois Gaston Ascier de Pompignan amused Edith and her sisters to no end, if for no other reason than they so enjoyed pronouncing the Martinique native's name. The Newport cold drove Monsieur de Pompignan away. Eventually a friend of Edith's grandmother recommended a French governess, Marie Rambaud, who had worked extensively in England and had reared Lady Alice Stanley, daughter of the Duchess of Devonshire. Soon Edith and her sisters were speaking French as much or more than English, and adhering to Mlle. Rambaud's strict routine of study, physical exercise, meals, and recreation, all scheduled with military precision throughout the day. Edith was never one to favor memorization or recitation whether in English or French, but her math skills were solid.

As children, Edith and Pauline had taken on the pet names "George" and "Willie" for their escapades in and around the house. Behind their grandmother's Newport home were drying grounds, an old stable with a victoria—the French-style carriage that was the choice of all the best families—and two horses. They acquired a number of pets, from collies and canaries to cats and two-toed kittens. They ran and played in a land of adventure perfumed by honeysuckle; surrounded in lilac, jacqueminot roses, English daisies, snowdrops, and hollyhocks.

In those days, the center of social activity was the Newport Casino. Fronting on Bellevue Avenue, the casino—loosely derived from the Italian for "tiny house"—was mere steps away from Edith's grandmother's home. The one thing that did not take place at the Newport Casino was any sort of gambling. This "casino" was a complex of shops and restaurants, and members and guests flocked to the shingle-style center of leisure to play billiards, attend dances and theater, or simply socialize over tea on the porch. The lawn tennis facilities were exceptional. In August 1881, a year after opening, the first ever US National Men's Singles Championship was held at the Newport Casino. There was no end of entertainments for Edith and her sisters, whether taking in a tennis match or strolling on the beach and watching the bathers. Edith adored the polo matches. She, Pauline, and Mlle. Rambaud almost never missed a chance to go to the grounds. There they would secure a seat on Deadhead Hill—the best views were available there—and watch the players, committing their names, and those of their ponies, to memory. William K. Thorn, the cousin of a man named George Washington Vanderbilt, was a noted player and team captain, and trained many of the younger players, including George's nephew, Willie Vanderbilt; and Willie's friend, Harry Payne Whitney.

The Vanderbilts were relatively recent arrivals on the Newport scene. George's oldest brother, Cornelius, had become the first of the family to buy property in Newport when he purchased The Breakers from tobacco magnate Pierre Lorillard, in 1885. Now, George's older brother Willie K. and his wife, Alva, were constructing the seventy-room Marble House, destined to make as much a mark on the shores of that island of Newport as 660 Fifth Avenue had on the island of Manhattan. The Vanderbilt name was now a common one in Newport, as were other Manhattan monikers. Nettie and Amos Pinchot—children of James Pinchot, whose Manhattan home Edith's family had rented—were familiar summer faces, as was Esther Hunt, daughter of architect Richard Morris Hunt.

The dancing school sometimes brought all of them together to learn the latest quadrilles. Edith's grandmother's home was always full of people, the site of dinner parties and teas, and Edith and other children were often called upon to wire flowers for elaborate centerpieces that put the sturdiness of the table to the test. When not invited to attend these fetes (or when festivities exceeded their bedtimes), Edith and Pauline—"George and Willie"—would sometimes venture out onto the tin roof above the dining room to gaze through the skylight upon the guests below.

Such was life in the Mauve Decade, that mallow-hued era that began in 1890 and took its name from the accidental discovery by William H. Perkin of the first synthetic dye. The young chemist had been seeking to synthesize quinine—for treatment of malaria—when, in 1856, he created the popular purplish aniline coloring. The shade grew in popularity before an entire decade was named for it, popularized early on by the likes of Queen Victoria, who wore the shade to her daughter's wedding in 1858; and couture icon Empress Eugénie, wife of Napoleon III, who reputedly favored purple because it matched her eyes. Gone were the plants, insects, and mollusks commonly used to dye fabrics, and soon society was awash in subtle, silky, violet tones bestowed upon the masses not by nature but by science.

One of the leading dishers of gilded dirt during this decade was a columnist who went by the name Cholly Knickerbocker. Cholly offered delicious details about the New York and Newport elite—with occasional reports about the colony abroad—filling society pages with celebrity speculation as viewed through his mauve-colored glasses. Cholly—then penned by a reporter named John W. Keller—was the pseudonym of a succession of journalists beginning in 1891 in the *New York Recorder*. For more than fifty years, Cholly would be the *nom de* several *plumes* who chronicled the lives of the

Four Hundred. "Cholly" was a nod to the northeastern pronunciation of "Charlie," and "Knickerbocker" had its roots in satire, not society. Author Washington Irving of *Rip Van Winkle* and *The Legend of Sleepy Hollow* fame had created the fictional Diedrich Knickerbocker as a writer and lampooner of early New York history and a demystifier of its early Dutch rulers, whom he labeled "Walter the Doubter," "William the Testy," and "Peter the Headstrong." Peter being Peter Stuyvesant, ancestor of the Dresser sisters.

Cholly Knickerbocker left no tiara stone unturned in his quest to document the lives that a nanopercentage of his readers lived. "Cholly Knickerbocker to Tell All" or "Exclusively Yours," the columns proclaimed, as the Cholly *du jour* offered a peek into the comings and goings of fabled families among various homes on the East Coast, highlighting hookups and hemlines along the way. There was nowhere to hide from Cholly's oft acerbic ink, no matter one's age or station. One New Year's dispatch, "Raid on the Low Cuts: Cholly Tells Us What the Dress Reformers Saw at the Grand Opera," detailed the preponderance of clavicular enticements on view in the box seats at the Met.

"It is said that spotters were on hand the other night to take notes of the quantity of shoulders exposed in the parterre," Cholly wrote. "Mrs. Cornelius Vanderbilt's dress was not so low, nor was Mrs. William Astor's, but they are both very thin, with unattractive shoulders. Mrs. Henry Sloan and Mrs. Benjamin Porter have superb busts, and their gowns were cut accordingly."

Cholly was an equal opportunity observer and ribber of society, and the Vanderbilts' escapades merited frequent mention. "The Vanderbilts, Who are Not Sportsmen, Buying up the Adirondacks," he once wrote. "Cornelius, the eldest son, never pulled a trigger in his life or got on top of a horse. Willie K. can cast a fly out of his parlor window and might still be able to kill a pheasant if it sat very still. Fred is a good fisherman, but doesn't shoot or ride, and George is a dilettante in books."

George was accustomed to speculation about his life, and especially his bachelorhood. He was engaged to be married. No—he was a confirmed bachelor. Wait—he was engaged again. He was *truly* engaged this time and it was an immensely suitable match. While Cholly's gaze may not have routinely fixed on the town of Asheville, the local press and visiting New Yorkers also fed the rumor mill. Theories about George's plans abounded. A hotel. A women's college. A school for "poor white children." An industrial and mechanical school. These academic rumors were not surprising considering the Commodore's end-of-life, million-dollar endowment of Nashville's Vanderbilt University, founded in 1873. And George had, in 1887, given $10,000 to Grace Dodge to fund what would become the Teachers College of Columbia University. "Here is your brain money," he wrote the philanthropist, "Now find the brains."

Fascination with his land acquisitions would only grow as time passed, as the site clearings gave way to rising foundations, and once-razed grounds burst forth in fresh plantings. The primary trio worked well together. Olmsted found George to be a "delicate, refined and bookish man, with considerable humor, but shrewd, sharp, exacting and resolute in matters of business." Olmsted's hard work at Biltmore was helped by the fact that he found George to be "frank, trustful," and "cordially friendly."

The so-called "dilettante in books" was beginning to resemble more of a gentleman farmer, but the farm was growing beyond anyone's earliest imagination.

In other news: Queen Victoria has gout, and George is engaged again.

■ ■ ■

"Mud in Asheville worse than any other place, by a good deal. Vanderbilt's place just right for forest management on a rather intensive plan. Hilly, but regeneration of conifer & deciduous both excellent and his house & grounds will be absolutely gigantic."
—*Gifford Pinchot, February 20, 1891*

As more and more acreage was finding its way into George's holdings, George now agreed with Olmsted's suggestion that some form of managed forestry was in order. Olmsted knew just the man for the job.

Recent Yale graduate Gifford Pinchot had returned from Europe where he had studied at the École Nationale Forestière in Nancy, France, and spent time in Germany. During his travels, Pinchot had met and studied with Sir Dietrich Brandis, considered the foremost expert in managed forestry in Europe, arguably the world. Gifford's interest in forestry had been seeded by his father, James Pinchot, who had made a fair fortune as a wallpaper merchant and land speculator. Gifford had grown up very comfortably at 2 Gramercy Square in New York and at Grey Towers, the family's country estate outside Milford, Pennsylvania.

The poor condition of the forests surrounding Grey Towers had deeply affected Gifford's father, who wanted to see them thrive again. James Pinchot became a founding member of the American Forestry Association, and his passion for the subject influenced his son. The turreted Grey Towers was one of Hunt's creations and Olmsted, a friend of the elder Pinchot, had been a guest there. The younger Gifford appeared a natural choice for Biltmore; however, he was currently mulling over an opportunity to work at the US Department of Agriculture's division of forestry under its chief, the Prussian-born Bernhard Fernow. Pinchot's mentor, Brandis, thought that managing a large tract of private forest might be the best way for Pinchot to begin to introduce the concept of scientific forestry in America. Biltmore could be an intriguing, if daunting, endeavor.

Olmsted met Pinchot at Biltmore Station when the twenty-six-year-old visited in October 1891. The two men talked as they made their way along Olmsted's Approach Road. Pinchot had long admired Olmsted, whom he once described as a "quiet-spoken little lame man with a most magnificent head and one of the best minds I have ever had the good luck to encounter." Two figures approached on horseback. They were George and his cousin Clarence Barker. When the group reached the esplanade, Pinchot found the view "gorgeous" and "was amazed and charmed by the situation & scale of [the] new place." However, there was something about the massive undertaking that felt off, as well. "Its setting was superb, the view from it breath-taking, and as a feudal castle it would have been beyond criticism, and perhaps beyond praise," Pinchot later wrote. "But in the U.S. of the nineteenth century and among the one-room cabins of the Appalachian mountaineers, it did not belong. The contrast was a devastating commentary on the injustice of concentrated wealth."

During his stay, Pinchot viewed 40 acres of gardener Chauncey Beadle's growing nursery, which already had 4,200 species of trees and shrubs. Olmsted had compiled a wish list of 43,382 plants culled from 669 varieties. Within Beadle's first year of work, he and his team had planted 40,000 trees and shrubs and were propagating even more. Later, Pinchot took a drive through Asheville with George and Clarence and went for a walk alone with George, whom Pinchot found to be "a simple minded pleasant fellow, full of his place." Pinchot later wrote that, "considering his associations and bringing up, he had a real sense of social responsibility and was eager to do more than merely live on his money." He also found George to be a "rather shy young man, too much and too long sheltered by female relatives, enormously rich, unmarried, but without racing stables or chorus girls in his cosmos." Biltmore was, Pinchot could see, "his heart's delight."

The following month, Olmsted met with Pinchot in Brookline, Massachusetts. The pair discussed Biltmore's forestal possibilities at length. Afterward, Olmsted wrote George, saying that Pinchot "would be glad to be identified with the undertaking, look to make his reputation upon it, and serve you with a degree of zeal that you could not expect to obtain from any one else." When Pinchot called on George in New York on a December Sunday after church, George was ready to offer him a position. He asked Pinchot if he would design a working plan for George's growing forest. Pinchot accepted. Fernow, at the Department of Agriculture, was not happy with Pinchot's decision and let him know that he did not believe the

Biltmore experiment would work. But by the end of the month, Pinchot joined George, Olmsted, Hunt, Hunt's son Dick, and Edward Burnett on the train for his first trip South as a Biltmore employee.

"Reached Biltmore about 6:30 & dined about nine," he wrote in his diary on New Year's Eve. "Very pleasant time. This traveling on private cars is something almost too good for words." While luxurious Vanderbiltian train travel was certainly a nice perk—Catharine Hunt, too, wrote of the joy of traveling south in one of George's cars, complete with a private cook—Pinchot would soon be back in the forester's world of converted farmhouses, pitched tents, and roadside inns.

Upon arrival, Pinchot got settled in the Brick House, a farmhouse on the property that had been renovated by Hunt's Asheville colleague Richard Sharp Smith. The residence was part of the property once belonging to a grist and sawmill operator named B. J. Alexander, whose holdings south of Best had been some of George's early acquisitions. Olmsted, Hunt, and George often stayed there while in town, as did McNamee and his wife and various family and friends. When Pinchot awoke the next morning, Hunt popped his head in to say, "Happy New Year."

"So 1892 opened," Pinchot wrote.

He began in earnest. At the esplanade, he saw chief engineer Thompson about maps. He rode the land with Olmsted, admiring the snow settling on the mountains, and despairing at what he referred to as the "sad lack of middle ages" of the trees. He assessed existing tracts and those George considered buying. When he wasn't working, he taught Sunday school, sat alongside Dick Hunt as they bested George and Burnett at whist, and he "fell violently in love with a fiery little black gelding by the name of Punch."

His efforts produced the "Biltmore Working Plan," the objective of which was to create a constant stream of forest products while improving the condition of the forest's health. George and Olmsted wanted Pinchot to present his results and the achievements at Biltmore at the upcoming World's Columbian Exposition in Chicago. No one had ever attempted this kind of scientific forestry management in the United States, where many still believed that forest resources were so unlimited that management was unnecessary. "When the Gay Nineties began, the common word for our forests was 'inexhaustible,'" Pinchot later wrote. "To waste timber was a virtue and not a crime." Pinchot was the first educated forester in America to have been born on American soil.

Pinchot's work attracted much attention—and affection—from George's niece, Florence "Adele" Sloane, the eighteen-year-old daughter of George's sister Emily. Adele adored both Biltmore and her uncle George. She had his dark eyes, passion for the written word, and preferred wearing her ebony hair in a Psyche knot.

"I have an easy natural figure . . ." the young woman wrote in her diary. "I have a moderately small foot, and I suppose a very well-shaped leg, only no one ever sees that . . . I suppose I am moderately graceful, and perhaps very much so on horseback; at least, so people tell me."

Adele loved riding, and Biltmore provided ample opportunity for that sport. When she saw George in New York—George at 640 Fifth Avenue, and Adele at 642 with her family—they reminisced ceaselessly about Biltmore, often to the chagrin of George's mother. "Why don't you all pack up and go back to Biltmore again, instead of always grumbling here?" the Vanderbilt dame would ask. And of course they would. George was only ten years Adele's senior, more like an older brother in that respect. She, too, loved books, languages, art. She was indeed her uncle's niece.

When she visited that spring, Adele found herself captivated by Pinchot. The six-foot-tall forester had a fit frame, prominent brow, and dark hair which he parted on the side. He was handsome and tastefully mustachioed, well educated, and spoke *to* Adele about things like science and spiritualism. Their paths and wickets crossed again in Bar Harbor, Maine, over croquet at George's Point d'Acadie manor.

Adele penned letters to Pinchot, often from New York, sharing that she was "Biltmore homesick."

"I think I would give anything I have to be down in Biltmore again," she wrote. She was tired of the forced conversations she endured in New York. She wrote him about the theater, music, books she'd read, even the consistencies of clouds. Some letters were laments for her prescribed life. "Most of my opinions have come from books. Experiences and real things are what I want now." She sometimes finished her letters with a flourish in French, one of several languages she spoke.

Pinchot may have returned Adele's correspondence but not her affections. Those were for someone nearer his heart and nearer Biltmore. Across the French Broad River from Biltmore was a summer estate called Strawberry Hill, where lived Laura Houghteling. Pinchot was clearly enamored of Laura, and Adele confessed freely to him in one of her letters that the mere mention of her rival's name "sends shivers up my spine." Be that as it may, nothing could keep young Adele from Biltmore.

In many ways, country estate life offered young women of Adele's station more freedom, especially on horseback and on hunts. While it might be scandalous for an unchaperoned young woman to attend the opera or theater with a man to whom she was not engaged, in the country she might take off on an hour's long ride, galloping into the unchaperoned wilds. Places like Newport and Bar Harbor were miniature seaside incarnations of New York society. ("I hate the gossip of this place," she wrote Pinchot. "I hate the formality, and sad to say, I dislike a great many of the people.") Her own family's estate, Elm Court, in the Berkshires, was more of a respite. But Biltmore and its land, at more than twenty hours' train journey from the small talk Adele had grown to loathe, must have been a refuge to any spirited, intelligent young woman. It was fitting that her favorite uncle, George—himself little interested in Manhattan maneuvering—was designing an estate that spoke to Adele's very soul.

■ ■ ■

For Edith Dresser and her sisters, that spring and summer were marked by loss and challenges, which would combine to change the course of the young women's lives. Winter had again been spent in New York, but as spring arrived, Edith's grandmother was not faring well. In April 1892, the family traveled back to Newport, again crossing the waters of the Narragansett on the Fall River boat, just as they had with their dying father. Life went back to normal at the red house next to the Newport Casino, if only temporarily. Edith's grandmother died in July, five days shy of her eighty-seventh birthday. She was surrounded by her grandchildren, for whom she had cared nearly ten years, and a black collie named Paddy that was reluctant to leave the ailing woman's side as her condition worsened.

Afterward, it was one last trip to her beloved New York City for the late Mrs. Susan Elizabeth Fish LeRoy where, at St. Mark's-in-the-Bowery on East Tenth Street, she was buried in the company of her people, the Stuyvesants, in a mausoleum once a part of the family's private chapel: "In this vault lies buried Petrus Stuyvesant Late Captain General and Governor in Chief of Amsterdam in New Netherland now called New York and the Dutch West India Islands."

Years earlier, Edith's grandmother had written a letter to be opened upon her death by her son, Stuyvesant, Edith's uncle. She left instructions that were both practical—"no pall bearers or unnecessary parade" at the funeral—and personal for those she was leaving behind.

It is my earnest prayer and hope that every thing will be arranged without trouble or publicity. That every one will feel satisfied that a just and equable [sic] distribution has been made—May all my dear children and grand children live in peace and love, mutually blessing and aidding [sic] each other. Their Uncle Stuyvesant will be the head to whom they must all look with reverence and love, and to whose tender care and consideration I commit the orphans and fatherless. . . .

Now my dear children—good bye to all. Stand by one another. . . . A house united can never fall.

In the wake of losing their grandmother, Edith and her sisters had just a month to vacate the grand house at 206 Bellevue Avenue in Newport, as it would be sold as part of their grandmother's estate. The sisters ascended into the attic to assess the many papers and pictures that lived in the recesses beneath the eaves, each carrying its own memory of lives gone, individuals past. Edith and her sisters knew they could not keep everything. Of the photographs they decided to save, one in particular captured their hearts—Grandmother surrounded by the four sisters. They also decided to save some photos of their parents and other family members. As for the rest of the papers and letters, the sisters went outside to the garden and burned them. Edith's Aunty King made arrangements to renovate a house in town, the Smith House, and once it was finished, the girls and Mlle. Rambaud, ever their guardian, could reside there. Until then, they were destined for Riggs Boarding House, run by an old Scotch landlord.

Spring turned to fall, and Thanksgiving approached. It would have been quite a lonely one for the girls had it not been for a Newport neighbor and welcoming friend, Edith Wharton. Wharton invited Edith and her sisters to Pencraig Cottage to share the holiday meal with her, her dogs, and her husband, Edward "Teddy" Wharton. At this point in her career, the well-traveled and quick-witted Wharton had already published a poem, "The Last Giustiniani," in *Scribner's Magazine*. She had spent a good deal of her youth abroad, and had a keen interest in design, which was reflected in her cottage decor. She understood the world that the Dresser sisters had been born into. She, too, claimed Knickerbocker lineage, via the Schermerhorn line. While the holiday was a sad one for Edith and her sisters, Wharton's invitation was a welcome one, softening the blow of a cold, lonely season.

Christmas found Edith still at Riggs Boarding House. She and her sisters decorated a small tree for a waitress who also lived at the house, a black woman who planned to bring the tree home for her young daughter. Aunty King made them dinner, but the year's end could not come soon enough. On the last day of that year, Edith and her sisters opened all the windows they could. It was time for 1892 to be carried away on the winds.

■ ■ ■

Shortly before Grover Cleveland's second inauguration, on February 26, 1893, the Philadelphia and Reading Railroad went bankrupt. What transpired in the following months and years would be the worst economic depression the United States had yet experienced: The Panic of 1893. The Erie Railroad failed in July; the Northern Pacific and Union Pacific eventually followed suit. As the depression worsened, stocks dove and runs on banks commenced. Thousands of companies and more than five hundred banks would fail. The rapid expansion and industrialization of the post–Civil War era was shrinking and buckling. As railroads curtailed expansion, the steel companies felt the pinch as well. There was plenty of inflation and little or no available credit. Unemployment skyrocketed.

As the depression descended, Edith, her sisters, and Mlle. Rambaud were a world away. The new year brought new adventure as the young women and Mlle. Rambaud set sail on the *Seguranca* for the Caribbean and South America in late January, bidding the cold Rhode Island winter and Riggs Boarding House farewell. Warmer— and more affordable—climes were on the horizon.

The ice floes of Brooklyn had given way to storms at sea and finally, thankfully, the smooth, blue waters of St. Thomas. Joyfully immersed in sunshine and native French speakers, the girls and their chaperone—whom they teasingly nicknamed "Boy" for the voyage— decided to push on to Rio de Janeiro. Their journey took them past Barbados to Martinique, where in St. Pierre they inquired about their old tutor Monsieur de Pompignan, who was away on business. They sailed by Santa Lucia and Guadeloupe, then the *Seguranca* turned inland at the mouth of the mighty Amazon and headed toward the city of Pará. Edith and her sisters were lucky enough to be snuck below deck to watch the greenest of the crew members be initiated at their first equator crossing. The long-standing naval tradition varies, usually featuring a Neptune and sometimes involving a "court" or even Davy Jones. That evening the young men were soaped up and shaved down with a wooden scythe by a senior sailor dressed as the god of the sea, and then ceremoniously dumped headfirst into a sail full of water. Edith was a long way from Newport, indeed.

Upon traveling farther south, the family stayed just outside Rio in Tijuca where, the sisters were informed, the reputation of their imposing heights had preceded them. Word had spread through the town that "twenty-four feet of American Girl was traveling down the coast."

The Dresser sisters' seafaring adventure lasted a few months. In keeping with the family love of pets, Edith's sister Pauline bought a parrot in Rio, but it did not survive the cold, damp return voyage north to New York Harbor. It was again back to Newport, where they hoped a renovated house awaited them. How long they would be able to stay, no one could know. The cold New York reality struck Edith as she stepped off the ship that Easter Sunday, April 2, and into a veil of city snow.

■ ■ ■

Also returning that month from points south was a fellow named William Bradhurst Osgood Field.

"Nothing can express the blueness of my feelings when I left Biltmore," he wrote his mother from his apartment in Hoboken, where he was entrenched in engineering studies at Stevens Institute of Technology. Reentry to student life proved jarring after his time in North Carolina, he added, so he took a Turkish bath to ease the transition to his usual daily existence. "I entered the house and the vacation became a dream of the past, and in five minutes I would not have thought I had ever had anything like a ride at Biltmore."

"Willie" to some and "Billy" to his mother and often George, Field hailed from a family known in New York and abroad, where his uncle Osgood was a respected member of the American colonies in

London and Rome. Field's mother, Augusta Currie Bradhurst Field, and his sister, Mary Pearsall Field, were well established in New York society. The Fields knew the Vanderbilts, though their own financial position paled in comparison. But Field and George shared interests beyond the size of one's bank account. Field, like his friend George, was a lover of the outdoors, an avid reader, and an obsessive collector of books and illustrations.

Field was one of several friends and family members who visited George during the construction of his North Carolina estate. While the house was not finished, the lands and nursery continued to grow. Chauncey Beadle filed a report in 1893 stating that, since coming on board in 1890, he had purchased 209,925 plants, had propagated yet another 2,935,615 and, closer to home, had wandered the woods and region to collect another 366,527 plants. All in all, an estimated 2,870,678 plants were eventually installed at Biltmore.

Meanwhile, Pinchot continued to explore and assess the Biltmore lands. An enchanting and promising tract of roughly 20,000 acres known as the Pink Beds—so named for its preponderance of mountain laurel and rhododendron—had been added to George's holdings the previous year. Pinchot happily noted that this acquisition would be a fine source of virgin hardwood. Another favorable tract on the far side of Pisgah would add another 94,000 acres to the forest if George secured it.

When the Chicago World's Columbian Exposition of 1893 opened that summer, those involved with the work at Biltmore were a significant presence there. Olmsted designed the Midway Plaisance and canal and Hunt the Administration Building. At the North Carolina exhibit in the Agricultural Building, Pinchot presented the work he and others had been doing at Biltmore, and also published a book that same year titled *Biltmore Forest: The Property of Mr. George W. Vanderbilt: An Account of Its Treatment, and the Results of the First Year's Work.* As a result, Pinchot's employment opportunities quickly increased and offers of private consulting began to trickle in.

As that year drew to a close, George welcomed his nieces Edith—his sister Margaret Shepard's daughter—and Adele, along with his aunt Virginia Vanderbilt Bacon and her husband to Biltmore. George's friend the composer and pianist Courtlandt Palmer entertained everyone in the evenings. George's cousin Clarence Barker, a talented performer and composer in his own right, was there as well. However, Clarence's bronchial struggles continued to hamper his health, no matter how curative the Asheville air.

Adele felt her lovesickness for Pinchot beginning to pass. Time at Biltmore was always a tonic, if also a reminder of what she felt lacking in her New York social life.

"I love to meet new people this way who are totally different from society men," she wrote in her diary. "If I marry a society man, it will narrow my life down to that set tremendously, and I will probably be very little thrown in with the sort of people whom I thoroughly enjoy talking to."

Fires became embers. 1893 became a memory.

"It has been so gloriously beautiful out today," she wrote on the first day of the year in the North Carolina mountains. "It made me feel wild."

■ ■ ■

Of course, challenges at Biltmore were to be expected along with progress. The winter of 1893 had been so cold that mortar would not set. Warming spring temperatures were encouraging, but heavy spring rains followed, flooding the clay pits. No clay, no bricks. An undertaking of this size could not be without danger, as during the first year of construction, when a powder explosion seriously injured a laborer and a foreman who were working to clear the site.

Personalities, too, proved difficult. In Olmsted's absence, he gave direction to Beadle and John Gall. Olmsted did not want any specific design element taken to a finished stage until the entire property was ready for its finishing touches. Otherwise, he believed, the grounds would look disjointed in the end. A disjointed appearance along the way was fine, but the final strokes should be considered together. Olmsted felt that Gall—whom Pinchot described as a "precise old person without much knowledge of trees and none of forestry"—aspired to make his own name as a landscape architect, and therefore didn't always follow Olmsted's instructions precisely. "He tries to improve upon them and blunders," Olmsted wrote.

Olmsted's plans were extremely detailed, from the smallest sedum to the tallest hemlock. Plantings were staggered so that the varieties themselves stood in proper relation to one another. He preferred the "soft dovetailing" of differing species at differing heights, rather than "direct lines of division." He wanted smaller plantings placed at the edge of larger ones to accomplish this. He told workers to break up anything too close to a proper row, and to create natural-seeming outlines. The hemlock line soaring above the evergreen was too straight. Get younger ones, or substitute some red cedars or yellow and white pines, which could be placed behind the hemlock groupings. Evergreen canes should be on the banks overhanging the water. Place juniper and yew near the bridle path. And if any water falls over the flat face of a dam, strike it with a sledgehammer so it looks less like a piece of masonry, and place a stone under the falling water to add "foam and sparkle" and "add to the purling sound." Olmsted painted his landscape from afar, while another hand held the brush, the shrub, the seedlings of promise.

George, too, was often away, whether traveling with Clarence in Japan or yachting in the Mediterranean and touring northern Africa and Europe with his brother Willie. Yet Biltmore remained in mind, and he not only brought home artifacts from abroad, but cuttings as well for the nursery from places like Gibraltar. Back at Biltmore, one by one tasks were completed. The shepherd's and gardener's cottages were among the first structures finished. In the village, a new passenger station was in the works, with permission from Southern Railway, and an estate office opened in the village, which was slowly beginning to take shape. As the house rose and its outline became apparent, it began to hold its own against the dramatic backdrop.

Hunt wrote Catharine that the mountains were "just the right size and scale for the chateau." George's original, more modest plans—the ones that were a good 100,000 square feet smaller—for his country retreat were now a distant memory.

But it was Olmsted's painstakingly conceived Approach Road that was truly the design linchpin, bringing the estate together, leading every visitor to the home along a winding wonder of towering, flowering fauna that, as Olmsted desired, should entice those traveling it "as paintings on the wall of a gallery." The landscape architect insisted that the arrangement of plantings and water features shouldn't be overly formal, but rather "with some caprice."

Hunt knew the value of the road's whimsically precise design as well, certainly aware of the impact it added to one's first sighting of the château he had designed. "Hasn't Olmsted done wonders with the approach road?" he wrote Catharine. "It alone will give him lasting fame. Please tell him so for me. If only Burnett, Pinchot and I succeed as well, what a blissful time is ahead for George in the fulfillment of his ideals; and may he live to a ripe old age to enjoy his and our work."

Both men, constantly pulled in so many directions, already so lauded, seemed to sense the lasting effect this great work at Biltmore would have on their legacies. Happily ensconced in the renovated Brick House, Olmsted once wrote his nephew and, later, stepson John Charles Olmsted about the work the team was doing. Olmsted knew that as he aged, his sons would play a larger role in the ongoing endeavor. He tried to communicate how Biltmore would affect John's life, as well, telling him that Biltmore "will, twenty years hence, be what Central Park has been to me. The first great *private* work of our profession in the country."

Hunt wrote to his wife, Catharine, "Nothing being spared by G.W.V. If it is not a success, the fault will lie with us, who are called upon to do our best." Biltmore was, Catharine knew, the "professional joy" of her lauded husband's career.

Everyone who came to Asheville wanted to get a peek at the

progress. Some of these people were invited; others were not. Local hotels, the Battery Park among them, actually had a limited number of passes available for guests who wished to wander the property. Some visitors attracted more attention than others, at least from Cholly Knickerbocker and the society pages. Eva Palmer—sister of George's musician friend Courtlandt—was one such visitor. When she traveled to Asheville with her mother in late 1894, the rumor mill kicked into high gear. Cholly, ever in the know, took to his desk to quash the tittle-tattle.

He opined, "Those infernal busybodies who make it their business to start false rumors see in this visit a positive determination on the part of the youngest Vanderbilt to marry Miss Palmer." It was a well-worn road, in Cholly's opinion, and traveled too often without good reason.

"So for about the twentieth time we have this very retiring young fellow engaged to be married. . . . The Palmers, who are all learned and studious, and George Vanderbilt who is extremely bookish, are old friends. . . ." As to any pending engagement, there was, Cholly assured his readers, "not a word of truth in it."

Curiosity about any of George's potential paramours was hardly surprising, especially in light of Biltmore. George was constructing a massive country retreat. Would there not be a Mrs. Vanderbilt anytime soon to help him entertain? In fact, there was one already. For the time being, the main woman in George's life continued to be his mother. All other energy was going into his home and retreat which, in many ways, would be as much or more hers as his. Catharine Hunt, who spent an increasing amount of time with the Vanderbilts as her husband continued work on Biltmore, found George's devotion to his mother "something beautiful to see."

She and others came, enjoying evenings at the Brick House, marveling as the home grew, limestone block by Indiana limestone block, brick by Biltmore brick, waiting for the day the grand lady's crown would be completed, rising above the ever-changing landscape.

4

Collaborations
and Consecrations

If Edith stepped out onto the iron balcony off the drawing room and peered between the two hotels across the street, she could glimpse the Avenue des Champs-Élysées, *la plus belle avenue du monde*, its grand expanse gracefully flanked by spectacular homes and enchanting gardens, its well-trod gravel populated by pedestrians and trotters.

In 1895, the Dresser sisters and their devoted Mlle. Rambaud resided at 15 Rue Vernet, a charming fifth-floor sublet with no elevator and this bit of view. It was steps away from that avenue of the Elysian Fields, one of the spokes extending out from the Rond-point des Champs-Élysées and the thoroughfare's centerpiece, the Napoleon-commissioned Arc de Triomphe.

The brood's first Paris apartment, at 61 Avenue Marceau, had been right in the middle of the American colony that the Franco-philic siblings swore they would avoid so that they could truly live *la vie Parisienne*. Life at that address had not been, however, without its diversions. There was the able Chef Henri Boulot, whose appetites also ran toward his assistant, Germaine, that is until Madame Boulot turned up at the apartment with a carving knife. Police had been summoned to remove another couple in the Dressers' employ when the pair spent too much time drinking and not enough time cooking and cleaning. And once a month like clockwork, a horse-drawn cart carrying a copper bathtub and heating unit arrived at the apartment building next to theirs. Deliverymen carried the wares in and, several hours later, carried them out, loaded them on the cart, and departed. This routine was for the older, fastidious monsieur next door who never missed his monthly bath. One bright spot in the sisters' lives was Mademoiselle Follette, a dog that Germaine gave to Edith's sister Natalie to keep her company during a bout of illness. In keeping with their newly adopted home, the sisters taught the pup to patriotically fall down and "die for France."

Paris in the 1890s could not disappoint spirited young American women who possessed a command of the language and an appreciation for the culture. Émile Zola, Paul Bourget, and Anatole France were in the bookstores. Grieg conducted. Paderewski played. Paris Salons brimmed with the works of well-known painters while the banks of the Seine were lined with artists of every stripe and all levels of ability. Even the advertisements for the newest wines or cabarets enticed passersby. The lithographic talents of Jules Chéret illustrated advertisements for the skater's Palais de Glace, the Folies Bergère, or the Moulin Rouge, earning him the title "father of the modern poster." Chéret and his compatriot Henri Toulouse-Lautrec captured the skirt-swinging, plume-topped, femme extraordinaire of the moment.

For the Dresser sisters and many other Americans, Belle Époque Paris provided a more affordable, yet still eminently stylish, choice of residence. After returning from South America to Newport and moving into the house their Aunty King had renovated for them, they examined their funds and found them sorely lacking—a mere fraction of the money available to them when their grandmother was alive. So that fall they set sail yet again, this time aboard the French steamer *La Touraine*, a speedy vessel which had once made the New York–Le Havre crossing in a brisk six days, twenty hours, and six minutes. What transatlantic travel lacked in South American equatorial rituals, it made up for in gustatory delights. The crossing prepared the Dresser palates well for France, with menus that included *artichauts poivrade, saucisson de Bologne, moules marinières, ris de veau princesse, tripes à la mode de Caen, côtelettes de mouton, po-*

tage Normande, filet de boeuf à la Portugaise and, to finish things off, a selection of *petit gâteaux* or a *baba Parisien*.

When they had bid adieu to Newport in 1893, Edith and her sisters left their faithful collie, Paddy, with William the coachman, who went to work with Mrs. Catharine Hunt at her Newport residence, Hilltop. Now, two years later, the Dresser girls found Mrs. Hunt's younger son Joe in their social circle, as he was beginning his studies at the Beaux-Arts where he would follow in the footsteps of both his architect father and older brother, who were immersed in the final push to finish the new American architectural masterpiece everyone was talking about: Biltmore House.

■ ■ ■

George wanted to honor and commemorate the men who were making his dream home a reality. In the spring of 1895, he summoned the world-renowned painter John Singer Sargent to Biltmore to paint portraits of Frederick Law Olmsted and Richard Morris Hunt.

Born in Florence, Italy, to American parents, Sargent had little formal schooling as a youth, but traveled extensively. He studied art at the Accademia di Belle Arti in the Renaissance city of his birth, and in Paris he studied in the atelier of French portraitist Carolus-Duran as well as at the École des Beaux-Arts. As his career developed, Sargent spent time in London and Paris and visited several times with Claude Monet in Giverny, where the older impressionist had committed his legendary water lilies to canvas.

By the time George commissioned him for the Olmsted and Hunt portraits, Sargent was already a sought-after portraitist and had, the decade before, painted several Vanderbilts: George's mother, Maria; Maria's brother Benjamin; Benjamin's wife, and one of George's dearest cousins, Virginia Barker Bacon. In 1890, Sargent had painted George: In the portrait, he stands with a bookish hunch, clasping a crimson-edged volume, his deep-set eyes peering out from beneath prominent brows, his dark-clad form and black hair almost disappearing into the ebon background.

Sargent traveled from New York to Biltmore with Richard and Catharine Hunt in one of George's private railcars. Olmsted was already in North Carolina, hoping to return home to Massachusetts.

Sargent was not the only reason Olmsted stayed. Olmsted was anticipating a stressful reunion with both George and Hunt. Though Olmsted and Hunt had worked together in a mostly harmonious fashion, their views of the evolving village were, according to Olmsted, "neither consistent nor reconcilable." Olmsted's desire for a New England approach conflicted with Hunt's preference for more of a French model. "I don't at all like Hunt's view," Olmsted wrote a colleague. "I don't like French villages. I do not think they are suitable to American habits but I am afraid that Mr. V. takes Mr. Hunt's view and I do not think it prudent to go away just before they are arriving." Olmsted stayed to sit for Sargent and stand up for his vision for the village.

Sargent arrived not to a finished home and landscape but to a set piece held together by scaffolding and mud. Somewhat chilly spring temperatures and persistent muck and chaos outside the doors forced the portrait sessions primarily indoors. Hours passed, Sargent occasionally stepping far back from both subject and canvas to take in the scene—present or imagined—then return to the work, palette in hand, decisive in his strokes.

"My campaign here announces itself ominously," Sargent wrote a friend. "Both wives prove to me that I must imagine thus [that] their husbands look at all like what they look like at present—totally different really." Neither the subjects nor setting met his expectations—the former in waning health, the latter still mired in struggling plant specimens and construction chaos. And whether or not she acknowledged it at the time, Catharine Hunt later wrote that "with the extraordinary inner perception of subconsciousness that marks so much of Mr. Sargent's work, he seemed to have divined, apparently without knowing it himself, how much more ill R[ichard] was than we realized. . . ."

Olmsted was now seventy-three, and he and his family already had concerns about his declining health and mental fitness. His nephew and stepson, John, wrote Olmsted's son, Frederick Jr.—who was attending to the completion of the esplanade—that "I am inclined to think that Father had better come home with Mother as soon as Mr. Sargent can let him off from the sittings." Hunt, too, though a few years younger at sixty-seven, was weakening. Sargent, consciously or not, seemed to have captured the encroaching infirmity of the two architectural masters. The persistently exhausted Olmsted had begun to show signs of memory difficulty, enough to alarm his sons. Finally, Olmsted could literally stand no more. His son Frederick Jr., who also sported a beard, eventually stood in for his ailing father, donning Olmsted's top coat so that Sargent could finish his work and Olmsted could leave for much-needed rest.

Sargent completed the paintings and George had his tribute in oil. In Hunt's portrait, the architect stands, gray-haired and goateed, one foot atop the pedestal of a Venetian wellhead, the house's magnificent stair tower in the background. The colors are muted, the wellhead appearing to get the most love from Sargent's brush. Catharine thought the portrait "represents a man thin and worn from suffering, and though it has a certain likeness, the fire, the vigor, the personality are all wanting." Olmsted, to the contrary, is set amid colors of forest and shrubbery, greens and russets engulfing his form as he leans on a walking stick. Sargent's view of each man imparted something elegant yet foreboding, majestic and final. In the end, both works turned out to be quite prescient. Sargent was a master, perhaps unable to keep truth from influencing his brush, seeing something in his subjects that perhaps no one close to the two masters wanted to face.

Time moved on. Plantings on the pergola beneath the south terrace, placed there by Catharine Hunt and George's mother, Maria, took root and climbed skyward, each increment of growth like the tick of clock, visual reminders that time—and the construction timetable—continued unabated. Workers came and went, as did trusted advisers. Earlier that year Pinchot, who had opened his own forest consultancy firm in New York, had broken the news that he would be reducing his role at Biltmore, and suggested to George that he replace him "in part at least by a resident German forester." George kept Pinchot on as a $1,000-per-year consultant.

Eminent forester Sir Dietrich Brandis recommended his former student and colleague Dr. Carl Alwin Schenck to pick up where Pinchot would at least partially leave off. Schenck was enjoying a vacation on the beaches of the French Riviera when he received a telegram from George with an intriguing offer: "Are you willing to come to America and to take charge of my forestry interest in western North Carolina?" At twenty-seven years of age, Schenck set off for the United States with the telegram in his pocket. He had arrived in April 1895 and spent his first Biltmore summer lodging with Frederick Law Olmsted and his wife, Mary. He enjoyed meeting the couple, and became fond of estate manager Charles McNamee and farm manager George Weston.

For his part, Pinchot was pleased with his first discussion with Schenck. However, in June, when Pinchot took his replacement out to Big Creek, a spot George was interested in lumbering, the men's more in-depth discussion there left Pinchot feeling less optimistic. He wrote in his diary that Schenck was "rather rash in statement and conclusions, but improving."

That month brought another, joyous visitor, George's dear niece Adele, now Mrs. Adele Burden, who had just wed in a spectacular—and spectacularly expensive—wedding to ironworks industrialist Jay Burden. The first stop on her honeymoon was her favorite uncle's estate. George had River Cliff Cottage, a home on the grounds which had been finished in 1892, prepared for the newlyweds. If there were any lingering romantic ghosts of foresters past, Adele exorcised them once and for all.

George wanted his home finished enough for a grand house party to be held over Christmas and New Year's. If it came to pass, the gathering would have one notable absence. George was in Bar Harbor when he heard the news about Hunt. The date was July 31, 1895, and though Hunt had been ill, the architect's death came as a surprise to all. Catharine had not even had time to call Dick to his father's bedside in Newport, a town that had benefited so greatly from the man's genius. George ordered work stopped until Hunt was buried.

Once work resumed, it did so in earnest, spending and schedules stretched to their limits. Charles McNamee and Richard Sharp Smith pressed on all fronts to get the house finished both inside and out. Workers clothed the brick exterior in limestone and began to bejewel the grand dame with ornamental sculpture. They used wire to attach roof slates to purlins that had been bolted to steel trusses—the lack of wood in the roof adding to the structure's fire resistance. Tiles on the ridgeline of the dramatically inclined roof bore a stamp of the Vanderbilt "V." A total of 287 train cars' worth of limestone—nearly 5,000 tons of the material by the time the exterior was complete—had made their way down from Hallowell Stone Co. in Bedford, Indiana, a region renowned for its quarries. It seemed that a little of Indiana was to be found in some of the country's most elaborate homes, including Willie K. and Alva Vanderbilt's home at 660 Fifth Avenue.

At Biltmore, the white limestone could catch the ample light, reducing the potentially overbearing appearance that a château of such scale might have. The house covered more than 4 acres—almost the same footprint as the original Grand Central Depot, which George's grandfather, the Commodore, had unveiled in 1871. Workers lifted the limestone into place with wooden derricks and geared winches. The blocks were crandalled by hand to increase surface imperfections and better absorb the sun's rays. Soon the rough-hewn stone was covered in scaffolding so the artisans could climb atop to finish the ornamental works around doors, windows, and balconies. Plaster models for stone carvings had been meticulously numbered; photos of all were kept at Hunt's office in New York. Now the subjects of those designs burst to life on the gleaming facade. Finials sprouted romantically around doors and windows. Carved capitals emerged. Life-sized

St. Louis and St. Joan D'Arc appeared upon plinths flanking the spiral stair tower, ready to stand guard. Two grand *rosso di Verona* marble lions slept in crates that would keep the big cats safe from the construction zoo around them. Gargoyles waited to spew mountain rain. Beautiful grotesques peered down from crevices and cornerstones. No two appeared alike: one grasping a mandolin here, another stroking his beard there. Acorns and oak leaves were scattered about the structure's surfaces as well, newly co-opted symbols of a family that held no claim to historical arms or crests of their own.

The interior, too, began to take shape. Furnishings, friezes, and tapestries soon found their homes within the cavernous space. Many surfaces showcased the tile work of Valencian master Rafael Guastavino y Moreno. Guastavino was no stranger to the Vanderbilt family before he came South to lend his magical touch to Biltmore House. A graduate of Barcelona's Escola Especial de Mestres d'Obres, Guastavino had honed his architectural and building talents in that city and Catalonia before coming to America in 1881. His signature technique—embedding very thin slabs of tile in beds of mortar—allowed him to create smooth, curved surfaces without the additional need of buttressing. This approach had been used for centuries in his native Spain and was now showcased throughout Biltmore House, perhaps most noticeably in the vaulted ceiling hovering over George's 70,000-gallon indoor swimming pool. Floors, ceilings, stairwells . . . the curves and domes were not only beautiful to behold, but fireproof to boot.

Guastavino had also recently worked with Hunt and Olmsted at the World's Columbian Exposition in Chicago as principal architect of the Spanish Pavilion. His talents graced places like the Boston Public Library's McKim Building and Carnegie Hall and the technique he mastered and the firm he ran with his son would eventually contribute lasting elements to iconic structures such as the Great Hall of Ellis Island and the corridors of the rebuilt Grand Central Terminal. In fact, an immigrant arriving in America for the first time would likely encounter Richard Morris Hunt's work at the base of the Statue of Liberty and then stand beneath Guastavino tiles at the Great Hall of Ellis Island. Truly, these two contributors to Biltmore House were as much a part of public American life as any artist or architect of the time. Their works were not relegated solely to the private dwellings and secretive salons of the wealthy, but were intrinsic elements of spaces through which all walks of people passed.

In 1895, Guastavino was also working on an estate of his own—"Rhododendron"—in nearby Black Mountain, complete with on-site kilns. He made the architecturally ironic choice to construct his three-story home of wood.

■ ■ ■

While Biltmore House itself may have looked like a château from the Loire Valley, the whistle-stop beyond the gates was beginning to take on the feel of an English manor village, as temporary structures were gradually being replaced with more permanent offices and shops. John Olmsted told his stepbrother Frederick Jr. that he didn't think George was going to finish the community before he opened the house. True, Hunt's exquisitely designed church was not yet done, but the outline of its growing structure, with its bell tower and pebbledash-coated exterior, was fast becoming the heart of George's unfinished model village.

Now thirty-three years old, George was anxious to move in. As of October 1895, though, his own room on the second floor remained incomplete. The northern "bachelor" wing was ready for guests, and would have to do as temporary quarters for the bachelor master of the house. Servants, for the time being, would stay above the stables. George panicked the day before their arrival because running water would not reach their quarters. The plumber, thankfully, was able to remedy the situation before workers were forced to begin toting buckets of water up from the basement. Dick Hunt and his wife, Margaret, traveled down to Asheville and joined George for dinner at the estate. Work remained: the stables, quarters above them, the village, the dairy barns, the market garden complex, and more. There was still much to do if they were going to be finished by Christmas.

They were not.

After six years of construction by more than a thousand workers, it was clear that there were more years of work to come, if George's finances held out. The scientific research arboretum that Olmsted so dearly desired had not materialized. The music room was bare and unfinished. Many works of the noted Austrian-born sculptor Karl Bitter—a Richard Morris Hunt favorite—had yet to be situated in their intended locations. Secondary staircases were unfinished, which would force guests and servants alike to use the same central stone staircase. Many interior wooden doors had not yet been installed. George's own room and some guest rooms were still incomplete and, perhaps most ironically for a bibliophile, George's library was nowhere near done.

Still, what visitors would see that Christmas holiday could not disappoint. The astonishing house boasted 250 rooms in all, among them 35 bedrooms, 43 bathrooms, and 3 kitchens, with 65 fireplaces augmenting the elaborate heating system that helped keep the 175,000-square-foot home warm. Its 780-foot facade and the rest of the exterior's limestone grandeur cloaked the use of nearly 11 million bricks. It may not have been in New York or Newport, but if this house didn't make an impression on the Four Hundred, nothing would, acorns or no: Biltmore was the largest house in America.

As Christmas approached, Asheville was buzzing about the arriving party and the grand opening of the magnificent house. George's mother was expected on the twentieth of December aboard George's private train car, the plush-seated, mahogany-paneled *Swannanoa*, with more friends and relatives following. Estate supervisor McNamee made arrangements for daily fish shipments from New York, enough for fifty people each day, or so he estimated. He instructed his purveyors to add lobsters to the order twice a week.

Webbs and Kissams, Shepards and Sloanes, Barkers and Vanderbilts headed South to celebrate the opening of George's not-quite-complete home. For those who had already visited the site, many improvements were immediately noticeable, while others were harder to see, such as the new Western Union line wired out to the house. A macadamized road now led from the village to the unfinished Lodge Gate that heralded the entrance to the estate. Young poplars lined the grand esplanade in front of the home, its large, central fountain no longer surrounded by errant stacks of tile or flanked by countless sheds and workshops. The ramp douce, visible to the left as the esplanade and home revealed themselves to a visitor's right, offered gently sloping inclines for horses and their riders as they headed to higher ground for country rides and hunts. At the home's entrance stood the pair of marble lions, finally free of their cages, roaring at the arrival of the season.

Stepping past the beasts, guests entered the home's vestibule and climbed the stairs into the main hall, gliding over the marble underfoot and admiring Guastavino's artistry soaring overhead. To the left was the grand staircase, reminiscent of the one in the Château de Blois in the Loire Valley. Gazing skyward up the 102 cantilevered steps and four floors that the staircase traversed, one saw a 1,700-pound wrought-iron chandelier which was held in place by a single, massive, physics-defying bolt. In the entryway, closer down to earth, was a sculpted bust of Richard Morris Hunt.

To the right off the main hall was the Palm Court, from which all rooms on the main floor radiated. The sunken space offered endless light and sky through its wood and glass dome, and promised a sunny respite from winter's chill. Karl Bitter's marble and bronze sculpture *Boy Stealing Geese* frolicked amid exotic plants. But the season's star was the banquet hall, 72 feet long by 42 feet wide, with three fireplaces at the one end and an organ gallery at the other, in front of which stood a 40-foot fir. The 70-foot ceilings easily accommodated the spectacular conifer.

On Christmas Eve, George, his family, and friends exchanged gifts. The following morning, George invited more than two hundred employees and their families to the house, where he distributed presents. Christmas dinner on the twenty-fifth was for family, and George's niece Gertrude—Corneil's daughter—dutifully recorded in her "Dinner Book" the twenty-seven relatives gathered at the massive dining table, which could have accommodated nearly three times that number.

At one head of the table sat George's mother and his oldest brother, Corneil, who himself had just finished rebuilding his cottage, The Breakers, in Newport, after it had been destroyed by fire several years earlier. (It had a mere 62,482 square feet of living space.) George and his sister-in-law, Corneil's wife, Alice, sat at the other end of the table. Gertrude sat between Ethel Kissam and George's beloved cousin Clarence Barker. George's brother Frederick and his wife, Louise, were there, as were George's sisters, Lila, Margaret, and Emily. Gertrude's cousin Adele was not in attendance, but her younger sister, Lila Sloane, was on hand and seated next to her uncle, George's brother Willie K. Other cousins and aunts and uncles were there, but others were conspicuously absent. Willie K. and Alva had divorced and their daughter, Consuelo, had been married to the Duke of Marlborough the month before in a union noted by many as the first Vanderbilt pairing with a non-American family. Despite the absences, it was as notable a Vanderbilt family gathering that Biltmore House would ever see.

Later that week more guests arrived, including George's book-collecting, engineer friend William B. Osgood Field. Field and the other guests in his party arrived three days after Christmas, a derailed train causing their own to pull into the station two hours late. The night was rainy and foggy as the tired guests aboard could see little in the darkness as the train detoured from the station to the house. The train stopped at the terrace, where George greeted them. Though a closer inspection of the home's exterior would best be done in daylight, the late arrival provided one benefit: Field got to see Biltmore in the moonlight. "No stage effect ever was more beautiful or perfect," he wrote his mother. He corresponded with Mama Field loyally throughout his travels, always devoting a particular amount of ink to his times outdoors, riding, shooting, enjoying life beyond the grip of the city.

Field had visited George during construction but could not help being awed by the improvements. In the Palm Court, moonlight poured down over the fanciful boy and his geese. Field turned into the ninety-foot-long tapestry gallery to admire the work of the Flemish masters. He stopped and paused to peer through the gallery's windows and onto the loggia beyond. There, again, was that moon. Its light cascaded over the loggia and "completed the intoxicating effects." Field headed to his room and stopped in to say hello to George's cousin Clarence. George's dear friend and traveling companion had been staying at Biltmore for several months. Field knew Clarence had been unwell, and though cheered to see him, Field thought the poor fellow looked worse than in recent memory.

Hard rain on the morning of Monday, December 30, 1895, kept most of the group inside. Field played several rounds of bottle pool and there were walks outside when the weather permitted, as well as golf, riding, and strolling. The next morning, the day of New Year's Eve, Field went on a quail shoot with a Mr. Waterbury and upon his return readied for that night's festivities. Dinner and chess led to dancing as the group swung and swayed to the sounds of the Imperial Trio—an ensemble usually in residence at the Kenilworth Inn. George took the hand of Mrs. Charles McNamee and led the others in the Virginia reel. The night wore on; waltzes and opera morphed into "Auld Lang Syne" as the group, Field wrote, readied to "dance the old year out, the old year of '95 that has been the hardest year of my life." The twenty-five-year-old engineer was adjusting to life after graduation from Stevens Institute and seemed to be looking for a purpose of some sort and, perhaps more important, someone to share that purpose with.

George's niece Gertrude offered a few final thoughts to her diary on this festive end to the year. "And at Biltmore too they are dancing," she wrote. "Bless them all."

New Year's Day dawned and Field went out for another day's

shoot. He treasured his time at Biltmore—it was never enough. This visit, too, and the gaiety surrounding it, were cut short. That afternoon, news arrived at the house that George's niece Alice, daughter of his sister Florence, had died from complications arising from pneumonia at 2 p.m. on New Year's Day. Alice had been just sixteen years old, and her death had occurred on the eve of her presentation to New York society. George's family decided to head home the very next day. Field and other friends joined them. The group left Biltmore at 11:30 on the morning of January 2, traveling in five private train cars, and arrived in New York the next day in preparation for the Saturday morning funeral. It was a private service held at the home of Florence and her husband, Hamilton McKown Twombly, at 684 Fifth Avenue. Police were stationed outside the home to keep prying eyes and unwelcome visitors at bay. George had also lost his fifteen-year-old niece Marguerite, his sister Margaret's daughter, to pneumonia a little less than a year earlier.

Winter wore on, the frivolity soon a memory. When George telegrammed Field in February it was not to invite his friend back to North Carolina, but rather to ask Field a somber favor. George's cousin Clarence, just thirty-one years old, had died at Biltmore. George hoped Field would serve as pallbearer. Field agreed. George headed to New York, accompanying the body of the cousin who had been like a brother to him, one who had been a companion during George's early days in North Carolina. The funeral was at St. Bartholomew's, where Clarence's coffin was covered with white and pink roses. Clarence's passing was also marked by a memorial concert at the New York College of Music, where a performance of Clarence's *Fantasia for Piano and Orchestra* was performed. It was much for George to bear. Biltmore's inaugural house party had ended on a tragic note, and now Clarence, too, was gone.

Work continued at the house through 1896, and the year brought more mixed events for George and his family. In August, his niece Adele suffered the loss of her first baby while living abroad in Paris.

That same month, his niece Gertrude married Harry Payne Whitney. She had written her uncle George and grandmother at Biltmore with the good news. If nothing else, such a sunny, optimistic announcement must have been very welcome by those who had seen so much recent loss.

While George was absent in New York and elsewhere, McNamee was as reliable an estate manager as George could want, Beadle's talents as a botanist continued to impress, and Carl Schenck was proving to be a sufficient successor to Gifford Pinchot. However, differences between the two foresters continued to emerge, despite Pinchot's departure from Biltmore. While in New York, George spoke with Pinchot, who wrote in his diary that George "was entirely in accord with me as to my directing the forest policy at Biltmore, and not Schenck." Whether on site or not, Pinchot's efforts had seen George's lands increase to well over 100,000 acres and brought to Biltmore a noted German forester with novel ideas about reshaping American forestry practice.

■ ■ ■

On the morning of Sunday, November 8, 1896, a crowd began to gather in the village of Biltmore. Eager parishioners seeking a place to worship mixed with the merely curious who were hoping to get a glance of the benefactor of this newly constructed church. They arrived in surreys, on horseback and on foot.

The Cathedral of All Souls rose alongside a looping road known as All Souls Crescent. Beside the church itself sat a parish house and a rectory. The structures stood out amid the growing village once known as Best. As with Biltmore House, George left no mason's stone unturned in his quest for beauty, design, and leadership in what would become the estate's house of worship. All Souls was Hunt's last church and one of only six he had ever designed. In New York, Vanderbilt family contributions had helped sustain the family's home church of St. Bartholomew's at Forty-Fourth and Madison, and the Vanderbilts had contributed substantially to the $400,000 required to build St. Bartholomew's parish house. But All Souls was all George.

On May 27, 1896, George had signed the deed to the church over to junior warden William Washington and others, keeping the deed to the rectory and parish house for himself. This was a common practice in the English manor tradition, and the relinquishment of the deed to the church itself was necessary before consecration could occur. Now, on this autumn Sunday, a new congregation awaited the blessing of the bishop, and All Souls Cathedral would be official in the eyes of the episcopal diocese.

As members of this nascent parish entered Hunt's creation, they walked over the newly laid floor, parqueted and perfect, and admired the heaven-grazing ceilings and majestic brick arches that separated the nave from the chancel beyond and the north and south transepts on either side. Translucent windows, mouth-blown and hand-leaded, had been created by Maitland Armstrong, a longtime friend of Richard Morris Hunt, and Armstrong's daughter, Helen. The baptistry and its font stood ready to welcome future members of this young spiritual community. Straight ahead was an enormous electric lantern, suspended by a chain and hovering over the communion rail. A humble yet graceful wooden altar stood before the congregants, and beyond it was a sanctuary framed by smooth, curved walls, while above the nave was a grand tower. Ornately carved stairs led to the pulpit. Each pew, offering kneeling cushions and seat pillows, accommodated about four people each. The congregants filed in and found places to sit.

As it turned out, the senior warden and benefactor of this new church would not attend opening-day services. George had been compelled to attend another church, many miles to the north, for a much more mournful occasion. His mother, Maria Louisa Kissam Vanderbilt, had died.

George had traveled down from New York just two days earlier with St. Bartholomew's rector, Dr. David H. Greer, who was slated to preach that first day at All Souls. No sooner had they arrived than news of George's mother's death reached them. They immediately returned to New York. The bishop of North Carolina, the Right Reverend Joseph Blount Cheshire, was already coming to consecrate the church. Now the Reverend Cheshire would be preaching as well.

George's mother had suffered heart failure during a stay in Scarborough, New York, with her daughter Margaret. Mrs. Vanderbilt had just attended her granddaughter Edith's wedding to Ernesto Fabbri, a well-traveled and well-heeled Italian linguist. Dr. McLane, the family doctor, took a specially chartered train to Scarborough as soon as he received the telegram that Mrs. Vanderbilt was not doing well, but his efforts were in vain.

George was Maria Louisa Vanderbilt's youngest child, and the pair had been devoted to each other. Now she would visit no more. The birth of George's new home had been entwined with the joy of new beginnings and punctuated by a spell of loss and endings. Hunt, Marguerite, Alice, Clarence and, now, his mother. Olmsted, though still at home in Massachusetts, continued to decline.

Those for whom Biltmore House should have been a refuge and a hallmark had but little time to enjoy it. Alone in his new house, George was surrounded by the faces of loved ones who looked down on him from paintings, some essence of their spirits captured by Sargent. At All Souls, the plain translucent windows, spectacular in their simplicity and practically brand-new, would soon be replaced with stained-glass memorials dedicated to those who had passed. Memories in oil spread themselves across canvas, and more remembrances would yet be fitted into the windows at the church.

A new era of George's life and the life of the house was just beginning, but he was alone and in mourning.

5

A Crossing of
Some Consequence

"On Thursday afternoon there was an immense crowd of carriages in the Rue Vernet before the door of the house inhabited by the Misses Dresser, who were giving an afternoon reception of the musical matinee order. . . ."

Outside these occasional formal entertainments, Monday afternoons at 15 Rue Vernet were for receiving, and the Dresser circle of friends included both seasonal and permanent residents. Gwendolyn King from Newport lived nearby. She was the daughter of Mrs. David King of Kingscote House in Newport and niece by marriage of the Dresser girls' own Aunty Mary—Mrs. Edward King. Edith's friend Florence "Flo" Van Dusen Reed and her younger sister, Gertrude, had lived in Paris most of their lives, and their apartment at 27 Rue Pierre Charron was a short stroll along the pleasant streets of the Eighth Arrondissement and down the Avenue d'Alma. Mrs. Reed made every effort to ensure that plenty of suitable young men stopped by the house, some of whom were brought along by Count Antoine Sala, whose father had worked for the French Legation at Washington.

While many in the Dressers' circle were French nationals, Paris bloomed with Americans in spring, including the prominent Brown family of Newport and Providence and their son, John Nicholas, who had become a topic of conversation between Edith and Natalie. The Brown family was a frequent fixture in Newport and abroad, and possessed a considerable fortune. Architect Richard Morris Hunt's son Joe and some of the other Beaux-Arts boys sometimes came by on Sunday nights for supper. Always present were Mlle. Rambaud and, of course, their canine mademoiselle, Follette, and her more recent counterpart, a French bulldog named Bluette.

If winters were for lessons and lectures, and spring for the bursting American colony, summers were for travel. Dinard, a seaside gem on Brittany's northern coast, the Côte d'Émeraude, was a favorite destination. Dinard sat due west of the eerily transcendent Mont-Saint-Michel, where the sisters had visited the Hôtel Veuve Poulard and sampled one of La Mère Poulard's (by French chef Annette Boutiaut) world-renowned omelettes. As the August waters swept in, the town magically transformed into an island, and once they'd receded, Mont-Saint-Michel was anchored to earth again. The waves of change were unceasing yet remarkable to witness, subject to the vagaries of the moon and capturing the imaginations of all who stood within earshot of their lapping rhythms. For the summer of 1896, a group of Paris friends joined the sisters in Dinard. There were picnics, day trips, and ample wandering of the countryside, seeking doors adorned with telltale mistletoe. In Brittany mistletoe grew on apple trees, and Breton tradition dictated that a sprig nailed above a tavern door meant a fresh batch of cider was available.

So the seasons of their adopted France passed and lives changed. The summer of 1897 would prove most different. Mrs. David King—Gwendolyn's mother—invited Pauline to be their guest in Newport. It was Pauline's first season and Newport—and the lavish Kingscote, a Gothic revival cottage orné—seemed an ideal place to come out to society, amid the myriad cotillions and the much-anticipated annual Astor Ball at Beechwood. Natalie, too, had her own reasons to return to the United States that summer, and went to stay with their Aunty King.

As for Edith, she decided to stay on the continent that summer, with her oldest sister, Susan, and Mademoiselles Rambaud, Follette, and Bluette. It would likely be a busier summer than usual considering the countless Americans crossing the Atlantic to celebrate Queen Victoria's Jubilee in London.

■ ■ ■

George was entertaining at the Berkeley in London in June 1897 when President William McKinley came to call at Biltmore House. The presidential train was on its way from Nashville, Tennessee, to Washington, DC, and made a quick stop in Asheville, which draped itself in its red-white-and-blue best for the short visit. There were several engagements on the commander in chief's schedule, including a reception and lunch at the Battery Park. Cobb's Orchestra provided music during a reception which featured fried frog's legs, brook trout sautéed in butter, filet of beef, and broiled white squab. For a sweet finish: fancy cakes.

E. J. Harding, auditor of the Biltmore Estate, was keeping an eye on things in the absence of George and Charles McNamee. When told of McKinley's desire to stop by, Harding said the president, his wife, and any cabinet members were welcome, but no media. McKinley objected. After some presidential pressure, Harding buckled and the press were allowed to join McKinley during his visit to Biltmore House. However, once the president departed, Harding fired off a letter to the local newspaper to clear up a few misconceptions about his initial refusal, which had already garnered negative public attention. George Vanderbilt had never invited the president to visit, Harding wrote. More pointedly, Harding added, "Admission to Biltmore House is a privilege granted only on rare occasions and to a limited number of persons."

Meanwhile, in London, George had procured excellent viewing for Queen Victoria's Diamond Jubilee parade. George's brother Corneil and his family were also in attendance. George's niece Consuelo, the Duchess of Marlborough, had left Blenheim Palace and taken Spencer House for the season. Queen Victoria had bested

King George III's record as the longest-reigning monarch, and the sixtieth anniversary of the day the now seventy-eight-year-old queen ascended to the throne transfixed London and her colonies—present and past.

George had been passing time in London attending exhibits and concerts, visiting friends, and enjoying dinners earlier that spring with painters John Singer Sargent and James McNeill Whistler, the latter of whom George had recently engaged to paint his portrait. During the Jubilee festivities, George hosted Charles McNamee and his wife, along with Dr. Samuel Westray Battle—who had cared for George's mother in Asheville—and his spouse. Joining the group was George's dear friend, the noted author Paul Leicester Ford. Afterward, George invited the entourage to join him aboard his yacht on a trip to the fjords of Norway, land of the midnight sun. George would likely head back to America in the fall, but no trip abroad was complete without a stop in Paris. There he saw his friend Field.

"What are you doing this winter?" George asked Field during a post-theater stroll across the Pont de la Concorde in Paris. "Will you go to India with me as my guest? I don't want to go alone."

George told Field that he wanted to see the Taj Mahal by moonlight. It was an offer that the adventure-loving Field could not afford—experientially or financially—to refuse. He felt fortunate to be George's guest on this East Asian adventure. George would return to New York in the fall and preparations for their trip would begin in earnest.

■ ■ ■

Another American was preparing to leave Paris and sail for the States that fall: Edith Dresser. The twenty-four-year-old was heading to the September wedding of her older sister Natalie.

Late summer had found Edith in the coastal town of Saint-Jacut-de-la-Mer when she received a cable with very exciting news: her sister Natalie was engaged to John Nicholas Brown.

"I never really dreamed that such a true happiness and blessing could befall us," Edith wrote her older sister. "It seems too good to be true and with the broad ocean between us it is hard to realize that really and truly you are engaged to that too adorable Johannes Nicholaus."

Edith and Mlle. Rambaud were anxious for more details. "You must be sure and tell us all the particulars; when and where and how it happened, what he said, what you said, what they said, what the world said!"

Edith wondered about the wedding date and said she was looking forward to seeing old friends in Newport and visiting with her brother, LeRoy.

"You are indeed lucky to have such a man, as he is one in a thousand," Edith wrote, "but I think we have often discussed his charms and merits, but now I love him more than ever because he has shown such good taste in choosing dear Nata for his bride."

The wedding was in Newport and Natalie looked beautiful in their grandmother's lace, worn over satin. While there were no bridesmaids or maids of honor, a bit of their Paris group was there as Joe Hunt served as one of John's best men. Aunty King hosted the bridal breakfast, and the newlyweds then set off on John's yacht *Ballymena* to begin their honeymoon.

Edith and her younger sister Pauline planned to return to Paris the following month, in October. Pauline had had a wondrous summer, the highlight of which was her coming-out ball at Kingscote, where Mrs. King had created a magical atmosphere. Staff enclosed the piazzas, adorning the spaces with red roses, peach blossoms, Scotch heather, and ornamental grasses. Silks were suspended from above and romantically backlit by electric lights. The Hungarian orchestra played, and Pauline and her friend Frank Andrews led the couples in a popular group dance known as the German cotillion, or simply "the German."

However, when Pauline went to New York to visit their brother, LeRoy, at Centre Island, she met up with Rev. George Grenville Merrill, a handsome young Princeton graduate she had known since she was a child. He proposed, she accepted, and Edith decided to stay stateside long enough to serve as her younger sister's maid of honor at her December 1, 1897, wedding at Trinity Church in Newport. LeRoy gave his youngest sibling away, and she, too, wore her grandmother's lace. The sisters' renovated house at Bellevue Court was opened up for the wedding breakfast, and with two of the four Dresser sisters married off in four months, Edith was ready to go back home to Paris.

Within a week, Edith and Mlle. Rambaud made the journey from Newport to New York by train, ferry, and carriage, and prepared to sail. Her newly married sister Pauline bid them farewell.

■ ■ ■

Fog sat atop the waters of New York harbor like a stubborn lapdog, its tails curling around the salt-soaked feet of Lady Liberty. It was December 8, 1897, and by the time the *St. Paul* got under way, she was already more than two hours behind schedule.

Yet another crossing. How many times had Edith made a journey such as this? Now just shy of her twenty-fifth birthday, she was going back to France again, after a brief stop in England. This crossing, however, would prove to be far from routine.

Elsewhere on the ship, Field settled his luggage in stateroom 103, which adjoined George's, and then made his way on deck. Field preferred the *Teutonic*, insofar as steamships were concerned, but his accommodations aboard the *St. Paul* and the ship's amenities were more than adequate. The Atlantic Ocean had some light traffic, and later in the day the *St. Paul* passed the *Germanic*, the two grand dames of the sea skirting each other's foamy wakes. By the next morning the skies had cleared and the *St. Paul* moved through relatively placid depths.

Field knew he would not even be on this particular journey were it not for George. Then again, George had confided to his twenty-seven-year-old traveling companion that he would likely have not made this particular journey had Field not agreed to come along with him. More than two hundred rooms and thousands upon thousands of acres of land were apparently not enough to keep George at home. Europe called. The East beckoned.

George's presence had hardly gone unnoticed by other passengers. "George Vanderbilt is on board!"

Field, amused, listened as the voices carried through the ship's ventilation system and out onto the second deck.

"Is that so? Which is he? Have you seen him?"

Such was George's life or, for that matter, the life of any Vanderbilt at the time. Field found the majority of his fellow passengers "thoroughly uninteresting, as usual." It was as though someone had ground Manhattan in a pepper mill and sprinkled her usual suspects on the decks of these floating hotels on the sea. A journey abroad was expected of members of the upper classes, if for no other reason than to keep one's conversational reserves well-stocked. With days and nights brimming over in formal dinners, afternoon teas, and theater and opera outings, conversation had been elevated to an art form. Excursions to far-flung destinations like India gave one something to talk about over cognacs, at intermissions, and in cigar-smoke-filled gentlemen's clubs. The faces of one's fellow travelers became familiar, if they were not already.

Among these familiar types was a traveler to whom Field was instructed to pay close attention: Miss Edith Stuyvesant Dresser, who was traveling with her companion and chaperone, Mlle. Marie Rambaud.

Those instructions had come from powers far greater than those of his traveling benefactor: George's elder sisters. The women were aware that Edith would be aboard and it was not surprising that they entertained Edith as a suitable match for their youngest brother who, at thirty-five, remained a resolute bachelor displaying little inclination that he would change his status anytime soon. Field was informed he should be more than George's companion on this trip. He should seek to help George land his life's companion. It was serendipitous that he, Edith, and Field were all aboard the same ship.

Perhaps Field might, for lack of a more genteel expression, attempt to thrust the two singles together whenever possible?

Field decided that part of his strategy would be to occupy the ever-present Mlle. Rambaud. This, he believed, would leave George and Edith time alone to become better acquainted. This also meant that Edith and Field would get to know each other better as well. George's sisters chose well by pressing Field into matchmaking service. Edith found Field a genial conversationalist and began confiding in George's traveling companion, perhaps making Field's task all the more feasible. Edith told Field that she had heard the "reports which were heralded of George's attentions."

Field listened. He liked Edith a great deal and believed that she would do well as the head of Biltmore House. Field was well acquainted with the beauty and splendor of George's country home and knew that its grandeur would be further enhanced by the presence of a proper mistress. But speculation in the society columns, the smothering expectations of the era and class, and the insistent maneuverings of well-intentioned siblings did not necessarily a marriage make.

If society made the tiny island of Manhattan shrink to a claustrophobic Lilliput, looming Gulliveresque in those circles were the Vanderbilts. And though not possessing great wealth, the Dresser girls were from a reputable family that was known and liked in those same circles. Edith's brother, LeRoy, was an entrepreneur and his latest venture, the firm Dresser & Co., had entered the New York financial scene earlier that year. Still, it remained a question as to whether the match would take. As Edith got to know Field— unwitting George's Cyrano—a bit better and the two talked more frankly, Field wondered about George's intentions. He confided his misgivings in letters to his mother.

"No one knows G.V.'s business as well as he does himself," Field wrote, "and I think his attachment, in whatever quarter it might lie, would be on a basis of business, as the rest hardly comes into his constitution."

Field knew his views were better kept quiet. "Be guarded how you read these things," he continued, "as my thoughts are sometimes not to be published."

Field did not have much time to work. The voyage from New York to Southampton was typically a week's journey. Meals, games, and walks often involved other guests and friends who were on board. It was challenging to matchmake over grilled sardines and Welsh rarebit. Other obstacles presented themselves, including sickness—common at sea—which caused Edith to excuse herself from dinner early one evening. The entertainments available to the upper classes were many, if not unlike those found at home in bars, games, sitting rooms, and libraries. On Sunday, passengers could attend services in the saloon, where an Irish purser lilted along beautifully with the prayers, and the smoking-room cashier offered hymns. Field enjoyed walking on the deck at night, thinking the moon quite like a balloon tethered to the cloudless horizon.

Lest the pampered first-class passengers forget that they were in the middle of the ocean, the Atlantic reminded them of its presence. Heavy seas proffered some sleepless nights of rolling and pitching, which strew George's books—constant companions—around his stateroom. George and Field weathered the weather and recollected the tomes. The following day, the weather cleared and Edith sat on the deck with Field, talking once again. She later joined him and George in their adjoining staterooms for enjoyable read-aloud sessions. They read Robert Louis Stevenson's "Will o' the Mill," a popular and appropriate short story about a boy who dreams of travel. Field read Rudyard Kipling to both Edith and George. The group played piquet. George won.

■ ■ ■

Catching a glimpse of the Isles of Scilly rising out of the waters to the southwest of Land's End and Cornwall's clawlike reach into the Celtic Sea, meant that Southampton and the end of the first leg of the journey were near. After docking, the group headed to London, where Field suggested to Edith that she and Mlle. Rambaud stay at Carter's Hotel. Field and George were off to Long's. (Both establishments were well regarded and easily found in that year's edition of the estimable *Royal Blue Book: Fashionable Directory and Parliamentary Guide*.) Once arriving at Long's, however, a waiting note shifted George and Field's plans. Whistler was in Paris with his unfinished portrait of George and wanted to know if he could please come to sit for him yet again. George and Field made plans to be in Paris within two days.

Their limited time in London was put to as good use as possible. The next morning, Field went off to collect Edith or, as he put it, "the girl G.V. is supposed to be in love with," and took her to Hatcher's bookshop, then Harmon the haberdasher. After shopping, Edith lunched with Field at Mansion House, then said good-bye for the afternoon so that Field could join George for a visit to the Hammam Turkish baths. Later that evening, Edith and Mlle. Rambaud rejoined Field, George, and other friends at The Princes Restaurant, a popular Piccadilly choice for the discerning diner.

Before leaving for Paris, George made a point of stopping at Bicker's bookshop on the way to Charing Cross station—a new Kipling was due out. The trip from Calais to Amiens was taken up again by the ruffs, sequences, sets, and tricks of the 36-card game or piquet, and George again won. The party was in Paris by seven that night. Once they'd arrived, Edith and Mlle. Rambaud returned to their home on Rue Vernet, while George and Field lodged one-and-a-half miles away at the Hotel Bristol on the Place Vendôme, a favorite of George's.

Whistler joined them for dinner. The sixty-three-year-old, America-born, Europe-based artist was a sight with his long, salt-and-pepper hair that framed his noteworthy eyebrows. The only feature that could upstage the rest was his formidable mustache. The artist was already well established in both Paris and London, and George and Field were rapt as Whistler regaled them with tales of his Parisian adventures.

That night, George stayed up chatting with Field. So much had happened since they had set sail from New York just ten days earlier. Not surprisingly, the conversation turned to marriage—whether to marry at all and, if so, when? Field noticed that George did not speak specifically of Edith Dresser at all, as if still resisting the life expected of him, albeit in his own quiet way. He told Field that he wanted to spend time seeing the world before settling down with a girl. And when he did, he imagined she would perhaps be ten years his junior. Field did not agree. For him, life and love should intertwine. He wanted a companion, someone with whom he could share those experiences he loved, someone with whom he could grow. The two friends retired, finally, at nearly 2:30 a.m.

Ah, but the gossip mill could wait only so long for a bit of grist. Paris in the late 1890s was hardly a place where one could successfully avoid the whispers and glances of Manhattanites. One could not swing a dead *chat* without hitting an American in Paris; a flaneur, perhaps; a man about town; or one of the countless students who were flocking to ateliers to study art; or the number of US transplants who cherished Europe's affordability over New York and Newport. Edith joined Field the next morning to attend services at the American Cathedral, and while strolling home, they encountered a New York acquaintance. By the very next day, word had spread in and among the Turkish baths and theater boxes and cafés of Paris's finest haunts that Miss Edith Dresser was engaged to be married . . . to William B. Osgood Field.

This delicious canard did not, however, alter Edith's social calendar or Field's secret mission for George's sisters. Edith invited Field to join her and her sister Susan for lunch. Field proved an amiable shopping escort for Edith—who in turn helped Field with some of his holiday buying—while George continued to hold very still for Whistler at his studio at 58 Rue des Champs. As Christmas approached, shopping and dining and exhibitions and concerts and theater dominated the holiday: Dining at Café Foyet, breakfasting and smoking at the Café des Cicles, enjoying a performance of Jean Richepin's "Le Chemineau" at the Odéon. George, Field, Edith, Susan, Mlle. Rambaud, Field's friend and fellow engineer Otis Mygatt, and Joe Hunt even spent a night at the Parisian circus.

Edith celebrated the season with George and Field. George presented Field with a copy of Keats. Edith stuffed George's stocking with an almanac and the latest edition of *Quo Vadis*, a historical novel set in Nero's Rome that tells the story of a poor, young Christian hostage of the empire and the Roman patrician who falls for her and converts, despite their differences in station. This, along with a small book on patience, may or may not have been the least subtle gifts ever presented a thirty-five-year-old bachelor of the Mauve Decade. Edith, Susan, and Mlle. Rambaud hosted dinner that evening, and Field, George, and their friend Mygatt joined. Joe Hunt was unable to make it, but he sent along a salad bowl full of greens, and presents for all, including a small train car marked "Swanannoa," in honor of the private car that ferried guests to George's Southern hideaway. After dinner, Edith led her guests to the salon, the tree was lit, and the Dressers presented small gifts to their dinner guests.

That damp clime, however, left George bedridden for days, fighting a cold as his time in Paris was coming to a close. Whistler was not yet done with him, and refused to add his telltale butterfly signature to the painting until he believed it to be truly complete. But the East awaited. Field went on a final shopping trip for George. "You see," Field wrote his mother, "When I have his cash account backing me, things go beautifully." Field began to believe that George "relies on me entirely." New Year's Eve saw the two friends departing for Dijon, the next leg of a journey that would take them to India.

George, book on patience in hand, left Paris and Edith behind.

■　■　■

Through Jaipur, Delhi, and Agra to Calcutta, Darjeeling, and the miles of dust and remnants of ruined palaces in between, George and Field's Indian travels took them from the ghats astride the Ganges to dancing in the ballroom of the Royal Bombay Yacht Club. George was proving far less adventurous than Field had hoped. When the pair visited the temple of Hathi Singh, Field unhesitatingly removed his shoes so that he could enter. George stayed outside. Mornings when Field wandered, George often remained at the hotel.

They visited Jama Masjid, one of India's largest mosques. Field was told it took five thousand workmen six years to build, roughly the same number of years—though five times the workmen—that George had hired for Biltmore. They dined with a maharaja who kept his five wives locked away on the fourth floor of his palace. While musicians entertained, bejeweled dancing women kissed their hands.

"I wish I could tell you how funny George is under these circumstances," Field wrote his mother. "They could do anything they liked with me, for I am in for it all, but poor old George remains George and has difficulty entering into the spirit of these things."

Mongooses engaged hooded cobras in street fights. Monkeys, parrots, and crocodiles dotted the landscape. Field and George traveled constantly, Field anxious to take it all in, to explore, to go out on hunts. He grew less and less surprised at George's behavior, his reticence, his love of napping and reading. He was amused by George's repeated need to instruct Field about what to do if George should die during their travels. (He had, in fact, purchased a $1 million life insurance policy before leaving.) After Field went on a shooting trip for black buck—George again staying behind—he noted that his traveling companion was a "funny chap . . . it is all I could do to get him out to see the beards I had shot for him." Once he did, though, George was very pleased with the pelts.

Field was alternately amused by George's aversion to trying new things and frustrated by his friend's changeable mind and mood, growing increasingly aware of the differences between the haves and the have-so-much-mores.

"George is too cold blooded to take any interest in anything here. He always says he has seen so much better. Wealth could not buy my temperament. He relies on me tremendously and is always showing me he is as glad that I am with him. You bet I show him the same thing. When the powers of money stop these people go crazy."

Money was first and foremost on Field's mind the longer the trip wore on, and he was beginning to find himself in a difficult position he wasn't quite sure how to rectify. While the Field family enjoyed comfort and standing, Field's own pockets were not so bottomless.

"It is a very hard position at times to be with one who can absolutely never think of expense," he wrote his mother, the person from whom he often requested money. Yet Field saw the potential downside to George's unique position. "You know I do not for a moment envy the position of GV. He is not one speck as happy as I am, and the spending of money gives him absolutely no thrill. Half the pleasure in life comes from learning to choose between things."

Yet George admired his friend's zeal for the new and undiscovered. He, too, corresponded with Field's mother, saying, "It is rare to see such genuine enthusiasm." Field saw George's kindness as well, and noted how his occasional petulant outbursts were followed by apologies and expressions of sincere thanks. Yes, George might rage against "heathen countries, and everything connected with them" or rail at rickshaw drivers and servants, but he possessed a self-awareness that was not lost on Field. George cherished the pair's friendship. During the trip, he surprised Field, taking his hand and saying, "Billy, you are the best fellow in the world. You are never cross, always happy and ready for any of my whims. I know how hard it is for you at times and I never can forget the kindness and undue consideration you show me. I only wish I could be a better companion to you."

"It is hard for me at these moments," Field wrote, "and always after they have passed, he calls me all kinds of endearing names, and himself all kinds of rotten ones.

"Poor old George," he wrote. Then, perhaps recalling his mission for George's sisters, he added, "If he only marries the right woman! But God help her!!!"

Their adventure came to an end in early spring. "GV is crazy to get back to Paris, and when he gets there he will be crazy to get back somewhere else," Field noted, noting George's restlessness and possibly boredom. Field wrote that George's anticipation of his return to Paris was "like a child to the circus. Why? I do not know."

By March, George had reached Paris and Field had traveled to Rome to attend to some family obligations with his uncle Osgood and aunt Kittie. There, hopefully, Field would recover from a fever he had contracted during his travels. Naturally, George wanted Field to return to Paris afterward to hit the museums and shows once again. George could not find an apartment to his liking in Paris so he was back at the always reliable Hotel Bristol, where his rooms overlooked the Place Vendôme. Field was to arrive in Paris mid-April, once his responsibilities were covered and he was on the mend.

In the meantime, George kept him abreast of his activities, including what he was reading—"Zola's *Paris* is distinctly inferior to his other works. It lacks spontaneity." He had seen Edith, he wrote, attending a performance with her and Mlle. Rambaud. He visited with and continued to sit for Whistler, whom George noted was rather ill though "charming as ever." George considered his days and nights a "feast of good things": concerts at the St. Eustache, drinks at the Café de Paris, walks through moody Paris *allées*, while performances of *Tannhäuser* and Rossini became the soundtrack of his stay. George's calendar epitomized that of a man of leisure. At one point he wrote Field that he "only went to the theater five times last week." The real world did intrude, on occasion, upon his consciousness. George ended one April missive to Field by asking, "Did you know there's a war on?" referencing the Spanish-American War that had begun that month. "And that's all the news I have."

And yet George's time in Paris eventually revealed itself to be better spent than perhaps anyone, Field included, might have imagined. George's correspondence took an exciting—if not unexpected—turn. Coded telegrams flew across the Atlantic and Mediterranean.

George wired Field, "Absolute Secret friends merriment conglobe roarers rather enviously home."

Field wired his mother, "Paris Masquerade with George seditious radiance hydraulic sealt."

How it all struck eyes unfamiliar with George's and Field's telegram ciphers is difficult to know. But the letters and cables grew into whispers which in turn morphed into gossip-column fodder.

The matter was finally settled. Field—and George—had been successful.

6

New Mistress

"Now that the long expected and much discussed marriage of George Vanderbilt is about to become a fact those people that have nothing else to do are counting up the eligible males that remain in the Vanderbilt family. . . ."

—New York Journal

Mr. and Mrs. Daniel LeRoy Dresser

announce the marriage of their sister

Edith Stuyvesant to Mr. George Vanderbilt.

On Thursday June the second, 1898,

at the Church of the Holy Trinity, Paris.

Edith and George's engagement would not be a particularly long one, but it would be a particularly watched one. Papers scrounged for details of the story behind their engagement, the parties the pair attended, their wardrobe, and honeymoon plans. Finally, all the false engagement rumors and endless speculation about George's potential paramours were put to rest. Ink spilled profligately throughout the society pages across the country and across the Atlantic about the confirmed match.

"Captured a Millionaire," the *Evening Wisconsin* announced.

"A Multi-Millionaire in Cupid's Clutches," the *Lima News* parroted.

"A Wealthy Benedict Who Surrenders at Last," chimed in the *Morning Telegram*.

"America's richest bachelor is going to wed. Even in the midst of war we must pay some attention to this stupendous fact," crowed the *New York Journal*. The *Courier* out of Syracuse agreed, stating that since much news had been of the preparations for the Spanish-American War, George's marrying the daughter of a military officer fit in nicely with current events.

Reports of how the pair met varied. One popular theory held that Mrs. Charles McNamee, while George's guest in London for Queen Victoria's Jubilee, spotted Edith and one of her sisters during the festivities and that the young women were subsequently asked to join the Vanderbilt party. Another hypothesis proclaimed that George had specifically booked passage on a westbound steamer in order to spend time with Edith at sea. In truth, their first meeting, and any prior to their confirmed, if unremarkable, December transatlantic trip, could very well have happened in any number of places or countries. The overlapping circles of society in and around Newport, New York, and the colony abroad were like a Venn diagram of the Four Hundred, intersecting seasonally, perpetually, transatlantically.

To be young, single, and of the right breeding in New York and Newport was to be watched, and Edith now found herself the center of unceasing attention. She had witnessed some of the fervor surrounding her sister Natalie's engagement to John Nicholas Brown. However, in the 1890s, the name "Vanderbilt" carried with it a kind of notoriety—good or not so much—that garnered particular fascination. Edith knew growing up that clocking the movements of New York's established families was pure sport for those who were on the outside looking in. Now she was the hunted one.

The media took aim at everything from Edith's appearance to her family lineage, from George's seemingly resolute bachelorhood to the couple's individual financial reserves or, in Edith's case, lack thereof.

Women of the day were often pitted against one another like racehorses galloping toward the finish line of a good marriage and a secure financial future. Edith's profile, sketched alongside those of her sister Natalie and another recently engaged young woman, dominated a large Sunday-edition spread of the *New York Herald* titled, "Three American Graces." Noting the women had "Come In for a Good Share of Pleasant Notoriety," the paper admitted it would be difficult to say which of the women were "of the greatest social interest." Nevertheless, the paper posited that Edith likely had the edge as she would become mistress of not only William Henry Vanderbilt's mansion at 640 Fifth Avenue but also of Biltmore House, George's "famous establishment at Asheville, NC, which is called the only palace in America," as a Utica paper so described it. "Biltmore would be regarded in any part of Europe as a suitable retreat for a prince or a monarch."

The juxtaposing of brides-to-be abounded, and coverage ranged from cordial to downright catty in its comparisons of Edith and her own sisters.

"They are still spoken of as the Dresser girls, as they have been for years and years at Newport," *Form: The Monthly Magazine of Society* said, referring to the four sisters. The article bemoaned the fact that Edith's wedding would be in France rather than New York, for in Paris, "it will be an event of interest only to the American colony." George gave Edith diamonds. Would she wear them? Was it a tiara? Someone told someone else who said they had most likely spotted George sporting a full beard. Would he keep it for the wedding? The Dressers' eldest sister, Susan, is still unmarried! Was Natalie's husband, John Nicholas Brown, richer than George? Was George going to build a villa in Newport?

"They are all fine big women and more or less good looking," the magazine continued, adding that while Edith was "so much less good looking" than her younger sister, Pauline, she was a good conversationalist, had an "agreeable manner," and was one of the "sweet-est girls of Newport."

Edith's appearance was relentlessly scrutinized. The *Washington Times* called her "A genuine daughter of the Gods, divinely tall," adding that with her "perfect French accent" she was as familiar in Paris as "Lady de Gray." She was "slender, with luxuriant, waving brown hair, dark hazel eyes, a clear rosy skin and bold, irregular features."

Another publication noted Edith had "the fine physique of the Dresser family, and is an extremely cultivated and agreeable woman." It was observed that at nearly six feet, she would likely stand a good head taller than her husband-to-be.

Good stock. Handsome. Fine physique. Stately carriage. Fine and big. Either Edith was engaged to be married or about to be placed on the auction block at the local state fair.

Conversely, George—"the most cultivated multi-millionaire in America"—was described as "remarkably swarthy" though "very delicate" as a child.

George's willingness to marry surprised many. One of his adopted hometown papers—the *Asheville Citizen*—called its famous neighbor's bride-to-be "handsome, accomplished and agreeable," but added that, "For him to strike out for himself in the matrimonial field amazes his own family as well as his friends."

The accepted party line was that George had sworn he would never marry while his mother was still alive. However, many had begun to wonder if they would ever witness his wedding day. He was inordinately wealthy, exceedingly cultured, charitable, and single—a catch if ever there was one. Yet rumored romances never evolved into anything serious, and this, combined with George's general absence from the dating scene, such as it was, led most to believe that his interests did not lie at the foot of an altar.

"So long this much-desired young man had set his face against the charms of matrimony," the *New York Press* wrote, "that he was looked on as almost unattainable."

"He was supposed to be a confirmed bachelor, having reached the age of thirty-five without having engaged his affections. His magnificent home, Biltmore, at Asheville and his large fortune have attracted many designing debutants and their moms but they have been forced to abandon their endeavors and he has capitulated only after he had fallen in love."

The *St. Louis Star* added that "members of the smart set have long predicted that George would always live a bachelor's life," and added that Miss Dresser was "handsome and accomplished but of modest means."

This last distinction captured much curiosity.

One spread highlighted "Extraordinary Tribute to the Talents and Personal Charm of a Young Woman in Whose Veins Flows America's Bluest Blood, but Who Boasts No Pride of Wealth. From Three Rooms and a Kitchen to Mistress of Biltmore, America's Most Palatial Manor. . . . It is a fairy tale. It is a romance."

Mr. Vanderbilt Has:
A fortune of $20,000,000
Biltmore, the greatest country house in America
A Fifth Avenue mansion
One of the finest picture galleries in New York
A series of solid gold plate
A house at Bar Harbor

Miss Dresser Has:
Beauty and cleverness
Splendid health and physique
High social position in New York and Newport
Descent from Peter Stuyvesant

One newspaper feature offered a sketch contrasting a typical army post quarters—a depiction that was a far cry from the lovely house the Dressers inhabited on New York's Washington Place, let alone their grandmother's home on Newport's Bellevue Avenue—next to a sketch of Biltmore House. "Those Dresser girls . . . are clever and attractive, yet they haven't any money to speak of."

Claiming that the Dresser girls did not grow up particularly beautiful, the paper remarked that they nevertheless had beautiful figures. "Tall and stately," the paper stated, remarking on their good taste in fashion, even by Parisian standards, and mentioning that "when they opened their mouths people liked to listen."

For her part, Edith maintained her discretion and did not want to open her mouth any more than necessary. When pressed for details about her special day, Edith declined to say very much except to comment on her dress and her attendants. She remained elusive with regard to her honeymoon, whether because she did not yet know the details or out of a guarded sense of privacy, something she and George seemed to share. "We mean all our marriage arrangements to be simple and quiet," she told a reporter.

Always in the plus column, as far as the media was concerned, was that Edith was Knickerbocker through and through, and this was a thoroughly American match, one that would bring together two very American families. Edith's mother had hailed from the storied Fish-Stuyvesant line; her father was a battle-tested army veteran. Edith had grown up comfortably, in that right-schools-right-manners-right-parties kind of way. "All the Dresser Girls are finely educated and are considered particularly brilliant," one paper asserted. Indeed, the press was quick to note that Edith was a direct descendant of Peter Stuyvesant, the legendary and surly, peg-legged Dutch governor of the island of Manhattan, and thus closely related to the LeRoy, Fish, and King families—all notable, and all long-lived in this land.

The loss of her parents made good copy as well. While the Dresser girls were not orphans in that Dickensian sense that conjures up workhouses, raggedy britches, and cold porridge, their familial losses were undeniable and surely felt just as deeply. To live through such a momentous occasion, and endure such intense scrutiny, would certainly have been easier were her parents or grandmother still alive.

Edith's life, with all of its joys and loss, remained one that was bereft of a loving parent's calming presence.

The focus on the couple's disparity of wealth was not limited to the press, however. George's friends were privately commenting on the topic as well. Among these individuals was a well-meaning Catharine Hunt, Richard Morris Hunt's widow, who took it upon herself to make sure that George's friend Paul Leicester Ford was in possession of all the facts about the woman George was going to marry.

Ford was an author whose accomplishments already included numerous historical works of biography, bibliography, and more, including *The Writings of Thomas Jefferson*. He had chronicled both the lives and written works of founders such as Jefferson, George Washington, John Dickinson, and Benjamin Franklin. He had established an entity called the Historical Printing Club and had brought historical research to the fore in many popular and academic circles. He also published novels, including 1894's *The Honorable Peter Stirling*, which had sold nearly 200,000 copies, a magnificent sales record then and now. In 1897, he had published the novel *Story of an Untold Love*. Ford's family was steeped in the written word, and Ford's father, Gordon Ford, had a library in the family's mansion on Clark Street in Brooklyn that was believed to be the most extensive private library in the country. It housed a renowned collection of Americana in a 50-by-60-foot space (built over the home's yard) that contained at one point an estimated hundred thousand volumes, more if pamphlets and other ephemera were included in the tally. Illness due to a childhood accident had resulted in ongoing fevers, physical pain, a hunched back, and a severe stunting of Paul Leicester Ford's growth—his height stopped well short of five feet. School, in the traditional sense, was thought not to be an option for the young man. A voracious, curious reader, Ford nevertheless grew up and grew brilliant among his father's tomes and papers. He published his first book, *Webster Genealogy*, about his great-grandfather, Noah Webster, on a hand press at the age of eleven.

His talents, charm, position in society, and fanaticism about books meant that he, like George, was a fellow collector and member of the Grolier Club of New York City. He was also a sometime chess adversary of George's. The two men valued each other's friendship and company tremendously. Ford had, a year earlier, joined George in London during Queen Victoria's Jubilee, and George had made sure to write Ford about the engagement to Edith, hoping that Ford could attend the wedding ceremony. Now Catharine, who knew the Dressers through their long association with Newport and New York society, sought to assure George's friend that Edith was indeed a suitable match.

"She is an old friend of mine, about 23," Catharine wrote Ford. "Fine looking, tall, slight, good carriage, sings, talks intelligently, is finished in all worldly and social matters and those who know her better than I claim for her a warm heart." Catharine added that while she had "heard last autumn that [George] had been very devoted," she had heard that Edith's response was more of a "courtesy."

"She is an orphan, her father was an army officer her mother, a member of the Fish connection, par excellence grand dame." Catharine remarked that Edith had been living in Paris "and is not well off." Still, Catharine believed that Edith had come to the marriage "slowly and truthfully." Her assessment of Edith's temperament was as conflicting as some of the newspaper reports of the day. "I have known her ever since she was a little child and seen always an affectionate fine nature," Catharine wrote, but added—apparently noting a perceived difference of opinion with others—"She is thought to be very cold."

Ford wrote her back that he was already "in the secret . . . I am glad to say, and have met and liked Miss Dresser. I think every one is pleased except Miss D" (most likely referring to Edith's oldest and unmarried sister, Susan). "But there," he continued, "I mustn't be scandalous in my first letter to you."

■　■　■

As Edith and George's June 2 wedding date approached, the weather was not cooperating: the Paris spring seemed perpetually gloomy and overcast. One guest who was not feeling quite in the spirit of things was George's best man, William B. Osgood Field. George had written Field in late May to say that his friend and original choice for best man, Jonathan Sturges, was ill and could not perform his duties. Could Field step in? It had been only a few months since George and Field had gone their separate ways after their Indian excursion—Field to Rome and George to Paris—and Field was exhausted and anxious to return to New York.

"Think of my staying over here six weeks for his old wedding and then having to pay my own expenses," he wrote to his mother. But, he added, "If you knew [George] as I do you would not wonder at anything he does. The truth is he does not know any better."

Of course, Field agreed. He had played such a large role in his friend's relationship thus far, and his friendship with George, despite any bumps along the way, was an important one to him. His friend sounded decidedly happy with his choice, one that had taken him years to make.

"I am entering on my new life without one doubt or fear and with absolute trust and confidence," George had written Field. "May the same be yours, Billy, is the best wish that can come from your devoted friend."

Field was trying his best to live cheaply, but his obligations as a best man were taking a toll on his patience and his pocketbook. He wrote his mother constantly, sometimes just to vent, other times to ask for more money. He was like the Nick Carraway to George's Gatsby: playing matchmaker, yet unable to keep up with his friend financially.

Still, he added while on a more philosophical bent, "In the long view and end I would not change places for all the world. Money can never buy his happiness."

As the big day approached, Field's devotion was put to the test. George wanted him at his side constantly, and the details George asked Field to handle were piling up: carriages, flowers, ribbons, music, ushers. Soon, it all began to come together and guests began to sail from New York, a number of them on the *Campania*. So many family and friends had set sail to witness Edith and George's wedding that Fifth Avenue must have seemed like a ghost town.

"New York without a Vanderbilt," the New York *World* headline stated a week before the impending nuptials. The brood had "deserted the metropolis." The guest list included the Duke and Duchess of Marlborough (the duchess being George's niece Consuelo), and family members on both sides, Vanderbilts, Sloanes, Twomblys, Kings, and more. Also attending was Chauncey Depew, a close family friend and legal counsel who had served as president of the New York Central railroad, chairman of the board for the Vanderbilt system of railroads, and soon-to-be New York state senator. George's brother Cornelius, the family patriarch, hosted a dinner in honor of the new couple. The Hôtel des Îles Borromées brimmed with expatriates.

As mandated by French law, there was a civil ceremony to legalize the union in the eyes of the state, in addition to the religious affair. The June 1 civil ceremony was in the Eighth Arrondissement on Rue d'Anjou, after which George also made a 2,500-franc donation to help orphans of the district. After leaving the *mairie*, civic duty completed, Field convinced George to buy a new hat, thinking his current one far too shabby for the occasion.

On June 2, 1898, George's carriage pulled up in front of the American Church of the Holy Trinity on Avenue d'Alma. He was right on time, with Edith's carriage following just behind. Inside the cathedral, ushers—Joe Hunt and Count Antoine Sala among them—stood proud in frock coats and white ties. George had gifted each of them pearl solitaire scarf pins. The bridesmaids, Florence Van Dusen Reed and Daisy de Montsaunit, carried white orchids and lilies of the valley. Edith, too, had gifted pearl pins to her attendants, which they wore on their mousseline de soie dresses of subtle green encrusted with dentelle jaune, large black hats completing the ensemble.

Theirs was to be a small, elegant affair, with attendance seeming minuscule compared to the outsize nuptial events that dominated the society pages of the day, including the recent weddings of George's nieces Adele and Gertrude. However, anything the wedding may have lacked in pomp it made up for in style and subtlety.

The *New York Herald* hailed the event as a "simple, tasteful affair" and noted that it was "a welcome relief to see that the nave had been left in all its grave dignity instead of being turned into a conservatory with flowers." Edith's older sister Susan received much credit for her role in planning the event. George's family sat on the right side of the church aisle, Edith's on the left. Aunty Mary King attended wearing black silk with steel paillettes. Rev. Dr. John Morgan, rector of Holy Trinity, performed the service, assisted by Edith's brother-in-law—Pauline's husband—the Rev. George Grenville Merrill. Shortly before noon, the clergy made their way to the chancel along with George and Field. George wore what Field considered to be a somewhat morose look as he watched the march up the aisle. *Damn it, George*, the best man thought as he and George stood at the altar awaiting Edith's arrival. *This is not your funeral. Look happy.*

The "March Nuptiale" began. Edith, her parents long departed, walked down the aisle on the arm of her brother, Daniel LeRoy Dresser, who towered over his younger sister. Edith strode toward the pair, every inch of her stature and form—ever so studied in the past several months—stylishly draped, the picture of elegance. She wore a high-necked dress of cream-colored satin with court train, the dress had lace flounces that had once graced the wedding dress of her grandmother, and the point-lace wedding veil had been worn by her mother many years before. Her loved ones were long gone, yet well remembered and present in their own way. She and George stood at the chancel steps and awaited the sacrament that would join them in the eyes of the Episcopal Church.

At the end of the ceremony, a sevenfold "amen" led into Mendelssohn's *Wedding March*, which swept the guests and newlyweds out of the church and onto the streets of Paris. Close family and friends went to 15 Rue Vernet where the Dresser family hosted a delightful déjeuner. Glasses were raised, toasts given, and rice tossed. Field picked a few grains out from inside his collar, exhausted and relieved. The couple departed on what would be a nearly four-month honeymoon journey. Field watched and smiled as their carriage pulled away.

"The wedding is over, the millionaire is settled, and thank God," Field wrote his mother. He was ready to go home.

Field wired his mother the next week, his telegram short and to the point, no codebook necessary:

"Sailed Germanic Happy."

■　■　■

Edith and George dashed off on their honeymoon, which included stops in Vienna and Venice, travels through the heart of the Tyrol, and a stay at the beautiful Villa Vignolo in the town of Stresa on Italy's Lago Maggiore. On Field's advice, George had traveled to Italy earlier that spring to investigate spots in and around Como. He had rented the villa for June and July, where the newlyweds could bask in the sun as it bounced off that nation's biggest lake, enjoy views of the Borromean Islands from their terrace, and stroll through gardens that had enchanted the nineteenth-century travel guru Karl Baedeker.

While on his honeymoon, George still thought of his friends. He took out some stationery from the Villa Vignolo and sat down to write Paul Leicester Ford. He was perhaps, even more than Field, George's most cherished companion. George wrote Ford that he was anxious to challenge him to another chess match, and hoped that one day he might be able to beat his good friend at billiards, another of their favorite pastimes. More important, George wanted to let Ford know how grateful he was that his friend was able to attend the wedding ceremony. "My glimpse of you June 2nd was tantalizing there were so many things I wanted to say and couldn't," George wrote, "but it gave me pleasure all the same to know you were there. . . ." Chess and conversation would have to wait until

George settled much more important matters. After all, he wrote Ford, "My wife has never been to Biltmore."

In late August, Edith and George boarded the *Augusta Victoria* bound from Southampton to New York. From there, they traveled to Lenox, Massachusetts; and Shelbourne, Vermont (the country estates of his sisters Emily and Lila, respectively), and stopped once more in Manhattan before venturing South. Edith took a moment to write a note to Field, to whom she had undoubtedly grown much closer over the past year. She thanked her friend and Galahad for the clock he had given the couple as a wedding present and, indulging in the pair's established confidant status, shared her joy as a new bride.

"I am so perfectly radiant that I feel a longing to see all my friends as happy," she wrote to the still-bachelor Field. "With renewed thanks believe me the very sincerely yours Edith Stuyvesant Dresser."

Yet another crossing, this time as a married woman. But this was just the start of the grander journey that Edith and George would make together. Their romance would take Edith further afield of the life she knew than she possibly could have imagined, far from the protocols and posturing of her breeding, to a place where she would truly come into her own.

The Dresser girl, the blue-blood orphan of "modest means," the military daughter who grew up with her name intact yet her future less assured, would now be the mistress of the largest house ever built in the United States of America.

And now she was heading home to her castle.

7

Forest for the Trees

Fall settled on western North Carolina like a shawl of burnt orange, bronze, and ruby. A five-o'clock shadow of naked branches rested on the faces of the mountains as they peered down, colder now, on the towns below.

George had wanted Edith to see Biltmore House while the weather was still good, as the surrounding landscape was equally as impressive as the house that sat upon it. He had thought summer might be best, but the honeymoon and travels had kept them away from North Carolina until the first of October. No matter. Autumn is arguably the best time of year in the southern Appalachians, that season when the lowering of the sun in the sky amplifies the evolving colors of the mountainsides. Peaks of biblically magnificent proportions burst forth with one final flourish of siennas, golds, and russets before turning to winter and slumber.

It was a Saturday afternoon, and Edith sat in George's private train car wearing a smart traveling gown of pearl gray. Her choice of color that day would be the only thing even near to drab about her arrival in Asheville. The pair journeyed stylishly, but had opted to travel with only his valet and her maid for the long rail trip. This small number of attendants belied the massive amounts of luggage that came with them: three large drays' worth of trunks, sporting equipment, and artwork. Many cars of furnishings and artwork had preceded them in September, adding to the already luxurious offerings awaiting Edith at the house and keeping the station agent and all who worked with him on their toes, all in anticipation of this, the couple's first homecoming.

News spread quickly through the small mountain town of the pair's impending arrival. George may have caused a stir years earlier when he began building his estate, yet today's curiosity was not directed at him, but rather at the woman who had, earlier that spring, become his wife.

Southern Railway blocked four trains at Biltmore Station so that George's car could deposit its passengers and goods. The conductor released George's car from the end of the train and its doors opened. George and Edith emerged, giving curious onlookers their first sight of Edith. Walking down the platform, she was a good inch or two taller than George, and this disparity was augmented by the English walking hat sitting atop Edith's head, waves of dark hair peeking out from beneath it. She wore her tresses slightly up, revealing her neck, long and lean, gracefully framed by a feather collarette. With her imposing stature and slim figure, Edith indeed embodied the ideal fashion of the moment, and her carriage, inspired by her grandmother and refined on the streets and in the salons of Paris, effortlessly captured the attention of all who lay eyes on her. Passengers aboard other train cars descended from their berths as well, in hopes of catching sight of the famous newlyweds.

Forester Carl Schenck, estate manager Charles McNamee, and farm manager George Weston met their boss and his new bride at the station. Edith and George made their way to a fashionable victoria and climbed aboard. Schenck, Weston, and McNamee led the way via sporty horse-drawn trap. As Edith and George embarked on the last leg of their long journey, Edith offered a smile for those who stood by at the station, and George gave a small tip of his hat. With that, they were off.

It was a gorgeous fall afternoon. The victoria proceeded through the estate gate and continued along the gracefully meandering Approach Road toward the house. Painstakingly envisioned by Olmsted with its three miles of myriad turns and carefully crafted runs, the road led visitors to believe—rightly so—that a great surprise awaited at the end of their nearly forty-five-minute ride. This was the landscape architecture equivalent of delayed gratification, leaving the sight of the house for that final turn around the bend.

The horses trotted over a road strewn with bridal roses, and then Biltmore House loomed ahead of their carriage. A giant floral horseshoe fashioned of goldenrod and late-season blooms was festooned with well wishes, harkening good luck for the couple. The closer Edith got to the château, the more the majesty of the mountains receded behind it, and the house soon dominated her entire field of vision, its spires scraping the late afternoon's autumn sky, eclipsing all else save for the boisterous crowd of people awaiting her.

Countless employees and servants stood on either side of the carriage as it made its way down the final stretch toward the house. As Edith looked on at the various groups assembled in her honor, she noticed that each person stood bearing a symbol representing their role on the estate: Gardeners hailed the couple with vegetable stalks. The estate's dairy workers were dressed in white duck and stood proudly alongside their Jersey calves. Foresters wore corsages on their coat lapels composed of small twigs and ribbons. All cheered as the carriage passed, while freshly picked blossoms danced against the fall sky as estate florists rained down roses and carnations.

Hurrah, Schenck thought at the arrival of the "new and young Mrs. Vanderbilt," later writing that "all was cheers and smiles and happiness." Schenck thought Edith's face, though not beautiful in a conventional sense, was "sparkling with kindness, sweetness, lovability, grace and womanliness. One could not help but love her."

Edith and George exited the victoria. Up to this point, estate workers had likely imagined Biltmore House the most elaborate bachelor pad ever built. Edith was now a part of the story unfolding at the magnificent home, a new bride about to cross the grandest threshold in the land. On the other side of that threshold, servants lined the hallway dressed in brand-new livery. One of the employees, a Miss Norton, handed over the keys to the castle. They were home. Biltmore House finally had a proper mistress.

It had been nearly three years since George had officially opened his home to family and friends. Since then, workers and artisans had added many finishing touches to the house. George's vast collection of art—whether Sargent paintings, or bronze sculptures from the hands of Antoine-Louis Bayre or Pierre-Jules Mêne; in part inherited from his father, in part collected on his travels—completed the setting. A Degas here, several Dürer prints there. George's collection of rugs warmed the house's near four acres of floor space. A visual treat awaited the eye, no matter the direction it might wander. Decorative flourishes leaped out from every crevice and capstone, each aspect of the house dressed to the nines in the luxury of the age.

Except, of course, for those parts of the house that had yet to be completed.

Edith may have been unaware before arriving at Biltmore House that parts remained unfinished. When she passed along the esplanade, kept in tip-top, neatly shorn shape by a horse-drawn lawn mower, the château's exterior would have given no clue as to any incomplete construction within. Upon taking her first steps into the grand banquet room, with its triple hearth and castle-worthy chandeliers, she probably did not immediately notice that the organ loft contained a single row of actual organ pipes and . . . no organ whatsoever. When she walked through the entrance hall for the first time, she may have been too distracted by the grand tapestry gallery to her left, or the magically glass-roofed Palm Court to her right, to notice the bare subfloor and brick walls of the unfinished music room.

Edith's bedroom was a chamber that would have delighted Louis XV, whose reign became synonymous with quality craftsmanship and ornamental flourishes which showcased the work of sculptors, painters, cabinetmakers, and other artisans. Edith's oval-shaped abode was dressed in lavenders and golds, its walls dripping silk and its windows dressed in floor-length velvet which framed the vistas beyond. Above Edith's canopied bed with its richly patterned quilting, the pastel ceiling was decorated like some fantastic Rococo Easter egg. The decor was, of course, presented as a fait accompli. One can only hope that Edith liked what she saw.

George's more masculine bedroom was located at the southwest corner of the house where he could survey the Deer Park below and gaze at Mount Pisgah seventeen miles away. The master of the house had a room of deepest red offset by furnishings of dark, hand-turned walnut. The feeling was Baroque, from its chaise to its desk, the latter with handsome chairs designed by Richard Morris Hunt. George's bathtub—with hot and cold running water—was marble. Hot and cold running water was not a common convenience in the nineteenth-century Appalachian home. Even among wealthier families whose homes had indoor plumbing, a "full" bath (rather than a water closet with a bathing tub in a separate room) was prized. Completing the regal feel of his personal realm, the walls of George's bedroom were as gilded as the age, a sparkling gold against a sea of scarlet.

His crimson lair and her velvet retreat were linked by a shared sitting room. The influence of Hatfield House in England, which George visited in 1889, was evident here in the details of the richly appointed space. Intricately carved oak paneling crept up the walls of the room to join with cornice friezes. The brass door locks were stunning, sturdy, and hand cast. No detail had been overlooked.

Night drew in. George's private train car headed back North. Soon Edith's sister Natalie and her husband John would come fete the newlyweds. For now, a celebration of Edith's arrival was limited to the estate's employees. Weston, the farm manager, led a group of employees in a torchlight procession, complete with band, along the elegant switchback of the ramp douce at the far end of the esplanade. George and Edith walked out onto one of the home's balconies and watched as the festive scene unfolded before them. Soon, fireworks illuminated the skies beyond the mansion, falling stars against the night sky. Suddenly, the peaks of the surrounding mountains erupted into flame as workers lit welcome bonfires.

Edith and George applauded and then retired for the evening, as the employees continued celebrating. The entire event, though intricately planned and meticulously executed, was a kind of holiday for them, and they carried their revelry well past the midnight hour.

A new era at the home had begun.

■ ■ ■

The welcoming attire of the employees on the day of Edith and George's arrival provided a visual clue of how much was now up and running at the estate. However, George's financial reserves were not as robust as they had been years earlier. Challenges remained. The water system connecting Biltmore to its private supply on Busbee Mountain, for example, was impressive yet finicky. Still, elsewhere there was progress.

Tenant farmers, their chicken coops, and the hens within them were getting a fair workout. George and Edith's kitchen required an estimated thirty dozen eggs per week. The estate's dairy advertised their milk for sale, boasting a herd of "high bred Jerseys"—more than two hundred from the Vanderbilt family farm on Long Island, all tuberculin tested, of course—that were under the care of the former inspector of the New Orleans board of health. "Perhaps you can buy milk a little cheaper," the ad conceded, "but just think it over."

Chauncey Beadle's impressive nursery operation continued expanding and gaining national attention. "Mr. George W. Vanderbilt has purchased the large herbarium of southern plants, collected and arranged by Dr. Chapman," the *Bulletin of the Torrey Botanical Club* reported in April 1896. "It will serve as a nucleus for the scientific collections in connection with the arboretum and systematically managed forest at Biltmore, NC." Though Olmsted's arboretum had never materialized, the herbarium added to an already impressive collection.

The Biltmore nursery functioned as a separate department of the estate now, with Beadle serving as its superintendent. Starting in 1895, Beadle had begun publishing the "Biltmore Herbarium," a pamphlet describing the exponentially increasing varieties of plants, shrubs, saplings, and other flora growing under his care. A true botanist and one who never stopped studying, Beadle made this list of specimens available at no cost to other students of his chosen and cherished field. Shortly thereafter, Beadle and Biltmore also began to offer plants, flowering shrubs, and more for sale to the public. The list was, in a sense, Beadle's way of not only sharing his knowledge with other science-minded growers, but also helped to build his and the estate's prestige in the horticultural community at large.

"The design of the catalogue is to effect exchanges with botanists and institutions," the opening page of an early catalogue announced, "but special specimens are gladly sent to any applicant." Most of the plants were indigenous to western North Carolina, with some "quite unrepresented in many of the largest herbaria."

From *Andromeda floribunda* Pursh, gathered on the slopes of Mount Pisgah at an altitude of about 5,500 feet, to the *Xanthorrhiza apiifolia* L'Her taken from the estate's swamps and moist thickets, the collection was astoundingly varied in name and origination.

Chief forester Schenck was a little more than three years into his job, and delighted in Edith's addition to the estate. The strapping German with bright eyes and upturned mustachio viewed the mistress's coming as a boon for his wife, Adele. Schenck believed Adele, sturdy in her own way and in little need of pampering, would nonetheless welcome any additional female company. Schenck also felt that Edith's presence in George's life would be good for the oft-reclusive Vanderbilt. "She had," he later wrote, "that fine social instinct that her husband unfortunately lacked."

When Schenck had first arrived, the grandness of the house and gardens contrasted with the over-lumbered wilds of the surrounding forests. Farms that had seen better days peppered the hills and valleys, as did homesites that Schenck thought had once been "owned by impoverished Southern landed aristocracy." Some of those individuals and families were still using the lands—whether living there or not—causing tensions. Shortly after arriving at Biltmore with

Edith, George had begun legal proceedings to remove some squatters from his game preserve. Those targeted by the ouster stated that they had been on the grounds for some seven years already and wondered why they should not be able to stay. For his own part, Schenck was in favor of a feudal style of management, so that those who lived on the grounds might also be able to produce in some fashion for the estate.

The scale of George's holdings also proved a challenge for Schenck. George now owned close to 125,000 acres. To manage those lands, to improve their health, Schenck needed help. However, even the most basically trained foresters were hard to come by as the United States had no school to train them—until now. Edith's arrival had come just a month after another auspicious event, the opening of the first ever school of forestry in the United States of America: the Biltmore Forest School.

Schenck had developed an intensive residency program that would train young men to be foresters, professionals who upon graduation could help maintain and sustain lands on either state or private grounds. His team of student rangers would live and work on the grounds of the Biltmore Estate and forests during their studies. When the Biltmore Forest School was about to take in its first students, Schenck received a letter from his friend and teacher, Sir Dietrich Brandis. "I hope you will soon have the management of a forest worth managing," the renowned forester wrote. "Neither Pisgah nor Biltmore are worthy of you."

However, Schenck and George were clearly on to something, and the forests could stand to benefit from the attentions of a dedicated corps of student rangers.

The depleted condition of the woods did not go unnoticed by knowledgeable visitors, including noted naturalist and Sierra Club cofounder John Muir, who spent three days with Schenck a month before the school opened. He wrote his wife, Louie, that he "had a grand time driving and walking over the Biltmore estate, royally entertained by the superintendents. The views, hilly and mountainous, are superb, but the forests are far inferior to those we passed through for 75 miles between Roan Mountain and Lenoir, and as for Vanderbilt's magnificent chateau and drives, I soon tired of them."

And a very short time after the opening of the Biltmore Forest School, Cornell University opened the New York State College of Forestry, headed up by the former chief of what was then known as the United States Division of Forestry, Bernhard Fernow. Within two years, Pinchot would help finance a forestry school at his alma mater, Yale. In what was once an unheard of field of study in America, three institutions were now seeking students.

What Gifford Pinchot—who succeeded Fernow as chief at the Division of Forestry—had begun, insofar as devising a plan for a truly sustainable management of Biltmore's forests, Schenck was continuing and augmenting as Pinchot's successor. The aim of Pinchot's Biltmore Working Plan had been not only to improve the condition of the forest but to do so with an eye to helping make that forest profitable. "Profitable sustained-yield forest management" was Schenck's charge now. He, too, wanted to make what was often called "conservative forestry" a paying venture for Biltmore. George craved that income as well. While Pinchot had been schooled in France, where the emphasis was more firmly placed on the scientific aspects of silviculture—the study of the growth and caretaking of forests—Schenck was firmly rooted in the German school's approach, which also heartily embraced the economic potential of managed forestry, including lumbering.

A revolution in American forestry had begun. Whether or not it would turn a much-needed profit remained to be seen.

■ ■ ■

Edith often ventured beyond the estate's Lodge Gate, and there she saw a proper village taking shape. After Richard Morris Hunt's death, his eldest son, Dick, had taken up the mantle alongside Biltmore's supervising architect, Richard Sharp Smith. Asheville had grown on the Yorkshire-born Smith, though his tweed suits and walking caps likely betrayed him as an Englishman to the mountain locals before any accent might register. Because of his involvement with Biltmore House, commissions for his talents grew throughout the city. In 1896, Smith had designed the Vance monument, a soaring obelisk dedicated to Buncombe County–born Civil War governor and dedicated Confederate Zebulon Vance. It now stood in Court Square in the center of downtown Asheville, the county seat. However, it was in the village that Smith's touch was most acutely felt. He had designed more than two dozen homes for the planned community, and his immediately recognizable pebbledash and stucco exteriors, with their half-timber frames, lent an air of uniformity to the growing hamlet, as well as a feeling that was more English than Appalachian. Smith's structures were set upon the design laid out by Olmsted and Hunt, streets fanning out gracefully from the anchor of the community, Hunt's quaintly resplendent All Souls Cathedral.

George may have been a world traveler but he found the man to lead his church much closer to his North Carolina home: Wheeling, West Virginia. In the company of Rev. Greer from George's New York City church of St. Bartholomew's and his friend Paul Leicester Ford, George had made his way to St. Matthew's Episcopal Church in Wheeling. The trip had been Dr. Greer's idea. He had encouraged George to visit Dr. Rodney Rush Swope there, and ask if he was interested in leaving the congregation he had served for eighteen years, and coming to minister to those at All Souls. He was.

On May 1, 1897, just six months after All Souls was consecrated, Dr. Swope began work in earnest. His salary of $4,000 was a lucrative one in those days by any estimation, but perhaps most especially for a congregation in a rural setting such as the one outside Biltmore's gate. For the year ending August 31, 1898, Swope reported 66 member families, 201 baptisms, and 210 Sunday school students, with Sunday collections from the parish totaling $1,544.47.

The reverend also quickly established a sewing school—organized by his wife—and a women's auxiliary. These were soon followed by the Biltmore Village Club for reading and games. Eventually a Boys'

Brigade was established, designed to offer gymnastics and exercise. This group had the unique benefit of training and performing drills under the instruction of a veteran of the Spanish-American War who lived in the area. Swope also helped to establish the Kindergarten for Colored Children, working closely with, and located at, the Young Men's Institute.

Opened in April 1893, the Young Men's Institute had become the heart of Asheville's black community. The key forces behind the institute were Dr. Edward Stephens, a British Guyana–born, multilingual scholar who led the black public school system, and Issac Dickson, a local businessman and the first black representative on the Asheville school board. Another crucial contributor to the YMI was George.

Stephens and Dickson had approached George in 1892 and asked him if he might contribute financially to a project that would focus on providing cultural, educational, economic, and other social resources for the black community. George agreed, and provided a loan of $13,000 to help develop what would become the Young Men's Institute. During the thirteen years that he was involved as a trustee, George would invest $32,000 in the project.

The organization's 18,000-square-foot building was designed by Richard Sharp Smith. With its pebble-dash facade, hipped roof, and quoin trim, the YMI building was much like many of the buildings in the village of Biltmore. Many of the institute's first members— black men who had worked on the building of Biltmore House itself—constructed the YMI building, which housed businesses and meeting spaces, including a drugstore, doctor's office, and dentist's office. The YMI celebrated its opening at the corner of Eagle and Market Streets two years before George moved into his house.

YMI offered educational and recreational programs, community resources, lectures, concerts, and more. Earnings from ticketed events often went to support these initiatives. Biltmore's estate manager, Charles McNamee, played an ongoing role at the institute, lecturing on topics as varied as astronomy and water quality. All members of the greater Asheville community were welcome to attend many of these events. Despite the institute's mission and membership, attendees were not treated equally. One evening's festivities, in spring of 1895, was titled "Old Time Songs and Ways," and advertised that "some of the oldest colored people in Asheville will take part. Seats reserved for white people."

By 1900, the Sunday school for black children would have seventy-five students in attendance. Swope continued reaching out to the black community, offering instruction in kitchen gardening and dressmaking. More groups sprung up for all members of the parish, including a Mother's Club, Neighborhood Club, and something termed the Happy Hour Club, whose first president was aptly named Miss Drinker.

All Souls offered music on par with any you might find in a big-city church. Even before the church opened, George had hired the Devonshire, England–born organist and choirmaster Caryl Florio. Florio had been a celebrated "boy soloist" at Trinity Church in New York City, and his teaching and performance résumé in New York and Chicago would be a boon to any music-minded congregation. He had at his fingertips a spectacular organ made by Geo. S. Hutchings & Co. which stood in a recess in the chancel's north wall. George Sherburn Hutchings was a Civil War veteran who had built organs for years, including a sixty-four-stop organ for the new Old South Church in Boston. With swells and stops and Clarabellas and Doppel Flotes, the organ in the industrial age allowed for expansion in both tonal variety and production. Shortly after building the organ for All Souls, Hutchings's company hired a young tuner by the name of Ernest Skinner, whose name would soon become synonymous with the instrument he worked to make hum.

Swope often felt challenged by a congregation that was "composed largely of sightseers and sojourners for a brief season." He did not feel the church was strong enough, from a parochial standpoint. A good part of the membership enjoyed a life of relative luxury—if not Vanderbilt luxury—and they were not accustomed to working for their church or its growth. He took to the newspaper to chide "the elite of his parish" who "have a habit of coming late to Sabbath services." According to one member of his congregation at the time, Swope "took off his gloves." Tourists were an added annoyance. They came in increasing numbers to gawk at the church that George had built, since few if any would ever have the opportunity to step inside his fabled house. "I want you to understand," the newspaper quoted Swope as saying, "that this is not a show place but a house of worship."

Since the church's opening, the south transept had been further transformed by the hands of stained-glass artisans Maitland Armstrong and Helen Maitland Armstrong, whose names were routinely mentioned alongside those of Louis Comfort Tiffany and John LaFarge. They had replaced three of the plain, leaded glass windows with memorial windows they'd created: one each for George's mother, Maria Louisa Vanderbilt; his architect and friend, Richard Morris Hunt, and his dear cousin, Clarence Barker. All the windows had been installed in time for Edith's first Christmas.

The younger Armstrong wrote that she and her father had wanted "to present both the Old and New Testament history, and at the same time to select, when possible, for each window a subject suitable to the individual commemorated." The window dedicated to George's mother occupied the center space, "Charity" its theme. Helen Maitland Armstrong described the late Mrs. Vanderbilt as a "good and lovely woman." The window's image is one of caring and devotion, safety and maternal protection. Three children huddle near the central female figure as she envelops them with her robes. Above her head three cherubs look on. George's mother was well remembered by many in New York as someone who had not forgotten her humbler beginnings before being married to arguably the richest man in the world. She was someone who was truly charitable, and not just with her pocketbook. The window's accompanying text read, "The love of God lives through eternity."

For Richard Morris Hunt, famed architect and, in many ways, a father figure to George, "The Building of the Temple" seemed appropriate. In the scene, young Solomon sits with a scroll of parchment resting upon his knees, discussing the text with Hiram of Tyre, who stands next to him. On the hill behind them looms Solomon's temple, Jerusalem's first, waiting to be finished. Beneath the image are the words "For glory and for beauty," two things Hunt had certainly enjoyed and, through his talents, shared with many others.

And for George's cherished cousin and friend Clarence Barker, a talented musician and composer, the Armstrongs chose a scene inspired by the first book of Samuel: A young David stands playing his harp before the mentally tormented King Saul, who rests his face in his hands. "So Saul was refreshed and was well . . ." the passage reads. Beneath this window are the words, "I will sing unto the Lord my King."

George had suffered many losses in a short time. Olmsted still lived, but his increasingly failing mind had predicated a move that same fall of Edith's arrival to the McLean Hospital in Belmont, Massachusetts. The memorial windows were a fitting and lasting tribute to those who had played a significant role in George's life. In the cases of his mother and Hunt, they had also played a great part in George's coming to this part of the world. It was fitting that George, so enamored of the arts, used his patronage as an expression of his own deep, abiding sentimentality.

■　■　■

Field and his family were among the guests invited to Biltmore House for Edith's first North Carolina Christmas of 1898. "Please bring your maid," Edith wrote to Field's mother, earlier that December, "as we have lots of rooms and the porter of our car will procure a berth for her in the adjoining car." Once in town Field, ever the outdoorsman, enjoyed an opossum hunt arranged by Schenck and his rangers. "Should you desire to have any quail hunt . . . please leave word at the house of Frank Potter at the side of the old chicken farm," Schenck told Field.

The employee Christmas party—already a favorite holiday tradition—was greatly enhanced by Edith's presence. She still remembered riding as a girl in a landau to West Twenty-Third Street and the home of her grandfather Daniel LeRoy, scouring the festively appointed drawing room for presents hidden beneath the sofa or behind the extravagant drapes. Now she had her own Christmas tradition on her own magnificent estate, to the delight of so many.

The tradition of giving presents to employees had well established roots going back centuries and was commonplace in feudal society. Though popular Christmas traditions like trimming the tree and exchanging gifts did not enter American culture until the mid-nineteenth century, the practices took hold fast and tight, especially in New York, where wealthy New Yorkers inclined to charitable giving—but who still wanted to keep their distance from the recipients of their aid—attended charitable holiday events on massive scales. An estimated 20,000 people attended one such Christmas event hosted at Madison Square Garden. The have-nots entered via Fourth Avenue, while the haves—decked in yuletide finery—filed in through the Madison Avenue entrance and made their way to box seats to watch flocks of hungry citizens eat food their donations had helped provide.

"The Rich Saw Them Feast" reported the *New York Times*, describing how wealthy attendees "looked on in happy sympathy" for the "biggest Christmas feast ever given in New York."

Even in their charity, the Four Hundred proved themselves overly extravagant.

Edith and George continued traveling in the new year. The pair could be found at their home at 640 Fifth Avenue in New York, strolling the avenues of Paris, enjoying the sea vistas of Cannes, soaking up the sun in Rome and Florence, and visiting with Edith's Aunty Mary King in Newport. There they also hosted Edith's older sister Susan, newly married to the Viscount d'Osmoy. They spent ten days in Pisgah Forest before leaving for their home in Point d'Acadie in Bar Harbor and planned to stay there until October. Naturally, when in London, George and Edith's names could be found in the Court Circular. (While Buckingham Palace covered nearly five times the floor space as Biltmore, the palace's gardens occupied a mere 40 acres.)

Fall and winter were for Biltmore. "Short stays here are too tantalizing," George once wrote his friend Ford.

That fall, however, necessitated a somber stay in New York. George's eldest brother, Cornelius Vanderbilt II, had died. News of Corneil's death had reached George in Bar Harbor. It was September 12, 1899, and he and Edith joined the family in New York City, along with close friends and countless onlookers who gathered for the funeral. Fifty-five-year-old Cornelius had had his third stroke in almost as many years, but this time the resulting cerebral hemorrhage—determined by autopsy—had claimed the life of George's eldest brother, the largest stockholder of New York Central Railroad and titular head of the Vanderbilt clan. Cornelius's body first remained at 1 West Fifty-Seventh Street, his mansion at the corner of Fifth Avenue, upon the bed in which he heaved his final breath. The lifeless body was covered with roses.

On the day of the funeral, onlookers gathered outside Cornelius's home, some out of respect for a man known for his charitable giving, others out of morbid curiosity. The police did what they could to give the family some semblance of privacy. The funeral was held at St. Bartholomew's, where Cornelius had been a member of the vestry and taught Sunday school. Rev. Dr. Greer officiated. Here, the crowds were even greater, especially since all were made welcome to attend the service.

"The poorly clad beneficiary of the dead philanthropist's bounty was made as welcome as any member of the fashionable set," the *New York Times* reported. "No rich man was more conscious of his stewardship." Cornelius's religious faith, charitable giving, and work ethic—despite starting life with an inordinate amount of wealth—were touted in every obituary, every society column.

"He takes with him to the grave the sorrowful respect of all who knew him," the *New York Times* added.

What he left behind, financially speaking, was markedly less than what his father, William Henry, had left to him, despite the fact that the "Vanderbilt system" was now perhaps playing an even more significant role in US transportation than ever. The saying "shirtsleeves to shirtsleeves in three generations" did not quite ring true in Cornelius's case. While their grandfather, the Commodore, left $90 million, their father, William Henry, left a hefty $175 million. Cornelius left behind a respectable $70 million. It was not time for the family to roll up their shirtsleeves and get to work just yet.

■ ■ ■

Edith had been happy to return to Biltmore in time for the turn of the century. She had written Field's mother that while they had enjoyed their summer in Bar Harbor, back in North Carolina the clime was transcendent with "A cloudless sky, a warm sun, and a fresh breeze."

"Everything looks more beautiful than ever (if possible), and we both are so happy to be home. We wanted to get where we could be quiet, and yet be out in the air."

The Vanderbilts closed out 1899 inviting only close friends and family to the house, among them Edith's sister Susan and George's friend Paul Leicester Ford.

George wrote Ford saying that he and "Mrs. V" would love to have him come visit. "We are not having any large house parties on account of mourning," George had written Ford, referring to Cornelius's death. George expected that they would be at Biltmore at least through the winter and if Ford could stay as much as a month, he would be most welcome.

Field, too, remained a frequent visitor to Biltmore House, though his motives for coming had perhaps changed as he had begun to admire George's niece, Lila Sloane, Adele's younger sister. But something else soon caught Field's eye, and he wrote his mother about it: Edith's appearance, her yellowish pallor and washed-out complexion. William, one of George's servants with whom Field was acquainted, confided that he had noticed something off about Edith as well.

"Mrs. V. is surely 'up slump,'" Field wrote his mother shortly after the turn of the century, "not very far gone but dollars to doughnuts there is something very much like the appearance of a woman in the family way."

After all, every castle needs a princess.

8

Births of the Century

The century had turned, its mauve fading now, as the country continued reeling from what was both a tumultuous and expansive period. Titans of land and sea, earth and transport, continued to dominate the industrial landscape. The United States was the largest steel producer in the world, and at the heart of that power was Andrew Carnegie and Carnegie Steel. John D. Rockefeller and his Standard Oil Company drove an American oil boom which overshadowed all other refinery efforts. Agricultural endeavors could now be undertaken on a scale—a profitable, large scale—never seen before. Karl Friedrich Benz in Germany, and Charles and Frank Duryea in the United States, had made the fanciful notion of a horseless carriage into a reality at the end of the nineteenth century, and the world was poised for a revolution in personal transportation. In New York City, transportation was soon headed underground as work on the rapid transit tunnel began.

Steel. Oil. Farming. Automobiles. These industries had produced some of the richest families in the world, and perhaps the most dramatic growth of cities and wealth as the United States had ever seen. Yet a feeling of uneasiness was also growing: Strikes for workers' rights. Pushback against corporate interests. Increased dismay and outrage at income disparity. Decades of work by suffragists like Susan B. Anthony, Elizabeth Cady Stanton, Lucy Stone, and Julia Ward Howe was shifting the women's rights movement into high gear, and the National American Woman Suffrage Association was now ten years old. Progressives who argued for social change found a growing audience for their message.

However, time, it seemed, stood still at Biltmore. As did much work on the house.

George began reducing annual expenditures to maintain the estate from nearly $250,000 to $70,000. It was said that George—who as a boy had diligently tracked every penny he spent—had ignored warnings from advisers to cut back on spending, especially during the construction phase. The press speculated that he had grown frustrated with the entire undertaking. The scientific museum that Olmsted had planned and considered an excellent idea for George in the arboretum remained just that—an idea.

Before George left for his life-changing voyage to Paris and India, his brother-in-law and oft financial adviser, Hamilton Mc-Kown Twombly, had warned George that Biltmore House would likely continue to cost him dearly, and was unlikely to ever pay. Yet Twombly's ire was more firmly directed at those who had advised George, including Olmsted's sons, who had taken over their father's role at Biltmore.

"The trouble with you landscape architects," Twombly wrote Fredrick Olmsted Jr., "is that you don't protect your clients from their own ignorant impulsiveness about matters in which they rely on your experienced judgement."

Frederick Jr. was quick to remind Twombly that he himself had fired Olmsted Sr. from a project when the landscape architect warned Twombly he was making unwise choices.

Frederick Jr. later wrote: "If we had known earlier that George Vanderbilt was spending more than his income on the Biltmore Estate and eating seriously into his capital, we could, and would, have urged methods of economizing—to any desirable degree—much more satisfactory in the net results, and less wasteful, than [what] inevitably happened when the annual expenditure was suddenly and arbitrarily cut to about a quarter of what it had been running."

While George drastically curtailed spending at Biltmore, that did not prevent him from purchasing land in New York City across from his home at 640 Fifth Avenue. The lot, once occupied by the Roman Catholic Orphan Asylum, was to be the site for two more town-houses at 645 and 647 Fifth, and its purchase was believed to be in an effort to protect the area from encroaching commercial development. George employed the services of Hunt & Hunt—brothers Richard Howland Hunt and Joe Hunt—to commence work on what would become known as the Marble Twins.

. . .

When guests arrived at Biltmore House, Edith often concealed the unfinished music room with some clever decorating. Fabrics and pillows and some of George's prized rugs made the bare floor slightly more inviting if one didn't notice the unfinished ceramic tile ceiling. However, one aspect of the house that had been completed since George opened his doors in 1895 was the library at the south end of the house—a room that must have certainly appealed to George's friend Paul Leicester Ford.

George treasured his visits with Ford, whether attending the opera at the Met or listening to Chopin played by the Polish pianist Ignacy Jan Paderewski during one of his famed recitals in New York. George and Ford often played chess. George had written his friend and sometime chess adversary that he had been practicing playing without his queen. When Ford visited, they did of course venture out, as no one could resist exploring the expansive estate, watching the ethereal afternoon light glimmering off the French Broad River or an autumn sunset throwing its pink shade across the forest. But perhaps George's favorite times with Ford were the quieter ones, those spent sitting in George's library, playing chess or discussing art or theater, surrounded by his most valued inanimate companions: books.

George's library was likely the only one in the country that could rival the one in which Ford first fell in love with the written word, that of his father, Gordon L. Ford, whose private collection was considered the most valuable in the country. George's library ably reflected his personal taste and abiding adoration for books and all things literary. Of George's estimated 23,000-volume collection, roughly 10,000 or so lived on these shelves. One New York City journalist to referred to George as the "best read man in the country," and based on the entries and dates in the notebook in which George recorded the volumes he had read, he averaged eighty-one books a year, roughly one and a half each week.

The two-story library was rich and ornate, encircled in Circassian walnut. The grand black marble hearth could help keep the room warm on colder mountain evenings. The sculptor Karl Bitter's work was showcased here as well, both in the bronze andirons and in his oak carvings of Demeter and Hestia—goddesses of earth and hearth, respectively—perched on plinths above the mantel.

To mark his literary treasures, George had helped create his own bookplate as well, entrusting his design to noted bookplate engraver Edwin Davis French. The central image was an oil lamp, and the inscription read "Quaero Ex Libris Biltmore": Inquire in the books of Biltmore. George often bought books from publishers in an unbound state, then had the volumes bound according to his own preferences. Riviere & Sons of London was one of his preferred binders and a favorite of the Grolier Club in New York. George's knowledge of the historical bindings was well respected. An 1891 issue of *Publishers Weekly* cited a *Daily News* exposé of "bogus historic bindings," in which a bookseller stated that while "falses" often passed unnoticed, "I take it that it would be almost impossible to fool either Brayton Ives, Robert Hoe, Rush Hawkins, Loring Andrews or George Vanderbilt."

The second story of the library could be reached by an ornate spiral staircase. Doors flanking the overmantel above the fireplace opened onto a secluded passageway which led to the living hall on the second floor. An insomniac guest could make a quick, secret trip from his bedroom on the second floor, to the living hall, and finally through those doors and down a circular descent into the library's cozy embrace of cloth and leather bindings, rich rugs, elegantly carved furnishings, sumptuous velvet, and gleaming iron and stone. Most convenient, this could be done without requiring the guest to get fully dressed.

Richard Morris Hunt's hand could be seen here as well, in a handsomely carved book stand and three carved sets of steps used for reaching the upper shelves. These steps were as elaborate as they were utilitarian, their swooping lines and ornamental flair echoing the elements of the spectacular Italian Baroque ceiling. The gorgeous six-stepped furnishings appeared designed to be more admired than stood upon. Eventually a large standing globe was added to the room. The den off the library was a favorite of George's, the stunning views of his lands surpassed only perhaps by those offered from his bedroom.

The 40-by-60-foot library was crowned by *The Chariot of Aurora*, a masterpiece executed by Giovanni Antonio Pellegrini, which once hovered over the eighteenth-century comings and goings in the Pisani Palace in Venice. The palazzo's Gothic floral style was cloaked in burnt orange, boasting striking mullioned windows on a facade that fronted the city's Grand Canal. The Pisani family eventually ended up overextending themselves on the construction and decoration of grand homes and had to sell one of the family mansions to Napoleon Bonaparte. Pellegrini, a child of Venice himself, had worked throughout Europe, and George had purchased Pellegrini's work from a Venetian family during one of his many trips abroad in search of furnishings, tapestries, and other artistic flourishes for his new home. The work was similar to the painter's *Allegory of Dawn*, eventually housed at the University of Oxford's Ashmolean Museum. In the painting, Pellegrini depicts Aurora, Roman goddess of the dawn, moving across the sky, ferrying a new day behind her. A torch in her right hand, angels and chubby cherubs below her, she sits atop clouds, draped in the whites and pinks of a new morning, backlit by the coming sun, the darkness of the previous night just barely visible beneath her.

The topics and titles in George's collection varied widely. Forestry, of course, was well represented, as scientific farming was a constant discussion at Biltmore. Art and architecture were long-time passions of George and Edith, both of whom had had the opportunity to see some of the most notable examples of these on their travels. More than a hundred of Honoré de Balzac's works lived among the stacks. A rare first edition of *Paradise Lost* by John Milton dwelled here, as did a copy of *Essays on Man: In Four Epistles to a Friend*, published in 1737 and featuring handwritten notes by the author, Alexander Pope. A rare edition of *Sibylline Leaves: A Collection of Poems*, by Samuel Taylor Coleridge, was a true find, and contained not only a first edition of *The Rime of the Ancient Mariner* but also Coleridge's own signed changes that he wished to incorporate into future editions. Another treasure was a first edition of Charles Darwin's epic contribution to science and evolution, *On the Origin of Species*.

However, in late 1899, Ford had mailed to George what was perhaps one of the most precious additions to his collection: a copy of Ford's most recent novel, *Janice Meredith: A Story of the American Revolution*. (Some in the press theorized that Edith had, in fact, been the inspiration for the book's heroine.) The book was not merely autographed by Ford, but had in fact been dedicated to George. When George first learned of the honor, he wrote Ford saying, "May you have many more literary and social hours under [Biltmore's] roof." Once George saw the dedication in print, he was moved by this public celebration of the treasured time these friends spent together at Biltmore House.

My dear George:

It begins, into the warp and woof of every book an author weaves much that even the subtlest readers cannot suspect, far less discern. To them it is but a cross and pile of threads interlaced to form a pattern which may please or displease their taste. But to the writer every filament has its own association: How each bit of silk or wool, flax or tow, was laboriously gathered, or was blown to him; when each was spun by the wheel of his fancy into yarns; the color and tint his imagination gave to each skein; and where each was finally woven into the fabric by the shuttle of his pen. No thread ever quite detaches itself from its growth and spinning, dyeing and weaving, and each draws him back to hours and places seemingly unrelated to the work. And so, as I have read the proofs of this book I have found more than once that the pages have faded out of sight and in their stead I have seen Mount Pisgah and the French Broad River, or the ramp and terrace of Biltmore House, just as I saw them when writing the words which served to recall them to me. With the visions, too, has come a recurrence to our long talks, our work among the books, our games of chess, our cups of tea, our walks, our rides and our drives. It is therefore a pleasure to me that the book so naturally gravitates to you, and that I may make it a remembrance of those past weeks of companionship, and an earnest of the present affection of

Paul Leicester Ford.

George wrote his dear friend a note of thanks.

"When Janice appeared a few days ago I was and still am much touched by the beautiful dedication you have written. Thank you dear fellow and come again soon and renew the talks, chess, drives etc."

Hopefully there would be many more of each. Aurora was watching and waiting. However, in the future, it was unlikely Ford would be traveling alone.

"There is no one of your friends I am sure who will wish you joy more sincerely than I do," George wrote his friend in the spring of 1900, congratulating him on his engagement to Miss Grace Kidder. "All of life looks differently and one's attitude toward many things changes . . . once a man is happily married. I only hope the future Mrs. P.L.F. will like Biltmore and its master and mistress as much as we feel P.L.F. does and that she will not keep you away from us. . . . Wishing you every possible happiness believe me as always your devoted friend, George."

■ ■ ■

By the summer of 1900, Edith's condition could no longer be kept secret. Schenck, returning after some months spent in his homeland satisfying a forestry service requirement that would permit him to keep his German citizenship, was thrilled by Edith's appearance. He watched happily as she, often attended by medical professionals and midwives, walked the grounds.

"Mrs. Vanderbilt's altered outlines forecast a great event. An heir for Biltmore was expected," he later wrote. "What an event for an estate on which the general manager, the chief clerk, the landscapist, the farm heads, and notably Mrs. Schenck and I, were without children and any prospects of them!"

Not all news was good. Schenck returned to discover that fires in the forest had destroyed several buildings. He was disappointed that there were not nearly as many new students for the forestry school as he would have hoped, and assumed that the new programs at both Yale and Cornell might be to blame. Still, Schenck still believed work in George's Pisgah Forest had some practical, on-site advantages that neither Ivy League school could offer.

On a positive note, the estate's piggery was up and running, and that year Biltmore's hogs performed well at a Chicago livestock show. The Berkshire hogs were particularly meaty, averaging 800 pounds each. "All honor to Farmer George Vanderbilt," a newspaper proclaimed. Lumber and dairy remained important, as well, if for no other reason than they had the potential to generate income. George had long envisioned a *working* estate, a self-sufficient enterprise that would not require constant investment of his dwindling inheritance.

Cornelius Vanderbilt II's window in All Souls was dedicated in July 1900. The Maitland Armstrong father-daughter team of stained-glass artists again brought their talents to the cathedral. "Behold the Man," read the inscription at the base of this new window for George's eldest brother. In this scene, Christ stands, draped in purple robes, with a Roman soldier to his right and a crown of thorns upon his head. Arching over the scene was the insignia of the ancient empire: S. P. Q. R. George's brother, a serious man and one of sacrifice for others, had become yet another memory in glass.

Edith's due date approached, and the soon-to-be-mother was pleased and healthy. She sat down to send Field's mother an update. "We are overjoyed at the prospect," she wrote. "If all goes as it has up until now there is no cause for alarm—I am very well, and we are most radiantly happy."

It was nice for Edith to have something to look forward to, as tragedy had struck her side of the family as well. On May 1, 1900, not quite three months after celebrating the joy of giving birth to her first child, Edith's sister Natalie had lost her husband, John Nicholas Brown. Typhoid fever was believed to be the culprit. That exceptionally contagious illness was caused by salmonella typhi and spread via food or water that had come in contact with the excrement of another infected individual. Though Almroth Edward Wright, a British bacteriologist, had developed a typhoid vaccine used by British troops during the Boer War, widespread vaccinations were still not common at the time. Someone exposed to typhoid would find themselves suffering from fever, headaches, and gastrointestinal distress. These symptoms were sometimes followed by intestinal hemorrhaging. Left untreated, individuals might survive roughly a month. So it was with John, who had been ill for just a few weeks before the disease finally won out. John's brother, Harold, received the news while traveling in Europe and immediately booked passage on the *Oceanic* to return to the United States. Stress, exhaustion, and the vagaries of travel merged mercilessly, and Harold caught pneumonia. He himself died less than two weeks after his brother, and he died childless. Natalie's infant son, John Nicholas Brown II, was now the heir to the bulk of John and Harold's shares of the Brown family fortune—estimated to be worth $30 million.

This "pink, chubby mite of humanity," as one paper described him, was dubbed the richest baby in the world.

Indeed, if he had any competition in that category, it was going to come in the form of his slightly younger cousin.

■ ■ ■

"Dear Billy,

"A fine healthy daughter put in an appearance last evening & received a hearty welcome," George wrote. "Mrs. V is doing splendid."

George was writing his friend from Biltmore House. Edith and George could have chosen to have their first child in Manhattan or Newport, of course, larger cities with more modern facilities that were closer to extended family and more easily reached by the throngs who would surely want to see this latest addition to the Vanderbilt family. Yet Edith and George chose to bring their first child into the world among the wilds of western North Carolina, in the privacy of their own home. Dr. Tucker of New York was on hand for the birth on August 22, 1900. Dr. Battle—who had looked after George's mother during their visit years earlier, and had helped establish the region's tubercular-healing reputation—watched over Edith during her accouchement. Biltmore House was more than adequate for any well-bred mother to occupy for the birth itself and the weeks of recommended convalescence that, according to the belief of the time, should follow.

Edith could sit up in bed, a new babe in her arms, and enjoy the view of the forests and mountains that had, years ago, bewitched her husband, and that would be some of the first sights that her newborn daughter's eyes would ever behold. This child was born to great wealth and privilege, but also to the land, and this mingling of the rustic and refined would shape her youth. Edith and George chose a name that joined each of their own families, two of the most well known—one for monies earned, one for lineage bestowed—in the United States: Cornelia Stuyvesant Vanderbilt.

American and European newspapers proclaimed the news of Cornelia's arrival to the world. But perhaps nowhere were people more enthused about the event than in Asheville itself. News broke

after midnight as reporters scrambled to get to the wires for confir-
mation. "Stork Comes to Biltmore," the five-cent *Asheville Citizen*
announced the next day.

"The little stranger is a Buncombe baby—pretty as new babies
go—but with the Buncombe birthright of the mountain's health . . ."
the newspaper wrote, referring to Biltmore's home county. (Named
for former congressman Edward Buncombe, "Buncombe" is the origin of the word "bunkum"—as in a load of—and was inspired by a
particularly long-winded, circuitous speech delivered by the politi-
cian himself.)

This monumental birth inspired poetry down the road in Charlotte:

> *The Biltmore Baby*
> *(To Miss Cornelia Stuyvesant Vanderbilt)*
> *Howard A. Banks in Charlotte Observer.)*
>
> *We love you, little heiress,*
>   *Baby Nell!*
> *Dainty, dimpled millionairess;*
> *You're the sweetest of the fairies,*
>   *Baby Nell!*
>
> *You're so noisy, red and funny,*
>   *Baby Nell!*
> *But there's not enough of money*
> *In the world to buy you, honey,*
>   *Baby Nell!*
>
> *And your pa was churchmouse poor,*
>   *Baby Nell!*
> *Though folks said he had some store—*
> *Till you knocked at Biltmore door,*
>   *Baby Nell!*

But dropped you through a crack,
Baby Nell!
In your papa's big, white shack,
Under Pisgah and the Black,
Baby Nell!

If your wee sock we could peel,
Baby Nell!
And your small pink footsies feel,
We'd find tar upon your heel,
Baby Nell!

So we love you, little heiress,
Baby Nell!
Buncombe county millionairess,
You're the sweetest of the fairies,
Our own Nell!

Conferring the "tar heel" moniker upon Cornelia was indeed a true Carolina honor. North Carolinians and Asheville residents clearly felt a kind of ownership over Cornelia. By extension, her birth solidified a growing feeling that George and Edith were more than just passers-through. This family now had a link to this area that could never be undone. George and Edith may have been from New York, Newport, and even Paris, but baby Cornelia was a child of Buncombe County, an Asheville baby, Tar Heel Nell.

People of her "native county . . . can wish for her no richer heritage than that she may have the quiet, unassuming kindness of her doting father and the beauty and goodness of her loving mother," a North Carolina paper trumpeted. "May her health be as rugged as the eternal hills about her and her whole life as peaceful as the scenes that attract the hundreds of thousands of pilgrims to her father's princely estate."

They also noted that, "a good portion of Buncombe is hers."

The extent to which Cornelia's eventual inheritance might rival or surpass that of her cousin John's depended on a number of factors, not the least of which was whether Edith and George eventually gave birth to a son, and if Biltmore did not completely deplete George's resources before Cornelia came of age.

For the time being, there was only joy. Edith's sister Natalie, though grieving herself, traveled with her young son, John, to Biltmore to see her new niece. She spent time with her younger sister, a new mother. The home's outdoor spaces were ideal for a quiet moment's reflection as they overlooked the majestic grounds and long-range vistas. There George sat on the loggia, breeze from the mountains he loved grazing his cheeks, beaming at the child in his arms.

Schenck described George at this time as "happiest of fathers." To Schenck's eyes, "there was nothing lacking from the perfection of all his dreams and schemes."

For Cornelia's baptism, George bought Edith an antique ring to commemorate the occasion. "A new fad!" the newspapers cried: the christening ring. Edith's was reported to be dull Burmese gold, set with a white opal, "of size suggestive of the diminutive closed hand of Mademoiselle Cornelia," and with a setting said to be identical to a ring Napoleon gave his empress Josephine. Though George had purchased the item from a European curio dealer, the interior, oddly enough, bore the engraving "E. D."—Edith's birth name initials. It was supposed to be worn on the little finger of the left hand and had the added bonus of distinguishing "the matrons who have been honored by the attentions of the stork."

Cornelia was christened at All Souls Cathedral. The babe received numerous gifts—ten carriages, for starters—one of which was a wicker contraption shaped like a giant swan with a silk interior. Other carriages had adjustable cushions, promising excellent views for the child. Some were designed with city travel in mind, others for country strolls. Cornelia would ride in the lap of perambulatory luxury.

The occasion of Cornelia's birth also provided a renewed opportunity for the media to write once again about Edith, who was not quite two years into her new life as Mrs. George Washington Vanderbilt. To this end, the *New York Times* ventured an opinion on Edith's affection for—or lack thereof—her new surroundings, stating that the "most magnificent estate in America has never possessed any charm for Mrs. Vanderbilt." The article added that Edith considered Biltmore "absolutely distasteful to her," but had managed, over time, "to endure it."

George, on the other hand, was "devoted to rural life" and his agricultural experiments, and was building a hospital and sanitarium for the community. The last part, at least, was accurate. The Clarence Barker Memorial Hospital and Dispensary, in the town of Biltmore, with a $20,000 endowment from George, would accept its first patients the following month.

The local papers had a much different take on Edith and her personality. They went out of their way to praise her as more than just the mother of an American heiress: "Those who do not know Mrs. Vanderbilt feel endeared to her for the philanthropic work she does among the poorer people around Biltmore, and her personal attention to the people associated in any way with her husband's estate. . . . Her very presence is sunshine to them."

■　■　■

Amid the great and growing forest of Pisgah, trees were taking root, soil was renewing itself; saplings were not only fighting, but surviving. However, much closer to the grand house, one more new tree had yet to be planted. This tree would stand in remembrance of one of the happier events ever to transpire at Biltmore.

As Cornelia neared two months of age, the family went to a quiet dell down from the house near the Bass Pond. Dr. Battle came with them. Together, the group brought along another babe, a sapling of *Magnolia acuminata*: "cucumber magnolia" or "mountain magnolia." It was hoped that the young specimen—already twelve feet tall—might soar to sixty feet or more by the time Cornelia reached her twentieth year.

The cucumber magnolia was of hardy stock and it thrived in the region. Seed cone fruits and yellow-green leaves topped off a tree known for its deep, wide-spreading roots. The plant was placed in the ground and covered with soil. Tiny Cornelia leaned over and laid a tiny hand on her special tree.

Just weeks earlier, another child of the new century had been born in Asheville. This child, a boy, was born up the road in a five-room house in downtown Asheville which his father had built. He was born in much simpler surroundings, and it would be years before his name would gain its own notoriety. Thomas Wolfe's renown would not come from his family name or from any grand inheritance but rather from his typewriter.

These two new Asheville citizens would make their own marks on the small mountain town, and it on them. Each of their stories would at once bind them to this spot and take them far away, once the call of something different grew too loud to ignore.

9

Trials and Toymakers

Now the mother of a healthy one-year-old daughter, Edith turned her attentions more fully to those beyond her gates. She was already becoming known and admired within the village and surrounding areas for her kindness, approachability and, like her husband, charitable acts. Edith would ride out on horseback to deliver baskets—of food, blankets, and other necessities—to pregnant workers, the sick, or those needing clothing or coats. Together George and Edith had worked to expand the parish school in the village, and Edith wanted to establish additional educational programs for the children of the workers on the estate. Edith arranged for a "school bus"—an outfitted wagon—to transport the children of dairy farmers living on the estate to school. She set up a sewing school in the Horse Barn. Both serendipity and determination helped Edith put another of her charitable social reforms into action.

Neighborhood children were likely among the first to spot the pair of artisans, two newly arrived women working diligently in their house in the village of Biltmore. The youngsters could see the women on their porch or through the windows facing the street, creating new and useful things from the bounty of the woods.

It did not take long for Charlotte Yale and Eleanor Vance to notice the tykes, eyes fixed, curiosity written in the furrows of their young brows. The women invited the youngsters in and showed them around. What started as a friendly invitation soon grew into a full-blown apprenticeship for the local children.

Come on in, was Vance's message. Eleanor Vance hailed from Ohio and was a graduate of the Art Academy of Cincinnati, where she studied with carver William Fry. A skilled artisan in her own right, she had studied in England with Thomas Kendall, restorer and carver to the royal family. Charlotte Yale was from Connecticut and knew her way around clay. Both women were adept at a variety of crafts, weaving and needlepoint among them. The pair had met while studying at Chicago's Moody Bible College. In that city, Vance and Yale felt the call of a powerful voice rising out of the postindustrial fray, one urging others to a life of service. That voice belonged to Jane Addams, cofounder, along with Ellen Gates Starr, of Hull-House in Chicago. When it opened in 1889, Hull-House became one of North America's first settlement homes, serving the poor by offering programs and education. Within two years, the settlement home hosted two thousand people a week. Hull House was also the home of The Chicago Arts and Crafts Society, founded there in 1897. Vance and Yale embraced Addams's call to service, befriended the social reformer, and were inspired to serve abroad as missionaries. However, Eleanor Vance's mother had been ill. The women brought her South, like so many others, to seek the recuperative powers of Asheville's mountain air and to see how they might put their skills to good use.

The settlement house approach, a burgeoning Arts and Crafts movement which popularized traditional craftsmanship, and Vance and Yale's arrival in Asheville all combined in happy coincidence. Though Asheville was meant to be only a brief, healing sojourn, the friends found a need for their skills there, and the vacation became their vocation. They would soon find they had something in common with one of the most well-known women in town.

Standing at the kitchen table which she used as a workbench, Vance initially began showing small groups of boys the techniques she had learned over the years. Word reached the ears of Reverend Swope. Shortly thereafter, in the fall of 1901, he helped the women establish what would become known as the Boys Club of Biltmore Parish. At 5 Oak Street in the village of Biltmore, the casual kitchen-table instruction took on a more formal feel as a small group of eager young boys began to learn a trade. The club had guidelines, including a constitution which stated that anyone participating had to be "of good moral character," and should "try to maintain the purity, kindliness, courtesy and mutual helpfulness that should prevail in a company of Christian boys." There was no smoking, no drinking, no cursing, and no chewing of one of North Carolina's biggest exports—tobacco.

Southern Appalachian traditions and artisanal pastimes—rivercane weaving, ceramics, wood carvings—were as much a part of the fabric of this culture as the clay was of the soil. Vance and Yale knew that they could build on the existing craft culture present in the mountains and show citizens that these skills could provide a living. There was, after all, not only talent, but need. The women wanted to harness that talent to alleviate that need. Vance and Yale began training the young people living in and around the estate and village, teaching them skills that might make it easier to put food on their tables, fires under their kettles.

Similar artisanal movements were taking root across the country. Elbert Hubbard, founder of the Roycroft Arts and Crafts community in East Aurora, New York, was a soap salesman who had met English writer, designer, and social activist William Morris while abroad on a walking tour of England. Hubbard soon evolved from Arts and Crafts acolyte into torchbearer. Hubbard published his own writings, and established the Roycroft Press to bring his personal philosophy to the public. His books and pamphlets sold by the millions and the press evolved into bookbinding, leather crafting, metalwork, and wood carving. When fans began coming to East Aurora to catch a glimpse of publisher Hubbard, an inn was built to accommodate them. The artisans who worked to furnish the Roycroft Inn became known as Roycrofters. The growing community espoused a creative ideology that emphasized style and expression, self-sufficiency and service. Theirs was a strong departure from the industrial age that had made tens of millions for the wealthiest families of the era.

"East Aurora," Hubbard's magazine *Fra* expressed, "is not a locality. East Aurora is a condition of mind."

The work Vance and Yale had begun in the community struck a chord with the down-to-earth Edith. By Christmas in 1901, the Boys Club was up and running, and in early 1902, Vance and Yale's young carving apprentices presented Edith with a bookrack as a thank you for her patronage. Edith thanked them in return by commissioning yet more work. Those who performed best were invited to Biltmore House to see some of the elaborate carvings there by Karl Bitter and others. Edith soon approached Vance and Yale about running a school for the community. Could they use some more formal support? Might she be able to assist them in expanding their small enterprise, to reach a greater number of children? Vance and Yale agreed. Reverend Swope had initially paid them each $970.83 per year. Edith arranged for additional financial subsidies, donated a large space in the village for the group, and within a few years a Girls Club was added. These programs would, by 1905, become officially known as Biltmore Estate Industries.

But Edith had yet more education in mind. In the fall of 1901, Edith had established the Biltmore School of Domestic Science for Colored Girls. The new institution was on Biltmore Road, just past All Souls Crescent. Enrollees had to be at least sixteen years old, and be interested in learning everything they needed to know to work in any area of housekeeping or service. Instruction was soon headed up by principal Mary Isabella McNear. The "classrooms" included a bedroom, dining room, kitchen, and laundry facility. The students could take courses in food preparation, housework, and laundering techniques, and would graduate with the kinds of skills that would enable them to find work in both private homes and businesses. The one requirement was that applicants needed to be able to both read and write, which limited the number of individuals eligible to apply.

Some young women walked up to two miles from their homes

for the opportunity to gain the skills needed to land work as maids, cooks, housekeepers, or waitresses. Students wore a uniform of a long full frock, with a blue and white gingham apron. A white collared necktie framed their necks; their hair was gathered and worn up, topped with a small cap matching their aprons. They learned to mend their own clothes, and how to prepare elegant meals as well as basic fare. George wasn't the only man in town with a private train car, and sometimes chefs from other locomotive kitchens— such as Dr. Seward Webb's *Elsmere*—visited the school to give talks and demonstrations.

There were many more applicants than there were spots available. The only tuition required was 10 cents per week. Students could purchase cookbooks below cost and in installments, if necessary. The school used as its guide *Mrs. Lincoln's Boston Cook Book: What to Do and What Not to Do in Cooking*, a favorite among home science schools.

On commencement day, diplomas and certificates were distributed, and Reverend Swope and Miss McNear addressed the graduates. Graduates created a society of houseworkers, a kind of support group for individuals in their line of work. Students also put their skills on display, serving supper at Edith's bazaar in the village to more than two hundred ticketed guests. They cooked a dinner for members of Asheville's black community, and in the process raised money for their orphanage.

Classes at both new establishments grew and garnered attention and praise beyond the estate itself. New classes in sewing, basketry, and weaving were eventually added to Vance and Yale's village school, and the students' work was displayed at the 1902 parish school year-end ceremony. The School of Domestic Science, too, had successes to share. One young graduate, Miss Annie Mae Nipson, did so well at her studies that after graduation she was hired to work in the largest house in America: Biltmore.

■　■　■

Late in the morning of May 8, 1902, Paul Leicester Ford was sitting at his desk in the second-floor library of his home at 37 East Seventy-Seventh Street in New York City. He had spent most of the morning working on a new book. His personal secretary, Miss Elizabeth Hall, sat at a nearby desk, immersed in her own administrative tasks. It was a large room, commensurate with both Paul's success and his vast collection of books, and stretched along the back of the four-story, Italian Renaissance town house.

When Ford's brother Malcolm arrived, he came straight to the study. Paul's secretary noticed Malcolm's entrance, but wasn't surprised to see him. He had appeared here many times before during the several years that she had worked for Ford. The low tone that the brothers employed was familiar enough to her ears. There had been ongoing tensions between the siblings. *He's probably here to talk about money again*, she thought. It was not her business. Elizabeth kept to her work.

Then she heard it. A shot. Her ears ringing, she turned to see her employer, Ford, hunched over in his chair.

Stunned, Elizabeth now saw Malcolm moving toward her. Terrified, she bolted from the room and stood in the hall. Her composure returning, she thought to go back inside. She could have sworn she heard a voice. Could it have been Paul's? Was he still alive? She listened. No, it was Malcolm's voice. She steeled herself and entered the room again.

Malcolm had moved closer to the doorway and stood facing her, still gripping the new Smith & Wesson .38 caliber, hammerless pistol. Elizabeth froze.

"Now," Malcolm said to Elizabeth, "watch me kill myself."

Malcolm placed the muzzle of the .38 against his chest and pulled the trigger. He fell to the floor, landing just feet away from his barely living brother. The sounds of the gunshots had carried down the stairs. The butler and maids now bounded upstairs to find the grisly scene, Elizabeth in the midst of it.

A frenetic parade of grief and panic followed. It was midday during the working week. The cries of those inside carried out the windows that May day and onto busy streets. Doctors soon arrived as well as the authorities, among them the New York Police Department's Captain Brown. By the time the family doctor, Dr. Emanuel Baruch, arrived, Malcolm was already dead. The scorched fabric on Malcolm's shirt attested to the entry of the fatal bullet. There were powder burns on his hand and body. Ford lay on the couch in the library, scarcely alive. Dr. Baruch summoned another physician, Dr. Julius Rosenberg, who lived nearby. Ford struggled to speak. He seemed aware of the people gathered around him, but was fighting to form words. There was little the doctors could do: Ford appeared to have been struck through the heart. Dr. Baruch felt certain he'd suffered massive damage to his arteries.

"How am I now, doctor?" Paul uttered. "How am I now?"

The doctors moved Paul upstairs to the third floor and worked to make him as comfortable as possible. Another twenty to thirty minutes passed, then the thirty-seven-year-old Ford finally succumbed. Before dying, Ford looked up at Dr. Baruch and spoke once more, one final time. He had forgiven his brother, and he hoped that others would do the same. Eventually Malcolm's body was also moved upstairs. The brothers lay at opposite ends of Ford's house, quieter and closer than they had been in some time.

The doctors immediately turned their attention to Ford's wife, Grace. Not yet married two years, Grace was nearly eight months into her pregnancy with the couple's first child. Dr. Baruch did everything he could to keep Grace away from her husband, concerned not only for Grace's health but that of the unborn child. She begged to look upon her husband once more. The doctors did not want to allow it, but had a difficult time preventing her from doing so.

The coroner arrived and it was not long before the newsboys took to the streets, their singsong calls rising up to the windows of Ford's home where his wife lay under medical care, widowed, pregnant, and in shock. That night, a Dr. Munroe came by to stay with Grace. Carriages came and went bearing grieving friends and concerned loved ones.

Reporters clamored for details about the circumstances surrounding the fratricide-suicide. Police captain Brown, who was already familiar with the tensions between the two brothers, told reporters, "The cause for Malcolm Ford's action can be explained by inference." It must have been a moment of temporary insanity, many believed. The gun Malcolm carried was discovered to have been newly purchased and used just this once.

Those who knew the men best would remember two very different brothers. The literary genius and the athlete. The able-bodied and the physically challenged.

Malcolm's amateur athletic achievements were well known. He was a member of the Manhattan Athletic Club and captain of the Brooklyn Athletic Association, and had begun competing in sports while still a student at the Brooklyn Polytechnic Institute. He shone in track and field and had been a world record holder in the standing long jump. He had notched championships not only in the United States, but in Canada, as well. Broad jumps, high jumps, dashes and quarter miles were among his ribbon-earning specialties. However, the boys' father, Gordon Ford, was said to have looked askance on his son's dedication to sport. The elder Ford's love was books, a love he passed on to his other children and especially to Paul, whose physical challenges made staying in his father's massive library all the more attractive.

Tensions grew between Gordon and Malcolm Ford, and the senior Ford eventually disinherited him, leaving his property and the bulk of his fortune to Paul, his other brother, Worthington, and their four sisters. When the elder Ford died, he left behind an estate estimated to be in the neighborhood of $2 million. His autograph collection alone was estimated to be worth nearly $100,000. Malcolm received none of it and had turned to litigation, claiming that his father's will was supposed to have been changed but never was.

Malcolm asserted that he and his father had reconciled once Gordon Ford had contracted typhoid fever. The resulting illness, Malcolm insisted, had changed things between the estranged father and son. However, the will had remained unchanged. Malcolm sued his siblings for what he believed to be his rightful share, to no avail.

With his days of record-setting athletic achievements behind him and no family money to rely on, Malcolm needed to earn a living. His latest venture, the *New Centaur*, a magazine aimed at the sporting world that Malcolm knew so well, failed to find an audience. Paul Leicester Ford, on the other hand, had been at work on yet another book. In the wake of the success of *Janice Meredith*, his novel set during the American Revolution, Ford had been fielding lucrative writing requests from outlets such as the *Saturday Evening Post*, and was anticipating *Janice Meredith*'s adaptation for the stage. Additionally, invitations continued to arrive from wealthy friends such as George Vanderbilt, and telegrams landed on his desk sent by President Theodore Roosevelt. His wife, Grace, was tall, lithe, and considered by many one of the more beautiful young women to come out of Brooklyn in some time. Paul Leicester Ford was a man at the top of his game.

The disinheritance had strained relationships among all the Ford siblings. Unable to cobble together a meaningful and secure living outside athletics, Malcolm had begun routinely asking his younger brother for financial assistance. At a time when one's quality of life, stature, and role in society were so closely tied to not only money, but family money in particular, Malcolm's entire sense of self must have felt drastically compromised. Cosseted by luxury and comfort from birth, Malcolm had little experience in creating prosperity on his own once that flow of financial support dried up. In a lengthy letter to the editor of the *New York Herald*, Malcolm's ex-wife wrote, "I think, as do his family, my husband was really temporarily insane when he committed the deed. . . . He certainly felt himself unjustly treated and had brooded over this for so many years that I think at last it unbalanced his mind." She continued for several paragraphs, noting that her husband "was a fatalist, and he had been known to remark that it took more courage to live than to die."

Two days later, the funeral was held in that same library, the two brothers reposed in black caskets. Grace sat near her husband's coffin, among a small group of family and friends. The five remaining Ford siblings—brother Worthington, and sisters Mabel, Emily, Kathleen, and Rosalie—stood by mourning two of their own. It was a small affair, though outside the home a crowd waited for the caskets to be brought out. The bodies of the brothers were taken to Grand Central Station, where they were loaded onto a northbound train. Paul and Malcolm were laid alongside their father, Gordon, and their mother, Emily, in the family lot of Sleepy Hollow Cemetery in Tarrytown, New York. Orchids, white lilacs, and white roses adorned Paul Leicester Ford's grave.

Grace's health rebounded and she gave birth to a healthy baby girl, Lesta. In the days and weeks that followed Ford's death, the papers detailed his career and associations. The clear consensus was that the writer and scholar had not yet come close to reaching the zenith of his abilities.

Remembrances of a different sort were arranged farther south at Biltmore, where Ford had spent so much time visiting with George and Edith. Schenck, too, remembered Paul Leicester Ford's visits very clearly. "I would rank him among the most bewitching gentleman whom I have ever met," Schenck wrote, "with his flashing wit, keen observation, and world-wide education."

How must the dedication of *Janice Meredith* have felt after such a violent loss. That fabric, that filament to which Ford eloquently referred, had been severed. Now, there would be yet another dedication at All Souls, another service to grieve a loss and celebrate a life. Richard Morris Hunt's simple Greek cross design, reminiscent of so many grander places of worship—St. Peter's Basilica in Rome among them—lent an air of peaceful solemnity to the church he helped George build. Its east transept would now house a scene to commemorate Paul Leicester Ford's life.

The window was again designed by Helen Maitland Armstrong and crafted by her father, Maitland Armstrong. Florence-born Helen looked to one of Italy's most celebrated painters for inspiration, and based her window on Michelangelo Merisi da Caravaggio's *Entombment of Christ*. Where many of the windows in All Souls would depict biblical persons, or moments from the Good Book that perhaps spoke to the individual being honored, this window was different. This window shows pain and loss, sadness and grief, as Jesus's mother, Mary, and followers including Mary Magdalene and Joseph of Arimathea, take Christ down from the cross and lower him into his tomb.

Caravaggio, the master of chiaroscuro, was an artist who could capture much beauty in the midst of terrific agony and pain. In his painting, his tenebroso effect draws the eye toward the subject with little background other than darkness to speak of. But Helen's glass interpretation was about light, light shining through her creation as the sun rose in the east, illuminating the memory of George's dear friend.

Paul Leicester Ford would forever be linked with Biltmore. The words he so lovingly shared with the world about how the place had inspired him would live on after him. George, now without one of his dearest mates, could sit alone among his volumes and read that dedication, perhaps hoping to hear his friend's voice again.

■　■　■

That summer finally brought happier times for George's family and friends, Field in particular. But it had also been an emotionally grueling bit of time for the romantic thirty-two-year-old.

Earlier, in March, he had gone again to Biltmore, arriving from New York with Edith, George, their niece Lila, and others. He sat down in his room, took a few sheets of embossed house stationery, and wrote his favorite confidante—his mother. Ten days into the visit, he was in a state.

"Again at Biltmore," he wrote his mother, "having the best time of my life and the worst time."

Poor Field. He had agonized over every encounter, parsed every word uttered from Lila's lips, read into her every gesture. Other guests came and went that March, including George's sister Edith and her husband, the linguist Ernesto Fabbri. Field stayed. He had come to settle things once and for all. Each morning, he and Lila took out two horses for a ride around the estate. In the afternoons, they went shooting together. In the evenings, when the other guests repaired to the billiard room, Field and Lila sat in the tapestry room together. When Dr. Swope preached during the Sunday sermon at All Souls—"By patience ye shall win your soul"—Field felt sure Swope was speaking directly to him. (He also noticed titters of subdued laughter coming from the rest of the group sitting near him in the pews.) Field had Emily—George's sister and Lila's mother—on his side. Emily had written her daughter about Field and levied no objections to the man.

Edith and George were preparing to sail for Cherbourg, France, at the end of the month. Field knew the clock was ticking. Field had played a crucial role in Edith and George's romance and, in turn, Biltmore had been a key factor in Field's budding romance with Lila. Here he had played golf and hunted game with the sporting Lila. Here he had admired her skill with a horse, talked and walked with her over the grounds. And here, finally, he had won the heart of his dear friend George's niece, after what seemed to the man an eternity of hoping against hope.

"I wish you were here to share, as I know you would, some of my more than happiness," Field finally wrote to his mother who was staying at the Hotel d'Alba on the Champs-Élysées in Paris. "Lila, the little darling, has accepted me."

Field could hardly believe it. "Straight through Lila has shown herself to be a woman and not a silly girl. I think she has satisfied herself that I am true and sincere," he continued. "God help me to remain so."

All smiled upon the union of William B. Osgood Field and Lila Vanderbilt Sloane. There was little snarking in the press about either party; instead articles celebrated Field's friendship with George and touted his affability, the many stamps in his passport, and his collection of Japanese and Chinese curios. After graduating from Stevens Institute, he worked as an engineer and helped former classmates Otis Mygatt and M. W. Kellogg establish their own firms, the Holophane Glass Company and M.W. Kellogg Company, respectively. However, his role in the working world had diminished significantly since receiving a sizable inheritance from his expat aunt Kittie, who had died roughly a year earlier in Rome. As for Lila, the press called her "a good angel of the slums of New York," who spent much time and money helping poor families on New York's East Side. Of course the newspapers could not resist lingering over the fact that all of Lila's lingerie was made in Paris.

The pair were married July 8, 1902, in Lenox, Massachusetts, at the Sloane country home Elm Court. Prior to the wedding day, armed guards stood watch over the accumulation of lavish gifts. In one day alone, six wagons full of presents for the couple arrived. After the ceremony and reception, newspapers reported that the newlyweds were "whisked off to a fairy land, otherwise known as Biltmore."

■ ■ ■

The newlywed Fields stayed at River Cliff Cottage on the estate grounds, where George's nieces Adele and Edith had stayed for their own honeymoons. While time spent at Biltmore was similar in many ways to a sojourn passed at a country estate abroad decades earlier, this estate south of Asheville was also very different.

Despite its setting in the wilds of western North Carolina, visitors to Biltmore felt as though they were stepping into a world where some of the oldest traditions of country life in both England and America prevailed. George's vision—the working estate, the village nearby—had already become an inordinately expensive undertaking, but it evinced an anachronistic charm, as if it were not just a country home, but a kind of monumental denial that time was passing more rapidly than some would have liked to acknowledge. It was at once outsize and quaint, a French château in the land of the Blue Ridge, with the English baronial farms and working tenants and neighboring village. In appearance and practice, it was a vestige of eras past, where one could cling to a fleeting way of life.

Yet, even if the idea of Biltmore seemed frozen in a time that would soon melt away, the house itself was technologically quite advanced. To be at Biltmore was to straddle these two very different worlds.

Guests could still receive breakfast in the comfort of their own beds, but rather than ring a bell attached to a rope and pulley to alert a valet or a maid, they pushed an electric, ivory call button. Though battery-powered systems had come into favor in some homes, Biltmore's system was elaborate and could be used to alert the maids, stables, or butler's pantry from many locations, both public and private, throughout the entire house. In the event that a guest or family member might feel peckish, a snack was a button push away. Traditional afternoon tea might still be offered in the grandeur of the tapestry gallery, but snacks could be requested from servants day or night, and could be delivered by either an electric or hand-cranked dumbwaiter. Hot food rose from the basement kitchen pantry to the first-floor butler's pantry and on to the second-floor hall near Edith's room. The electric dumbwaiter boasted a capacity of 250 pounds. Flower arrangements, too, could rise from the bowels of the house, thanks to a hidden trapdoor in the floor of the Palm Court.

The house had a passenger elevator near the grand staircase at the home's entrance, which featured oak paneling, ornate wrought-iron swirls over the glass windows, and brass lamps. A freight elevator at the north end of the house near the servants' stairs hauled everything from guests' steamer trunks to coal and firewood. These were installed by Otis Brothers & Co., which had also installed the elevators in the Eiffel Tower, Balmoral Castle, the Kremlin, and the Washington Monument. Hunt had been more than familiar with elevators, having designed the Tribune Building in New York which, in 1875, contained what is believed to be the first express elevator installed in a commercial office building. With Biltmore staff providing roughly one footman for every three guests, several changes of clothes per day for each, and eight to ten courses per meal, the elevators and dumbwaiters got a fair workout.

For recreation, those at Biltmore might still wish to visit the stable complex and set out for an afternoon of hunting on the estate. But if they so desired, they could also enjoy two lanes of indoor bowling or swim in the 70,000-gallon indoor pool—complete with underwater electrical lighting.

Heat was generated by boilers built by the John D. Clarke company out of New York. The boilers used both wood and coal, and the hot air headed up through pipes which, in turn, heated water to create steam. Shafts ran like spines through the entire house, from subbasement to the fourth floor, carrying steam-heated air. Natural convection and the laws of physics wafted it upward, and there it would find its way out of wall vents, warming the chilly noses and toes of visitors. Water was heated by a horizontal tubular return system. But the energy needs of the house were astounding. Roughly 25 tons of coal were burned in two weeks alone during the winter of 1900.

Entertaining scores of guests involved storing massive quantities of food, and Hunt wanted the refrigeration system to be able to handle any party that the Vanderbilts could throw. The ammonia gas, mechanical refrigeration system was capable of keeping up to 500 pounds of meats and vegetables and 50 gallons of liquid at a chilly 40 degrees Fahrenheit—the approximate temperature of modern refrigerators. Walking through the basement—should one venture down on the way to the gym or changing rooms—one found two walk-in coolers in the hallway. The main kitchen, butler's pantry, and pastry kitchen all had refrigerators as well. There was also an ice-making plant. All these conveniences stood in marked contrast to life as it was lived by ordinary people of the time, who made do with regular deliveries of ice blocks from the local purveyor. Iceboxes would continue to be commonplace in many American homes well into the mid-twentieth century, and the first domestic refrigerator in the United States would not be marketed until 1913, when Fred Wolf introduced his Domelre (*Dom*estic *el*ectric *ref*rigerator).

With an estimated 2,388,828 "cubical feet" of space to serve, Biltmore House's systems and amenities were on the scale of, and had more in common with, those at a large hotel rather than a typical American country home. The three kitchens and forty-three bathrooms, for starters, required a great deal of water at a time when having on-demand hot water and indoor plumbing was not a given for many, especially in the rural South. Hunt designed many of the lighting fixtures himself—including the "Crown of Light" chandelier in the banquet hall—and he made sure that the house would have enough electricity to power 180 electrical outlets, 288 fixtures, and other electrically powered items, such as the refrigeration units and internal call system.

The New York firm of Hatzel & Buehler were the masterminds behind the electrical wiring and call boxes throughout the house. John D. Hatzel and Joseph Buehler had worked at Thomas Edison's first generating station. The debate between the alternating and direct currents raged on as George was constructing the house. Rather than choose between Edison's direct current system and Westinghouse's Tesla-designed alternating current system, George had both systems installed. The alternating current could actually be used to generate direct current, which could in turn be used to run not only the house itself, but also to power aspects of the village of Biltmore. The lower voltage of the stepped-down direct current made the swimming pool's underwater lights a luxurious—and safe—possibility. Though alternating current would eventually win out nationwide, Edison's trademark lightbulbs would continue to glow throughout the house.

The laundry complex was impressive, with washing "machines" that could spin and extract, all powered by overhead belts. Heated drying racks accommodated the family's and guests' numerous linens. The laundry alone had a separate electric system to warm its hot water.

So while all was peaceful precision and luxury above stairs, the churning subbasement made Biltmore House hum. Over the years, changes and upgrades were made as they became necessary. As early as 1901, a rusting issue threatened the refrigeration system's brine tank, through which the chilled ammonia gas–confining coils circulated. Workers eventually installed a gas generator with backup batteries. The magnificent electronics switchboard was a sight unto itself, six feet by seventeen feet of gleaming marble dripping with wiring.

The home's timekeeping system, designed by Boston's E. Howard & Co., relied on technology indispensable to train stations across the nation, the Vanderbilt railroad system among them. Wall clocks in the servants' areas and elsewhere in the house were perfectly synchronized with an outdoor master clock that looked down over the stable complex. No matter where your station placed you on those grand estate grounds, time passed, each tick unrelenting.

■ ■ ■

Queen Victoria had died in 1901 at the age of eighty-one, bringing an official end to a near sixty-four-year reign and an era that bore her name. Edward VII succeeded her as king of the United Kingdom of Great Britain and Ireland, and of the British dominions, and as emperor of India. On American shores, though, a tarnish had already begun to settle on the Gilded Age. Those who had earned their wealth—the upstarts, those of much humbler beginnings, such as the Commodore—were two generations removed from those who now enjoyed it. Many wealthy scions lost the ability to earn. For those, it would soon be once again back to shirtsleeves.

The capacity of individuals to adjust to changing times increasingly defined their ability to succeed in life and commerce. Malcolm Ford could not. George's challenges—financial, certainly, and perhaps others which stemmed from an exhaustion with the gargantuan estate—appeared to be increasing. As for Edith, her attentions were never far from the larger community surrounding her own, rarefied realm.

It would still take some time for the Gilded Age to fully yield to the Progressive Era, for the rage for Louis XV flourishes to fade away and be replaced by an appreciation of the simple elegance of the Arts and Crafts movement. The artificial would give way to the natural; that which was of the elite, would soon be of the people.

Edith strode deftly between these two worlds, one of Victorian elegance, the other of rugged mountain simplicity. She may have appeared to live a life of the elite, but to those beyond the iron gates of the estate, Edith quickly emerged as one who was decidedly of the people.

10

The More Things Change

Edith gave more than money to Vance, Yale, and the students they served. She constantly looked for ways to increase the school's output and reputation and showcased items that the students made when influential friends visited the house. In 1903, one of those friends included Alice Roosevelt, daughter of President Theodore Roosevelt.

The president knew Edith's brother, LeRoy. Both had homes in Oyster Bay, Long Island, and the two men corresponded on topics ranging from politics to bear hunting. After becoming the youngest president in U.S. history in 1901—following President McKinley's assassination—Roosevelt had several southern trips in the works. LeRoy tried to arrange big game hunts for Roosevelt in the fall of 1902 in places like Mississippi, Tennessee, and the Black Mountains of North Carolina.

In Mississippi, LeRoy had promised Roosevelt "plenty of bear, deer, turkey and 'bob-cats,'" and also told Roosevelt he felt that the "Republican party can make great strides down there." As to a potential outing in Memphis, Roosevelt wrote LeRoy that, "Bear and wildcat are exactly what I need," and hoped that they could keep the hunting party limited to "just as few people as possible; you and I and [Stuyvesant] Fish," and perhaps a few other friends. "But the fewer the hunters, the better the sport."

However, the hunt that garnered the most press for the sportsman-in-chief was the one during which he shot no bear at all.

The president passed through Asheville in early September, and after an address in Court Square, hopped in a carriage and visited Biltmore House. The November hunting trip in Mississippi that Le-Roy had been working to arrange came through, but once on the hunt, Roosevelt wasn't having much luck. After his fellow hunters located and tethered an injured black bear to a tree, Roosevelt re-fused to pull the trigger, considering the move unsportsmanlike.

Cartoonist Clifford Berryman depicted the bear-sparing incident in *The Washington Post*, and it caught the eye of Morris Michtom, a Brooklyn-based seller of sweets and stuffed toys. He and his wife, Rose, created a stuffed bear: "Teddy's Bear." Roosevelt okayed the use of his name, and—thanks in no small part to LeRoy Dresser—the Teddy Bear was born.

Now fewer than six months later, Roosevelt's daughter was guest of honor at Biltmore House. Clever and at times mischievous, Alice garnered attention for everything from her societal debut within the halls of the White House to smoking on its roof. She was a reader, a sometimes player of the horses, and was known to carry a snake in her purse. With a mass of raven hair swept atop her head, and dis-tinct brows looming over a penetrating gaze, she was a celebrity in ways that previous presidential offspring had not been.

When Edith organized the 1903 Biltmore Charity Bazaar, her efforts received a significant boost from the presence of this special guest, who helped increase exposure for Biltmore Estate Industries and in the process raise some money for the community as well. Turnout was indicative of the excitement among locals and other members of Asheville society. Edith worked at the parish house of All Souls each day for the week leading up to the event, ensuring that it went off smoothly. The result was described as a "fairyland," with booths manned by Edith herself and other prominent fixtures in the Asheville social scene. Vance and Yale worked alongside Reverend Swope's wife in the American stall. Adele Schenck—the forester's wife—was aptly dressed as a fräulein and presided over a Dutch windmill. There was an astrologer's tent, a Russian tent—complete with attendants in traditional dress—and a Japanese tea garden. The presence of Alice Roosevelt, though, elicited perhaps the greatest excitement from participants and patrons alike, and helped Edith and the other volunteers exceed their fundraising goals.

As Edith flourished, her brother, LeRoy, floundered. He was now, in the parlance of the times, "a bankrupt." LeRoy headed Dresser & Co. and had been founder and president of a young bank, Trust Company of the Republic. During his tenure, the firm underwrote a $4,750,000 loan for the United States Shipbuilding Company, a merger of seven shipyards and, eventually, Bethlehem Steel. Additional funding was coming from investors in France and England. When the shipbuilding company went down, it took LeRoy's company and his investors' money with it. All entities soon came under investigation. LeRoy personally—and very publicly—lost hundreds of thousands in the stock of the trust company, and suffered a much damaged reputation. Testimonies and media coverage featured affected parties which spanned the social register and globe, including J.P. Morgan & Co., and Bethlehem Steel and its primary stockholder, Charles M. Schwab.

In a hearing before a special examiner in New York City, LeRoy claimed that in order to sell his Bethlehem Steel plant to the Shipbuilding trust, Schwab had extracted terms so favorable that he had effectively taken control of the Shipbuilding company. While the Shipbuilding trust had been driven into bankruptcy, Schwab looked to make a tidy profit. Tales of dummy investors—including very young men without bank accounts of their own—dummy incorporators, syndicates, and former money-movers who now resided in Sing Sing prison spiced up the proceedings.

LeRoy appeared to be in over his head. Nothing in his background had prepared him for such a complicated business transaction. To make matters worse, he admitted, under oath, that he and his underlings had never independently verified the financial statements of the other shipbuilding companies, accepting them instead at face value. In truth, most of the firms—with the exception of Bethlehem Steel—were indebted, unprofitable entities, doomed to fail. It looked as though it would be a long haul for LeRoy, as coverage of the financial scandal was unyielding.

"The fall in reputations in the Wall Street district lately has been quite as marked as the fall in stocks," the *Financier* remarked. "The methods of mendacity set forth in Captain Dresser's testimony are a shock to the credulous; but sober reflection will tend to show that the whole movement in Wall Street for the last two years has been leading up to such a culmination."

The press also hinted that by lending the Dresser name to the various business concerns, LeRoy had hoped to make it easier to raise funds. LeRoy took issue, however, with reports that the names of his sisters Edith and Natalie—who had married conspicuously wealthy husbands—had also been bandied about in order to raise money.

"My sisters, Mrs. George W. Vanderbilt and Mrs. J. Nicholas Brown, had nothing whatever to do with my business," LeRoy told the press. "I never said they would back me in any of my business undertakings." However, the scandal would not leave Edith and Natalie unscathed, as reports surfaced claiming they had paid 90 cents on the dollar to keep Dresser & Co.'s creditors at bay. If this were all true, this meant they were throwing good money after bad.

Forester Schenck had met LeRoy shortly after he had become president of the United States Shipbuilding Company, during what Schenck believed might have been LeRoy's first visit to Biltmore. The group spent time at the estate's "Three Day Camp," a lodge where Schenck had some of his best memories of his time with the Vanderbilt family. Trout fishing, trail riding, and climbing up to Looking Glass Rock filled their days during LeRoy's visit.

It was around that time that Schenck remembered coming across a telegram at Biltmore House. He claimed to have opened the missive purely by accident, believing that it was for him. In fact, the telegram had been meant for George. It read:

"Have bought for you 100,000 shares. Roy Dresser."

At the time, Schenck confessed his mistake to George. The episode may have been forgotten by George, but the contents of the telegram came back to Schenck now, several years later, as the winds of fortune blowing from points north were shifting dramatically. If the stock purchase had indeed gone through, this would now indicate substantial losses for George.

■ ■ ■

Who is the man on a horse named Punch?
Riding along at the head of the bunch?
Giving no time to eat our lunch?
'Tis the man who looks like the Kaiser!

So went the words to a song sung by Schenck's forestry students. They had nicknamed their forestry professor—with his German heritage, fit frame, and "imperial" mustache—after the German emperor and king of Prussia, Kaiser Wilhelm II. Whether sporting the traditional forestry service uniform from his home country or not, Schenck's commanding presence, renowned temper, and facial-hair flourish gave him a ruggedly regal air in his role at the Biltmore Forest School. Lectures and long rides added both to his workload and his diversion as he taught his enthusiastic young foresters. Mornings were for classroom instruction and afternoons for exploratory rides—sometimes twenty miles—into Pisgah Forest. Students studied for an intense twelve months, then worked for six months in a kind of work-study program in order to gain practical forestry experience. Two hundred dollars tuition, $330 room and board, and bring your own horse.

From fall into spring, classes—held six days a week—were taught in Biltmore. In summer, school was conducted deep in Pisgah Forest in the area known as the Pink Beds, where the rhododendrons and mountain laurel lent a rosy springtime hue to the woodland floor. Schenck kept a two-story summer residence there, with a view of Pisgah Ridge and ample space for his wife Adele's vegetable garden.

Students did their own cooking and lived sparsely, some with set-tlers who still remained on George's land, others in austere cabins aptly bestowed with names like Gnat Hollow, Rest for the Wicked, Little Bohemia, Little Hell Hole, and Big Hell Hole. On Sunday, Schenck's cabin-cum-schoolhouse served as a church for students and other area residents, and Schenck was known to play the organ. There was a small commissary amid the cabins and, on that day of rest, if all went well, there was a fresh meat delivery.

Schenck may have been stern, but he knew his students needed to unwind, so he introduced evenings of "Sangerfest." Traditionally "singer festivals" or contests, the loose interpretation of this phrase involved nights of drinking, singing, games . . . and more drinking. One student, Douglas Sayre Rodman, wrote songs for these occa-sions, including "Schenck's Grenadiers" and "The Man Who Looks Like the Kaiser." He also penned "Down Under the Hill: Song of the Biltmore Forest School," which best captured the essence of these nocturnal imbibing sessions:

Down under the hill there is a little still and the smoke goes curling
* to the sky . . .*
You can easily tell by the sniffle and the smell there's good liquor in
* the air close by . . .*
For it fills the air with a perfume so rare that it's only known to a
* few;*
So wrinkle up your lip and take a little sip of the good old
* mountain dew.*

With no English-language texts on forestry in existence, Schenck created, and began to publish, his own lectures covering topics such as silviculture, forest policy, and forest protection. State by state, he described items like wooded acreage, timber use, and fire frequency, and broke down federal, state, local, and private ownership of lands. He knew the number of mills and their output, whether industries such as leather, paper, or pulp were operating, and if an active forestry movement existed. In these lectures, he took his students on a tour of forests and their management, from states like Alabama in the South to territories such as Alaska in the north.

On afternoon rides, students assessed George's vast acreage, marking trees to be felled and those to be spared. They learned to grade the quality of firewood, which could later be sold. Perhaps most important, they reforested, planted, transplanted, and nurtured saplings. They built much-needed roads for the transportation of materials and machinery, and also learned the workings of a lumbering operation, running sawmills and studying various aspects of logging, milling, and retail lumber management.

Back at the estate, however, the hope that lumber would provide a significant profit had not yet been realized. George reduced his investments in this part of the estate, and his enthusiasm appeared to be flagging. When Schenck had approached George with a budget in 1902, George told his head forester to borrow money from the bank and pay back what was owed from earnings.

Behind the scenes, George may have also been influenced by Gifford Pinchot. Schenck remained, even long distance, at increasing odds with his former coworker, who now served as head of what was now known as the US Forest Service (previously the Division of Forestry and Bureau of Forestry).

Once in his new post, Pinchot had hired Schenck as an agent of the Forest Service to survey lands in the South. Yet their differences over the methodologies of forestry had only grown. Schenck believed that lumbermen who profited from the sale of timber should be consulted in a cooperative, rather than confrontational, fashion. But Pinchot's boss—Theodore Roosevelt—regarded these men as lumber barons, great decimators of the woods. One such argument found Schenck and Pinchot standing face-to-face in the nurseries of Biltmore, standing on the tracks of the Southern Railway, debating their views on managed forestry. Schenck told Pinchot that on examinations, Schenck insisted his foresters-to-be at the Biltmore Forest School demonstrate a clear understanding of the practices of logging and lumbering and added that that those answers carried more weight than a knowledge of strict silviculture, or the healthy cultivation of forests. Hearing this, Pinchot was at a loss and called Schenck an antichrist.

Pinchot ended Schenck's role as an agent of the Forest Service in 1902. A year later, Pinchot had gone so far as to write George asking him to shut down the Biltmore Forest School. George did not. When George took Schenck aside and showed him Pinchot's correspondence, Schenck was hurt by the accusation that, as he later wrote, his teachings were "antagonistic to the development of forestry in the United States." Undeterred, Schenck continued working. Now reports of LeRoy's financial downfall came on the heels of Pinchot's maneuverings and George's cutbacks. As news broke and stocks plummeted, Schenck was haunted by memories of LeRoy's telegram, and became concerned that George's losses were extensive. Schenck noticed that nonpaying farms on the property were closed. Staff was reduced. Schenck wondered just how much time he and his school had left on the grounds of the Pink Beds in the Land of the Sky.

■ ■ ■

For Edith and George, any financial losses they were experiencing were compounded by personal ones. That summer the world lost two artists. James McNeill Whistler died July 17, 1903, and Frederick Law Olmsted followed just six weeks later on August 28.

George had written Whistler hoping to arrange some additional sittings that summer. Whistler's oil rendering of Edith, *Ivoire et or: Portrait de Madame Vanderbilt*, had been completed in 1902 and displayed at the 12th Exhibition of the Société National des Beaux-Arts in Paris. Knowing that George and Edith would be attending *Le Salon du Champ-de-Mars*, as it was more commonly known, Whistler had arranged to display the portrait there as a surprise for his patrons. The oval canvas cradles Edith's torso, a wide white ruffle about her neck. Her aquiline nose gently sets off her fine features and upswept hair. The *Nation* was impressed, noting the manner in which "the head rises with infinite grace and distinction . . . what character there is in the face." The *Portrait of George W. Vanderbilt*, which had been commissioned before George married Edith, had yet to be finished to Whistler's liking and remained in the artist's studio at the time of his death. Whistler had depicted George standing amid a muted palette of slates and umbers, riding crop in hand. Whistler was buried in Chiswick, outside London. Edith and George were able to attend, and George served as an honorary pallbearer.

In many ways, Olmsted had been gone from them for several years now, dementia having taken its toll, and he had spent his last years at the McLean Hospital in Massachusetts.

"You cannot think how I have been dreading that it would be thought expedient that I should be sent to an 'institution,'" Olmsted once wrote. "Anything but that." When he decided to stroll about McLean's grounds, he hopefully found the setting to his liking—he had helped choose it, years earlier.

Edith and George were still not back from the continent in time for the holidays, which meant, according to one newspaper, that Christmas at Biltmore would be "like the play of Hamlet with Hamlet left out."

Hamlet, in this case, was Edith, and any noel in the growing *hamlet* of Biltmore without Edith on hand to distribute presents was a sadder one, indeed. In her absence, Reverend Swope oversaw the festivities. Though the Christmas tree's boughs weighed heavy with presents for the employees of the Biltmore Estate and their children, the mistress who was always the hostess of the holiday occasion was away with her husband and daughter Cornelia, and keenly missed. A separate celebration was held and a tree decorated at the Clarence Barker Hospital. That tree was named in honor of Cornelia.

Also absent from the annual fete was Biltmore Estate manager Charles McNamee, though he sent a telegram from Seattle to be read to those gathered. The press linked Charles McNamee's resignation from Biltmore to George's order of "a curtailment of expenses in every department." While out West, McNamee would look after George's interests there. George had not yet named a successor to McNamee's position.

Edith and George stayed in Europe for the early part of the year as well, enjoying a spot at the "America" table alongside George's niece the Duchess of Marlborough and the US ambassador, for a leap year celebration at The Princes Restaurant, a noted London eatery. They spent time in Paris as well, and made a spring appearance at the royal court. Former Biltmore guest Theodore Roosevelt was reelected in November.

George and Edith planned to return from Europe to be at Biltmore for the winter. A 500-ton coal order had already been signed. The leap year passed and 1905 arrived, finding Edith's brother LeRoy still in the midst of litigation. Even if she and George were removed from any direct involvement in the proceedings, Edith had to contend with seeing her husband's name again in the *New York Times*: "The bankrupt head of Dresser & Co. and brother-in-law of George W. Vanderbilt."

Still, the year did bring welcome visitors, Edith's sisters Natalie and Pauline among them. Since the tragic death of her husband, John, just months after Natalie's son was born, Edith's older sister had been traveling with the young boy, who enjoyed playing with his cousin Cornelia. The pair were now nearly five years old. Pauline, Edith's younger sister, did not yet have children of her own, but always enjoyed seeing her two siblings. Their oldest sister, Susan, still resided primarily in France, though she and her husband, the Viscount d'Osmoy, had made the cross-Atlantic journey to Biltmore in the past. When Pauline visited along with Natalie that spring, she stayed in the rose- and gold-hued Louis XVI room and indulged in reading, enjoying views from the loggia when the weather cooperated, and marveling at the views from the Breakfast Room—a much less formal room than the banquet hall. She enjoyed, as did Edith, time with her sisters and with young John and Cornelia.

Visitors to Biltmore House often signed the "Nonsense Book," which featured sketches and musings from the family and their guests. George wrote this of his young daughter:

> *There once was a dear little Girlie*
> *With hair so soft and curly,*
> *"The pleasure is mine!"*
> *With a bow so fine*
> *Would lisp this dear little Girlie.*

The sisters did not stay long enough to see Edith and Cornelia drive in that May's Floral Parade. Edith led the way in her red-and-green decorated trap—created with the magic of peony and fern—with her young daughter by her side. Participants hailed from as far off as Philadelphia and New York. Frederick Law Olmsted Jr. was on hand as well. Despite the heavy competition, Edith won top honors for her carriage's springtime decoration, and entertained guests afterward at the house.

The passing of time and of dear friends continued to be chronicled in the colored glass of All Souls. A window was soon unveiled for the man who shaped the estate and the village, sculpting vistas and views and strolls and greens out of what he had originally thought to be a blighted, overworked, and underutilized landscape.

The window, titled "Jesus and the Doctors in the Temple," was unveiled in May 1905. This tribute to Frederick Law Olmsted stood across the church—from east transept to west—from the window honoring his colleague at Biltmore, Richard Morris Hunt.

George and Edith's New York life changed as well. The mansion at the northwest corner of Fifty-First and Fifth Avenue, where George had grown up, where William Henry Vanderbilt had entertained, was no longer the couple's residence. George had decided to lease the property for ten years to Pittsburgh's Henry Clay Frick, who hoped having a Manhattan residence would allow him to keep a closer eye on his holdings in U.S. Steel. Frick, like George's father

William Henry Vanderbilt, had a love of art and sought to expand his collection.

Frick was, according to novelist Edith Wharton, one of the "lords of Pittsburgh," part of the stream of new residents entering New York's evolving social dynamic but, as she wrote, "their infiltration did not greatly affect old manners and customs, since the dearest ambition of the newcomers was to assimilate existing traditions."

"Conformity," she wrote, "is the bane of middle class communities."

The noted novelist was no mere observer of the idiosyncrasies and mannerisms of the Four Hundred. She, herself, had been born into that world. Wharton had visited Biltmore in 1902, and clearly found it enjoyable enough that here she was again, at Christmastime 1905. Her lives had intersected with those of George and Edith over the years. Edith likely never forgot Wharton's kindness to the Dresser sisters that first holiday season after losing their grandmother. Wharton, too, was a friend of Field's. She had gifted Field and Lila a two-volume set of Dante Gabriel Rossetti as a wedding present.

The woman who chronicled the fabulously cloistered lives of the privileged yet stilted upper echelon of New York society welcomed a reprieve from city life. Wharton herself had left New York City, shedding some of the Victorian remnants of her childhood and building a home, the Mount, in Lenox, Massachusetts, in 1902. There she had written the novel *House of Mirth*, which had just been released. When she arrived at Biltmore for Christmas of 1905 she presented a signed copy to George.

Wharton's friend the novelist Henry James had stayed at Biltmore earlier that year, in February. James had been living abroad, and the past several years had been professionally fruitful ones for him. In that time, he had published such novels as *The Ambassador, The Wings of the Dove,* and *The Golden Bowl.* These followed the success of titles such as *Turn of the Screw, Portrait of a Lady,* and *Daisy Miller.* He had also made a reputation for himself as a critic of literature and art and occasionally lectured on the work of Honoré de Balzac. When he had arrived at Biltmore, the weather, his mood, and his health combined to make a very gloomy experience. Keeping mostly to his room at Biltmore House, he wrote both to his nephew, Henry "Harry" James III, and to Wharton.

James arrived during a snowstorm—"The land all buried, and the dreariness and bleakness indescribable," he wrote Harry. Soon after arrival he had what he described as a "sharp explosion of gout in my left foot." He was adhering to a regimen of bran footbaths and aspirin in hopes to stop the gout short. As to the house, he found little solace in its "huge freezing spaces" and thought the creation to be "based on a fundamental ignorance of comfort and wondrous deludedness (though now, I think on poor George Vanderbilt's part, waked up from) . . ."

"Pity the poor Biltmorean!" he wrote Harry, complaining that he was lonely, that his room was freezing—with "a hideous plate glass window like the door of an ice-house"—and devoid of curtains. James rang his bells in vain, but no servant came to call on him. He hobbled on his gout-ridden foot down the long hallways in search of hot water and a bath. But he was determined to see his visit through before heading south to the warmer climes of Charleston, South Carolina.

"I shall weather through even the tortures of Biltmore."

While there, he corresponded with Wharton, congratulating her on *House of Mirth* and its "compact fulness." He told Wharton that he had still not ventured outdoors and rarely departed his room in what he termed a "colossal heartbreaking house."

James had nothing ill to say of his hosts, "the good George Vanderbilts," but remained struck by the juxtaposition of the massive house against its natural surroundings. He could not restrain himself from criticizing the home, stooping to an unkind expression of the sort of casual racism that marked the era.

"I mean one's sense of the extraordinary impenitent madness (of millions) which led to the erection in their vast niggery wilderness, of so gigantic and elaborate a monument to all that *isn't* socially possible there. It's *in effect*, like a gorgeous practical joke. . . ."

James admitted to Wharton that he had not done justice to the house "as a phenomenon (of brute *achievement*)." He had finally made it down to luncheon, he later wrote Wharton, and confessed that he felt "a bit shabby at failing to rise to my host's own conception of the results he has achieved."

Wharton, on the other hand, likely fed her longstanding love and knowledge of art, architecture, and books when visiting Biltmore. She had already published the nonfiction book *The Decoration of Houses* with Ogden Codman Jr., and had herself penned other nonfiction titles *Italian Backgrounds* and *Italian Villas and Their Gardens*. Wharton believed that her "Ruling passions" were: "Justice—Order—Dogs—Books—Flowers—Architecture—Travel—a good joke—& perhaps that should have come first."

She could indulge most of those passions at Biltmore, where holidays were a spectacular time. Meals were a multicoursed and indulgent affair. The dining table in the banquet hall could extend from 7½ feet to 40 feet, if necessary. The damask tablecloths were embroidered with George Vanderbilt's monogram, the china boasted a gold-and-burgundy border, and when the flames emanating from one of the hall's three fireplaces were just right, the Baccarat crystal would catch their reflection. Of the many courses served on special occasions at Biltmore House, oysters made a frequent appearance—as they likely had at the nation's first Thanksgiving. George was particularly fond of roast turkey. Ellen Davis, a chef from nearby Avery Creek who worked at the house, used to simmer the turkey, covered, on top of the stove to render the fat before placing it in the oven for a finishing roast.

Another Christmas came and went. "Hamlet" had returned, and Edith and her presents were a welcome sight at the dairy, in the village, and among the employees and their children. The same year that Wharton visited Biltmore for Christmas, author O. Henry published a much different Christmas story, one that perhaps would have rung true with many of the citizens living in the shadow of the great house and glow of its kind mistress. "The Gift of the Magi" was a soon-to-be timeless and moving story of a poor young couple who sacrifice their only prized possessions in order to give each other a costly Christmas present, and in doing so, exhibit the truest of loves.

It was a reminder, in this time of tarnishing gilt, that should all else crumble, memories of gestures made, thoughtfulness considered, and seeds of inspiration planted, might outlast all.

■　■　■

The effect of Biltmore's artistic and cultural legacy had already begun to spread through the town of Asheville. By 1906, the Young Men's Institute had raised enough money to buy out their lease from George and established their first board of directors. Richard Sharp Smith, supervising architect of Biltmore House and Richard Morris Hunt's boots-on-the-ground appointee in his absence, had decided to stay put in the South, his English roots and New York life now things of the past. His personal brand of architecture began to shape the look and feel of turn-of-the-century Asheville beyond the limits of the Vanderbilt lands. He did stick close to the estate in some respects, however: He met, fell in love with, and married Isabella Cameron, a young woman of Scottish origin and a member of the household staff at Biltmore House.

Rafael Guastavino's firm continued growing with commissions throughout the country—Biltmore House had elevated its profile tremendously. Guastavino and his son lent their trademark touch to hundreds of buildings, many of them open to the public, such as the Cathedral of St. John the Divine (the largest cathedral in the world and one of the five largest church buildings in the world), the Metropolitan Museum of Art in New York City, and Guastavino's tile was the centerpiece of the City Hall subway station which had opened in 1904. But it was in Asheville that the Valencian master began what would perhaps be his most remarkable creation. He had set his sights on building a grand church.

He did not think that the Roman Catholic community in Asheville had a space befitting its community so he began collaborating with Richard Sharp Smith to design and build a Spanish Revival structure that would become the Church of St. Lawrence. Constructed with no beams of steel or wood, the church's dome would one day loom high over the downtown area.

If George had not yet, as Henry James suggested, woken up from any "deludedness" regarding life in the largest house in the country, 1907 likely woke him and investors across the United States to the possibility that their stockpiles could dissipate rapidly. The Panic of 1907, occurring in mid-October, affected bankers and investors everywhere. An attempt by Augustus and Otto Heinze to gain control of the copper market, including expanding their majority stake in United Copper, had gone awry in spectacular fashion, and within a week stocks that had once soared were now in free fall. The New York Stock Exchange plummeted nearly 50 percent from its peak the year before. Many banks and trusts ceased to exist after that day, including the Knickerbocker Trust Company, which lent the moniker "Knickerbocker Crisis" to the event. From amid the chaos, a savior emerged: Millionaire J. Pierpont Morgan orchestrated a consortium of bankers to loan money to the NYSE so that it could continue to operate.

It is difficult to know the full extent to which the earlier Shipbuilding trust failure and Panic of 1907 affected George's finances. He had already closed his poultry operations the year before, in 1906. Timber prices also fell in 1907, in the wake of the panic. Schenck had done what he could to improve transport for felled trees to leave the forest and make their way to market. By 1905, he had 80 miles of road and 198 miles of trails that he had either improved or had built from scratch. Nevertheless, George was beginning to consider selling the bulk of his extensive wooded lands, if there were a suitable buyer. Yet he had also found another *seller*. Mr. Charles Collins, an African American man who had refused to sell his cabin and 6 acres to George more than ten years before, finally acquiesced. He sold his land with log cabin to George for $2,000. The *Washington Post* reported that George had once offered the local man $10,000, which Collins refused. The domicile had long been known as the cabin Vanderbilt could not buy—resulting in the printing of souvenir postcards depicting the site.

If George and Edith felt the pinch of reduced finances, they hid it well. They had been again in Paris, and were expected back once more in time for Thanksgiving. President Roosevelt was also expected in the fall for a hunting expedition. George's lands were considered the largest private game preserve in the United States, and deer; quail; fish; and the seasonal favorite, turkey, were a draw for sportsmen—whether invited onto the lands or not. A local United States Circuit Court judge was also expected on the hunt, should it come to pass.

In George and Edith's absence, a hunt of another kind had been conducted on the estate: a hunt for burglars who on more than one occasion had chloroformed residents of the village of Biltmore in an attempt to burglarize them. Bloodhounds followed the trail of the handkerchief-wielding thieves straight to Biltmore House itself, but there the trail grew cold.

■　■　■

The evolving Progressive Era and Arts & Crafts movement dovetailed nicely with the efforts of Biltmore Estate Industries, now located at 8 Plaza in the village—a space donated by Edith in 1903. Schenck, too, took an interest, and sold wood at a discount to Vance. He had sent the teacher pictures of Roycroft furniture which, in turn, she shared with her woodworking boys as a model of "simple, well made furniture." The outfit enjoyed brisk sales, notably to springtime tourists "on their way North from the Southern resorts." However, it was not a self-sustaining enterprise, and goods were often sold for less than it cost to create them.

Yet Edith's guiding hand and her support for Vance and Yale's school was unwavering. Edith had brought a carving instructor from Belgium to stay for three months, and in 1906 suggested that a weaving program be added to Biltmore Estate Industries' repertoire. Edith herself rode out on her horse to educate herself about textiles by observing the work of local weavers. Textile design and creation had been a mountain practice for generations; there were ample varieties of berries and roots in this biodiverse region to use for dyes. Edith also sent Vance and Yale on a fact-finding trip to England and Scotland, where they located a loom. Edith bought it and had it shipped to North Carolina. Edith thought wool fabric for sale on commercial markets would be a smart investment for Vance and Yale's outfit.

Edith continually looked for other ways to increase exposure for Biltmore Estate Industries, and such an opportunity came during the Jamestown Exposition of 1907. It had been three hundred years since the first successful English colony had landed in the New World, and to celebrate, a tercentennial event was planned for Virginia. Edith, whose family had been in the United States nearly that long, intended to showcase the work of Vance, Yale, and their students at that event. She arranged for the creations of the boys and girls to be displayed at the Biltmore room of the North Carolina building at the Jamestown celebration. With its columns and porches, and built of North Carolina pine, the building was considered one of the loveliest at this once-every-hundred-years expo. Eight students traveled with Vance and Yale to Jamestown, and the Biltmore Estate Industries display also featured work by Edith's daughter, Cornelia. Already a budding artist in her seventh year, Cornelia enjoyed sketching in the skylight studio on the Biltmore House's third floor. When Edith herself appeared at Jamestown wearing an ensemble she announced had been fashioned by students from the school in the mountains, it was one of the best advertisements the school ever had.

"Mrs. Vanderbilt in Homespun," the *Chicago Tribune* headline read. "Rich Woman, by Wearing Dress Made by North Carolina Mountain Dweller, Revives Lost Art."

Edith was in many ways a woman of two worlds, one of luxury and one of simplicity. She was hostess to wealthy friends and relatives, and helper to the impoverished residents of the village and the hills and hollers beyond, where her neighbors here were laborers, shop owners, and farmers. She saw to it that Cornelia spent as much time with the children of estate workers as she did with the privileged children of visiting family and friends. Cornelia had been to Paris before her first birthday, but future birthday parties included the children of estate employees. The young girl was growing up as a child of the mountains, often accompanying her mother on trips to check in on sick or pregnant employees.

Perhaps it was Biltmore's vast emptiness, hinted at in the writings by her friends Henry James and Edith Wharton, that compelled Edith to move beyond its gates and to insert herself into the life of the village. Maybe it was her own mother's shunning of society, her father's down-to-earth welcoming nature, or her grandmother's entertaining of missionaries in her home. Somehow Edith had acquired an appreciation, a respect, for what was referred to as the "service class." While George had chosen to come to the area for his health, for his mother, for the beauty, or simply to do something different with his name and his wealth than what was expected of him, Edith had ended up in western North Carolina solely by virtue of marriage. Yet she now spectacularly bloomed where she had been matrimonially planted.

11

High and Dry

If George's finances had been adversely impacted by the Panic of 1907, that year's Christmas celebration, one of the more elaborate in recent memory, gave a different impression. Fifty wagons full of holly, mistletoe, and other evergreens arrived at the house. There were three separate celebrations, the largest of which brought nearly a thousand people—employees, their families, and friends—from near and far, by horse, wagon, and foot.

The rafter-scraping tree towered more than 30 feet high in the banquet hall. Hanging from it were five hundred incandescent lights, and more presents than ornaments. The lights remained dim, however, until seven-year-old Cornelia stepped forth and flipped the switch to illuminate the festive arbor. She was her mother's daughter, ever the approachable hostess. She cavorted with the other children and led them in games and dancing. George and Edith arranged for a brass band to play during the festivities and, following the home's now well-established tradition, everyone received toys and clothing. The gifts were not limited to the younger attendees, and the needs, if not wants, of the adults on hand were given as much consideration as Edith and George distributed blankets, clothes, and other useful items to employees. Edith kept track each year of which children got what gifts so as not to duplicate a present. Fruits and nuts and hundreds of pounds of candy sweetened the affair, and George shook every hand.

Later in the day, Edith held a tea for choir members from All

Souls, and a Christmas dinner was held that evening for family and friends. The family's impact on the area was already undeniable, and the attraction of estate employment had resulted in a popular ditty sung by some of the local young boys:

> *When I grow up, if I don't get kilt,*
> *I wanna work for the Vanderbilts.*

However, future festivities at the estate and elsewhere in town would likely be tamer—or at least more private—and not solely because of any belt-tightening. Asheville officially dried up in the fall of 1907, and the state of North Carolina followed suit in the spring of 1908. Asheville, not unlike other locales, had gotten a jump on Prohibition, and it would be the last Christmas for years that a citizen of that town could legally buy alcoholic beverages. The temperance movement had brought women and children to the streets, lawmakers to secluded hand-wringing sessions behind closed doors, taverns to their knees, and voters to the polls.

Places like the Eureka Saloon, opened at the corner of West College and Lexington in 1896 by A. G. Halyburton and now run by John O'Donnell, began to feel a sobering pinch. O'Donnell and other tavern keepers would have to find new ways to keep their customers—tombstone carver W. O. Wolfe, young Thomas Wolfe's father, once counted among them—well lubricated. To that end, a series of tunnels were being burrowed in and under Asheville's sloping fairways, allowing even the most well-heeled, illicit drinkers to venture from the lobbies of respectable hotels into the basements of boarded-up saloons without being spotted.

"Drop in and refresh yourself at the Eureka," O'Donnell's ads had read in more free-flowing days, inviting citizens to stop by his newly acquired establishment. In addition to beers like Schlitz and Dixie, O'Donnell carried a wide selection of whiskies including Old Barbee and J. R. Riper's. O'Donnell also boasted that he was the sole agent in town for Green River Whiskey: "The kind without a headache."

No more. A fresher, more irritating headache was here to stay for the foreseeable future.

■ ■ ■

From Schenck's point of view, cash flow on the estate in general, and in his forestry department specifically, had been drying up to a mere trickle. He had had difficulty securing money for his payroll, and sometimes offered his own promissory notes to the bank in order to keep things functioning. Schenck had begun viewing George's entire estate venture as a "rich man's hobby" with "no grounding in economics." He felt sure that the enterprise—from village to piggery, from forest deep to mountain high—was "destined to fail."

With work on the estate at a standstill, Schenck began to feel his own role would soon meet an end. He decided to go to Germany and elsewhere in Europe to visit his mother, friends, and colleagues. He happily greeted his forestry students when he returned to Asheville, but the financial forecast remained cloudy as the school and associated lumber accounts were in the red. George had ordered horses to be sold and the grooms who cared for them to be dismissed. Schenck also noticed a change in George and Edith's moods.

"George Vanderbilt was very nervous," he later wrote, "and Mrs. Vanderbilt was in tears whenever I called on her." Schenck also felt a change in George's demeanor toward him. "I had the feeling that somebody, during my absence, had succeeded in undermining Vanderbilt's confidence in me and, what was worse, in the outcome of his and my enterprise in forestry."

Then came the day that George instructed Schenck to try to sell as much of Pisgah Forest as possible, leaving a scant several thousand acres or so around the house. George promised to pay Schenck the standard agent's commission if he were successful in finding any buyers.

With his future at the estate growing ever more uncertain, that summer of 1908 Schenck nevertheless began preparations for a three-day forestry celebration the coming fall. He invited those who worked in, profited from, and preserved forest lands. "Rejoice with us," his missive began. "On the 26th day of November next we shall celebrate the twentieth anniversary of forestry at Biltmore, together with the tenth anniversary of the Biltmore Forest School. Rejoice with us, and make our hearts glad by your welcome presence. . . ."

Meanwhile, Edith and George made arrangements for an extended European stay. American money went much further in places like Paris, where both Edith and George felt at home and could stay in their own apartment or with friends and family. The costs of running an estate as large as Biltmore were greatly reduced if no one were living there. Schenck and his rangers would continue to live frugally in the woods that George hoped to sell.

Schenck had one last favor to ask of Edith before she and George departed. Schenck had received a letter from the Greys of Canada: Governor General Earl Grey; his wife, Lady Alice Grey; and their daughter, Lady Sybil. They wrote saying that they hoped to stop by for a visit on their way north after a stay in Bermuda. Schenck could not imagine entertaining the family in the modest cottage he and his wife shared in the Pink Beds. Edith happily arranged for the visitors to stay in Biltmore House. Schenck entertained as well as he could. There was so much that the land and the surroundings had to offer that cost little more than an adventurous spirit and some sensible shoes. There were horseback rides and motorcar trips. Schenck took the earl hunting around the estate. All in all, it was a successful sojourn for the Canadian family. Shortly after, George and Edith closed up the house and took Cornelia, now almost eight years old, and headed North. From there, they would set sail for distant and affordably charming shores.

At home and abroad, 1908 developed into a turbulent one, professionally, personally, and legally. Several miles north of the now-empty estate, on Haywood Avenue in downtown Asheville, the new Catholic Church of St. Lawrence was almost done. Its creator, however, would not see it finished. Rafael Guastavino died that summer

Bibliophile, aesthete, and patron of the arts, George Washington Vanderbilt was twenty-five years old in 1888 when he visited the mountainous region of Western North Carolina with his beloved mother and became enthralled with the notion of acquiring land in the area.

Orphaned as a child and not endowed with great wealth, Edith Stuyvesant Dresser nevertheless claimed lineage to several of the famous founding families of New York City.

To bring his dream to fruition, Vanderbilt hired two giants in the field of design. Frederick Law Olmsted (left) was the father of landscape architecture—renowned for his work on New York City's Central Park and many other great American public spaces. Architect Richard Morris Hunt had designed grand homes for wealthy families, but had also created public spaces and monuments as well—like the pedestal for the Statue of Liberty. Poignantly, Biltmore became one of the last works for both men.

Gifford Pinchot (top) served as Biltmore's forester before becoming the first chief of the U.S. Forest Service.

His successor at Biltmore was German-born forester and founder of the Biltmore Forest School, Carl Schenck.

Soon after a transatlantic meeting aboard the steamship *St. Paul*, George and Edith—shown here in her 1898 engagement photo—wed and returned to a grand welcome by the staff of Biltmore Estate.

George's love of books was shared by two chums: Paul Leicester Ford (top) was a noted man of letters; William B. Osgood Field was a sportsman, adventurer, and engineer.

Cornelia (left), George and Edith's daughter, is seen here with her mother. She inherited her parents' compassion for the less fortunate.

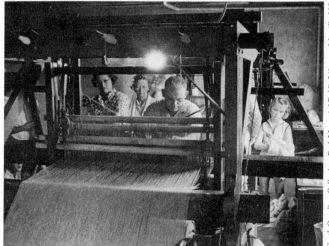

The 1916 flood (top) dealt a severe blow to Biltmore's nurseries, forcing their closure. George and Edith's early investment in the community ultimately led to Biltmore Industries, purveyors of locally crafted fine wood carvings and homespun fabrics.

Grove Park Inn at Foot of the Sunset Mountain, Asheville, N. C.

Influenced by the burgeoning Arts and Crafts movement, the sumptuous Grove Park Inn—built on Sunset Mountain in Asheville—signaled an aesthetic shift from Gilded Age opulence. The inn was financed by E. W. Grove's "chill tonic" empire. Billed as a cure for malaria, the quinine-infused concoction promised to make "children and adults as fat as pigs."

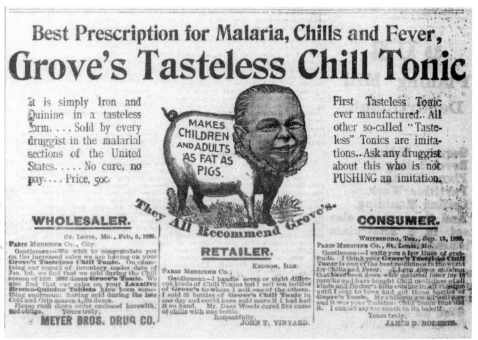

Best Prescription for Malaria, Chills and Fever,

Grove's Tasteless Chill Tonic

It is simply Iron and Quinine in a tasteless form. . . . Sold by every druggist in the malarial sections of the United States. . . . No cure, no pay. . . . Price, 50c.

MAKES CHILDREN AND ADULTS AS FAT AS PIGS.

First Tasteless Tonic ever manufactured. . All other so-called "Tasteless" Tonics are imitations. . Ask any druggist about this who is not PUSHING an imitation.

They All Recommend Grove's.

WHOLESALER.

St. Louis, Mo., Feb. 6, 1899.

PARIS MEDICINE Co., City.

Gentlemen:—We wish to congratulate you on the increased sales we are having on your Grove's Tasteless Chill Tonic. On examining our record of inventory under date of Jan. 1st, we find that we sold during the Chill season of 1898, 2660 dozen Grove's Tonic. We also find that our sales on your Laxative Bromo-Quinine Tablets have been something enormous; having sold during the late Cold and Grip season 4,200 dozen.

Please rush down order enclosed herewith, and oblige, Yours truly,

MEYER BROS. DRUG CO.

RETAILER.

KEDRON, ILLS.

PARIS MEDICINE CO.,

Gentlemen:—I handle seven or eight different kinds of Chill Tonics but I sell ten bottles of Grove's to where I sell one of the others. I sold 35 bottles of Grove's Chill Tonic in one day and could have sold more if I had had it on hand. Mr. Dave Woods cured five cases of chills with one bottle.

Respectfully,

JOHN T. VINYARD.

CONSUMER.

WHITESBORO, Tex., Sep. 13, 1898.

PARIS MEDICINE Co., St. Louis, Mo.

Gentlemen:—I write you a few lines of gratitude. I think your Grove's Tasteless Chill Tonic is one of the best medicines in the world for Chills and Fever. I have three children that have been down with malarial fever for 12 months and have bought Chill medicines of all kinds and Doctor's bills coming in all the time until I sent to town and got three bottles of Grove's Tonic. My children are all well now and it was your Tasteless Chill Tonic that did it. I cannot say too much in its behalf.

Yours truly,

JAMES D. ROBERTS.

Cornelia's 1924 wedding to British diplomat John Francis Amherst Cecil may well have been the most glamorous wedding ever to take place in the small North Carolina mountain town.

An 1895 postcard shows how the estate appeared in its infancy, when Olmsted's trees were still immature. The house appears on the right hill; the white structures to the left are the greenhouses of the lower walled garden.

Work on the house progressed for roughly six years. Stonecutters—shown perched on ladders and scaffolds—were employed by James Sinclair & Company, a New York contractor that had built Vanderbilt homes in that city. A special rail spur, constructed at a cost to George of nearly $80,000, ferried men and materials via locomotive to the worksite each morning.

Images culled from the personal scrapbooks of architect Richard Morris Hunt show the Palm Court, George's indoor garden (top); the fireplace in his personal library (left); and the equally stunning fireplace just outside his bookish lair, in the tapestry room.

Knowing that the estate would one day grow into his vision, Olmsted planned for astonishingly diverse views. Formal sweeping vistas contrasted with glimpses of the house framed by mature vegetation and watery reflections.

According to Olmsted's plan, the approach to the house is an exercise in sustained suspense—a long, winding trip through a canopied forest beginning at the Lodge Gate (top) that ultimately leads to unexpected grandeur. This portion of the façade mimics the staircase inside the house. Look closely and you'll spy statues of St. Louis and St. Joan of Arc.

No home in the United States has ever come close to beating the size of the 175,000-square-foot Biltmore House. But its greatest achievement may well be the fact that it has survived into the twenty-first century while other Gilded Age masterpieces have long since disappeared.

at his home in nearby Black Mountain, just a year prior to the completion of his masterpiece. He was fifty-five years old.

Guastavino had been suffering from diabetes, but a recent onset of a severe flu—deadly in those times—had proven too much for his strained health to handle, and a priest was summoned to perform the final Catholic sacrament of last rites. Those who had come to know and work for the transplanted Spaniard thought of him not solely as a renowned architect but also as a philanthropist. He gave freely of his talents, time, and money. The new church's cost was carried to a great extent by Guastavino himself, who worked on the project exuberantly and without pay. When completed, the church's copper-sheathed, sky-dominating dome, measuring 58 feet by 82 feet, became the largest freestanding elliptical dome in all of North America.

Guastavino left an architectural legacy of structures throughout America and his son, Rafael Jr., continued his father's work. (In fact, the following year, 1909, Guastavino Jr. would complete the dome of New York's St. John the Divine.) Guastavino-tiled arches soared above the heads of the rich and poor alike, whether in private homes or in public New York City subways. From Biltmore to Boston, from Grant's Tomb to the soon-to-be-built Grand Central Terminal, the Guastavino touch was everywhere reflected in dome and tile, forever sealed in ceramic and mortar. An accomplished musician, Guastavino had been composing a special mass that he wanted performed at the opening of the new church. He did not finish the work, but when the high requiem mass was eventually celebrated at St. Lawrence, sections of that composition were sung in his honor. His collaborator Richard Sharp Smith served as a pallbearer. Guastavino's body was placed temporarily in a vault at Riverside Cemetery while his church was finished. He was later interred in a crypt in a small chapel to the left of the altar. Those who worked with him knew that there were finishing touches and details that Guastavino intended to make but had never had the chance to execute. These ideas would now rest with him forever. Biltmore had lost another of its artistic masters.

On the legal front, George found himself on the receiving end of a lawsuit pertaining to his lands. This time, the plaintiff was not a poacher, or a squatter, but rather a former employee. The gentleman in question had worked for the Biltmore and resided on the estate grounds. According to the ex-worker's complaint, George had cheated him out of a land deal and the man was determined to get justice in one form or another. The most recent hearing, however, was to assess the former worker's sanity. He had vociferously threatened that, if monetary reparations were not made, he would burn Biltmore to the ground.

Troubles in love and money continued to plague Edith's brother, as well. Between 1903 and 1907, Natalie had advanced more than $67,000 to help her brother. Though his bankruptcy had been discharged in 1907, LeRoy was still struggling to regain his reputation in the business world. The press had taken a renewed interest in LeRoy's personal life after his wife was found that summer living in Sioux Falls, South Dakota. Sioux Falls had long been a destination for those seeking a quick-ish—if not quickie—divorce. The town had become slangily known as a divorce colony and one could legally dissolve a marriage after a short, ninety-day residency there. Sioux Falls soon had hotels, restaurants, and a booming lovelorn business. One cluster of rental houses had been nicknamed "Divorce Row." (As if to keep affairs in balance, there was a growing business in remarriages as well.)

To avoid notice during her stay, Emma used the name "Mrs. A. M. A. Stewart." She had initially taken up residence in the Cataract Hotel, where a fellow lodger spotted Emma and revealed her true identity. While waiting out her residency, Emma had enrolled in a stenography course at the Sioux Falls Business College to brush up on her typing and shorthand. Once her identity had been made public, Emma was tracked down by a reporter from the *New York Times* who found her studiously reviewing her class notes. "I have made no secret of my being here, but I do resent being dragged into publicity on Mr. Dresser's account," she told the reporter, noting that she had successfully avoided contact with the papers during the height of LeRoy's legal trials in New York City. "I lived with Mr. Dresser until a year and one-half ago, when he deserted me," she said. She added that, "His [financial] failure occurred six years ago, which disproves the suspicion that I am separated from him because he lost his money."

She wanted a skill, she explained, and hoped to be able to support herself and help care for her teenage children, Susan and Daniel Jr. Emma also proudly pointed out that since moving into a modest home on Sioux Falls' Prairie Row, she had begun mowing her own lawn. This was a far cry from the life she and LeRoy had been living at their estate in Oyster Bay, Long Island. Since then, the pair had resided in a New York City apartment, and even spent a short period of time with Emma's mother. It wasn't long before the two went their separate ways and LeRoy took up residence at the New York Yacht Club.

The papers delighted in highlighting the divorces among the Vanderbilts; "The Vanderbilt Curse," it was sometimes called. George's brother Willie K. and his wife Alva—now Mrs. O. H. P. Belmont—had parted, and their daughter, Consuelo, was separated by this time from the Duke of Marlborough. George's nephew Elliott Shepard had split with his wife. George's nephew Alfred—Cornelius's son—also went through a very public split in 1908. His wife, Elsie, had filed for divorce, accusing Alfred of an affair with Mary Agnes O'Brien Ruiz, the Cuban attaché's wife. The alleged indiscretions took place aboard Alfred's private train car, the *Wayfarer*.

There were, however, bright spots among these darker romantic pairings. George's niece, Lila, was still happily married to Field and living in one of George's now completed "Marble Twins" at 645 Fifth Avenue. Field and Lila divided their time between Manhattan; Lenox; Massachusetts; and Westfield, Field's farm in Mohegan Lake, New York. Edith and George had now been together a respectable ten years, despite facing what seemed to be more upheaval each day. A bright spot was Cornelia. She continued growing, leggier and longer, looking more with each passing year as though she would inherit her mother's stature . . . and, perhaps, her father's restlessness.

■　■　■

"Statesman! Lumberman! Engineer! Forester! Come! And be welcome!"

Thanksgiving 1908 arrived. The Biltmore Forest School had been in operation for ten years, and Biltmore welcomed guests for a weekend of outings in and around the estate's forests to celebrate the milestone. It had been more than twenty years since George had looked over these ravaged lands with the enchanting vistas and decided to put down some very large stakes. This first-ever American school of forestry was no longer alone in its educational mission but, as it operated solely on private lands, it remained unique. To commemorate this "tin" anniversary, Schenck hosted the Biltmore Forest Festival from November 26 through the twenty-eighth. "Do not don your best!" his invite warned.

Schenck took the lead for the weekend's activities, ably helped by Reverend Swope, Chauncey Beadle from the nursery and landscaping, Dr. A. S. Wheeler from the agriculture department, and Charles Waddell, who ran the estate's electrical section. Schenck, his students, and other estate employees guided visitors on a variety of excursions, during which Schenck described his views on "practical forestry." Visits to Chauncey Beadle's domain, the herbarium and nurseries, took place on Friday, and guests were also treated to a visit to the Biltmore Dairy, and other small farms. There were educational outings into the forests, showcasing new growths, including an impressive second growth for the well-performing yellow pine, some of which now dated to the estate's initial clearing. Guests received economic as well as scientific context for the developments they witnessed. Newspaper correspondents wrote with gleeful fascination about how students become "cruisers," stalking the forest and estimating marketable board feet along the way before chopping a single trunk. The modified, notched ax handle the student rangers used to assess measurements like merchantable height, diameter, or volume became known even beyond the estate as a "Biltmore Stick." Educators, visitors, and lumbermen listened to Schenck describe how students learned which trees to cut, which to leave, how to lumber, and how to plant. On horseback and on foot, students covered miles, felling trees and harvesting tanbark, mapping acres, grading lumber, and preparing their choices for market.

Groups set off in carriages to inspect the new plantings of white and yellow pine, ash, oak, hemlock, maple, chestnut, walnut, and poplar, and to lunch beneath the newly expanding canopies of the forest plantations. It was like a carriage ride through time, studying the 1899 plantings of locust, cherry, sugar maple, and basswood, followed by a look at the progress of those planted in 1907 and 1908. There were sporting activities, featuring fishing and shooting contests. Finally, the adventurous and physically fit among the festival's attendees embarked on a sunset hike to the lodge atop Mount Pisgah, which offered incomparable views from 5,700 feet above sea level, and a night sleeping beneath a glittering gathering of stars.

The festival was a great success which received national coverage. Still, Schenck must have wondered if it would be his last dance in the Pink Beds. Edith and George had to return sometime, and when they did, Schenck knew hard decisions were coming.

■ ■ ■

The following year, 1909, the inventor Wilbur Wright circled the Statue of Liberty in his airplane and Carl Schenck circled Chauncey Beadle in a fit of frustration and anger. Both events made the papers and captivated witnesses.

Passengers aboard the *Lusitania*, docked in the harbor of lower Manhattan, got quite the show from the deck of the massive ocean liner, its four sentry-like stacks standing at attention for Wright's flyover. First launched in 1906, the *Lusitania* held the record for being the world's largest ocean liner, but the White Star Line was planning two new ships which would best her: The *Olympic*, already under way in Belfast, and another, even more mammoth vessel, the construction of which had just begun and once completed would give new meaning to the popular term "floating city."

Still in Paris in early 1909, George and Edith had hardly escaped the financial worries they had left in America. Buncombe County had telegrammed George to inform him that Biltmore was behind on its county taxes, and the county wanted at least half the amount due as soon as possible. The amount in question—$24,000—had been due in October, and expected by December. Now it was January. The county had been unable to pay teacher salaries in the first half of the month, a clear indication how much the area depended on George's tax dollars. Legally speaking, the estate could be seized and sold, but it was unlikely to happen. "It is unjust to publish Mr. Vanderbilt as a delinquent," a Greensboro paper pointed out, "when so many others are in the same boat." Edith wrote Schenck about how popular her muskrat skins had been in Paris and asked Schenck for more. "The lagoon is full of muskrats," Schenck had written Edith. He would be sure the trappers saved the best for her and thanked her for the "fine edition of Dickens" that Edith had mailed him. They planned a Dickens evening with the Wheelers upon George and Edith's return. By spring, Cholly Knickerbocker's "Society Gossip" column reported that George and Edith would be returning to Biltmore after the Easter holiday, and would stay through spring and early summer. A litany of challenges awaited the couple upon their return, among them one final conflict with Carl Schenck.

With such tremendous holdings, brimming with game of all kinds in its forests and riverbeds, the acreage surrounding George and Edith's house were a tempting destination for hunters and gamesmen. The leasing of hunting and fishing rights was one way to offset costs at the estate. In March 1909, Schenck had done just that, leasing hunting and fishing rights on 80,000 acres of the Pisgah Forest to a consortium of men, with members from Asheville, Chicago, New York, and other locales, who comprised the Biltmore Rod and Gun Club. The group now looked forward to using those rods and guns to hunt on George's land and pluck fish from his waters. There was a lodge available, game was plentiful, the streams hopped with mountain trout, and members would pay dearly to hunt there. The lease was for ten years at $5,000 each year. Schenck had made the deal, acting as the leasing agent and believing the action within his rights and responsibilities as chief forester. Schenck did not, however, mention it to George, who was not happy when he learned of the lease upon his return. He did not think Schenck had the right, no matter his position, to enter into any such agreement. He chastised Schenck and repudiated the lease.

The following month, in early April, another blow struck at the heart of the forest. Fires erupted at multiple locations throughout the lands near George and Edith's house, spreading rapidly. Residents of the housing suburb that George had developed between Biltmore and Asheville, an enclave called Victoria, were also threatened. Residents there worked with firemen to try to keep the blaze at bay, and Schenck's student rangers joined the firefighting effort. The fact that several fires appeared to begin at roughly the same time in more than one location on Vanderbilt properties raised suspicion. Witnesses reported seeing individuals fleeing the scene of newly erupting flames, which sprouted *after* the rangers and firemen had battled most of the blaze. The consensus was that the fires were set intentionally, and Schenck offered $100 to anyone who could help find the culprits. The fire consumed nearly 10,000 acres of land. Striving young poplars, notable among the reforestation efforts, were destroyed. Estimated market value losses varied, ranging from $250,000 to $300,000: Virgin timber reduced to ash. Years of reforesting work up in smoke. Armed guards now patrolled the remaining timber tracts.

Just a week later, another fire erupted, this one at the nearby Kenilworth Inn. When it was originally built, almost eighteen years before, George had been the principal stockholder in the venture. Again, Biltmore's rangers sprung into action. Desperate guests, jumping from the windows of the burning hotel, landed in blankets held by the forestry students. The hotel faced estimated losses of $250,000 but was insured for only $72,500.

The fires stoked frustration and suspicion. Newspapers hinted that the flames were a result of the enmity of neighbors, but there was generous sympathy for George and Edith. The litigious ex-employee who had publicly threatened to burn Biltmore to the ground must have crossed many a mind.

By early June, newspapers broke the news that Chief Forester Schenck was leaving Biltmore. His resignation would go into effect November 1, 1909, even as the forestry program continued garnering praise. Less than two weeks after Schenck's end date, newly elected president William Howard Taft lauded Biltmore's efforts in a speech in the coastal city of Wilmington, North Carolina. "You have within the boundary of your state a gentleman named Vanderbilt who goes before everyone in the science of forestry," the president told the crowd, "and I congratulate you on having that example, that thereby you may formulate laws which shall preserve to you the timber of your state."

Before leaving, however, Schenck appeared in magistrate's court to answer for yet another fracas that had resulted from the hunting and fishing lease: one involving estate superintendent Chauncey Beadle. Beadle had become one of the estate's longest-running employees, and he and Schenck had had their ups and downs. They socialized—Beadle attended a stag dinner party hosted by Schenck—but when they disagreed about how the estate should be run, the arguments became heated. When Schenck turned up at Beadle's office and allegedly threw the botanist to the floor and began pulling on his leg, Beadle filed charges. Judge Gudger in Asheville heard the case, and Schenck was fined $1.00 and "costs."

Schenck spent the remainder of his time in Asheville keeping busy. When there weren't blazes to attend to, the wily forester was evading US revenue officers who had learned of a whiskey still within view of Biltmore House. They asked Schenck to serve as a witness to the violation, but Schenck was not interested in cooperating. When a deputy marshal showed up at the estate to serve Schenck papers, Schenck scampered into the woods he knew so well. Eventually it was revealed that a novice moonshiner, T. C. Whitaker, had asked a more experienced local for help in distilling his hooch and, in turn, that "expert" had ratted Whitaker out to the revenuers.

Affairs between George and Schenck were settled, to a certain degree, roughly a year after Schenck left George's employ. Schenck sued George for unpaid salary and overdue lumber accounts. The former employer and employee settled the two suits out of court with the total paid to Schenck reported between $12,000 and $15,000.

Schenck's fourteen-year stay at the estate had been both innovative and memorable. He had searched the lands for radium for Thomas Edison—a friend of his cousin, pharmaceutical chemist George Merck—who was convinced the rocks in and around the estate might supply what he needed for his own experiments. Schenck had educated young men who would make fine foresters in both the private and public sectors. Schenck had enjoyed sleeping under the stars, whether escorting George, Edith, and their guests on camping trips to the Pink Beds or at the Buck Spring Lodge. He would remember the sight of pink rhododendron, and the voices of black construction workers singing "Jesus, Lover of My Soul" as the swing of their hammers created order from chaos, roads and safe passage in the midst of the ancient Appalachian undergrowth.

"This first breaking of virgin soil, it is true, came to a close in 1909," Schenck later wrote. "But who will deny that, within the short span of its lifetime, the ground was effectively broken for private forestry to flourish in due course throughout America?"

After leaving Biltmore, Schenck approached Merck for funding contacts so that he could take his unique Biltmore Forest School on the road. Within four years, however, Schenck's teaching adventures in America would come to an end. "Retrospectively, let me assert that the Biltmore Forest School died at the right time," he wrote. "It died when it had reached the apex of its career. Be it man or tree or institution, it is better to die too early than too late."

Shortly after Schenck left Biltmore, so, too, did Gifford Pinchot leave his job as chief of the US Forest Service. Pinchot had originated that post under President Theodore Roosevelt, with whom Pinchot shared a similar conservation vision and close relationship. Pinchot shared neither with Roosevelt's successor, President William Howard Taft. When Department of the Interior agent Louis Glavis accused his boss and Taft appointee, Secretary of the Interior Richard Ballinger, of corrupt practices regarding claims on coal-rich lands in Alaska, Pinchot sided with Glavis. Things boiled over in late 1909 when the affair went public.

Pinchot wrote a letter to Congress, which Senator Jonathan Dolliver read on Pinchot's behalf. There was "imminent danger that the Alaska coal fields still in government ownership might pass forever into private hands with little or no compensation to the public," Pinchot wrote. He wanted these issues made public, "unless there are secrets which the people of the United States are not entitled to know concerning the source, nature, and progress of claims made for portions of the public lands."

The Ballinger-Pinchot controversy resulted in Taft dismissing Pinchot for insubordination. The president wrote Pinchot in a January 7, 1910, letter: "By your conduct you have destroyed your usefulness as a helpful subordinate of the Government."

In the eventual Senate investigation, Ballinger was cleared of wrongdoing, but his reputation did not emerge unscathed. Pinchot was out of a job and the conservation policies enacted by him and Roosevelt seemed at risk. The brouhaha and subsequent siding that followed the affair revealed the first fissure in what would become a massive rift within the Republicans, one that would carry into the presidential election of 1912 and lay the foundation for the formation of the Progressive Party.

Pinchot and Schenck, each passionate and knowledgeable in his own way, encountered difficulty fitting their views on forestry into the existing political and cultural landscape. For an important snapshot in time, however fleeting, they each had found their place at Biltmore, and benefited from the auspices of a family that was, whether or not purposefully, far ahead of the times. Pinchot and Schenck's impact on American forestry would outlast any echoes of dissent and distrust.

■ ■ ■

With no forest school to subsidize in any way, George continued lightening his financial load and had recently sold off his herd of Berkshire hogs. Dr. Wheeler, the farm manager, explained to curious members of the media that George was no longer interested in raising the animals, many of which had been originally imported from England and Europe. A local farmer, William Cocke, bought all the hogs, around thirty in all. The entire piggery was moved to Cocke's Blue Ridge Berkshire farm in Beaverdam, just outside the city. The animals' lineage would continue to garner attention in future breedings and sales. One of George's hogs, Loyal Lee, had been a prize-winner for Biltmore and had sired offspring which included the 617-pound bruiser Loyal Highclere. Though the hogs were award winners, they were not satisfactory income generators.

George soon sold the water rights from his Busbee Mountain supply to the village of South Biltmore, a growing area that had recently taken root across from the estate. He had also, just after the first of the year, sold all of his electric lines, associated equipment, and existing contracts to the Asheville Electric Company, making the firm the official owner of all the power lines on the estate which supplied not only the house, but also homes and businesses in the village and the Kenilworth Inn.

George and Edith did not seek to close the parish school which they had established in the village nearly twelve years earlier. However, the passage of school bonds and the formation of new nearby public schools made the school, in its current form, redundant. The building that once housed the school would be leased to another Asheville teacher who intended to operate a boys' school in its place. This would also alleviate the $1,000 per year in taxes associated with the property. But this decision meant that the family would soon, however, need another place for Cornelia to complete her schooling. In addition to tutors and much educational travel, Cornelia had attended the parish school alongside the children of the estate workers and other community members.

George was not divesting himself of everything, however. He had purchased a Stoddard-Dayton automobile in 1907, which he had brought to a home he rented in Washington, DC. And when news spread in 1909 that George had purchased a Chalmers-Detroit touring car to use on the estate, the citizens of Asheville and Biltmore hoped the estate roads would now be open to motorists, something George had long forbidden.

And still, the Vanderbilts' charitable giving and community involvement continued, despite the larger cutbacks. One day, an African American locomotive fireman, George Logan, spotted George's private railcar, the *Swannanoa*, attached to the train he was working. Logan knew whose car it was. His family had sold their land to George years earlier. Now, however, he was having trouble making payments on his new home, and needed $500 to salvage his situation. Logan snatched a piece of scrap paper and pencil and quickly jotted down a note, which a sympathetic porter agreed to deliver to George. Soon after, Logan was instructed to go within the week to the Biltmore offices in the village, where he would find a check waiting.

Biltmore Estate Industries and the School of Domestic Science escaped the chopping block. Edith's interaction with the community did not abate, and Biltmore Estate Industries—the weaving division, especially—was fast gaining national attention, if not large profits. Between 1906 and 1909 she and George had allotted more than $12,000 to the Industries. Sales during that time had grown from around $1,600 to a little over $6,000. White and blue counterpanes, a traditional favorite coverlet, were a popular offering, and sales were increasing. This simple yet quality work contrasted with grander designer fare of the moment available in boutiques. There one might find hats with brims a good three feet in diameter, covered in black and pearl-gray felts, and often festooned in Chantilly lace, bows, and plumage that would make even the proudest peacock seethe and flap in feathery envy. Though they may not have trafficked in such fanciful garb, Edith, Vance, and Yale's efforts were successfully reestablishing handweaving's place in the market.

"This summer," one newspaper noted, "many fashionable women have surprised their friends by declaring that they preferred running a hand loom to playing bridge."

■ ■ ■

Ten years into the new century, the planet Earth passed through the tail of Comet Halley, and the nation lost two very different but very capable chroniclers of its cultures' haves and have-nots.

The man who had brought "The Gift of the Magi" to the world had come to Asheville just three years earlier, in 1907, to visit his childhood friend Sara Coleman. Greensboro-born William Sydney Porter—better known as O. Henry—headed West to the mountains where Coleman now lived and also wrote, often adopting the dialect of her home in the southern Appalachians. O. Henry, a former bank embezzler who had done time in the Ohio State Penitentiary in Columbus, had become noted for his literary portrayals of the have-nots, the working classes. His tales of difficulty and despair made him popular and ran in stark contrast to the writings of society stalkers like Ward McAllister and Cholly Knickerbocker. While those columnists wrote of the Four Hundred, New York and Newport society's most elite families, O. Henry penned a collection of stories—"The Gift of the Magi" among them—aptly titled *The Four Million*, a number he undoubtedly believed to be more reflective of the world in which he lived. In it, he detailed the experiences of a population with stories he felt worth telling, lives worth chronicling: from newsboys to showgirls, bums to butchers, secretaries to streetwalkers. After happening upon one of O. Henry's short stories, Coleman had written him a letter inviting him to visit. He did, and they married that year. It was a late-life romance for both of them; he was forty-five, she was thirty-nine. Now, three years later, Mrs. Porter buried her husband in Riverside Cemetery, in the Asheville neighborhood of Montford.

O. Henry's death came not quite two months after that of the man who had named the Gilded Age. On April 22, 1910, Mark Twain died, a copy of Thomas Carlyle's *French Revolution* lying nearby on his bed. "Give me my glasses," the exhausted author had scribbled on a piece of paper for his caregivers. Then, after nearly seventy-five years on this earth, he left it. His birth had coincided with the passing of Comet Halley, and now his death was punctuated by Earth's next encounter with that cosmological phenomenon. 1910's appearance was a particularly close passing, and apocalyptic theories spewed like stardust across the globe, with French astronomer Camille Flammarion warning that the cyanogen gas in the comet's tail would bring an end to all living things on planet Earth. Songs were written, voodoo comet cures were hawked, and one distraught prospector in San Bernardino, California, became so panicked by the idea of Earth passing though the comet's tail that he nailed his feet and one hand to a cross, convinced the end of the world was nigh.

But Halley passed, humanity endured, and stars faded, Twain's and O. Henry's among them. Halley's tail disappeared into the night sky, embarking on a seventy-six-year journey that would keep it at cosmic bay until its next earthly sighting.

By 1910, the number of boardinghouses in Asheville had exploded, from 55 in 1900 to 137. One of those newish boardinghouses was run by Thomas Wolfe's mother, Julia Elizabeth Westall Wolfe, who had hung her welcome sign outside a house at 48 Spruce Street in 1906. Young Thomas spent much time there with his mother, observing the people who came and went in the rented rooms and breathing porches of the house known as Old Kentucky Home. In 1900, the year young Wolfe and Cornelia Vanderbilt were born, tuberculosis was one of the top three leading causes of death in the United States. That epidemic continued to bring visitors and leading doctors to the mountains of North Carolina. Hotels, too, were often at capacity in the summer months as visitors poured in from all directions.

For the Vanderbilt family, however, a change of scenery, a change of home, and a daughter in need of a change of schooling conspired to keep them away from Asheville more and more. George, Edith, and Cornelia often spent time in the nation's capital, and had rented a house at 1707 New Hampshire Avenue several years earlier. As early as 1908, Biltmore Estate Industries had made its debut in the capital at Washington's Arlington Hotel with a sale of the school's wood carvings, embroideries, homespun fabric, and baskets. Washington was closer to North Carolina than New York City, and the city also provided excellent schooling options for Cornelia, who would soon be starting high school. There was also an active social scene with which George and Edith were already familiar, and excellent museums to satisfy even George's well-honed tastes. In 1912, George bought a home at 1612 K Street in Washington, DC, which was formerly owned by Senator Matthew Quay of Pennsylvania and which added a fresh mortgage to George's ledger.

The Vanderbilts continued to travel—and spend—overseas as well. Edith had been sitting for noted Italian portraitist Giovanni Boldini, a friend of Whistler's who had moved into John Singer Sargent's Paris studio when that painter relocated to London. Boldini told Edith he wanted her dressed in a black gown, and that she should bring along a chinchilla boa and a black picture hat. The Ferrara native lamented to *American Art News* that the increasing popularity of automobile travel had made his subjects restless, and that getting women to pose had become a challenge. "Their features lack the calm necessary to a successful painting," Boldini told the publication.

"But Mrs. Vanderbilt," Boldini stated, "has the repose of a statue."

George paid a reported $15,000 for the full-length portrait, and when the Paris Salon of 1911 arrived, Boldini sketched the arrangement of paintings he desired for four portraits and a still life that would hang in Salle 13. At the center of the five paintings in the position of greatest honor was "Mme G. V."—Edith's exuberant and dramatic portrait, complete with boa.

Whenever away, George stayed in touch with Chauncey Beadle, who had emerged as an indispensable part of estate management and life. George still did not have a buyer for the bulk of Pisgah Forest, though he had, in 1911, managed to sell timber rights to 20,000 acres. The reported price was in excess of $500,000.

On February 20, 1912, Beadle wrote George, his employer now of twenty-two years, in Paris. It had been a severe winter, making it difficult to work in the forest, he wrote. He appreciated George's "encouragement" insofar as Beadle's "effort to exploit the Pisgah Forest property with the Federal Authorities."

Spring found George and Edith in Paris. Assessing their travel options for the trip back across the Atlantic, they had a chance to book passage on the maiden voyage of the White Star's newest, most luxurious ocean liner.

A ship named *Titanic.*

12

Final Crossings

Chauncey Beadle, in his letter of February 20, seemed to agree with George and Edith's travel plans, saying, "a trip on the *Titanic* reminds me of the wonderful experience Mrs. Beadle and I enjoyed on the sister ship *Olympic*. It is truly a wonderful experience on a floating city."

There was a certain prestige to making the maiden voyage on a new ship, especially one with the amount of hype and coverage that the *Titanic* was receiving. John Jacob Astor and his fiancée, Madeline Talmage, were expected on board. William Carter planned to bring his 35-horsepower red Renault motorcar, completely dismantled and crated for the journey.

White Star chairman Joseph Bruce Ismay and his firm certainly seemed to have left no luxurious detail overlooked in what was widely regarded as a "floating palace." First-class baths included the divine Vinolia Otto Toilet Soaps. If you wanted to relax, one dollar would buy you a bath—Turkish or electric, your choice—or a deck chair. Supplies were ample, especially for the kitchen. Among the items stowed on board were 12,000 dinner plates, 4,000 aprons, 75,000 pounds of fresh meat, 1,000 pewter forks, and 100 pairs of grape scissors. A bugler announced dinner for the lucky first-class passengers, who would dine on caviar, lobster, Egyptian quail, and—hence the scissors—fresh grapes.

The ship, designed by Thomas Andrews, was massive, all 45,000 tons of her, a triple-screw liner with three million rivets and sixteen watertight bulkheads making the possibility of sinking almost unthinkable. At the first sign of any sort of breach, the crew would be able to quickly close the troubled compartment.

Yet early in the morning of April 15, 1912, the *Titanic* and more than half of her passengers—1,517 souls—sank into the North Atlantic.

When Adele Burden woke that morning and saw the news of the horrific disaster aboard the *Titanic*, her thoughts immediately turned to her uncle George and aunt Edith. She had had so many happy memories at Biltmore, her own honeymoon among them. Could it be that they were among the more than 1,500 lives lost? A higher percentage of first-class passengers were saved, and George and Edith would have certainly traveled first class. Perhaps they had made it safely aboard the *Carpathia*?

Upon receiving her mail, Adele spied a letter from her aunt, George's cousin Jennie, more formally known as Mrs. Virginia Purdy Bacon. Adele opened the letter and began to read. The news was unexpected, but most welcome. George and Edith had, in fact, changed their plans at the last minute.

Adele sat down to write a letter of her own, this time to George. "That was such a burden off my heart," George's niece wrote. "We cannot be too thankful that you were safe on the *Olympic*."

Edith later explained their decision in a letter to Paul Leicester Ford's sister Emily Ford Skeel. "For no reason whatsoever we decided to sail on the *Olympic* and had only 18 hours to get ready in. We were homesick, and simply felt we must get home, and changed our ship, as I say, at the Eleventh hour!"

George's nephew Alfred Gwynne Vanderbilt—Adele's cousin—had also changed his plans, but the press incorrectly reported that he boarded the doomed ship. The Fabbris—George's niece, Edith, and her husband, Ernesto—were also aboard the *Olympic*.

A much relieved Adele wished her uncle the best upon his return to America.

"Just a few lines to welcome you to Biltmore and may you all live for many years happily within its beautiful grounds and enjoy its restful and peaceful surroundings. May it be your refuge, dear George, in times of trouble which come to all men and which none can escape."

Europe beckoned yet again the following year, and though the family had formally transitioned to a less grandiose lifestyle within the nation's capital, Biltmore remained a respite from city life for George and Edith.

"Next week we go to Buckspring Lodge," George wrote Emily Skeel in July 1913. He had just returned to Asheville from abroad to find two volumes of Noah Webster—an ancestor of the Ford family on their mother's side—waiting for him, courtesy of Emily. She had blossomed into a first-rate editor and scholar in her own right; the Noah Webster project had been a passion of hers for years. George enticed her to come visit. "Not only is the road to the lodge now finished but nine miles beyond down to the Pink Beds making six miles of panoramic road with all the inspiration these mountains possess."

George and Edith had maintained contact with both Emily and her brother, Worthington, in the years following Paul Leicester Ford's death. The couple often invited Emily to stay with them at Biltmore and tried to catch up with Worthington when they were at their home in Washington, DC. In his letter, George lamented to Emily that he had in fact missed Worthington in Washington the winter prior.

"You and he," George wrote, "are a link with the past that I don't want to let go."

By January 1914, Edith and George were back in Washington again for the winter. They made the most of their time there, attending dinner dances, hosting family and political players at their home on K Street, attending the National Theatre. When George's niece Gladys, the Countess Széchenyi, was in town with her husband, he and Edith hosted a tea dance and supper in their honor at the Shoreham Hotel. They, along with DC's other luminaries, helped fill the society page of the *Washington Post* and feed insider scoops to the *Washington Times*. Here, too, Edith made charity a priority.

"The entertainment to be given Thursday night for the benefit of the Diet Kitchen will take place at the Playhouse, instead of at Rauscher's, as originally announced," the *Washington Post* reported in late February 1914. The Diet Kitchen was an organization that focused on the welfare of the infants of the capital city, providing care and nourishment at different "stations" throughout the city for the poorest of children. Fundraisers such as these were much needed and much watched, and Edith served on the board of at least one such group hoping to establish a new Diet Kitchen station. "The entertainment," the article continued, "which will be given under the auspices of Mme. Dumba, Mrs. George Vanderbilt and Mrs. Edward Rowland, will bring together one of the smartest assemblages of the winter." And so it did.

Tableaux vivants were still all the rage, though their popularity had begun to take hold earlier in the prior century. To create one of these "living pictures," participants dressed in elaborate costumes and used props and sets to replicate famous paintings or scenes from history. Edith had hosted masques and tableaux at Biltmore. As popular in New Orleans as they were in the Yorkshire countryside, no house party was complete without tableaux. When the curtain rose at ten o'clock, the Playhouse was past capacity, with guests standing to watch the evening's program, which begun with a tableaux entitled "Egyptian Frieze."

Edith spent most of her time at the party occupied with her responsibilities as hostess. Throughout the night, she drew many a gaze for her ensemble, a white gown with lace and silver brocade. She completed the evening's look with a necklace of diamonds alongside a string of pearls. Her dress, and the charity event, were both a rousing success. The roster of attendees featured ambassadors from Germany, Italy, and Austro-Hungary; the Countess von Bernstorff; and ministers from Sweden, the Netherlands, and Denmark. Society reporters eyed every lady of prominence in the room—including the first lady, Mrs. Woodrow Wilson; and Mrs. Marshall Field—and dutifully documented each yard of silk, every carat of each gem.

"Beauties of Washington Society Dancing Like Woodland Fairies to Aid Children of the Needy" the *Washington Post* proclaimed. "Gathering Is One of Most Brilliant of the Whole Winter Season." The event also featured a variety show with dance performances. Supper was served at midnight. Then came dancing till dawn.

However, Edith's time in DC was not all fundraisers and ball gowns. George had not been feeling his best for some months now, and though he appeared to have run-of-the-mill digestive issues, his discomfort became untenable, and it was soon clear that George had more than simple gastrointestinal difficulties. He required an appendectomy.

In 1914, appendectomies were fairly commonplace, with the history of the modern appendectomy dating to around 1890. There was no reason to expect that anything would go amiss. The Vanderbilts lived in the nation's capital, and they had access to the best doctors, the best hospitals, and the best care that money and their name could buy. Dr. John Finney performed the removal of George's inflamed organ, assisted by Dr. James Mitchell. After the procedure, there were no particular concerns. The doctors thought the procedure had gone well, and Dr. Mitchell reported that George was resting comfortably and that Finney, the lead surgeon, was "entirely satisfied with his condition." Soon it would be life as usual in Washington and, later that year, the family would return for a stay at Biltmore. Although the US government had passed on George's most recent offer to sell Pisgah Forest, there were hopeful signs of negotiation. Best of all, George was on the mend.

One Friday morning in early March, Edith sat with George in his bedroom of their home at 1612 K Street. George sat up to read the papers and talked with Edith. Around midday, George asked his wife if she could fetch him a drink and another newspaper. Edith obliged. When she returned to George's room, the man with whom she had been conversing freely all morning was now unresponsive. Every attempt she made to rouse him failed. Panicked now, Edith called for the doctor. But by the time Dr. Mitchell arrived, George was gone.

Edith was gutted. Just two days earlier, the doctor's glowing appraisal of George's recovery had made the papers. Now, the man who had traveled to the far corners of the world, often far from the reach of medicines and modern care, the man who feared death from tuberculosis, had in fact lost his life to a myocardial infarction. A pulmonary embolism had formed after the appendectomy, causing George's heart to fail.

George Washington Vanderbilt died on March 6, 1914, in his bedroom, his wife, Edith, within his fading grasp. He was fifty-one years old.

George's brother Frederick came down from New York to help Edith with the arrangements. Edith's sister Natalie was already there, and Pauline made her way down the East Coast to join her sisters and young niece. Natalie knew all too well the devastation of losing a partner so suddenly to illness. Now she held on dearly to her son, John Nicholas Brown II, as Edith would to her daughter, Cornelia. Edith and Natalie also knew better than most what it was like to lose a parent at such a young age. Cornelia was not yet fourteen years old.

Edith wired Reverend Rodney Swope, who immediately left Biltmore for Washington, DC, where services were held at the Bethlehem Chapel in Washington's National Cathedral. Many imagined George's body might be brought back to Biltmore and buried beneath his church, but in death George was destined to rest where others of his Dutch clan had gone before.

Following the service in Washington, George's remains were placed on a train headed for New York City. The locomotive pulled into what was now the new Grand Central *Terminal*—just opened to the public the previous month—a structure in its third incarnation yet still synonymous with his family name. Family and friends made their way to 2 West Fifty-Second Street, the home of George's sister Emily. Afterward, the group began yet another journey. George's hearse was followed by roughly twenty-five automobiles as the caravan proceeded south through the streets of the city that George's family had impacted in so many ways. At the southern tip of the island, the cortège boarded the ferryboat *Richmond*. The funeral procession continued across the same waters that George's grandfather, the Commodore, had chartered as a poor, young river rat.

The ferry docked. The casket emerged. Edith and Cornelia walked with the family as the procession made its way to the stone edifice where other final journeys of George's family would end. Bishop Greer from St. Bartholomew's presided over the services at the Moravian Cemetery at New Dorp, near the humble farm where the Commodore had been raised. George was placed in the family mausoleum at the bottom of Todt Hill, the completion of which he himself had overseen decades earlier, with the help of his friend and architectural north star Richard Morris Hunt. The grounds of the surrounding acreage originally donated by Commodore Vanderbilt and George's father, William Henry, had been carefully designed by George's friend and landscape visionary Frederick Law Olmsted. Finally good-byes were said and prayers intoned. The mausoleum was sealed once again.

Edith and Cornelia again boarded the ferry. It pulled away from the island, and wind rose off the Hudson. Another crossing. Edith would make the return trip without the man whose life she had enlarged in ways he may not have been able to imagine. They had made countless trips together, traversing lands and seas and cultures. They had also made a home on the banks of a river far from the Hudson, creating a gem of a life in the crowning moments of an age that could not long survive. So many remnants of that age were already crumbling under the weight of their sumptuous guise, opulence yielding to irrelevance.

But Edith would not let go so easily. Their fates, hers and the mountain gem's, were intertwined now more than ever.

It was up to her to safeguard George's legacy. By her efforts, Biltmore would either endure or lapse into obscurity, just another dissipating ripple in the tide of wealth and privilege which the world had at once fetishized, vilified, admonished, and envied.

On public buildings throughout Asheville, flags flew at half-mast.

The *State Journal* out of Raleigh called George's death "a very direct and heavy blow to North Carolina," and the *Asheville Citizen* wrote that "no individual death which has occurred in this section in recent years was a greater loss than is the passing of George W. Vanderbilt." On March 16, Junius Horner, bishop of the Missionary district of Asheville, took Swope's place on All Souls's pulpit and celebrated a memorial service in honor of George. The Sunday bulletin remembered the man who had forever altered their community:

"Courteous in manner, dignified in deportment, kind in heart and pure in morals, he was beloved by his friends, honored by his acquaintances and respected by everyone. The place he occupied in the life of this community and in the history of this church can never be filled. That place will know him no more; but wherever there is nobility of character, wherever there is gentleness of spirit, wherever there are all the things that make for Sweetness and Light, there George Vanderbilt has found his home."

In the weeks and months after his death, the papers seized on every aspect of George's estate. Within a week, the *New York Times* had predicted how the estate of one of the city's most well-known residents would be settled: George's estate was estimated at $50 million, the bulk of which would go to Edith and Cornelia. Cornelia was set to eventually receive the estate of Biltmore and would receive the entirety of a $5 million trust and its income, originally left to George by his father, William Henry Vanderbilt. There were other houses, of course, in Bar Harbor—which came with some thirty-odd acres of its own—in Washington, DC; and in New York. Edith was to receive $250,000 in cash and another $1 million life insurance policy and all of Pisgah Forest. However, a final balancing of the ledger and examination of George's true financial position was still in the very early stages.

In his will, George had not forgotten his employees. His trusted estate manager and adviser Charles McNamee and his wife, Julia, would each receive $2,000 per month for the rest of their lives. Some other employees were also given annuities.

The estate included furnishings, clothing, cars, and the remarkable art collection. George's father had been a lifelong collector of art, filling every inch of 640 Fifth Avenue with notable paintings, sculptures, and more, some of which George had already loaned to the Metropolitan Museum of Art. Jean-François Millet's *The Sower* was among the treasures, as was a painting by that master of the French landscape Jean-Baptiste-Camille Corot. Eugène Delacroix was represented and, of course, there were paintings by John Singer Sargent. The one Sargent had painted of George's sister Margaret, Mrs. Elliott Fitch Shepard, George left to his niece Maria Louise Schieffelin. George left his cousin Fredericka Pulitzer the portrait of her by James C. Porter, which had been reproduced by *Harper's Weekly* for her wedding announcement to Ralph Pulitzer, son of the New York *World* publisher, Joseph. There were also paintings by George's friend and sometime Paris dining companion, James Whistler. George left Whistler's painting of Edith, *Ivoire et Or: Portrait de Madame Vanderbilt*, to their daughter, Cornelia. The painting that Whistler had done of George years earlier in Paris, during that fateful visit in which George had brooded over the prospect of marriage, dining frequently with then–Edith Dresser and her chaperone, Mlle. Rambaud, as he prepared to depart for India with his friend Billy—*that* painting, George had left to Edith.

About $6 million worth of property, including the family home at Fifth and Fifty-First Street, where George spent his childhood and where he and Edith and Cornelia often stayed, would go to George's nephew Cornelius III for the sole reason that Cornelia did not possess the necessary Y chromosome. That was where the art collection would reside. George's father had been quite direct: "Residence and art collection should be retained and maintained permanently by a male descendant of his bearing the name of Vanderbilt."

Regarding Cornelia's inheritance, George left specific guidelines as to how the trust and properties should be handled until she was ready to take it over. George appointed Edith and his brother Willie K. trustees of his estate and managers of Cornelia's share in it until Cornelia's twenty-fifth birthday, and an Egerton L. Winthrop Jr. was appointed special guardian by the county of New York to represent Cornelia's interests. At twenty-one, she would receive any income accrued and reinvested from the $5 million trust. And at twenty-five, she would have access to the principal—a privilege not granted to George in his lifetime. George made provisions for her education and care, of course. At least one newspaper labeled Cornelia the "Hillbilly Heiress," one of the wealthiest little girls in the world.

Though the will was filed in the state of New York, Edith would soon find that there was plenty of curiosity about the future of George's estate in Asheville and the village of Biltmore as well. Shortly after the initial reports of George's death, the North Carolina newspapers began to speculate as to what might happen not only to his lands but also to specific holdings and projects, most specifically, All Souls Cathedral.

"Close associates here of Mr. Vanderbilt, without having definite knowledge of the provisions of his will, say . . ."

These early reports on the future of the village and the church appeared to have been based on not much more than hearsay and wishful thinking. *The church will be fine; the facilities will be provided for. The memorial hospital, named for George's cousin, Clarence, will undoubtedly be fine.* Additionally, reports asserted that much of the land surrounding Biltmore was to be included in an "Appalachian National Park Reserve." The specifics of that, too, remained to be seen.

Clarity came once George's will had been filed and made public. Two months after George's death, a North Carolina newspaper reported news that unsettled the small community. The financial maintenance of All Souls Cathedral—reputed to have possibly the highest-paid choir in the South—had *not* been included in George's will. In fact, there was no mention of either All Souls Cathedral or the Clarence Barker Memorial Hospital. Many in the community wondered what might become of the Vanderbilts' church.

In early April, Edith and Cornelia made the long trip back down to Biltmore. It was time to go home. More changes awaited Edith when they arrived in Asheville. The longtime housekeeper, Emily King, left that year of 1914. She had married William C. Jones, a North Carolina native, fruit purveyor, and clerk at George's estate. The Joneses had decided to leave Asheville and venture to the small town of Apopka, Florida. There the pair opened an inn in the burgeoning citrus-growing region of the country, and were up and running in time to offer Christmas dinner: 50 cents a head. When it came time for the former housekeeper to choose a name for their new venture, she found herself gripped by nostalgia: She named it the Biltmore Inn. The Joneses' hotel would eventually be one of many in the country to boast the name "Biltmore," a name with a history far from the groves of the Sunshine State and one of many Biltmore hotels that would eventually spring up in Florida, New York, and far beyond.

Edith somewhat eased the minds of the local residents. Although the care and maintenance of All Souls Cathedral was not provided for in George's will, Edith let everyone know that she intended to support the institution. She would continue to pay not only the rector's salary but also the salary of the organist, all told a contribution of roughly $5,000 each year.

Biltmore House and the surrounding village—let alone the other properties—may have seemed to outside eyes to be a tremendous inheritance for any wife or daughter. However, Biltmore was perhaps George's greatest liability. Intact, that is. Broken up and sold off, it might net a tidy sum for the booming resort locale of Asheville. It was still too early to tell if Cornelia's birthplace would survive long enough to eventually be handed over to her. Biltmore House and the remainder of George's holdings needed attention. Curiosity naturally extended to George's family and what it was that they planned to do in the wake of this tragic and unexpected loss, and whether or not they intended to stay. Edith, grieving her husband and left to care for her young daughter, knew that significant challenges—both emotional and fiscal—lay ahead.

For all his riches, George Washington Vanderbilt was in many ways leaving behind an architectural albatross, one that would require a good deal of care and savvy financial maneuvering if it were to survive in one piece. Edith did not want to see it abandoned or destroyed, sold off or parceled out, turned into a hotel or a sanitarium. This was not merely a house, but a monument to the talented men who had made it a reality. It had reshaped the lives of not just a family, but an entire region. But Edith knew that in order to ensure that it could be preserved as their family's home, she would need help.

13

Washed Away

The realities of George's estate began to crystallize into a post-probate financial assessment that was significantly less than the $50 million figure initially bandied about. Not including his real estate in North Carolina, Maine, and Washington, George's net estate was valued at $929,740.98. He had repeatedly tapped and drastically reduced the value of his million-dollar life insurance policy, and the monies due Edith were now closer to $640,000. A mortgage of $65,000 remained on the Washington, DC, home at 1612 K Street. Edith's $250,000 bequest had to be reduced to closer to $178,000. Buncombe County valued the home and forest at $2,592,306 and valued George's additional personal property—from art and musical instruments to livestock and cash on hand—at $149,715. There was not enough money to cover the generous bequests he had made in his will to employees and others. The railroad magnate's son held just $11,125 in stocks and bonds—the majority held with the Bar Harbor Water Company.

The estate would still pass to Cornelia one day, but for Edith, Biltmore's preservation must also have been about protecting all George had worked for—in truth, the closest thing to work George had ever done in his life—his passion, his legacy. It would all be lost to memory and sliced up by the surveyor's transit if Edith did not find a way to reduce the estate's financial burden and maintain the integrity—if not the ownership—of all that she and George had worked to create.

Edith decided to pursue George's long-held desire to sell the forest. Several factors combined to motivate her.

One of these was the passage of the Sixteenth Amendment to the United States Constitution, which altered Article I, section 9 of that legislative document and forever changed income tax in the United States.

Taxation had been a sore spot among Americans since the country was just a collection of bickering colonies. The idea of taxing income—as opposed to merely goods—had been in play since the Civil War. The Revenue Act of 1861 was proposed during the first session of the nation's 37th Congress. House Resolution 54 passed, and Abraham Lincoln signed the legislation into law in his first year in office. This act was designed to raise money to support the Union troops during wartime. It imposed a flat tax of 3 percent on income exceeding $800 and constituted the first-ever federal income tax in the United States. But it did not raise the kind of money that its architects had hoped it might, and enforcement was spotty at best. In 1862, new legislation created a Bureau of Internal Revenue within the Treasury Department, and luxury taxes were added. Two years after that, in 1864, the creation of a progressive income tax rate taxed 3 percent of any income between $600 and $10,000, and 5 percent of any income above that. New taxes on goods—including the tobacco tax—were also implemented. By 1872, after roughly ten years, these income taxes were repealed. Until 1913, federal taxes were raised primarily from tariffs on imported goods and excise taxes on items such as alcohol and tobacco.

In 1909, President Taft suggested a tax on income. In July 1909, the Sixteenth Amendment passed but four years elapsed before Wyoming became the thirty-sixth state to ratify it. On February 3, 1913, it became law. Its first full year in effect was 1914, the same year of George's unexpected death.

The Sixteenth Amendment states:

"The Congress shall have power to lay and collect taxes on incomes, from whatever source derived, without apportionment among the several States, and without regard to any census or enumeration."

The gist of it all was that with the ratification of the Sixteenth

Amendment, all income was now fair taxable game. Individuals could be taxed, no matter the population of their state—a factor that had been an issue in prior taxation efforts. (A flat tax in 1894 had been rejected by the Supreme Court for that reason: the taxes being levied were not proportional to the population of each state but were, instead, a direct tax.)

Now, regardless where the income originated, where one lived, or what that state's population was, the federal government could tax you based on *all of* your income: wages, dividends, rental payments, and so on. Later that year, the government levied a 1 percent tax on net personal income in excess of $3,000 annually, and a 6 percent surtax on income that exceeded $500,000. The effect on members of the Four Hundred could not be overstated.

While this new legislation provided a challenge to Edith and others of her economic ilk, other recent legislation proved helpful to her situation. That legislation was the Weeks Act.

The Weeks Act authorized the federal government to purchase private lands in order to help ensure the health of watersheds and river headwaters. The importance of protecting large swaths of forested lands from fire was also a consideration. With this legislation in place, there could be cooperation between the US government, corporations, and individual landowners to protect the forests and the waters that ran through them.

Once Congress passed the Weeks Act in 1911, the government planned to purchase lands in the southern Appalachian region, and set money aside to do so. This piece of legislation would prove to be a game changer for Edith's financially beleaguered estate.

Edith and others—presidents and foresters alike—admired what George had managed to accomplish with Pisgah Forest. In a sense, the lack of significant profitability from lumbering had resulted in a forest that had rebounded. In the hands of Pinchot and then Schenck—despite their differences—the land had become a model for private forestry and instruction that was unique in America. Land that had fallen victim to a blind-cutting timber

craze and been left denuded of its former glory had begun to reju-
venate, to take root, to sheathe the slopes in green and gold once
more.

George had died nearly six years after first instructing Schenck
to try to sell off as much of the forest as possible. There is little evidence to suggest that Schenck pursued the sale of these lands to any
great degree; his negligence perhaps a reflection of his professed belief in the wisdom of concurrently managing the lands *and* turning
a profit from timber interests. But once Schenck had left his post,
George took up the idea again, and was willing to part with land in
four different counties, holdings that included the beloved summit
that had first caught his eye decades earlier: Mount Pisgah. Clearly
he prized that peak and her surroundings. He had wanted upwards
of $600,000 for a tract of roughly 90,000 acres.

However, initial assessments did not work in George's favor. When
the National Forest Commission first came to Asheville to inspect
the land, estate superintendent Chauncey Beadle greeted them and
showed them around, from the twisting banks of the French Broad
to the rustic, chestnut-beamed magnificence of the Buck Spring
Lodge. The commissioners came, assessed and, ultimately, passed.
This decision—*not* to purchase George's land and add it to what was
then called the Appalachian Forest Reserve—came not quite a year
before George's death. The fact that George had already negotiated
the sale of timber rights on various tracts of that same land may have
influenced the commission's decision.

Though smaller sales of timber rights had been pursued in the
past, in October 1912 George entered into an agreement with a gentleman named Louis Carr. George sold the timber rights on 69,326
acres to Carr and gave him a twenty-year lease. Though the price for
the timber rights was $831,912, that money was to be paid in install-
ments: $10,000 upon signing, another $10,797.80 by May 1, 1913,
and then $41,595.60 in total to be paid each year—in two annual
installments—through 1932. However, only $41,595.60 had been
paid before George died. Edith needed that money now. So though

the National Forest Commission had recently passed on the sale of George's lands, Edith resolved to try again.

"I now confront the question of what disposal I shall make of Pisgah forest, which, under the terms of my late husband's will, has passed to me without qualification or condition," Edith wrote in a May 1, 1914, letter addressed to the Secretary of Agriculture. "This letter constitutes my formal offer for the sale of Pisgah Forest to the Government for National Forest purposes."

She enthused about her husband's role as a pioneer in the practice of forestry in America. "I keenly sympathize with his beliefs that the private ownership of forest land is a public trust, and I probably realize more keenly than any one else can do, how firm was his resolve never to permit injury to the permanent value and usefulness of Pisgah Forest."

Edith wisely noted that this offer was a reduction on the last option that she and George had executed a year earlier. While George had asked for between $5.75 and $12.75 per acre for lands that were both under timber contracts and those that were left uncut, Edith now asked for a flat $5.00 per acre for the 86,700 acres being offered.

"I make this contribution towards the public ownership of Pisgah Forest with the earnest hope that in this way I may help to perpetuate my husband's pioneer work in forest conservation, and to insure the protection and the use and enjoyment of Pisgah Forest as a National Forest, by the American people for all time."

The commission, attracted by the price and the value it represented, must have certainly wondered when, if ever, another private seller would have such a large single tract for sale in an area that the forestry division had itself identified as a target for conservation. Edith's offer was persuasive. Within a month, 86,700 acres of Pisgah Forest were bound for the Forest Commission's hands. The sale price was $433,851. The sale of the lands to the government left more than 10,000 acres around the house itself—ample by any estimation—and may likely have eased some local speculation about what Edith intended to do with the property. Edith had added in her letter that "it would be a source of very keen gratification to me if the tract retained, as a national forest, the title of 'Pisgah Forest' which my late husband gave it." The government obliged, and Pisgah National Forest became the first national forest established under the Weeks Act.

Under George, Pinchot, and Schenck's stewardship, Pisgah had been enjoying a rebirth. That name long associated with Moses's trek up from the plains of Moab—the peak east of Jordan from which he first glimpsed the Promised Land—would now be the name of the first national forest in the United States of America ever created from the purchase of private lands. Pisgah would belong to Biltmore no more.

Despite the tasks that demanded attention back in North Carolina, Edith and Cornelia spent more time in Washington, DC, at the house on K Street which—along with its mortgage—had been left to Edith. Cornelia attended Miss Madeira's School, an all-girls school founded in 1906 by Lucy Madeira Wing. Biltmore was not far from their minds. Chauncey Beadle, who had known Cornelia her entire life, stayed in touch with his young friend while she was away. He wrote her letters detailing the buds, blooms, and fall shades of life on the estate.

Their summer of mourning came and went, and early in 1915 the pair went to visit Edith's sister Pauline. Edith leased the Bar Harbor property, which likely alleviated some financial strain. Trials and difficulties at home were amplified by mounting fears abroad. Roughly a month after Edith sold the forest lands, Archduke Francis Ferdinand of Austria-Hungary was assassinated. By the end of August, the Allies of Britain, France, and Russia were at war with the Central Powers of Germany and Austria-Hungary. A Great War was beginning, and citizens of the United States wondered when, or if, they, too, would be drawn into the bloodiest conflict the planet had ever known.

In February 1915, Germany declared the waters surrounding the British Isles a war zone. In late April, a sterner warning came for citizens of America—not yet engaged in World War I—in the form of a notice sent from the Imperial German Embassy to the State Department, stating that "travellers sailing in the war zone on ships of Great Britain or her allies do so at their own risk." German submarines stalked the waters off the European coast. The newspaper reports caused some to cancel their tickets. George and Edith's nephew Alfred Gwynne Vanderbilt took the threats in well-heeled stride. Three years had passed since Alfred, George, and Edith narrowly avoided going down on the *Titanic*. In 1907, Alfred had watched from the deck of his yacht as the new ocean liner *Lusitania* steamed into New York on her maiden voyage. Now it was 1915, he had business abroad, and he intended to go. He and other passengers received anonymous telegrams warning them not to travel on that grand ship. Many remained undeterred.

When a torpedo fired from the German submarine *U-20* struck the ship on May 7, 1915, she sank in less than twenty minutes and took nearly 1,200 souls with her. Among them were Elbert Hubbard, founder of the Roycroft Arts and Crafts community in East Aurora, New York, and Alfred. Alfred's second wife, Margaret, could not accept his death on the *Lusitania* and stayed locked away in the Vanderbilt Hotel—which Alfred had built in 1912—before finally returning to her home on Fifty-Seventh Street. She sent cable after cable across the Atlantic to those she knew hoping that someone, anyone, might have heard about or, God willing, laid eyes on her husband. She offered $5,000—a fortune in 1915—for the recovery of his body. She never had reason to part with that money. Alfred's body was never found.

The Vanderbilt family mourned the loss of one of their own, and the episode sent a shudder through a country that wondered how long President Woodrow Wilson and Congress could keep the United States out of the war.

■ ■ ■

The nervous strain has become so great that I can bear it no longer. . . .

That evening, Mr. C. W. Gould raced to hail a taxi as soon as he'd read the letter waiting for him when he arrived at his New York City apartment. The note was from his client and close friend Daniel Le-Roy Dresser, Edith's brother. Once Gould read the words, he dashed down to the street.

The cab made fast for St. Anthony's Hall at 434 Riverside Drive, part of the Delta Psi fraternity suite of rooms located uptown at Co-lumbia University—LeRoy's alma mater—where Gould knew Le-Roy had been staying. He tried the door—it was locked. Soon after, the club steward arrived and managed to open it. The two men entered and proceeded up to the library. There they found LeRoy lying on the floor in blood, a .38 caliber revolver at his side.

The steward had seen LeRoy just hours earlier, sitting in the library, reading. By the time Gould and the steward had entered the room, LeRoy had been dead for nearly an hour.

Edith's brother, divorced from Emma, had married a pianist and actress named Marcia Baldwin just before Christmas. The union had caught many friends and family by surprise when it was announced in March. LeRoy had first met Marcia while he was staying at his sister Natalie's house in Newport, and it was there the couple honeymooned before returning to New York. Marcia was staying with her mother in Brooklyn while LeRoy stayed in Manhattan, ostensibly looking for a home for himself and his new wife. While LeRoy's financial difficulties had been ongoing for years now and were of little surprise, the news of his suicide came as a shock.

His troubles were revisited now in the press. The Trust Company of the Republic had failed more than ten years earlier, followed by the United States Shipbuilding Company. The first setback had cost LeRoy most of his fortune and resulted in his bankruptcy. It wasn't until 1907 that he had been purged of his bankruptcy status. He had worked hard to pay back what he owed, but then vindictiveness seized him and he sought to litigiously harm those he felt accountable for his downfall. He had managed to reestablish his old firm, Dresser & Co., and at the time of his suicide was working to gain backing for his latest venture—a manufacturing company for steam generators—but was having little luck. Friends in Newport would later recall that he had taken the Shipbuilding failure very hard. He had pinned much of his hope for a return to prosperity on the steam generator patent and its potential manufacture on a large scale—all to no avail.

"Anyone who has known Dresser for the last six months will understand why he took his own life," Gould told the coroner. "It was purely a case of money troubles."

The night before his death, Marcia had received a love letter from her husband. She was now a widow and in seclusion. LeRoy left behind her, an ex-wife, two children, and four sisters: Edith, Natalie, Pauline, and Susan. It was July 1915. For Edith, not quite a year and a half had passed since she'd lost George.

That Christmas might have been a somber one if Edith were a different kind of person with a different circle of family and friends. However, Edith planned for a festive group to be at Biltmore House, and would not abandon the yule traditions she and George had so long enjoyed sharing with their employees.

On December 23, Natalie, John, and the boy's nanny were among a group heading south by train. Natalie was able to arrange an extra car on the train which included two drawing rooms. Aside from the "poor dining car service" (which Natalie always noticed on the Pennsylvania Railroad), it was a comfortable, if long, trip. The train arrived at Biltmore at one o'clock in the afternoon before Christmas Eve. Edith and Cornelia—with drivers and motorcars in tow—went to the station to meet their guests. After a long day's travel and festivities, Natalie sat in her guest room and took out her diary.

"After a very warm welcome and greetings all around we tucked ourselves in and started for Biltmore House," she wrote, "a drive of 3 miles through the beautiful park like grounds, winding in and out until we came to the great Esplanade and saw before us the magnificent house itself built by Richard Hunt."

The weather was warm and bright, especially when compared to the New England weather she and John had just left. They enjoyed lunch and then drove up the road to Asheville for some last-minute holiday shopping. Tea, dinner, and dancing followed, as did much needed laughter. Christmas morning found Edith, Cornelia, Natalie, and John emptying their Christmas stockings before going to 11 a.m. services at All Souls. After lunch, the group assembled in the beautifully decorated carriage house, where a large tree stood surrounded by estate employees and tenants. Now a young woman of fifteen years, and ever as gracious and warm as her mother, Cornelia distributed the presents to those workers and families gathered. That evening, and the three days that followed, were full of games, "moving picture shows," spontaneous theatrical performances—featuring cousins Cornelia and John—fancy dress balls, and quiet talks in the winter sun.

But more than anything, the visit served as tribute to the resilient spirits of the Dresser sisters, the children they were raising, and the friends they kept close.

"So ended a day many had dreaded," Natalie wrote in her diary on Christmas Day, "but by doing and thinking of others, we had forgotten self."

■ ■ ■

After the holidays, Cornelia returned to school in Washington. By that summer, Edith and Cornelia were back at Biltmore, where Edith continued pondering her next financial steps. Summers in the South are known for their afternoon, air-clearing downpours, and while Asheville's plateaued location amid slopes and valleys sometimes protected it from passing storms, warm-weather rainfall in the mountains was not only good for the farms but also quite beautiful. But the citizens of Asheville had seen more than their fair share of wet weather in the summer of 1916. Early in July, a six-day rain had monopolized the skies and now, on a Saturday in mid-July, a steady rain fell yet again. It took more than a little ground soaking to alarm folks, but what they likely did not know of was another storm, one that had formed in the Gulf of Mexico and had already wreaked havoc many, many miles away. This storm, too, would find its way toward the western half of North Carolina, hiking up the Blue Ridge Mountains, bringing its own dose of rain.

Meanwhile, a hurricane grew in the southeast Atlantic, and had already sunk a naval collier—the USS *Hector*—off the coast of Charleston. The coasts of both South Carolina and Georgia had already bowed beneath the force of its winds. That storm, too, tracked through the midlands and headed toward the mountains. East of Asheville, in Hickory, North Carolina, there was much rain and damage. Even nearby Yancey and Mitchell Counties had felt the effects of the rain. The local newspaper coped with some downed wires by hooking up to Atlanta and the Associated Press rather than to the Washington wire. By the time the hurricane reached the western part of North Carolina, the winds seemed tolerable. The rain was not the heaviest anyone had seen, but it just kept coming. The French Broad River, full but not bursting, showed little agitation. Its waters were already high due to recent rains, but the Long Man's mood had not yet turned malevolent.

Sunday, July 16, was a different story.

At first, the rain appeared to be subsiding, but land will only absorb so much water before it sloughs off what it can no longer bear, and the rivers are then forced to swallow it up. Until they can't. At the headwaters of the Swannanoa, the river broke her banks and threatened the new bridge just constructed at Biltmore. She had long met the French Broad in the village, their waters mingling. But now that confluence of Swannanoa and French Broad waters began backing up. Tiny streams and creeks, watery arms incapable of carrying the extra load past ground-soaked banks, became clogged with wood and debris. The water table, full to the brim, could take no more and sent leftovers to the streets, to the rivers. Dams burst, banks gave in. Bits of land sagged and buckled and floated away. Soil, flotsam, and water rushed downstream.

Not one but two Category 4 hurricanes—the one from the Gulf

and the other from the Atlantic—had moved inland and were arriving in the western part of the state, bringing rain that would not stop. The practice of anthropomorphizing weather events with names was not yet a standard practice. However unnamed, these two storms would be forever remembered.

The Monday morning news coming out of Asheville was grim. "Worst Flood in History of Section," the front page of the *Asheville Citizen* proclaimed, calling it the "greatest catastrophe [Asheville] has ever known." At least five were confirmed dead from Asheville and Biltmore and several others were still missing, including two young nurses. The rivers were still rising. By Tuesday morning, the death toll had climbed to eleven. Hundreds of people were homeless, scores of houses had been washed away, and countless people were now missing. Manufacturing plants had been damaged or destroyed, there was no train service in or out of the area, and wires were down. The village and the estate of Biltmore were cut off and reeling from what the French Broad and Swannanoa had wrought. North Carolina was not the only state affected. Waters were still rising in Virginia, Tennessee, and West Virginia. Columbia, South Carolina's Pee Dee, Wateree, and Congaree Rivers were feeling the effects of what had happened beyond their borders. Streams surged, and many crops paid the price. Nearer to Asheville, the Catawba and Linville Rivers burst their banks. Trickling tributaries and quiet creeks quickly morphed into raging terrors, a clamor of rushing horror where babbles once echoed. Landslides tumbled down the sides of mountains and hills, threatening everything in their path.

At this point, the estimated loss of property stood at around $1.5 million in and around Asheville and Biltmore. The cost multiplied greatly—closer to $10 million—if nearby Transylvania and Madison Counties were taken into account. Adding irony to tragedy, the National Casket Company, one of the town's largest businesses, was practically submerged, its wares bobbing among the dead and the debris. The watery chaos consumed warehouses and shacks alike, carrying them away in a fury of rapids. The detritus of lives upended coursed down the rivers and creeks, some meeting sudden, splintering ends as bridges and other concrete structures stopped them in their tracks. Asheville, the Land of the Sky, a good half mile above sea level, was an island.

Miles away, 263 passengers on the *Carolina Special* sat, stuck, near Nocona, just below the hard-hit town of Marshall, where more than one trestle bridge was now gone. The Southern Railway officials had suspended train service coming from the east, citing mudslides on Saluda Mountain as part of the cause. Years of topsoil and humus, branches, and deadwood had sloughed off, blocking tracks. Nothing would move until the mountain slides were cleared. The Saluda slide hurled boulders the size of train cars onto the tracks, and the Catawba River had overflowed. The train was in the thick of trouble. The water came up on them quickly and all those aboard could do was wait and watch as the floodwaters rose—over the banks, approaching the tracks, eventually crawling beneath the passenger cars themselves. This was too much for some, who fled the cars and scrambled up the hillsides in search of higher ground. One of these passengers found a farm, a mule, and a car with a bit of gas. A reporter from the Associated Press made his way all the way back to Asheville. When at last the water stopped rising, the wheels of the train stood in several inches of water and remained unable to move. Meager dining car provisions did not last long, and the following morning, the passengers assessed their situation. There were no houses to be seen, but soon farmers came down out of the mountains, bringing honey and ham, and offering sandwiches to the stranded. Automobiles, once they were able, traveled to the train with blankets and even some bacon.

Back in the village, waters had begun slowly creeping into All Souls. The train depot was filling, its tracks gone from sight. The fast-rising waters in the village took most citizens by surprise, including three young women—Mabel Foister and Charlotte Walker, nurses, and Charlotte's younger sister, Marion, a student of fifteen years old. The sisters had lost their mother years earlier, and Charlotte was like a guardian now. The three women were boarders of Captain

James Lipe, a military veteran and superintendent of skilled labor at Biltmore—one of George's earliest hires. That day, the young women joined up with the captain, two of his daughters, and a Mr. Thompson. The captain's oldest daughter was Mrs. Milholland, and Kathleen Lipe was just shy of eighteen years of age. Together, this small group headed across the village green and toward the lodge gate of the Biltmore in search of higher, drier ground and perhaps supplies. The water was around their ankles at this point, but began rising faster as they reached Lodge Street. Mrs. Milholland made it across the street safely, as did Mr. Thompson.

Then a rising wave unexpectedly poured down Lodge Street and none of them could evade the torrent as the waters carried them off. Mrs. Milholland and Mr. Thompson disappeared down Hendersonville Road and soon landed in a tree. The others, who had not managed to get across Lodge Street, caught the brunt of the current. As they were swept past the village green, the captain, his daughter Kathleen, and the three young women scrambled desperately for the trees. Those trees, imported from England and transplanted here to George's model village, had grown relatively undisturbed for nearly two decades. Captain Lipe and his tempest-tossed party hit a sudden stop as they were flung into the branches. They held fast.

Frank Lipe, the Captain's son, had set out earlier to find his father and sisters. He spotted the elder of his sisters in a tree with Mr. Thompson and started to make his way toward them, tree by tree. He had almost reached them when the water carried him off to a bank well above the waters. Milholland and Thompson held on. Near the estate's lodge gate, Captain Lipe, his daughter Kathleen, and Mabel, Charlotte, and Marion clung for hours to the tree that had snagged them. Captain Lipe's home—which they may have regretted leaving—would have provided no better shelter. Shortly after they left, it was washed away.

For nearly four hours, Charlotte had been holding Marion, her younger sister, as close to the tree as she possibly could. Finally, weakened by the ceaseless pounding of the water, Charlotte's grasp gave way. Mabel tried unsuccessfully to help Marion, her efforts bested by the churning waters. Both she and Marion were ripped from what little safety they had found and washed away. For the moment, Captain Lipe held on—to the tree and his daughter Kathleen. He managed to remove his coat, which he used to tie his daughter to the tree. Then he was gone, swallowed by the water.

Onlookers on higher ground had been watching the terrifying scene unfold. Now they watched as Kathleen, exhausted, hung suspended by her father's coat. The prospect of reaching her while the waters still swirled seemed implausible. Time passed, waters rose, and Kathleen's coat harness sagged. Suddenly, a small craft—just a few timbers lashed together—with two men aboard headed for Kathleen. They had almost reached the tree when their makeshift ferry cracked in two. One man jumped for the tree, reaching it safely. The other man swam hard for the shore. A Mr. Cooper, another employee of the Biltmore Estate, set out swimming toward the pair. Dodging debris and carrying a rope, he reached them. He hurled the rope toward the man, who tied it beneath Kathleen's arms. Just then, the waters rose to fetch her, snatching her from the precarious safety of the tree. She washed away from the boughs, but the knot held. From All Souls Cathedral emerged a proper boat with three men aboard, fighting vigorously against the seething floodwaters. When they pulled Kathleen aboard, she was barely conscious. The men navigated their way through the mayhem toward Biltmore Hospital, and Kathleen was safe. So, too, were her sister Mrs. Milholland, and Mr. Thompson. However, the fates of her father, Captain Lipe; and of Mabel, Charlotte, and Marion, remained unknown.

As soon as she was able, Edith organized workers from the estate to help provide relief and to search for the missing. Edith provided food for all those who had volunteered to look for Captain Lipe and the young women, and she worked her way through the village as best she could, arranging for blankets, supplies, and nourishment. The volunteer efforts soon paid off, but in the most somber of ways. The floodwaters had lodged the corpses of the two orphaned sisters beneath some shrubs and undergrowth on the south side of the estate. The search party had not yet turned up Mabel, but volunteers assumed that she, too, had suffered a similar fate. No expense would be spared, Edith said, to find the body of the heroic Captain Lipe.

The region had suffered a flood nearly seven feet higher than any in history—a figure which could be only estimated, since many of the area's gauges had been washed away. Railroad cars sat covered in water, with their tracks and railbeds washed right out from under them. One such track was left standing in midair, like a railroad through the clouds. The French Broad River had proved worthy of the translation of one of its Cherokee names: "Where He Races." The Swannanoa River, though small by comparison, proved its power, menace, and extreme unpredictability. The death toll climbed to twenty-nine by Wednesday, but the total would eventually reach upward of eighty. The bodies of Captain Lipe and Mabel Foister were eventually found. Mabel lay beneath bushes on the estate; Captain Lipe's body was not recovered until July 20, roughly a half mile from the Biltmore entrance. Receding waters brought relief and sadness, and as sun and time pulled back the cloak of the floodwaters and the full scope of devastation was laid bare. Damage estimates across the state reached $15 to $20 million. Mountain Island Mill, a large textile mill in Gaston Country, washed away completely, leaving no sign that it had ever existed.

An important leadership role now fell to Edith, the Biltmore Estate and, by extension, young Cornelia, who would one day inherit this wounded landscape. The estate's crops were damaged, and its farming interests suffered as silt blanketed nearly 100 acres of corn. Machinery, rusting in the damp fields, would need to be replaced. Three hundred acres of Biltmore nurseries were completely destroyed, so much of Chauncey Beadle's dedicated efforts and meticulous care gone. "We are heavy losers," Beadle later wrote an acquaintance, "eighty-five percent of our nursery stock having been destroyed: but the material losses are nothing to the loss of life which occurred right in our midst. It was so appalling."

Weeks afterward, some houses were still half-underwater, and the hospital and church were bursting with those in need. There were now countless homeless. Incomes and livelihoods continued to be threatened as businesses puzzled over how they might possibly come back from such a tragedy.

For Edith, it had been a trying few years. George's sudden death in 1914. Her nephew Alfred's tragic end in 1915. Then the suicide of her older brother, LeRoy, the man who had walked her down the aisle when she married. And just when she was beginning to make her peace with these new circumstances, as finances and life seemed to be approaching some semblance of normal, nature had dealt a blow of biblical proportions.

14

Homespun
and a Great War

"Makes Children and Adults as Fat as Pigs."

So proclaimed the small bottle's label and its ubiquitous advertisements. The cartoon image accompanying the disturbingly enticing text featured a pig's corpulent body topped off with the head of a grinning child, joined by a lace collar. Like some porcine centaur, this was the image that sold bottle after bottle of Grove's Tasteless Chill Tonic. Yours for a mere 50 cents, Grove's tonic claimed to be the "Best Cure for Malaria, Chills, Fever. On the Market over 20 Years. 1½ Million Bottles Sold Last Year. No Cure, No Pay." This odd piglet-child had bankrolled the creation of Asheville's latest and most fabulous resort hotel: the Grove Park Inn.

Tennessee-born Edwin Wiley Grove was a teenager during the Civil War. In his early twenties, he took a job at the local pharmacy in Paris, Tennessee, and began to think about how he could set himself apart. Grove worked, planned, and eventually bought his employer's small business, renaming it Grove's Pharmacy. His imagination was fixed on what he thought would be his financial salvation: tasteless quinine.

This was an era of curious remedies for aggravating ills and their symptoms. Tar Heel Cough Syrup. Electric Bitters. Shiloh's Vitalizer. Acker's Blood Elixir. Magnetic Nervine. There were also the ever-present offerings of the Lydia E. Pinkham Medicine Company, with its patent-protected Pinkham's Vegetable Compound, which claimed to offer relief from menstrual cramps, menopause, and depression. Pinkham's single-handedly brought attention to conditions affecting women, which were roundly ignored by the male-dominated medical profession.

Noted for its antimalarial properties, quinine was a bitter—if somewhat effective—powder to swallow. It helped with fever; it reduced chills. It was no cure-all, but it alleviated some symptoms. Grove set to work on a formula that would make the popular treatment more palatable. The first of these he named Feberlin, which required a prescription for purchase. He kept at it, choosing to add sugar, lemon, and the all-purpose medicinal additive, alcohol. And so Grove's Tasteless Chill Tonic was born. It required no prescription, and transformed Grove from struggling small businessman into malarial magnate. Near the turn of the century, sales of Grove's bottles of Tasteless Chill Tonic were greater than those of Coca-Cola.

Grove formed the Paris Medicine Company and relocated to St. Louis, Missouri. His product list expanded to include Grove's Laxative Bromo Quinine, touted as a treatment for the common cold. When he needed manufacturers for his new tablets he approached Parke, Davis in Detroit. The business grew, as did Grove's bank account. Whenever exhaustion occasionally set in, Grove's doctors—like so many other physicians—recommended a stay in a small mountain town in the Blue Ridge Mountains. He packed up some Chill Tonic—which Grove would later advertise as a restorative for "energy and vitality by creating new, healthy blood"—and headed for the breathing porches of Asheville.

During one such trip, Grove invited a young Parke, Davis employee, Fred Seely, to join him. There, Seely promptly fell in love with Grove's daughter, Evelyn. Seely left Parke, Davis for good and went to work for the Paris Medicine Company and the father of his bride-to-be. Seely went on to manage his father-in-law's firm, and the pair expanded their business ventures, investing in real estate and, eventually, publishing, distributing a daily newspaper, the *Atlanta Georgian*.

In 1909, Grove bought 408 acres in Asheville, a large swath of which was on Sunset Mountain. It was the perfect site for a resort in a town whose tourist population was still fed by tuberculosis fears and had been buttressed, in the early 1900s, by the construction of Biltmore House and the development of the village. Not unlike a young George Vanderbilt decades before him, Edwin Wiley Grove found himself marveling at the panorama that surrounded him from atop Sunset Mountain. He, too, was charmed by the endless sky and the silver-green ranges that basked in the late-afternoon tangerine glow that had given this mountain its name.

In 1912, Seely and Grove unburdened themselves of the unprofitable *Atlanta Georgian*, palming it off on William Randolph Hearst for $200,000, and turned their attentions to the building of a resort hotel. After soliciting designs from several architects—Richard Sharp Smith's firm among them—Grove was still not happy. He wanted a certain kind of inn, with an older, homier feel. The Old Faithful Inn in Yellowstone National Park was an early source of inspiration for Grove who, though he insisted upon modern amenities, did not want flash. When son-in-law Seely—who had studied architecture—whipped up a sketch, Grove was on board. They hired an architectural engineer out of Atlanta—G. W. McKibbin—who transformed Seely's ideas into formal structural plans for a grand new hotel overlooking Asheville and the mountains beyond.

The granite walls, four feet thick in spots, grew rapidly. Mules and steam shovels and wagons hauled men and mortar and rock. The roof would be fireproof. Jagged, uncut stone would protrude dramatically from the facade and chimneys. Italian masons—some of whom had worked on the construction of Biltmore House—now helped erect the stone walls of the hotel. The Grove Park Inn opened in July 1913, its earliest guests receiving complimentary bottles of Grove's Elixir. Furnishings had been provided by Elbert Hubbard—a friend of Grove—and his Arts and Crafts Roycrofters out of East Aurora,

New York. The wood artisans created chairs, sideboards, and stunning clocks. The copper shop fabricated lighting fixtures—seven hundred electric fixtures in total.

Two grand fireplaces, each 36 feet wide, anchored the 120-foot lobby or "Big Room" (eventually dubbed the Great Hall), each of them requiring 20 tons of boulders to construct. When finished, the Big Room became the prime relaxation spot for guests, who rested in red leather-upholstered rocking chairs and enjoyed complimentary yet tasteless quinine. One-piece rugs—four hundred of them—throughout the hotel were fashioned at the Tapestry Works of Aubusson, France. The rugs in the Big Room alone were valued at $5,000. Advertisements proclaimed "The finest Resort Hotel in the world has been built at Sunset Mountain, Asheville, NC." Secretary of State William Jennings Bryan gave the address at the inn's grand opening. "I have never seen any structure to equal this," Bryan said to the crowd. "I congratulate these men. They have built for the ages." Toasts were made, praise heaped, and in keeping with Asheville's early adoption of prohibition, grape juice was served.

In January 1915, after the Grove Park Inn had been in business only about eighteen months, Fred Seely leased the Grove Park Inn from his father-in-law. Seely had been prepared to leave the now flourishing resort and take a job in Washington, DC, but an offer from his father-in-law to manage the sprawling property proved to be precisely what Seely craved. He advertised the hotel in places like New York City, where he maintained a booking office. The hotel already had an impressive reputation. The stunning setting and quality furnishings—including oak-and-copper smoke stands and American Beauty vases designed and handmade by the Roycroft School—enticed discerning travelers. Branding was a consideration, so the omnipresent "G.P.I." logo was carved into the back of every chair placed in the hotel's massive dining room. The chairs were wooden, simple in design, with straight backs. At the Grove Park Inn, there were no signs of the frilly over-the-topness of the Victorian Age, only the rustic appeal and handmade charm of the Arts and Crafts movement. Seely seemed to understand that maintaining a certain decorum of elegant simplicity within this homey atmosphere was key.

From the moment he had taken over management of the Grove Park Inn, Seely sought to put his own stamp on the operation. He had opinions and was not shy about sharing them. No writing in the Great Hall, he strongly urged his guests—you might spill ink on the rugs. Please use the designated Writing Room. Women were not to be seen smoking in public areas. Seely bought a Skinner organ for the resort's Great Hall. Ernest Skinner had gotten his start working for George Hutchings, whom George had hired to build his organ for All Souls Cathedral. Now the student had become a maestro of pipes. Ernest Skinner himself came to town to ensure that the installation went smoothly, only miles north of where his former boss's commission still accompanied Sunday worship.

In some respects, these two iconic Asheville structures—Biltmore House and the Grove Park Inn—were at opposite ends of the design spectrum, the town, and an era. South of downtown Asheville was Biltmore; to the north, Sunset Mountain and the Grove Park Inn. Biltmore House was smooth, scored, gleaming limestone, while the Grove Park Inn was rough, unpolished granite boulders plucked right from the earth. Subtle stenciled rose motifs lined the walls of the Grove Park Inn's palm court, while wrought-iron fixtures and bronze sculptures were featured in Biltmore House's court. Marble surfaces and coffered ceilings greeted the rarefied Biltmore guest, while wicker rockers welcomed whomever wanted a reservation at the Grove Park Inn.

In other respects, the destinations had much in common. Both embraced the beauty of their surroundings. Both displayed uniquely captivating—if quite divergent—architectural design. Both were playing a role in the still evolving tourist economy. Each was magnificent in its own way, and they both embraced the growth of the arts and crafts movement: Grove and Seely through their design and furnishings, and Biltmore—more specifically, Edith—through the Biltmore Estate Industries and her schooling efforts in the village.

■ ■ ■

Once the floodwaters had subsided and Edith had assessed the damage to the estate and to the village—which was substantial—she had contacted her trusted local adviser, Judge Junius Adams of the Asheville firm Adams & Adams. She asked him to study all the estate's debts and its holdings and make a recommendation. Adams advised selling the village and eventually the industries. However, Adams also believed that a bit of patience was needed, as pursuing this path too aggressively with the specter of a Great War looming on the horizon was inadvisable. Still, they had made some progress. In March 1917, the Southern Railway Company had paid $175,000 for 110 acres of estate lands. The railway's right of way would pass very close to the entrance of the Biltmore Estate itself and included parcels of land that held Biltmore's greenhouses. There were plans for a new terminal facility and passenger waiting area.

From the time Edith first became aware of Eleanor Vance and Charlotte Yale and their small woodworking class in the village until now—roughly seventeen years—the outfit had developed into an integral part of the life of the village and of Asheville, impacting many lives along the way. Biltmore Estate Industries had established itself as a resource for quality mountain woodworking crafts, yarns, and handwoven fabric more commonly referred to as "homespun." Sales and notoriety now reached far beyond the city limits of Asheville. In 1914, Edith had purchased another mill, from J. H. Wright and the Reems Creek Woolen Mills, up the road in Weaverville. In 1915, Biltmore Estate Industries had won the Gold Medal for Hand Made and Hand Carved Furniture at the Panama-Pacific International Exposition held in San Francisco. Fashions featuring fabrics spun on Biltmore Estate Industries' looms had been featured in *Vogue* and *Harper's Bazaar* magazines, and were worn by noted public figures like the Schwabs, Thomas Edison, Henry Ford, Amy

Du Pont, President Wilson, Elbert Hubbard and, of course, Edith's socially prominent sister Natalie.

However, Biltmore Estate Industries had outgrown its current facilities. The success and popularity of the school and its products had the outfit figuratively and literally bursting at the seams. Additionally, its instructors had moved on. Shortly after George's death, in 1915, Vance and Yale had moved to the nearby small town of Tryon to start another school and woodworking shop, the Tryon Toy-Makers. Biltmore Estate Industries was growing fast and without its original leaders at the helm. Orders placed in January 1917 had not yet been filled. Now it was April. The busy enterprise had grown in size and renown, but remained essentially a philanthropic venture for Edith. Still, it did have value on the market. It, too, could be sold to help support the estate. To whom the property would go, however, would be important to Edith should she decide to go that route. Something so cherished, something that Edith had watched grow from the ground up, ought to go to the right buyer. That buyer, it turned out, was up the road at the Grove Park Inn.

The Grove Park Inn and the Biltmore Estate were already doing business together. All of the milk and cream that the resort provided their guests came from the Biltmore Dairy. When Seely initially approached Edith and began discussing with her the possibility of taking over all of Biltmore Estate Industries and moving it to Sunset Mountain, Edith was not immediately convinced. Selling Biltmore Estate Industries was not like selling land. This was akin to selling an idea, namely that every choice, every project embarked upon by people in her position should give back to the community. She may not have always stated this, but with each action she had taken with the development of that homespun shop in the village, she had made it clear that this was more than just an investment of money, it was an investment in people. The school and industries had been investments in her neighbors and in their future.

Seely had ample business experience and had seen the profits flowing in from his father-in-law's line of products. But Biltmore

Estate Industries was not Chill Tonic. Seely eventually convinced Edith he would make a "suitable guardian" for the child she had nurtured so long. The workers, some of whom had started studying with Vance and Yale as children, would remain. Seely initially offered $10,000 for the Industries. Chauncey Beadle told Edith he thought $12,500 was more like it. He managed to negotiate for somewhat better terms and Edith sold. Once the deal was done, Seely commenced the building of five new workshops next to the hotel, expanding the Grove Park Inn's footprint on Sunset Mountain. He hoped to have the workshops ready by September. (One of the workshops' early projects would be to add arms to the inn's original Roycroft dining-room chairs.) Seely decided to announce his acquisition publicly. In April 1917, he wrote an open letter to the newspaper discussing his views on the newly acquired Biltmore Estate Industries.

Seely acknowledged the tremendous strides that Edith, Vance, and Yale had made in the years since Edith first took it upon herself to foster the school in the village. It had gone from being a small workshop to a fully operating school, eventually overtaking a small electrical works building on the Biltmore Estate when that shop in the village could no longer suffice. After that, a building that had once housed George's automobiles was transformed into a weaving shop. It took an estimated nineteen motors to run all the machinery now required to prep hardwoods like walnut and cherry before the pieces were passed to the trained hands of the carvers. The entire business had gone from selling goods locally to selling local goods across the nation. "There is no question," Seely wrote, "but that woodcarving as it has been revived at Biltmore is finer, more perfect and more sincere that nearly anything we find by artists of olden times."

He estimated that in the coming year, Biltmore Estate Industries would go through twelve to fifteen thousand pounds of wool. He rightly praised Edith for taking what he thought to be initially a "crude" homespun industry and, through her commitment, turning it into something quite extraordinary. She was kind, yes. She had been determined to take on this enterprise and do it in the best way in order to turn out products of the highest possible quality while giving an opportunity to local boys and girls who, otherwise, might have little in the way of schooling or trade development available to them. Seely noted, "Nobody but a person of her wealth could have done it."

Might she have spent that money differently, directed it toward the house, the dairy, or set it aside? Yes. She might have. Clearly mere philanthropy was not her aim, either. She could have given the money to any local charity and let them see what they could do with it. She had instead taken an interest that was more than financial. Seely observed that Edith's success with Biltmore Estate Industries came with additional burdens. In a sense, its very success made it necessary for her to turn the business over to someone else. Seely did not think Edith could take the business to the next level. The sale would also mean alleviating a little more of the responsibility that had fallen to Edith since George's death, a situation aggravated by the merciless flood the year before. Now with the sale of Biltmore Estate Industries, Edith would have more money and fewer financial—and administrative—responsibilities.

Under Seely's watch, the homespun fabric offered by the Industries would continue to be known on the marketplace as Biltmore Homespuns. The storefront in the village of Biltmore would remain open for business. Seely would drop the word "Estate" from the business's full name, once operations moved to their new home at the Grove Park Inn, but the name "Biltmore" would remain. Edith agreed. Seely knew that it would take a few months at least before he could move all of the materials and machinery to their new home behind the Grove Park Inn. Once there, however, he believed that the inn's existing sales and shipping departments, along with other business facilities that served the inn and its guests, would help ease the transition.

By May 1917—just a month after sealing the deal with Edith—Seely began advertising for supplies and the personnel to shape them into products worthy of the reputation of Biltmore Industries. He did not delegate this task, but instead handled the search personally. He placed an ad in the Asheville papers for a wool spinner and hand-loom weaver: "Call Mr. Seely, Grove Park Inn. 4771-5-7." In Tennessee, he advertised for wool. "Wool wanted for cash," read his newspaper ad. Seely sought 5,000 to 10,000 pounds of wool direct from sheep farmers.

Seely intended to modernize the equipment while maintaining the educational aspect of the industries as well. Seely felt confident that it would not be long before product demand doubled. The shop's carvings found their way from mountain workshop to the halls and sitting rooms of the Grove Park Inn and the homes of senators who dwelled on Fifth Avenue in New York City. Hanging in a place of honor in the Grove Park Inn's Great Hall was an eagle, released from its cherrywood bonds by a young woman carver from North Carolina—a "mountain girl," as the newspapers liked to say.

Under Seely, the reputation of Biltmore Industries spread, and the Grove Park Inn continued to attract notable guests and visiting dignitaries, including the "Four Vagabonds"—inventor Thomas Edison, automobile mogul Henry Ford, industrialist Harvey Firestone, and naturalist John Burroughs. This group's annual camping excursions to wilderness spots ranging from the Adirondacks in the north to the woods of Tennessee in the south, started in 1915 and would continue through 1924, give or take a camper or two. Their entourage might contain up to fifty vehicles, complete with staff, cooks, and photographers. Burroughs observed, "It often seemed to me that we were a luxuriously equipped expedition going forth to seek discomfort." In August 1918, their two-week combination camping/ road trip took them "into the land of Dixie" and included a day's rest at what Burroughs called "the wonderful Grove Park Inn," as Seely's guest.

Down the road in Tryon, North Carolina, Vance and Yale were busy with their newly established Tryon Toy-Makers and Weavers. There they—and the young students they trained—crafted hand-carved toys and homespuns. They maintained a correspondence and close friendship with Seely, whose advice they clearly valued as their business grew. He, too—often addressing them in letters as "sisters"—appreciated their skills and counsel as he took over the Industries from Edith. "She is such a direct, sincere and fair minded person that we felt sure she would be happy to know the real facts of your word," the pair wrote to Seely several years after his purchase of the enterprise. "You will find her from now on a helpful and true friend to the Industries."

The Grove Park Inn was a significant client as well, and the Tryon Toy-Makers's "Morris the Horse," "Kicking Rabbit," "Sawing Cats," and other fine toys and linens could be found throughout the resort. Edith, too, stayed in touch. This pair of socially progressive women who simply wanted to give people a way to express themselves and make a living had managed, with Edith's help, to launch an entire industry that was now poised for department-store contracts. A young man named George Arthur, who had started years earlier in their tiny village workshop, was now general manager and superintendent of the Biltmore Industries at the Grove Park Inn. Virtually everyone working in the new facilities had started in Biltmore alongside Vance and Yale. Now those three women—Edith, Eleanor, and Charlotte—had to let it go and let it grow.

And so Edith witnessed another part of her life in Biltmore, her work in the village, slip away. There must have been relief, there must have been some sense of closure. There must, too, have been some sense of pride mixed with loss. The forest that surrounded her home was still there, but only a fraction of it now belonged to the estate. The village, so carefully laid out, still recovering from the flood, was now 110 acres smaller since Southern Railway had come along. Now she saw Biltmore Estate Industries go, something she had built and nurtured. So much of what was a part of the estate when she first rode down that flower-strewn road as a new bride was no more.

■　■　■

That same April Seely bought Biltmore Industries, a friend of his—and occasional visitor to the Grove Park Inn—President Woodrow Wilson, made an announcement that many felt was inevitable, though nonetheless alarming.

"The world must be made safe for democracy," Wilson said on April 2, 1917, as he stood before Congress and told that legislative body that the United States had broken off diplomatic relations with Germany. The war an ocean away felt closer now. Wilson did not go so far as to declare war, but stated that "preparations for war are being made."

Within four days of Wilson's speech, the United States officially declared war on Germany. London's St. Paul's Cathedral hosted a service honoring the United States' decision to enter the Great War, attended by King George and Queen Mary along with a number of cabinet members and ambassadors. The Stars and Stripes waved alongside the Union Jack on countless streets in the United Kingdom, outside pubs and shops, homes and factories, even on the Victoria Tower of Westminster.

Edith's nephew by marriage, William Henry III—whose father, Alfred, had died aboard the *Lusitania*—was himself serving as a midshipman in the US Naval Reserve at a mere fifteen years of age. However, even before the American soldiers went off to war, Edith had already begun volunteering for the war effort. In early 1916, when United States allies Britain and France were deep in the brutal trenches, Edith formed an Asheville branch of the American Relief Society. The group assisted with the war effort abroad, making bandages and gathering supplies for British soldiers, Edith serving as local president. As that summer arrived and she and Cornelia were at home at Biltmore, Edith continued her support of the local National Guard and beseeched the same relief society she had founded to provide hospital supplies for US soldiers stationed on the Mexican border. Edith and George had enrolled as life members in the North Carolina branch of the American Red Cross when it formed there in 1906, and now Edith hosted a gala in support of the organization at the Country Club of Asheville. Even when she was not in North Carolina, Edith remained active in the war effort, chairing benefit balls and making donations. But her volunteer efforts were not always glamorous charity events. "Buy a forget-me-not and save a Belgian baby," she implored passersby on the streets of Washington, DC. As a charter member of the American Red Cross Refreshment Corps in their DC chapter, she worked in the canteen at Union Station serving soldiers. She also paid for a young nurse from New Jersey to travel abroad and volunteer for the Red Cross.

Edith and others across the state of North Carolina knew that the National Guard was in need of a training and mobilization site. Before the official declaration of war was made, Edith had offered 120 acres of the Biltmore Estate as the site of just such a mobilization camp. She made her offer to state officials who sent the word along to Washington. The same month Edith accepted Seely's offer, she found herself entertaining Colonel H. J. Slocum of the United States Army, along with a party of other fact finders. The group was on orders from the War Department to inspect the estate. Maj. Francis Clemenger, a local Asheville officer, was eager to have Biltmore serve as a mobilization camp for the growing volunteer army. Slocum, staying at the Battery Park Hotel with his wife, liked what Edith had to show him of the site. The location was desirable, fitting snugly between two rivers. There were forests beyond and varied terrain, level where needed. All in all, excellent training grounds.

The possibility that a training camp could be located at the estate was big news and meant big business. "Biltmore Likely to Get Big Government Training Camp," the *Asheville Citizen* proclaimed on the front page of the paper the day after the inspection. "Government May Accept Mrs. Vanderbilt's Offer of Splendid Camp Site." It was already the lead story, though no formal acceptance had been made. The government had several issues to assess, including the climate, water availability and purity, and any danger of malaria. (There was, of course, an ample supply of Tasteless Chill Tonic available nearby). All these had to be considered before anything was set in stone.

The army was expected to stay for a year, though there was also the possibility that the camp might become a permanent training facility after the war was over. A selective conscription bill was before Congress, and the possibility now existed that more soldiers beyond the current crop of volunteer forces might use the area, with all the horses, munitions, and vehicles that went along with them. Though Slocum believed the site too small for a full division, a brigade could easily set up camp there. For the time being, six thousand soldiers were anticipated—three regiments of 2,000 men each—and the town had already begun in earnest to raise money for the necessary facilities and their supporting infrastructure. An estimated $15,000 to $20,000 in funds was going to be necessary to provide the camp with everything it would need, including pipes to carry an extended water line from the city source out to the site on the estate. In 1917, there were fewer than six thousand men living in Asheville. Therefore, adding another six thousand bodies to that number—grown men who would be training day in and out, men who would need to be fed, bathed, and have clothes laundered—meant that the water supply issue was no small one. It could change the face of the city, village, and estate entirely.

Seely had already volunteered to help with the fundraising, donating $500 of his own money to the cause and taking on the role of chairman of the collecting committee. Coca-Cola followed suit with a matching donation of $500. The needs were great: mess tents, latrines, bathing and sleeping facilities, administrative buildings, and electricity to support it all. While patriotism played some part in the fervor surrounding the potential arrival of the camp, the more business-minded of the community saw the influx of government war dollars as a potential long-term boon for the city as well. As soon as soldiers collected their pay, they would at some point spend that money outside the gates of the estate. No wonder other cities— Raleigh, Greensboro, Wilmington—were vying for the camp as well.

The US government would eventually construct upwards of 32 cantonments, or training camps, throughout the nation to turn men into soldiers. And while several of these were situated in the southeast, none were built in Asheville. The closest camps were in Charlotte, North Carolina, and Spartanburg and Greenville, South Carolina. But that did not mean the Asheville area was completely exempt from duty. The Kenilworth Inn, overlooking the village of Biltmore and recently reconstructed after its 1909 fire, served as a military hospital. Every free patch of lawn was used for rehabilitative drills for recovering soldiers, and officers and staff were housed in Asheville and the village of Biltmore.

Edith remained a unifying and supportive force in grand fashion in Asheville. On August 8, 1917, a group of men stood in the shadow of the grand Masonic Temple in downtown Asheville. Crowds watched and waited as the four hundred guardsmen stepped off. The group made their way across Pack Square and continued through the center of the mountain city, crowds of Asheville citizens cheering as the First Regiment band led the military procession down what was now known as Biltmore Avenue. As the boisterous patriotic affair neared the village of Biltmore, the marchers turned toward the plaza green. There Edith sat "reviewing" the soldiers who marched past in their parade dress as regimental tunes kept time. Then Edith hopped in her motorcar and joined up with the troops as the procession continued toward the village green. There she hosted more than three thousand adults and children gathered to watch a day of contests for the local national guard.

By the time the sky opened up above the festivities, no one seemed to care—Edith least of all. The soldiers pitched their tents in Biltmore's village green, and members of the four invited units prepared to compete. The cavalry was up first, for a rescue race. Close formation, calisthenics, and bayonet drill competitions followed. But nothing entertains a crowd more, despite the clouds of war and rain weighing heavy on everyone, than a good old-fashioned tug-of-war. Company B took on the Field Hospital Corps. With one pistol shot the men were dug in, the white handkerchief slowly inching its way toward the victorious Field Hospital Corps team. Edith stayed from start to finish that day, handing out cigarettes, congratulating winners of the various events, and declining offers of shelter from the rain. Edith then hosted a luncheon for the soldiers after the competition.

War continued. That December, Biltmore Industries held its traditional Christmas sale featuring homespun items and beautifully carved wood objects. The firm was doing well, boasting between four and five thousand dollars' worth of woodworking stock and about two thousand dollars' worth of Biltmore Homespuns. A pall hung over the season, however, and there was sadness beyond the battlefields of the Great War that winter. On December 2, 1917, Reverend Dr. Rodney Swope died. The sixty-six-year-old rector was remembered by the *Asheville Citizen* as an "energetic friend" and one who "did not dogmatize" and who "accomplished much in that quiet and modest way which endeared him to hundreds of people."

15

Freedoms and Flappers

World War I left its mark on Biltmore House and its wide circle of friends and family. George's dear friend William B. Osgood Field did his duty in various capacities and locations. Among other roles, he served in the US Army Officers' Reserve Corps and in the Signal Officers' Reserve Corps before being assigned assistant to chief of the Military Intelligence Division in Washington, DC, eventually earning the rank of major. He stayed in touch with Edith, who wrote "Dear Willie" from her home in Washington regarding his latest assignment in the capital. "Thanks a thousand and one times for sending me the photograph of 'my soldier boy,'" she wrote her old friend. "I know you are going to make good and that you will find the work intensely interesting."

In 1918, Edith leased four buildings in Biltmore Village and family property on Staten Island to the US government. When the Spanish flu epidemic came on the heels of the war, Edith opened her home to Red Cross women workers. As with other sicknesses in other times, Edith rode out with soup and other supplies for estate workers suffering from the flu. More than fifty Biltmore employees served during the war, and Edith commissioned a service flag in their honor: blue stars for those who returned safely, gold for those lives lost, all mounted on a white background with a bold red border. It would hang in the banquet hall.

The Great War ended on November 11, 1918, as the eleventh hour of the eleventh day of the eleventh month arrived, and hostilities ceased all along the Western front. What economic boom existed in America during the war seemed to evaporate with the last gunsmoke of battle.

The presidential election of 1920 saw a Democratic governor, James M. Cox, running against a Republican senator, Warren G. Harding—both of them newspaper editors, both from Ohio. Cox's running mate was recent assistant secretary of the Navy Franklin Delano Roosevelt, and Harding's was Calvin "Silent Cal" Coolidge. (Biltmore guest Alice Roosevelt is famously credited with stating that Coolidge looked as though he had been "weaned on a pickle.") Almost as important as what the candidates themselves had to say was the point of view of another demographic: women.

With the ratification of the Nineteenth Amendment to the Constitution on August 18, 1920—"Proposing an amendment to the Constitution extending the right of suffrage to women"—the presidential election of 1920 became particularly historic. (It would also be the last time voters listened to the campaign speeches via phonograph.) When November 2, 1920, arrived, women cast their votes for commander-in-chief alongside men for the first time. The Harding-Coolidge ticket won handily, routing Cox and Roosevelt with nearly 30 percent more of the popular vote—a winning margin that has not been bested since.

Shifting tides for women were felt far from Washington, DC. Edith's former sister-in-law, Alva—now Alva Belmont—had evolved from social-climbing strategist of the Four Hundred to become a women's suffrage activist. She founded the New York Political Equity League and was on the executive committee of the more militant National Woman's Party. Within months of women voting for the first time, Alva would be elected the organization's president. Alva supported the cause with both pen and pocketbook. Local elections also saw increased opportunities for women, Asheville included. Public meetings in Asheville on women's suffrage had been happening for decades, and the North Carolina Equal Suffrage

Association in Asheville was the state's first, officially ushering tar-heel women into the movement in 1894.

Black Mountain native Lillian Exum Clement, who attended high school and college in Asheville, was a twenty-six-year-old law-yer in the year 1920, and the first woman in the state to ever open her own law office. Influential Asheville Democrats knew which way the political winds were blowing that election year, and asked Clement to run for Buncombe County's seat in the North Carolina senate. "Brother Exum," as she was sometimes known, accepted the chal-lenge and won the election by a landslide even greater than that of President Harding—10,368 to 41—making her the first female leg-islator in North Carolina.

"I know that years from now there will be many other women in politics," Clement said, "but you have to start a thing."

However, another feminine first had occurred before those historic November elections. In late October 1920, Edith was elected presi-dent of the North Carolina Agricultural Society, which ran the State Fair, among other things. The decision was unanimous, making Edith the first woman in the history of the state to ever hold that office.

"There are a few women in the United States whose interest in agricultural and related social problems is noteworthy," the *Durham Morning Herald* reported, "and among them Mrs. George W. Van-derbilt is conspicuous."

The media applauded the choice, citing Edith's role in a number of agricultural pursuits, including the Boys' Corn clubs and the Girls' Canning clubs, and the importance of citizens of a commonwealth who "know how to transform wealth into welfare."

Days later, on October 28, 1920, Edith the newly elected pres-ident stood alongside Cornelia and others as a bronze marker was placed at the entrance to Pisgah National Forest.

"This portion, eighty-three thousand three hundred and ninety-eight acres was formerly Pisgah Forest established by George W.

Vanderbilt in 1891 and the earliest example of forestry on a large scale on private lands in America. Acquired by the United States 21st May, 1914."

Edith watched as the legacy of George's land was honored. She had played an important role in his endeavors, and now, like so many other women of 1920, was embarking on her own.

Edith had followed Junius Adams's advice on streamlining affairs at Biltmore in order to protect the financial futures of herself, Cornelia, and the estate. To that end, the village of Biltmore was now up for sale—every bit of it.

Up to this point, those living in the village could not buy the homes in which they lived. The entire village—homes, offices, shops—belonged to the Vanderbilts. Edith had sold some tracts to the Southern Railway Company, and others, but the current sale would be of a much higher order. The war was past, the time was now. Indeed, Adams suggested selling more than just the village itself. He suggested offering up another 1,500 or so acres of land that bordered the road heading south to Hendersonville. Taxes on this and the other lands were taking a financial toll on the family's budget, and these particular tracts could be sold off as residential lots.

The value of the offering attracted outside attention, and when George Stephens of the Appalachian Realty Company arrived in Asheville from Charlotte earlier that year of 1920, he was ready to do business. The brisk sale included most of the structures throughout the village: homes, the post office, various shops. All Souls, the heart of the village, was not part of the deal, nor was the Clarence Barker Memorial Hospital. Everything else, about 50 acres, was available. Stephens spent a reported $1 million to secure it for his company.

Stephens intended the village of Biltmore to stay the way it had always been, and to preserve George's initial vision for it. The houses were going on the market and existing occupants—some of them estate workers—would be given the option to buy. Stephens's firm planned to enact certain restrictions which would preserve the village's character, one that would keep the overall look and feel of the community. Shortly after the sale, the Southern Land Auction Co. announced it was auctioning "50 Choice Residential Lots" in South Biltmore overlooking the village. *Get in on the ground floor. . . . Buy them Saturday afternoon at your price. Sell them when developments start at 100 to 500 per cent profit*, the ad promised. One five-room house went up for sale on Biltmore Road, walking distance from the village, for $3,100. The village of Biltmore was no longer part of the estate of Biltmore.

Edith was likely relieved, and planned to convert the money earned from the real estate holdings into bonds. Edith's sale raised obvious questions in the community. Was the estate beginning to scatter, to be divided? First thousands of acres had gone to the federal government to form Pisgah National Forest; and now the sale of the village, the station, and residential lots. Were these steps leading to the inevitable end that so many other wealthy homesites— Vanderbilt homes among them—were currently facing?

That July, Edith and Cornelia postponed a house party for a group of New York and Washington debutantes, and sailed for France to attend the funeral of her sister Susan's husband, the Viscount d'Osmoy. While abroad, Edith enjoyed a brief Parisian reunion with her darling "Boy" and former chaperone, Marie Rambaud. In August, Edith, Cornelia, Natalie, and John returned to the United States on the *Aquitania*, accompanied by Myron Herrick, the US ambassador to France. This resulted in Edith and Herrick being romantically linked in the press. Edith and Cornelia returned to an estate that may have been smaller, but was still facing lingering challenges.

"Did Vanderbilt dream a fool's paradise on those North Carolina hills?" the *Kansas City Star* asked. "He is dead; the dream is dust and ashes."

■　■　■

In 1921, the year after women attained the vote, Vanderbilt family friend and Biltmore guest Edith Wharton published a novel titled

The Age of Innocence. The book, which described the stifling life of New York City society—which Wharton had known as a young woman but now critiqued as an adult and author—became her most successful title to date. Wharton became the first woman to receive what was fast becoming one of the most prestigious recognitions in American letters: the Pulitzer Prize.

Established by former *New York World* editor and owner Joseph Pulitzer in 1917, the prize was initially described as being for books depicting the "wholesome atmosphere of American life, and the highest standard of American manners and manhood." Though jurors had wanted to give the prize to Sinclair Lewis's *Main Street*, at least one member of the committee objected, feeling that Lewis's book—about a college-educated woman who moves with her husband and her ideals to a small Minnesota town, only to find it smothering, gossipy, and provincial—did not meet the "wholesome" part of the prize's requirements, and thus Wharton became the winner.

Fans of Wharton's may have disagreed that *The Age of Innocence*— the story of an engaged society man who falls in love with a scandalous woman—fit the bill any better than *Main Street*. To some readers, the book was a nostalgic look at the way things used to be, a time when men were men and women were corset-bound husband fodder. One reader's romantic reminiscence was another's claustrophobic comment on societal mores that were clearly on their way out. When Wharton had learned that her novel was chosen over Sinclair Lewis's *Main Street*—and under what circumstances—she was disappointed and a bit perplexed.

"When I discovered that I was being rewarded—by one of our leading Universities—for uplifting American morals," she wrote Lewis in response to his congratulatory letter, "I confess I did despair."

In a later book, Wharton would slyly refer to the commendation as "the Pulsifer Prize."

■ ■ ■

As Edith entered the room, striding confidently and elegantly toward the dais, the crowd erupted in applause; they supported her before the first words ever left her lips.

Making her way up to the speaker's stand was a challenge that February morning in 1921. The crowd gathered was thick and pressing in from all sides. Edith had been invited to address the General Assembly of North Carolina in the state capital of Raleigh in her role as head of the state fair. The legislative body convened at eleven in the morning, but seats were filled to capacity before that hour, and people were bursting into the aisles by the time Edith arrived at noon. After parting the throng of well-intentioned assembly persons, Edith took her place on the speaker's stand between North Carolina governor Cameron Morrison and General Julian Carr, who had nominated her to succeed him as president of the state agricultural society.

Many eager onlookers were surprised by her appearance, expecting a more matronly woman of forty-eight years rather than the tall, attractive woman before them this morning. Flashes of white silk were visible beneath Edith's suit, an expertly tailored ensemble fashioned from golden-brown fabric hand-woven at Biltmore Industries. Her homespun attire was neatly finished with a brown fur collar, and a small, corded turban with a discreet black veil sat atop her head. From one of her wrists hung a platinum and diamond watch, a four-stranded pearl bracelet draped the other. She wore a bejeweled eyeglass chain around her neck and no gloves. As a result, many an eye caught the sizable topaz and amethyst stones adorning the little fingers of either hand.

Carr stood to introduce Edith. It was, Edith told the crowd, her first speech. Still, Edith clearly knew how to read her audience. It was overwhelmingly male, and many of them suspicious of the increasing array of roles for women in government and politics. Her comments today, she explained to the curious throng, would be like a modern skirt: Long enough to cover the subject, yet short enough to attract attention. Laughter and applause emanated from the crowd, which included Judge Junius Adams and twenty-year-old Cornelia. Towering and thin like her mother, Cornelia, too, wore the homespun apparel of her hometown, opting for shades of green.

"This is a day when women have come into their own," Edith said, "and each one of us must shoulder her responsibilities along with the men." She noted the continued obligations of women to their homes, and that they must live up to the examples of those who had founded the government before them. "So, gentlemen, I at once assume a responsibility in thanking you in the name of my fellow sisters for what you have done, for in conferring this distinction upon me, you have included them."

In addition to speaking on behalf of the state fair specifically and agricultural policies in general—"No single factor can exert a greater influence in this accomplishment than the State Fair"—Edith discussed the need for good roads. She endorsed Governor Morrison's proposed policies to develop and improve byways across the state.

"Our governor has a splendid and far-reaching program for road construction," she stated. For Edith, new roads meant the "opening up of many regions at present difficult of access and consequently undeveloped." First and foremost in her mind was her own region of western North Carolina. Farmers needed good transportation options in order to get their produce to markets. The beauty of the southern Appalachians attracted tourists from the North and helped feed the tourist economy, which would be aided by increased accessibility from the East and South. "In connecting county seats with hard surfaced roads we will be able to connect our industries, farm products and commodities with the outside markets," she continued, "this bringing comfort and an improved scale of living to the people of the remote and hitherto neglected localities."

Toward the end of her address, Edith's comments took a patriotic turn.

"We as a nation, are confronted with problems such as heretofore we have never encountered but we can and will face them, and to the best of our abilities overcome them," she said. "The will to do is half the battle and strength comes with the knowledge of our power and being thus armed we will go forth fully prepared to meet emergencies and with the satisfying assurance that victory is to be ours."

The crowd broke into rousing applause at the end of Edith's historic speech. Afterward, Carr had a few words for the members of the executive committee of the state fair

"I've been president of the North Carolina State Fair three times," Carr said. "I've trotted around here at a good pace last year for an old spavined horse, but now," he said, acknowledging Edith, "I'm going to present to you a thoroughbred."

The October fair was still eight months away but Edith was off to an auspicious start. One newspaper hailed her debut speech as "the smartest 15 minutes' speech to a joint session of the general assembly heard within the historic walls of states in a long time."

The woman who had spoken so eloquently about the need to develop better roads put some existing highways to quite the test: Later that year, Edith claimed a new driving record, making the trip from Washington, DC, to Asheville—a 601-mile route—in 18 hours and 40 minutes.

■ ■ ■

Edith continued developing her own political skills as Biltmore and her own small family seemed to be, for the time being, eluding financial danger. She indeed set a strong example for her daughter, Cornelia, who also reached an important milestone on August 22, 1921: her twenty-first birthday. A party was in order.

Early on that celebratory morning, a gathering of estate workers assembled in front of the house to wish Cornelia well. Though she and her mother had been spending more time in Washington since her father's death, and had downsized their living quarters at Biltmore—moving into a renovated apartment in the bachelor's wing of the house—Cornelia and Edith were still a welcome sight on the estate.

That night, Cornelia and Edith hosted a fancy dress ball and grand masquerade. Invitations had landed in mailboxes all along the East Coast and farther afield. Cornelia's dear friend Rachel "Bunchy" Strong came down from Cleveland, Ohio, for the affair. She made a magnificent addition to the festivities, costumed as a dancing girl from the "Orient," crowned by a headdress of beads and feathers. Edith was an elegant vision, her own beaded headdress accenting the long, delicate slope of her nose. The costumes of all the guests ran the gamut from geishas and gypsies to sultans and nurses. More than two hundred invited friends and family stood admiring one another's festive attire until a large, curtained sedan chair carried into their midst captured their attention. The fringed curtains hanging from the chair's canopy parted, and Cornelia emerged dressed as a Renaissance page. She wore a bolero jacket with glittering buttons, the romantic lace flounces of her blouse peeking out from beneath it. On her feet, she wore buckle shoes with a low heel. About her waist hung a bright pink scarf which matched the color of the vibrant ostrich plume extending from the jaunty velvet cap which sat at an angle upon her head, dark tresses framing her face.

The birthday girl and her guests enjoyed dinner in the banquet hall and later danced to the Garber-Davis Orchestra in the sunken winter garden. Music was always a fixture at Biltmore bashes, and Cornelia's was no different. While the Vanderbilts had the advantage of hiring live musicians, the phonograph had come a long way since 1878, when Thomas Alva Edison patented his version. Edison had spoken "Mary Had a Little Lamb" into his invention, the sound of his voice etching its way into tinfoil and into history as he stood in his Menlo Park, New Jersey, laboratory. "I want to see a Phonograph in every American Home" stated an ad for his Edison Speaking Phonograph Company.

Not everyone was immediately captivated with technology's advances. Just months after Cornelia celebrated "reaching her majority," author Willa Cather gave a speech in which she presciently waxed philosophical on the subject of the phonograph. "We now have music by machines, we travel by machines," she said. "Soon we will be having machines to do our thinking."

. . .

The North Carolina State Fair in October was a success, and once back at Biltmore, Edith and her adviser, Judge Adams, had more plans for part of the remaining lands still under Biltmore's umbrella. Edith, Adams, and a select group of others formed the Biltmore Estate Company which would develop about 1,500 acres of land into golf courses, homes, and a country club. The Country Club of Asheville—originally founded as the Swannanoa Country Club—had been around since 1894, and was the oldest private golf club in the state. Still, there was room for another in this growing city. There was talk about town that one of the reasons that particular country club didn't suit Edith's needs was because they refused to let her smoke on the premises.

The new private club would stand in the shadow of Biltmore House, whose property was now in the neighborhood of 12,000 or so acres. Only the best architects would be consulted in the design and building of the facilities. Donald Ross, the famed Scots golfer and course designer who made the United States his home, would lend his talents to the development of the new links. The plans were grand; however, just a year after the Biltmore Estate Company was formed and the 1,451 acres were transferred to the company, it became clear that there was not enough capital available to complete the golf course and clubhouse in the manner in which the investors had envisioned.

Luckily there was someone who could help, someone who was already involved as a trustee: Cornelia. Cornelia advanced funds from her own inherited monies to enable the club to be completed. By 1923, the development surrounding the club and future homesites—named Biltmore Forest—would have a charter. The lots available for purchase would be 3 to 5 acres in size and could not be divided for twenty-one years.

On July 4, 1922, the Biltmore Forest Country Club opened.

Lunch was $1.00. The golf course was a hit, with nice rolling expanses and a decent selection of hazards. At the time, Ross had declared it his masterpiece. Cornelia herself started off the play on the Ross course, driving the ball over the green.

■ ■ ■

Cornelia's time in Washington, DC, had not ended with her graduation from Miss Madeira's School. It had proved romantically fruitful. Tar Heel Nell had met an Englishman and fallen in love.

The Honorable John Francis Amherst Cecil was a diplomat of no small standing, the son of Lord William Cecil of London—once gentleman usher to the King—and the Baroness Amherst of Hackney. The family's peerage was notable. Cornelia's fiancé, "Jack," was a direct descendant of William Cecil, Lord and eventually 1st Baron Burghley, who served Elizabeth I, the Virgin Queen, as principal secretary, lord treasurer, and chief minister, and was one of her most trusted advisers. As for Cornelia, she may have been the great-granddaughter of a ferryman and born far from the glamour of New York and Newport, but she was nevertheless considered a kind of American royalty in her own right.

Newspapers across the country and the Atlantic mooned over the engagement. "She does not deny rumor. . . . He says 'Not yet.' . . . Friends of Both accept the Match as a Fact," stated the *New York Times* on March 6, 1924: ten years to the day that Cornelia lost her father. On this sad anniversary, it seemed, the family would relish some joyous news. The announcement of the engagement appeared on the front page of the *New York Times*—above the fold.

Much like her mother before her, Cornelia had little to say to the press of her engagement. Jack was still working in Washington; and Cornelia, living in the family home there, promised news as soon as there was any to give. In the absence of her commentary, the couple's "friends" were happy to provide some copy. To celebrate making the engagement official, Edith hosted a house party at Biltmore, then returned to Washington and instructed her personal secretary, William Ashby, to release the date to the press: Tuesday, April 29, 1924. Preparations for the wedding commenced.

While Edith had her choice of high-end stationers, she opted to give her business to companies south of the Mason-Dixon line. Engravers Adolph & Dungan of Louisville, Kentucky, handled the design; and a local firm, Inland Press of Asheville, the printing. Invitations were simple and elegant, calligraphy on plain background: "Mrs. George Vanderbilt requests the honour . . ." Inland Press had a sizable order to fill: Edith and Cornelia and Jack and his family invited 500 people to the ceremony at All Souls, and 2,500 lucky people received an invitation to join the newly married couple at the reception that followed.

The Kenilworth Inn, Grove Park Inn, and Biltmore Forest Country Club welcomed out-of-town visitors. Forty-three guests and their attending staff stayed at Biltmore House, including Cornelia's bridesmaids. Groomsmen stayed nearby at the Biltmore Forest club. Cornelia's longtime friend Bunchy stayed in Cornelia's room with her. Edith's secretary, William, had his hands full with arrangements but still thought to ask the Biltmore Fire Department if they could spray down the village streets with water to reduce dust and dirt kicked up by motorcars.

Edith did what she could to get Biltmore—now nearing thirty years old—in order. Preparations at the house included making soon-to-be family members from England feel welcome. To that end, upon entering the home, guests stepped beneath a large Union Jack and an American flag draped over the doorway leading into Biltmore's entrance hall.

Not for many years had so many Vanderbilts traveled en masse such a long distance from points north. Vanderbilt. Twombly. Webb. Brown. Fish. Dresser. New York's oldest families and most venerated names traveled down the East Coast with trunks and servants to celebrate the grand occasion.

Cornelia's wedding portrait captures the twenty-three-year-old standing at the foot of the grand staircase of the house in which she was born. Striking and languid, she leans against the massive lime-stone walls, the staircase rope in graceful swoops behind her. She is awash in crinkles and folds of tulle and satin, her dark lips contrasting with the white ensemble. Her chin-length hair, the fashion of the day, parts like curtains as it hangs down from her headpiece. Her magnificent headpiece reaches almost down to her eyebrows, framing her dark eyes, ebony-hued and serious, reminiscent of her father's. But her frame is luminous and serene, commanding yet feminine, like her mother's.

The night before the wedding, the servants gathered to serenade the couple. Underwood & Underwood came down from Washington, DC, to photograph the wedding; and a second pair of photographers, the husband-and-wife team of Harris & Ewing, captured the myriad VIPs, family members, and friends descending upon Asheville for the event. George Harris and Martha Ewing, he a former newspaper reporter, she a colorist, had a studio on F Street in Washington. Running what would eventually be the largest photographic studio in the United States, the two had already photographed presidents and dignitaries. It was Theodore Roosevelt, in fact, who had suggested to Harris that he open his own studio. Harris's specialty was capturing the quiet moments that made a grand affair personal: Edith walking with Representative and Mrs. John Hill near the church. Cornelia arm in arm with her cousin Sue Fish at the train station. Houseguests sitting beside the magnificent marble lions in front of Biltmore House. Wedding party members standing outside the elaborately detailed arch of the house's main entrance, awaiting the bride-to-be, gargoyles perched overhead. Cornelia and Bunchy exiting the house, all smiles, veil in tow.

The lines of Cornelia's white satin dress were simple and straight, with a rounded neck and long sleeves covering her arms. Point lace covered her face, a more elaborate feature of the veil, which included nearly four yards of tulle. Orange blossoms held the lace aspect, passed down from Edith's side of the family, in place, forming a small cap atop her head. The orange blossoms were from her dear friend Chauncey Beadle. Chauncey the azalea hunter, Chauncey who wrote her at school of the blooms and buds and fallow times at her childhood home. In Cornelia's hands was a bouquet composed of lilies of the valley and white orchids. She walked down the aisle, her white satin flowing tulle and train gliding behind her. Bunchy served as Cornelia's maid of honor. She wore a striking Lanvin dress, very bouffant in style, with two rows of pearls around her neck and an organdy bow in back. The eight bridesmaids wore green-flowered Japanese silk dresses in simple straight lines, white horsehair cloche hats, and white kid shoes.

Spring blooms plucked from throughout the gardens of the estate burst the constraints of the chancel of All Souls. The fresh-cut blossoms created a heady aroma as the sounds of the magnificent organ, James Alderson at its helm, played "O Perfect Love." It was as complete a picture as any bride could want, except for one missing element—George. Proudly walking Cornelia down the aisle was Edith, tall and grand, clad in chiffon, with an elegant turban atop her head and a white ostrich boa draped around her frame. Through christenings, births, and deaths, George's absence was surely felt, yet his presence as well, in every pane of stained glass, every ray of light.

"The First Bride of Biltmore," Cornelia's aunt Pauline called her. Pauline's husband, the Rev. George Grenville Merrill, presided over the wedding ceremony, and Pauline read a poem commemorating the special day, calling her niece "the beautiful Cornelia who knew all the mountain people . . . who loved the house and grounds . . . who was loved by all."

The "mountain people" attended alongside everyone else—that was the way Cornelia had wanted it. The *New York Times* described the wedding as having an "almost feudal character." Employees and tenants and their families waited with dignitaries in the same receiving line to wish Cornelia well. They and their families were not only invited to the ceremony, but to the lavish reception as well. Edith and Cornelia sent a car to ferry "Old Frank," the family's longtime gatekeeper, and his wife to the wedding. Chauffeurs and servants stood alongside lords and sirs, farmers and dairy workers mingling with the governor of North Carolina, Cameron Morrison. Onlookers from the village waited outside to catch a glimpse of the happy proceedings.

After the ceremony the couple left the cathedral and strode beneath an arch of spring blossoms held by the children of estate workers, and was greeted by Polly Ann Fowler, a three-year-old cupid sporting a hunter's bow and wearing a draping, one-shouldered, makeshift toga. Back at Biltmore House, a huge bell of flowers hung over the wedding party as they stood in the tapestry gallery. The centerpiece on the impeccably appointed table was a miniature horse-drawn coach sitting atop moss and flowers. Arched bouquets were at either end of the table, and the coach itself was emblazoned with the initials "C. V. C."—Cornelia Vanderbilt Cecil. The coach was fitted with a tiny bride and groom inside. Gifts stacked up in profusion, the exotic and the handmade. Locally made marmalade and handwoven baskets from nearby citizens stood alongside the Dresden china and diamonds.

Following the reception Cornelia changed into her send-off ensemble. A richly embroidered gray coat from France and a black straw cloche hat completed the last look many would have of her until she returned from her honeymoon abroad. The couple's car was decorated in high newlywed fashion with a distinctly Biltmore touch: alongside the streamers, trailing behind the vehicle as it spirited the couple away on the first leg of their honeymoon, was a pair of white slippers, their heels lovingly smeared with black tar. Rose petals and rice fell from above as the couple left the reception to head to Buck Spring Lodge on Mount Pisgah, long a favorite spot of the family, one that George and Edith had enjoyed on many an occasion. After that, they were off to Europe, where Edith joined them briefly.

In August, the White Star Line's *Adriatic* docked in New York and Edith disembarked impeccably clad in black and white chiffon. She proceeded to tell customs officials that she was a plain farm woman. "I have no interest in society, and would much rather live on a farm," she announced to the press gathered there to report on the latest arrivals from abroad. Edith added that she had been running a dairy since George's death, and planned on continuing to do so, now with the help of her new son-in-law. When asked if dairy farming was profitable, Edith enthused that it was. "It is just a matter of getting it going."

Cecil had a promising future ahead of him in the diplomatic service, but had resigned his post as first secretary of the British Embassy in Washington, DC, after serving in the diplomatic branch for eleven years. In the course of his career, his travels had taken him to London, Cairo, Madrid, Prague, and Washington. And now to Asheville, for a grand adventure in dairy farming.

■ ■ ■

Just ten months after Cornelia's grand wedding, Biltmore's newest resident arrived: Eight-and-a-half-pound George Henry Vanderbilt Cecil was born at Biltmore House early on February 27, 1925. George came into the world in much the same manner as his mother had, in Biltmore's Louis XV room, arriving to the expected society fanfare and media coverage. Children of the estate's tenants cheered outside the home and left gifts for the baby. Biltmore had yet another heir. The community of All Souls christened the new addition.

Edith, now a grandmother, was adding to the family as well. Eleven years after George's death—and after being linked to a host of suitors including Myron Herrick, Governor Cameron Morrison, and General John Pershing—she was marrying Rhode Island senator Peter Goelet Gerry. The recently divorced Gerry seemed a good fit socially. The Gerry family had been influential in the Newport and New York communities for decades. (In keeping with the constant intersection of society families, Gerry's sister Mabel had attended dance class in Newport with Edith's sister Pauline.) Edith's new fiancé was the grandson of Elbridge Gerry, the fifth vice president of the United States—under President James Madison—and a signer of the Declaration of Independence. (Due to his incessant fiddling with voter districts in Massachusetts to shape them in his favor, Elbridge Gerry infamously inspired the term "gerrymandering.")

Edith and Senator Gerry were married in an intimate, early morning ceremony in London at the Savoy Chapel. Due to Gerry's political obligations, the pair would spend much time in Washington, and when in Asheville, Edith could stay at the lodge on Mount Pisgah while she was having a home of her own built in the newly developing Biltmore Forest, where she and Cornelia held controlling interest.

That year, 1925, presented another milestone. According to the terms of her father's will, Cornelia could not come into full possession and control of her inheritance until she turned twenty-five. On August 22, 1925, already a wife and mother, Cornelia became vested in her estate. The trust fund which once passed from her grandfather William Henry Vanderbilt to her father, George, was now fully at her disposal, along with some property in New York, Biltmore itself, and the remaining surrounding lands that were not turned over to Pisgah National Forest.

To celebrate this fiscal milestone, Cornelia and Jack threw a grand fete for hundreds of friends and family. Asheville would be well represented on the guest list, as would Washington, DC, and New York. Three hundred estate employees and tenants—as with most estate celebrations—were included in the Friday festivities. The group had their own garden party with the new mistress of the manor, some of whom had known Cornelia since she was a child.

Members of the estate's dairy presented Cornelia with a massive ice cream birthday cake from the Biltmore Dairy, an enterprise which contributed not only to the estate's income but to its celebrations as well. Resting on a two-foot-tall base, the cake measured about four feet high and contained 26 gallons of fresh ice cream. Sandwiched between were layers of chocolate parfait, topped off with a vanilla mousse and a confectionary bedazzlement of lilies and roses. "May your joys be as many as the sands of the sea," read the inscription. That afternoon employees danced to Guthrie's Orchestra. Cornelia kept the party going on Saturday night with a second group of three hundred guests. The ball was held in the fresh air of an Asheville summer evening, the heat of the dog days kept at bay by altitude, breeze, and the levity of the occasion. It was the largest party the house had seen since Cornelia's wedding, and Edith, too, was there to receive the guests. That night featured dancing in a garden pavilion to tunes courtesy of the Charles Freicher Orchestra. Japanese lanterns dotted the landscape, illuminating silhouettes against the summer night sky. A midnight supper completed the grand affair, and Cornelia the heiress was now Cornelia the mistress of Biltmore House.

In 1925 the Jazz Age was at its height, and Biltmore was as much in the ballyhoo of the day as anywhere else in the country, due in no small part to Cornelia, whose flair for partying took on dramatic proportions. It was the same year F. Scott Fitzgerald published *The Great Gatsby*, a glitteringly tragic tale that celebrated the period's excesses. Cornelia was coming into her own as an adult just as the world was falling in love with jazz. She was the perfect age—and had the bank account—to enjoy the best the Jazz Age had to offer. F. Scott Fitzgerald was credited with naming this heady time in America's between-war days. The 1920s were, for many, a time to let loose, with hemlines rising as fast as bottles of illegal hooch were emptying.

"Ain't We Got Fun?" the popular foxtrot tune asked, and people everywhere from West Egg to Asheville answered an exuberant "yes" with every hop of the Lindy, bob of the hair, and akimbo bend of their knees. The call of the age was relentless. Women had the vote, bootleggers had the booze, and speakeasies were the scene. The Jazz Age brought young people to the cities. Cars looked snazzier, music sounded catchier, people felt freer. The goals of Prohibition were hardly realized as the liquor flowed and parties raged.

Stories abounded that in order for Cornelia to receive the full measure of her vast inheritance she had to make Biltmore her primary residence, but George's will stated no such thing. The *New York Times* insisted that both Cornelia and her husband were interested in the management of the estate and that since marriage Cornelia "has maintained residence at Biltmore House and is understood to have declared that she will live here permanently."

Yes, she started polo teams and engaged with the local community, as she always had. She had grown up watching her mother care for the estate families, start schools, and visit with families in the surrounding areas. Edith had raised Cornelia to view their less fortunate neighbors as a part of her life, not merely ornaments that existed solely to make her world more glamorous.

The independence and assertiveness of her mother, the willingness of her father to do something different than those of his societal echelon in New York and Newport—both took root in Cornelia. She was both her mother and her father's daughter. The estate was still her home; she had learned to walk in its halls, she had swum in its fountains, ridden hard across its acres, and grown up with the village children. But the spirit of the age was intoxicating. Jazz and freedom and cigarettes and speakeasies called to many a young woman in the 1920s. Perhaps some of those jazz rhythms moved Cornelia, imbued in her a sense of wanting something more. Maybe, like a number of women of the time, she would choose a different path altogether, one not wholly expected of her.

16

Glimpse of a Castle

In his State of the Union address of 1928, President Calvin Coolidge had cast a rather rosy hue on the country's financial outlook. The Dow Jones Industrial Average, in particular, was in the midst of what was the longest-lasting bull market the country had ever seen. For Cornelia and Jack, that meant the $5 million trust left her was enjoying ever-increasing returns. Life at Biltmore House was good, as was the time they spent in their home in Washington, DC.

That year, the City Hall building was dedicated in downtown Asheville, just one of many structures that were part of a sustained construction boom during the 1920s. Architects still found themselves attracted to the area. One such architect, Douglas Ellington, left many of his structural marks throughout town. The North Carolina–born man had put his abilities to good use during World War I as part of the newly established "camouflage unit," using his artistic talents to conceal important structures from enemy eyes. Like groundbreaking architect Richard Morris Hunt decades earlier, Ellington had studied at the École des Beaux-Arts in Paris. He had an office in Pittsburgh but by 1926 was back in North Carolina, this time in Asheville. His melding of Art Deco and Neoclassical flair shone amid the growing downtown skyline, notably evident in the pink-domed and -tiled Asheville City Hall, and the S&W Cafeteria with its glazed terra-cotta and green-and-blue roof.

Elsewhere in town, Fred Seely invested more time and money into Biltmore Industries. The firm's fabrics continued earning a high-profile following and two new colors—Coolidge Red and Hoover Gray—had even been especially designed for the president's wife and the vice president, respectively. Homespun cloth was advertised in *Vogue* and offered for sale at Lord & Taylor. Its popularity—which Biltmore Estate Industries had helped spawn years earlier—reached as far as Tinseltown, where the Hollywood Tailoring Company offered Carolina Homespuns to residents of the entertainment capital. Asheville's population would grow roughly 76 percent between 1920 and 1930, and as the decade approached its close the number of residents hovered around 50,000.

One building whose time had come to an end, however, was the Battery Park Hotel, George's old stomping ground. It became a victim of progress and expansion in 1924 as E. W. Grove, the Tasteless Chill Tonic magnate, prepared for yet another undertaking: an arcade. This type of indoor shopping center had yet to truly catch on in the United States, with the Providence Arcade in Rhode Island, opened in 1828, as a notable retail trailblazer. A new Battery Park Hotel would be built in place of the old one, and across from it would be a shopper's dream on the lower floors and a private men's club in the tower above. Grove, who died in 1927, never saw the Arcade bearing his name completed, however. Work on the Grove Arcade continued after his death and was finished in 1929, but not in the manner Grove himself had originally planned. Before the tower could be completed, the financing ran out—as it had begun to run out for so many.

What had been a record-setting stock market took a turn in late October 1929. New, more horrifying records were achieved as investors dumped stocks in a frenzy. A disconcerting Thursday led to an even bleaker Friday and Monday, culminating in Black Tuesday: October 29, 1929. Fifteen thousand miles of ticker-tape papers were spat from machines as stocks recorded losses of $25 billion. With the crash of 1929, the boom around Asheville, which had already shown signs of slowing, finally screeched to a halt, as it did in so many other parts of the United States.

But not all Asheville natives had a bad October 1929. Thomas Wolfe was perhaps, along with Cornelia, Asheville's most famous citizen to date. Though the writer had spent years away from his hometown—at the University of North Carolina, Harvard, and New York University, along with nights in New York City's Chelsea Hotel and travels abroad—Asheville had clearly been first and foremost in his mind as he worked on his first novel.

Editor Maxwell Perkins had an eye for prose. Ernest Hemingway and F. Scott Fitzgerald were among the writers he had ushered through the publishing process at Charles Scribner's Sons. Perkins took what was originally Wolfe's 294,000-word, door-stopping tome and pared it down . . . to a still-whopping 223,000 (626 pages). The result was *Look Homeward, Angel*, Wolfe's novel about life in the mountain town of "Altamont" and the goings-on at a boarding-house called "Dixieland." His mellifluous sentences poured one over another, describing in sumptuous detail many a barely veiled reference to Wolfe's hometown. Upon publication, Asheville's families tore through the book looking for versions of themselves. The Vanderbilts would also find fictionalized versions of themselves within Wolfe's pages. From the breathing porches of Montford to the wide lawns buffering the stately homes on Kimberly Avenue to the speakeasies surrounding Pack Square, everyone who could afford, borrow, or nick a copy of Wolfe's novel read it and were at once titillated and scandalized. It was still early in October when Wolfe was first able to hold his novel in his hands for the first time. The six-foot-seven-inch man of so very many words was now developing a reputation to match his imposing stature. His career began to take off as the fortunes of so many others would begin to come crashing down.

It had been five years since that glorious day in the sun at All Souls Cathedral when Cornelia and Jack Cecil had married. The '20s had roared in and Asheville felt its heady force as much as anywhere. But that era felt a world away now, in America's post-1929 existence. Despite any national financial setbacks, Biltmore House did not become any less expensive to manage, and was now completely in Cornelia's care. Though her twenty-fifth birthday had come and gone in 1925, Edith and her brother-in-law, Frederick Vanderbilt— as trustees of Biltmore until Cornelia came of age—had delayed transferring the title to Cornelia until 1929. The house and, perhaps more important, its furnishings required costly upkeep, and though the limestone facade may have continued to gleam in the afternoon light, the luster of objects within needed ongoing attention were they not to fade with now limited fortunes.

Within a month after the stock market crash, Cornelia and her husband, Jack, reached out to Cornelia's cousin—John Nicholas Brown II, her aunt Natalie's son—who had become a knowledgeable art collector. Without stating precisely why, Jack said Cornelia wanted a suggestion as to who might be able to assess Biltmore House's treasures. From the tone and persistence of the letters that followed, one senses an urgency, as if the couple had taken a practical look at their expenses and realized that the home was too costly to maintain without an infusion of steady income.

"Thank you ever so much for all the trouble you have been taking in hunting out 'spooks' to tackle the rugs, tapestries and prints," Jack Cecil wrote his cousin-in-law, referring to the battery of appraisers. "You remember we agreed not to take on the cataloguing of the library, anyhow at present."

In a series of correspondence, Jack reviewed with Brown a list of individuals who could help adequately appraise items of value at Biltmore House. For starters, Brown had suggested Maurice Dimand, associate curator of decorative arts at the Metropolitan Museum of Art, with whom Brown would try to meet on an upcoming trip to New York.

"Mr. Dimand sounds exactly the man we want," Jack wrote. Then, referring to the reduced level of hospitality currently available at Biltmore House, Jack added, "I should be delighted to put him up here—if he won't mind picnicking."

A Miss Ellis seemed like a good choice to assess the house's countless prints—Dürers among them—however, Jack added, "I suppose I should have to put her up at the club for the sake of my morals!" But Miss Ellis, sadly, proved unavailable. Brown dedicated himself to the task of helping his cousins, and Jack was clearly grateful. "Thank you again, John, a thousand times for helping us. Hope you and Aunt Nata are well. Off again to Washington for the weekend this evening. Yours ever, Jack."

Ultimately, the task of tracking down reputable experts to catalogue and estimate the value of prized collectibles proved more difficult than initially expected. Brown wrote on Cornelia and Jack's behalf to Charles Niver of Harvard about the engravings. "My cousin, Cornelia Cecil, wishes to have somebody make a list for her giving the title, the engraver, the painter and if possible one significant remark about each."

Brown confessed that he did not believe the engravings to be particularly valuable. Nevertheless, Brown approached yet another contact, Joseph Breck, curator at the Met, saying Cornelia "wishes to complete the cataloguing of the art treasures in Biltmore House as soon as possible." Brown added that he still hoped Mr. Dimand would be available to help them and reminded him of the ongoing relationship between the museum and the Vanderbilt family. "Let me call to your attention that the Metropolitan Museum has enjoyed for many years the George W. Vanderbilt Collection of pictures. I should very much hope that it would see its way to rendering this service to Mrs. Cecil." Brown then wrote Mr. Dimand once more, citing the "collection of very fine antique oriental rugs," which contained "many rare and beautiful examples."

After much effort on Brown's part, the Met finally replied that it was against museum policy to perform this kind of cataloguing for private individuals. Jack, too, received a similar verdict from Breck. "Terribly distressed," he wrote Cornelia's cousin. Dimand had other suggestions, including a professor of fine arts at New York University. "Good authority," Jack wrote to Brown, "but expensive."

Luckily, Jack had also written Ella S. Siple at the Cincinnati Art Museum regarding the home's tapestries. After some nudging, a response was finally received. Siple could come to Biltmore in February 1930. What she found impressed and surprised her. Among the tapestries she catalogued that had long hung in the Biltmore House gallery was a sixteenth-century Flemish set of *Venus and Vulcan* tapestries which Siple and other experts believed had been lost from record for nearly fifty years. In fact, George had arranged for their purchase during a sale at the Hôtel Drouot in Paris in 1887—around the time that Siple and other experts lost track of their whereabouts.

"I found them hanging at Biltmore House," Siple wrote of the highly discussed works in a journal article she published in 1938. Along with the report of her findings, Siple included what she firmly believed to be the first-ever photographs of the long-lost tapestries.

If, in fact, the culmination of events of 1929—the stock market crash and the transfer of the home's title to Cornelia—prompted the heiress to seek some financial relief via the sale of some of the home's artifacts, it may have been a not-yet-acknowledged bit of good fortune that appraisers were difficult to come by. It may never have occurred to Cornelia, Jack, or anyone else at the time that keeping Biltmore House just as it had always been might someday prove even more valuable.

■ ■ ■

A crowd gathered and the press waited. Photographers snapped pictures of the family and others who had gathered on this unique day.

It was March 15, 1930. There, enduring still, stood Hunt's masterpiece, framed by Olmsted's magical flora and cradled by the ancient forests. Cornelia and Jack stood alongside those assembled before the grand entrance to the house. The heyday of luncheons and hunts, swimming parties, grand banquets, Christmas feasts, and more was years past. Now the doors through which authors, inventors, artists, millionaires, presidents, and royalty had passed would be thrown open to everyone who had an extra two dollars in their pockets (one dollar for children under twelve). Those long intrigued by the castle on the hill, but without the benefit of an invitation to step inside, could now walk her halls, marvel at her collections of artifacts and tapestries, gaze at her architectural flourishes, and take in her vistas from the loggia. Biltmore House was opening to the public.

A deal had been struck between the Asheville Chamber of Commerce and Edith's adviser Judge Junius Adams to open the house to paying tourists. The situation was mutually beneficial to both parties. The town would get a much-needed, post-crash boost in tourism while the family would get income to help defray the costs of managing the estate—taxes alone were $50,000 per year. The most financially successful aspect of any of Biltmore's operations at the time was the dairy, but even that was not enough to offset the estate's massive expenses.

After the particulars were ironed out, the opening date was set. At that March press conference, Jack and Cornelia looked out on the crowd from behind the small microphone standing before them. The announcement was not long and would be broadcast. A Pathé sound and picture crew were on hand, as were the president of the Chamber of Commerce and Asheville mayor Gallatin Roberts, whose name would be the first entered into the house's registration book.

"Mr. Cecil and I hope that through opening Biltmore House to the public, Asheville and western North Carolina will derive all the benefit they deserve," Cornelia said to the crowd gathered, "and that the people who go through the house and the estate will get as much pleasure and enjoyment out of it as Mr. Cecil and I do in making it possible." Cornelia added that opening the house was "a fitting memorial to my father.

"After all, it was his life's work and his creation."

Photographers captured a photo of the moment. Where once Edith, whose grace and easy manner had charmed villagers and visiting dignitaries alike, had stood as mistress of the manor, now stood Cornelia, the child that had completed the royal tableau, welcoming visitors as lady of the house. By her side was Jack Cecil, the British diplomat who embraced this hidden little corner of the world. And the two young boys, the latest generation to be brought into this rarefied world. An image of the family together, one of their last, a gathering representing the life that once was.

That day, three hundred people from twelve states stepped past the lions and through the doors. Cornelia's two young boys, George and his younger brother, William—just born in 1928—had guests. The doors swung open and those outside could see firsthand what they had only read about in the papers or heard about at the drugstore counter. For many, it must have been a welcome reprieve from the hardships of the Depression. For others, perhaps what they saw was more of an affront. But the town needed new business, the Chamber of Commerce agreed, and the house needed as much income as it could muster.

Trusted employee Herbert Noble had cataloged the home's prized contents and oversaw a team that monitored the mass of visitors now traipsing through the main rooms on the ground floor and some bedrooms on the second floor. The gardens and grounds surrounding the house, still lovingly managed by Chauncey Beadle, were open to all who wished to wander. Later that spring, Junius Adams ordered brochures and postcards to help promote the house beyond Asheville. That first year, nearly 40,000 individuals visited the house. The forest had been sold, followed by Biltmore Estate Industries and the village, all part of an incremental unburdening of expenses. Yet what may have initially seemed a giant limestone albatross now perhaps showed the potential to generate revenue on its own.

The passage of time had rendered many such large homes obsolete. In New York City, the old Vanderbilt mansions were falling victim to the wrecking ball, dwarfed by the towering buildings rising up around them as the architectural legacies of the Four Hundred dwindled. The Hunt-designed mansion at 660 Fifth Avenue that George's brother Willie K. once shared with Alva had been demolished in 1926. The real estate developer who had bought the design gem planned to erect an office building in its place.

In Europe, British landowners—titled or not—were facing a similar crisis. Some four hundred high-value residences in England were either sold or razed in the first decade after World War I, a trend that would continue through and after World War II. Taxes played a role in England as they had in America, specifically the so-called "death tax" which called for a sliding scale payment of duties on inheritances. For an estate valued at $50 million, for example, 40 percent would be due when the estate passed to the next generation. Many families lost country houses and more.

"Out of every £100 that I get, I have to pay £60 to the state," Lord Astor told the *New York Times*, lumping in additional taxes levied against him beyond the death duties.

And so he closed Cliveden House on the Thames. He was hardly alone. "From Kent to the Cotswolds, from Cornwall to the Berwick border," the paper wrote, "old families are being uprooted from the broad acres on which they have lived for century after century."

The Duke of Devonshire lost the house bearing his name in Piccadilly, and the site was soon replaced by apartments and shops. Grosvenor House, once home of the Duke of Westminster, was converted to a hotel and additional smaller rentals. The family of the Marquess of Lansdowne did not resort to tearing down their ancestral home in Berkeley Square, London. They sold it to a notable figure of the nouveau expat riche, H. Gordon Selfridge, the American department store magnate of London's Selfridges.

■ ■ ■

Later that year, in November 1930, patrons arrived at the entrance of Asheville's Central Bank and Trust Company to find a notice posted on the door. The bank—the largest in the western region of the state—was closed on order of the board of directors, the note read, for the "conservation of assets." The news was troubling, since the bank's last statement had reported more than $18 million in deposits. Four banks in North Carolina were reported closed on that one day, leaving nearby Hendersonville completely without a bank.

In the aftermath of the Central Bank and Trust Company failure,

Asheville's former two-term mayor, Gallatin Roberts, was indicted for using public funds to try to save a private institution—the ailing bank. His second mayoral term had ended in a citizen-demanded resignation once it was revealed that the bank had closed with $4 million of city funds on deposit. Auditors looking into the bank's affairs charged that Roberts's administration had issued a number of city and county bonds, the proceeds of which had been used to shore up the bank's finances, despite the millions in cash already on deposit.

About a week after his indictment, Roberts was on the fourth floor of the downtown building that housed the bank, speaking with friends and colleagues. He left the discussion to go to the washroom. There, he took out a pistol and shot himself in the head. An attorney in a nearby office heard the shot and summoned a janitor. The fifty-two-year-old man lay in a heap on the floor, the resulting trauma and blood making it initially impossible to identify him. His suicide followed that of Arthur Rankin, a former vice president of the bank; and the attempted suicide of J. Charles Bradford, a cashier, who had slashed his own throat with a razor, but survived.

In the aftermath of this latest tragedy, Police Chief W. R. Messer retrieved three letters written by Roberts. One, written to city attorney George Pennell, contained instructions for funeral arrangements and Roberts's personal affairs. In the second letter, addressed to the people of Asheville, Roberts asserted his innocence. The contents of a third letter, written to his wife, were not made public.

Though the city's debt grew inordinately, the city of Asheville chose not to file for bankruptcy. It would, instead, pay off what it owed, slowly and steadily, as best it could.

After Biltmore House opened to the public, Cornelia and Jack took a trip to the Florida Keys, followed by journeys to London and New York. Cornelia longed to find a publisher for a book she had written about a young Elizabethan girl whose life takes her to the Carolinas. The young girl who had participated in the exhibits Edith organized for Biltmore Estate Industries, and who had been raised in a home with a notable collection of artworks and books, had apparently nurtured her own ambitions to be an artist and writer.

But Cornelia craved something more, something that she was not finding in the grounds she rode so often on her horse or in the town that had embraced her since birth. Maybe Cornelia's life had gotten too small, too familiar. Maybe her independent spirit could no longer be contained, even in 175,000 square feet. Perhaps she wanted to leave her own version of Altamont behind.

■ ■ ■

Edith remained involved in Biltmore's management, though her recent marriage to Senator Gerry kept her more often in Washington, DC, and Rhode Island. The year after Biltmore House opened, Edith and Gerry bought a home at 62 Prospect Street in Providence, Rhode Island, where she was closer to her sister Natalie and nephew John. The Italian Renaissance building had been built in 1863. Its facade was Philadelphia brick, red in color, striking in lines. The home was square except for a large curved bay encapsulating all three floors on the Prospect Street side. The couple also had a home at Lake Delaware Farm in Delhi, New York. When in Asheville, they could stay at Frith House—Edith's newly constructed home in Biltmore Forest—or at the Buck Spring Lodge.

In the years since marrying Gerry, Edith had made an immediate impact on the Washington political scene. Less than two years into their life together, she was elected president of the Congressional Club, whose membership comprised women in public political life—primarily the wives of members of Congress and the presidential administration. The club held fundraisers and published congressional cookbooks, but perhaps one of the more memorable events she oversaw during her tenure was a baseball game between the Republicans and Democrats of the House. President Coolidge attended.

She had spoken on a "dawn-to-dark" radio broadcast presented by the Democratic National Committee prior to the 1928 election, promoted as "the most elaborate political program ever broadcast in a single day in the history of radio." Edith was first on the schedule, speaking at 10:30 a.m. Her talk was titled, "Why Governor Smith Should Occupy the White House," referring to New York Democratic presidential hopeful Al Smith. On Mother's Day of that same year, she addressed Gold Star mothers at the Arlington National Cemetery. She was a familiar political face in Providence as well, whether speaking alongside her sister Natalie at a meeting of the Young Women's Democratic League of Rhode Island—held at, of all places, the Providence Biltmore—or hosting more informal yet impactful meetings of what came to be known as the "Edith Gerry Club."

Peter Gerry had been in public office since being elected to the US House of Representatives as a Democrat in 1913. The Rhode Islander entered the Senate in 1916, and had spent ten years as the Democratic whip. A "Wilsonian moralist," Gerry was unsuccessful in his bid for reelection in 1928. (Al Smith, too, was beaten handily by Herbert Hoover.) However, not all of the press in the aftermath of Gerry's defeat was about the election results themselves.

"Capital Wonders Who'll Be New First Lady of Fashion," read one headline. The article was accompanied by a photo of Edith, a shimmering turban atop her head, her lips painted, and a feathered shawl draped over her shoulders. "With Mrs. Peter Gerry stepping out of official Washington life," the paper wrote, "there is an opportunity for some other senator's wife to assume the role of First Lady of Fashion."

The article discussed the growing size of Washington wives and the "problem of diet" for ladies in the political world of Washington's nonstop dinners, teas, and luncheons, where "life conspires to make the average woman lose her figure as rapidly as possible."

With styles in the 1920s and 1930s favoring simpler, straighter lines, Edith's near six-foot frame and flair for fashion made her just the kind of high-profile figure that designers of the day wanted to see wearing their clothes. "Though Washington has many famous and charming women, it has remarkably few who are distinguished for their originality or extraordinary taste in dress," the paper opined.

Though Edith often wore clothes designed by the top houses in Europe, she also embraced trends at home. Ready-to-wear lines were becoming increasingly common—Bergdorf Goodman had opened their ready-to-wear women's department in 1923—giving Edith more shopping options on the American side of the Atlantic. Her panache had been evident from the beginning of her public life, and Edith never shied away from sumptuous velvets, the finest silks, and flashy lamés. At home, she would lounge in a floral-printed, gold silk lamé robe, with hints of metallic green. Her broad yet feminine shoulders could easily handle the long, sweeping lines.

The French house of Callot Soeurs provided her with a pleated, chiffon dress, billowy and cinematic, with brocade accents at the hem, cuff, and closure. For cold Washington winters, she could don her Paul Poiret coat of velvet, silk, and metallic embroidery, skirted in fur and trimmed in faux-pearl beading. Metallics were a favorite of hers. She shopped at France's House of Worth and found a lamé cape that combined both silver and gold fibers for a shimmery finish. She paid attention to every detail, down to her accessories. Though gloves were no longer considered a necessary item for the modern woman, the gold metallic yarn employed by the Surrealist-inspired Italian designer Elsa Schiaparelli in her gloves added a dreamy Dalí-esque edge to many of Edith's ensembles.

"Her social and sartorial leadership here was inevitable," the newspaper continued, noting that despite her husband's political setback, Edith would continue to be a fixture on the DC social scene. This was true enough. Edith's husband did not seem to be finished with his Washington career, and Edith had spent a great deal of time in the city before she became a senator's wife. Moreover, what was clear to all was that Edith's élan was hardly dependent upon her wardrobe.

"Mrs. Gerry was an outstanding figure here," the paper noted, "not because she tried to be, but because she couldn't help being."

. . .

Edith's constant maneuvering, selling, and strategizing in the years following George's death had still not resulted in an income steady enough to eradicate all financial concern. The house's future remained in question, despite potential income from curious visitors. Junius Adams also began crafting a negotiation between Cornelia and the house trustees—Edith among them—to plan for Biltmore's security.

In 1932, Adams finished negotiating the deal that would see the house and land of Biltmore placed in trust under a newly established Biltmore Company, with Adams serving as president. Cornelia contributed $3.8 million of her own inheritance into a trust to support the estate's ongoing maintenance. She received half the shares of the company and arranged for the rest to go to her sons, George and William.

Belt-tightening continued. In the early 1930s, the wages of the home's longtime butler, Herbert Noble, had been cut from $175 per month to $100, and the rest of the staff underwent similar reductions, with the cook instructed to stick to a sixty-cent-per-head-per-day budget for those at home. "Mrs. Cecil had lost quite a lot of her money," Noble wrote in his log, "and her dividends were not paying much. . . ." While Noble's wages dropped, his responsibilities increased as tourists continued coming to the house, and he needed to make sure it looked its best. "This we all accepted in a spirit of loyalty to Mrs. Cecil," he wrote, "as no one was to blame for the Depression."

Adams had given up his home in Biltmore Forest—and lost his mayoral position—in the financial aftermath of the 1929 crash. He continued work with his law firm and eventually moved onto the estate and resided at one of the existing homes there, Farmcote. He committed himself, among his other responsibilities, to the development of the purebred Jersey herd of cattle. Also still living on the estate was Chauncey Beadle, the only person who had been with the Biltmore Estate longer than Edith—and he had arrived in 1888, ten years before she did. He resided at Eastcote, as he had since 1900. From assisting Frederick Law Olmsted, to managing the nursery and, finally, after the departures of Charles McNamee and George Weston, acting as superintendent of the entire estate, Beadle had been as much or more a part of Biltmore House and gardens as anyone—even George himself.

Cornelia's trips to New York and abroad without Jack were signs of a growing relationship strain. Just as he had commented on the comings and goings of Vanderbilts decades before her, Cholly Knickerbocker now commented on what he called the "coolness" between Cornelia and Jack, noting that Cornelia would spend more time in New York where Edith had an apartment and where Cornelia could spend time indulging her artistic calling. Something shifted permanently in their relationship around 1932, and Jack moved into the bachelor quarters at Biltmore House. Cornelia was seldom seen. In her increasing absence, the company, trustees, and trusted managers such as Beadle managed the estate for her and her children. Cornelia still received income from what remained of the $5 million trust of her grandfather William Henry Vanderbilt, and income from her shares in the Biltmore Company. Going forward, Jack would receive a modest income as well.

Many members of the Four Hundred—including several Vanderbilts—had brazenly paved the divorce path before her. Nevertheless, the scramble for details, whether mundane or salacious, remained as popular a pastime in 1934—when their separation was made official and public—as it had at the turn of the century. In fact, fascination with celebrity of any kind was only increasing as media coverage expanded over the airwaves. Cornelia needed a new start, a new town, perhaps even a new name. While she was studying art and spending time in New York, she had gone around town using the name "Nilcha." She dyed her hair a shocking pink. (One society reporter insisted this change was due to Cornelia's belief in numerology.) Junius Adams traveled with Cornelia to France to oversee the final steps that would end her marriage to Jack Cecil that had been celebrated only ten years earlier.

She had come into this world in the Louis XV room, as had her two sons. She had enjoyed exploring the lands, talking azaleas with Chauncey Beadle, entertaining children at Christmas, coming into her own as a woman and mother. Biltmore had been the site of the most transformative moments of her life, yet it was Jack Cecil, an Englishman, who now remained at the house and would continue to do so. Reports of the divorce stated that the two would share custody of the children, George, now eight years old, and his younger brother, William, just five.

"The Strange Matrimonial Disaster of Cornelia Vanderbilt," one paper proclaimed in a two-page spread. "Why the 'Perfect Marriage' of the $50,000,000 Heiress Has Suddenly Made a Detour into the Divorce Courts without a Harsh Word or a Breath of Scandal."

The article's author seemed almost disappointed at the lack of more acrimonious details surrounding the end of the Vanderbilt-Cecil union. He referred to Cornelia as the "unspoiled mountain maiden" and Cecil as the "faultless young English aristocrat." Their marriage was ending, as the paper added, "like so many others, in a Paris divorce court."

To some, she was no longer Cornelia. She was Nilcha, the fuchsia-haired artist and writer living the café life. To others, she would always be Tar Heel Nell, the Biltmore baby, a down-to-earth woman who, like her mother, welcomed all into her home, no matter their station.

She was gone now, and would never return.

17

You Might Go Home Again

Edith immediately began stumping for her husband's reelection campaign. Putting her charm, connections, international flair, and language skills to good use, she took to campaigning—in French—before citizens of French-Canadian and Portuguese descent living in Rhode Island. Her efforts and those of her husband paid off; Gerry was reelected to the US Senate in 1934.

Biltmore remained a concern, and in Cornelia's absence, it was as though Edith was again mistress of the house, if an often absent one. The first year Biltmore House opened to visitors, ticket sales earned $64,000 for the estate. However, as Asheville struggled to rebound from its financial downturn, so did Biltmore House. Ticket sales drastically declined in the depths of the Depression.

By the time author F. Scott Fitzgerald arrived in Asheville, the Jazz Age he had popularized and embodied had come crashing to an end with the economy. Fitzgerald was among those facing sobering realities in the early 1930s—both literally and figuratively. In the summer of 1935, he visited with friends in nearby Tryon, North Carolina, and then transferred to the Grove Park Inn. Winter found him down the road from Asheville at the Skyland Hotel in Hendersonville. There he wrote "The Crack-Up," a very personal exploration of his struggles with depression and his flagging career. The following year he came back to Asheville, this time with his ailing wife, Zelda, whom he checked into the Highland Hospital on Zillicoa Street just north of downtown. An icon of the age, at times a creative and productive artist and writer in her own right, at other times driven to despair, Zelda may have been bipolar, an illness that was little understood or known at the time. Highland was known among the wealthy set as a popular spot to come for treatment. After leaving Zelda at Highland, Fitzgerald proceeded to check in once again to the Grove Park Inn. (He first tried the Old Kentucky Home—Thomas Wolfe's mother's boardinghouse—but Julia Wolfe turned him away because of his visibly drunken appearance.) At the Grove Park Inn, Fitzgerald took two rooms for himself—numbers 441 and 443—at the front of the mammoth granite structure with views of the entrance, rather than at the back with a view of the mountains. (It was alleged that here he could better track the comings and goings of guests, many of them women.)

Fitzgerald would sleep in one room and write in the other. He had made a major decision: he believed the time had come for him to sober up. To keep the alcoholic demons at bay, he resolved to tame his intake. No hard alcohol. No more of his beloved gin. Just beer, perhaps only about fifty ponies (quarter pints) or so a day. Fitzgerald's experiment did not go as he'd planned. He drank. He broke his shoulder while swimming. He became increasingly depressed. In 1936, he turned forty and by this time was employing a nurse. He deigned to do an interview with the *New York Post*. He knew people thought he was washed up. Maybe a bit of press might help. The visiting journalist Michel Mok was struck by what he found on the fourth floor of the Grove Park Inn, but he was not lacking for material, either. Mok titled his piece, "The Other Side of Paradise," riffing on the title of Fitzgerald's debut novel.

"Long ago, when he was young, cocksure, drunk with sudden success, F. Scott Fitzgerald told a newspaper man that no one should live beyond 30," Mok wrote. "That was in 1921, shortly after his first novel, *This Side of Paradise*, had burst into the literary heavens like a flowering Roman candle."

On his fortieth birthday Fitzgerald—whom Mok referred to as a "poet-prophet"—sat in his room with Mok and his nurse. Mok observed and took copious notes. If Fitzgerald were trying to stay off the harder stuff, he certainly wasn't that day. Mok watched as the man made trip after trip to the drawer of his desk where he kept a bottle. "A series of things happened to papa," Fitzgerald confided, "so papa got depressed and started drinking a little." Something, he told Mok, had "snapped." *Confidence*, Fitzgerald mentioned to Mok. *That's* what a writer had to have in spades. He referenced Thomas Wolfe and Ernest Hemingway. *They* had it, Fitzgerald thought, but Fitzgerald believed that he had long lost his.

Fitzgerald was tired and antsy. When he got up to leave the room, Fitzgerald's nurse turned to Mok. "Despair, despair, despair . . ." she said. She also told Mok that her employer wasn't working much. Fitzgerald returned to the room carrying a birthday cake. He wanted to celebrate. When Mok's frank account of his visit with Fitzgerald was published shortly after, in September 1936, Fitzgerald was suicidal. He downed enough morphine to kill himself, but was revived by his nurse and a doctor. The following month, Maxwell Perkins, Fitzgerald's editor, was so concerned about his author's condition that he prevailed upon another writer—then Pulitzer Prize–finalist Marjorie Kinnan Rawlings—to check in on him.

"Are you near Asheville?" Perkins wrote in September 1936. "If you are, I should like to have Scott Fitzgerald see you, for I think you would do him a great deal of good. He is in a very defeatist state of mind, has been for years. . . ."

Rawlings, herself a fan of Fitzgerald's work, had been, she wrote Perkins, "deeply shocked at the feature story" in the *New York Post*. She was in nearby Banner Elk, North Carolina, working on another book of her own. That book would eventually become *The Yearling*, a bestselling and Pulitzer Prize–winning coming-of-age story about a young boy's tender relationship with an adopted fawn. After some back and forth with both Perkins and Fitzgerald, Rawlings made it to Asheville. She had suggested a possible trip to Pisgah Forest to look at pottery, but when Fitzgerald responded to her in October, he was not up for a trip. "In short," he wrote, "Papa is an invalid, and if you want to see him enough you can always find him pacing up and down in his room at the Grove Park Inn." He suggested some good places where Rawlings could purchase liquor. She found him at the hotel, where they talked and drank. Later she wrote Perkins that they had had "a delightful time."

Fitzgerald was alternately buoyed and sunken by his drinking and girl-watching. During one particularly unhinged episode he fired off a loaded gun in his room and the Grove Park Inn kindly asked him to pack his bags, his books, and his ponies, and leave.

Not all of Fitzgerald's Grove Park Inn musings were in vain. From the Inn he wrote his daughter, Scottina, who was fifteen years old at the time and had just begun high school. Fitzgerald summoned what little faith in creativity he had and wrote a letter of encouragement to his daughter, stating that "nobody ever became a writer just by wanting to be one.

"Nothing any good isn't hard."

Life remained hard for Scott and Zelda, Asheville proving no balm for either. In 1940, F. Scott Fitzgerald died of a heart attack in Hollywood. He was more than halfway through writing a new novel, *The Last Tycoon*. Eight years later, a fire at Highland Hospital in Asheville took the lives of nine women—Zelda among them.

■ ■ ■

Thomas Wolfe was headed back to Asheville. After the success of *Look Homeward, Angel,* Wolfe released *Of Time and the River*, whose million or so words were severely trimmed by Perkins. Its criticism frustrated Wolfe and he traveled to Europe, where *Angel* had been a success. He had attended the 1936 Summer Olympics in Germany, sitting in the American ambassador's box. Though just nine years had passed since Philo Taylor Farnsworth had successfully demonstrated the concept of television, the Nazi Strength through Joy organization installed television screens throughout the Olympic Village and Berlin, the first time the Olympics would be broadcast. One critic said that the athletes looked "like humans floating in a milk bath."

Wolfe's writings against Nazism followed the year after, likely influenced by his time there and the growing fervor he noticed surrounding Adolf Hitler, leader of the Nazi Party and führer of Germany. Wolfe published a three-part series on the topic—"I Have a Thing to Tell You"—in the *New Republic* the following year. While at the Olympics, Wolfe cheered on a young, African-American track star who won four gold medals: Jesse Owens. Now, there was a homecoming of sorts in the spring of 1937, when Thomas Wolfe returned to his hometown. With attention heaped on him from all sides, he found it difficult to get a moment's peace and secluded himself in a small cabin outside Asheville in the town of Oteen.

Wolfe stayed just several months in Oteen before traveling again, this time in the American West. He became ill while on the road in Canada and landed in a Seattle hospital. Symptoms worsened, among them horrific, blinding headaches. Needing more advanced treatment, Wolfe transferred to Johns Hopkins Hospital in Baltimore. There, after conducting exploratory brain surgery, Dr. Walter Dandy determined that Wolfe had contracted pneumonia which, in turn, had aggravated an old tubercular lesion on his lung. The specter of tuberculosis had loomed over Wolfe his entire life. The "lungers" (as he had described Dixieland's boarders in *Look Homeward, Angel*) had stalked the halls and porch of his mother's boardinghouse, young Thomas in their midst. Now, decades later, Wolfe's own battle with the illness was coming to a tragic end as it spread to his brain and soon manifested itself as tubercular meningitis.

Wolfe died less than a month before his thirty-eighth birthday; the official cause was acute cerebral infection. His body was taken to Asheville and his funeral held at a packed-to-the-rafters First Presbyterian Church. Many residents of "Altamont" came to pay their last respects to one of the town's most famous native sons. Any resentment borne toward the man who had so openly revealed his neighbors' peccadilloes was suspended if not entirely forgotten. Several hundred more came to Riverside Cemetery, where Wolfe was buried a stroll away from the grave of author O. Henry.

So as one favored turn-of-the-century child—Cornelia—left Asheville's embrace, another, Thomas Wolfe, had returned for all time.

■ ■ ■

Cornelia sat quietly in the courtroom, perched on the bench with her hands folded, her fit frame clad in black. Her lover, Guy Baer, sat next to her. She was blond now, thirty-seven years old, and he just a bit older. His hair was somewhat unkempt, perhaps what one would expect from an artist. Across from them, also opting to dress in dark clothes, was another woman, this one with dark hair—the reason for Cornelia's presence at these proceedings.

About four years after officially leaving her marriage and leaving Biltmore to others to manage, Cornelia found herself embroiled in a marriage dispute of another kind. In Switzerland, Cornelia had taken up with Baer, an artist. Whether or not Cornelia's romance with the Swiss painter had already turned heads, the coverage of Madame Baer's charges against the couple certainly had. She named Cornelia as co-respondent in a suit filed against her husband. She accused her husband of not only desertion and "improper relations" but also of taking their daughter, Gladys, and holding her in an attempt to force a divorce. She claimed that Cornelia and Baer had begun seeing each other in 1934, the year Cornelia's divorce from Jack was finalized in Paris. According to Madame Baer, when she refused her husband's request for a divorce, he refused to let her see their daughter.

Cornelia did not say much at the proceedings. She confirmed statements describing her lineage and her former husband. That was all. Witnesses appeared. Cornelia and Baer's lawyer, Edouard Sillig, stated that Cornelia had recently gone so far as to have her surname changed in the English courts to that of her paramour: Baer. The couple had hoped that these hearings would be held away from the public eye due to the "honorable" nature of the families involved. But it was not to be, judging from the extensive coverage in the *New York Times* and other newspapers. If Cornelia had hoped that divorcing

Jack and putting an ocean between her and East Coast society would dim the glare of the spotlight that shone on her most of her life, she was mistaken. Her behavior abroad continued to captivate the press, perhaps now even more. Though only a handful of media were present in court, word spread quickly, and the wires were a-titter with the latest chapter in the life of Cornelia Vanderbilt.

The District Court in Vevey, Switzerland, made a swift decision. Within days the affair was settled and Cornelia was fined 50 Swiss francs for "complicity" for the role she played in the disruption of the Baer marriage. She was also sentenced, along with Baer, to pay his wife's lawyer 200 francs. It would be a year from this judgment day before any divorce decree could be handed down.

In the end, Cornelia never married Baer, nor did she give up on finding love again. She returned to London and found a home in the much-desired Kensington neighborhood where she was often spotted in her garden. When she did turn her interest toward Biltmore House, in 1939, it was for financial reasons. She dispatched her lawyer, T. E. Chester Barratt, to Asheville to recover her stake in the Biltmore Company, and to agitate for the sale of the estate. There were still six hundred people working at the estate, primarily in the dairy operations which, for the first time in 1936, had managed to turn a profit.

The Biltmore Company did not want to go through with the sale, and instead sent Barratt back to Cornelia with a $200,000 payment meant to cover her share of the family homestead on Staten Island, New York. With the assistance of her advisers and attorneys, Edith had again just barely managed to keep Biltmore whole, just as the world was being torn apart yet again.

■ ■ ■

World War II reached Hawaiian shores on December 7, 1941, and its impact began to be felt not only by those who boarded carriers and transports bound for Europe and the Pacific, but also by those left behind at home. There was no corner of American life into which the war could not seep during those years, no refuge from reminders of the horrors that so many were suffering. Family members and paramours waited anxiously for the return of loved ones, hanging on every censored piece of V-mail, dutifully seeking metal to scrap, carefully rationing what there was to go around, doing their best to do their part.

It was a time of repurposing. "Use it up, wear it out, make it do or do without," was the motto of the time. From clothes to factories, new lives were squeezed out of existing businesses and the people who worked for them. A factory that made pots and pans might switch to making munitions. Young women went to work in numbers never before seen.

The following spring, a train pulled into Asheville carrying 242 Axis power diplomats, their staff, and families. Hailing from Italy, Bulgaria, and Hungary, they headed to the Grove Park Inn. The US government had reached an arrangement with the hotel to house these diplomats and treat them well in hopes that an exchange of US diplomats overseas might be arranged. That was accomplished within roughly a month of the guests' arrival. A new batch of visitors arrived shortly after—not diplomats this time, but 155 Germans and 63 Japanese. Later that summer, and as the residency of the Axis guests was nearing its end, the US Navy leased the hotel for the recuperation and rest of US seamen.

Biltmore House, too, again felt the effects of wartime. Jack Cecil, still a British citizen, had returned to England in 1939 to serve as minister of information during the war. His and Cornelia's sons, George and William, were schoolboys of fourteen and eleven, respectively, when fighting began in Europe. In 1941, the pair left school in Switzerland and headed to London. In 1943, George enlisted in the British navy; William intended to do the same once he was old enough.

There was a growing need in the United States to protect not only her citizens but her culture. Washington, DC, was particularly at risk for attack, and elected officials analyzed what could be done for its citizens and the valuable artifacts that resided in the capital. One senator proposed painting the brilliant white edifices in the capital city a dull, drab gray so as to render them less visible from above. The nation's archival documents were a high priority for protection, as was the artwork at places like the National Gallery.

David Finley, director of the gallery, was prepared. By October 1941—two months before Pearl Harbor—he wrote donors and others that the gallery had "made arrangements to secure space in a suitable building about 500 miles from Washington." That building was "as nearly fireproof as is possible in this type of building," and said that "it has been requested that the exact location be kept confidential." That location was Biltmore House.

Finley and Edith had been friends for years, and in 1939, Edith had shipped Whistler's painting of George to the Corcoran Gallery for storage until the National Gallery could put it on exhibit. Since Peter Gerry had been reelected once more in 1940, Edith was spending much time in Washington, DC, and was heading up the Senate Ladies group in the capital. Under her guidance, the group spent a good deal of their time making surgical dressings for the war effort. Reaching out to Edith about evacuating art to Biltmore House was an excellent option, and David Finley and the gallery's chief curator, John Walker, met with Junius Adams and Chauncey Beadle at Biltmore House to see if it might be a serviceable repository for some of the nation's most valuable artistic possessions. It was.

In 1943, the home was closed to visitors partially due to a gasoline shortage and ban on pleasure driving. Jack and the boys were overseas. Ticket sales at the house had declined steadily after the opening year and rebounded somewhat in 1940 and 1941, but prospects for a steady stream of tourists during the war were dim. Under the circumstances, the fact that George had never completed the music room now proved a boon for this new wartime venture; its bare state would make an ideal spot for storage. The evacuation of the gallery began, followed by a careful installation at Biltmore. The caravan of precious cargo made its way from Washington, DC, southward in January 1942, its declared value $26,046,020. First, a train car full of

Italians, Dutch, Spaniards, and others pulled into the station. Rembrandt was on board, as were Donatello, Botticelli, Perugino, Titian, Van Dyck, Velasquez, Vermeer, Giotto, and Raphael. Next, a procession of trucks whisked the guests to their new home. The artwork was escorted and babysat, never alone, during its entire sojourn in the mountains. These new residents sat quietly on the floor in the music room, and stood proudly in the downstairs kitchen. Unknown to many, deep in southern Appalachia lay some of the country's most remarkable artistic treasures.

By the summer of 1944, four Asheville hotels were being used as redistribution centers for soldiers returning from the war. In the fall of that year, Finley let Edith know that the National Gallery's art could be safely sent back to its home in Washington, DC, and thanked her "for the valuable service which you have rendered to the National Gallery and to the country in a time of need." The works arrived safely back in Washington, and Finley stated in a press release that "there will be no special ceremony, but a feeling of great thankfulness on the part of the Gallery and the public that the Raphaels and Botticellis and other works of human genius are safely home again." Edith wrote her friend that it had been "a great privilege to be of any service."

In August 1945 the war came to an end in the skies over Japan as a new atomic age began. The horrific conflict and the industry it spawned helped wrest American from the grip of the Great Depression. Loved ones finally returned home, others were lost forever. Everyone wanted life to go back to normal, but the world had forever changed.

Having done its wartime duty, Biltmore House stood empty.

■ ■ ■

In 1945, clothiers Best & Co. bought and demolished 645 Fifth Avenue, one of the Marble Twins that the Hunt brothers had completed for George in 1905, and where Field and Lila had lived. Two years later, in 1947, bulldozers came for George's childhood home at 640 Fifth Avenue. Any remaining art was packed and transferred to the Metropolitan Museum of Art. Cornelius Vanderbilt III—George's nephew—had inherited the Vanderbilt mansion upon George's death. He died in 1942 and his wife, Grace, eventually sold the imposing structure to developers. Workmen tore away at what was one of the last standing Vanderbilt homes on Fifth Avenue, now completely surrounded by skyscrapers. Only 647 Fifth Avenue remained, though its tenants, the American Express Company, had renovated the building in the late 1930s. In the process some of the structure's more elegant elements were supplanted by more commercial architectural features such as large plate glass windows. New York City's Vanderbilt Row was no more.

In the summer of 1947, Cornelia and Jack's sons, George and William Cecil, drove to North Carolina to see their father, who had returned to his adopted home after the war. William, now in his twentieth year, had not seen the house since he had left at six years of age. He was planning on a career in the British navy, but Jack Cecil wanted his youngest son to see what his American inheritance looked like before he settled permanently on a life in London. That same year, Cornelia made another request to settle her finances and extricate herself from the estate. She would receive $2 million from the Biltmore Company in exchange for her shares. The Biltmore Company, unable to provide a lump sum payment, began paying her in installments.

Two years later, Cornelia found love again. She remarried in October 1949 to Captain Vivian "Vi" Francis Bulkeley-Johnson, a World War I veteran and London banker. It was in her Kensington garden, it is believed, that she first caught the eye of this confidential secretary at the Rothschild Bank of London. He was fifty-eight, she was forty-nine—though she listed her age as forty-three. There was little fanfare as the two strolled through the back door of the registry office in Kensington to give official notice of their intention to marry. "We wanted not fuss or bother," Bulkeley-Johnson told the press. "I am, of course, just a nobody. My fiancé has had all the publicity she needs for the rest of her life, so we just want to get married in a quiet sort of way." It was the second marriage for both of them. A friend of the couple commented to the newspapers—using yet another newly acquired name for Cornelia's new life—"Mary and Vi will make a perfect couple. They are so quiet." Cornelia would remain in England, first in a four-story brick home in Kensington, London, then leaving the bustle of the city behind for a more pastoral life at a home called the Mount, in the village of Churchill, lying northwest of Oxford.

By the middle of the twentieth century, many changes came to those who had been a part of Biltmore's more than half century of existence. Gifford Pinchot had dedicated his life to advancing the interests of forestry and conservation. His views on silviculture seemed to extend beyond trees to humans, as he served as delegate to the first and second International Eugenics Congress and was a member of the American Eugenics Society advisory council. During his time under Roosevelt, Pinchot was involved with a report on conservation which the president approved and sent on to Congress. The report included recommendations relating to "eugenics, or hygiene for future generations."

"If our nation cares to make any provision for its grandchildren and its grandchildren's grandchildren," one of the report's recommendation stated, "this provision must include conservation in all its branches—but above all, the conservation of the racial stock itself."

After leaving Washington, Pinchot served Pennsylvania as commissioner of the the Department of Forestry, secretary of the Department of Forests and Waters, and twice as state governor: from 1923 to 1927 and again from 1931 to 1935. His impact on forestry was remarkable, and his lifelong dedication to the field helped put the concept of conservation on the policy map. Just a slice of his time in Washington, DC, netted huge results: Forest reserves included 56 million acres in 1905, and by 1910 were 172 million acres. He died of leukemia in 1946, shortly after finishing his autobiography.

In 1949, George's great friend, best man, and traveling companion William B. Osgood Field died at his farm in Westfield, New York. Lila had passed away in 1934, after which Field spent more of his time away from the city. The couple had raised four children and continued enjoying the outdoor life that had, in many ways, brought them together decades earlier at Biltmore House. Field remarried twice, first to Erika Segnitz, a union which ended in divorce, and a second time to his nurse, Mary Hemenway, who remained with him until his death. In 1950, Jack Cecil, still unwed since his divorce from Cornelia, continued to live at Biltmore. Young George had begun working on the dairy operation and joined his father in Biltmore's bachelor wing. By then, Cornelia received her final payment from the Biltmore Company in exchange for her shares. Her separation from the estate was now complete. Edith, by now seventy-seven, suffered a coronary attack and, while recovering, lost her sister Natalie, who had been ailing for some time. Cornelia wired her cousin John, from Oxfordshire, when she heard the news of her aunt Nata's death. William sent word from Cambridge, Massachusetts, where he was attending Harvard. Jack sent condolences from the family in Asheville.

Just a few months later, in July 1950, Junius Adams sat down to write Edith with more news from the estate. On Independence Day, Chauncey Beadle, a fixture at the estate for more than sixty years, had died. Adams called Beadle's passing a "shock," adding, "It will take a long time to adjust ourselves to Biltmore Estate without him." The funeral was at All Souls. A solemn breeze blew through the azalea gardens and beyond, for all those who had lost a caretaker, a manager, and a friend. The following year, 1951, forester Carl Alwin Schenck returned to the United States and was celebrated from coast to coast. A redwood grove in California's Prairie Creek Redwoods State Park was named for him—signposts there honor George and Pinchot as well, for their contributions to forestry—and, closer to Biltmore, a plaque in honor of Schenck was placed on the site of the Biltmore Forest School.

Edith returned to Biltmore in 1955 for the wedding of her

thirty-year-old grandson George. Jack Cecil had died a year earlier and missed seeing his eldest son marry. Cornelia was on vacation in Italy when she got the news that her first husband had died. Jack was sixty-four, and had become much more a part of Biltmore than had Cornelia. Both his sons, George and William, were at his side when he died. The Englishman was buried in the United States, in nearby Fletcher, North Carolina. George Cecil's wedding would mark Edith's last visit to Biltmore. Three years later she died at her home at 62 Prospect Street in Providence, a little more than a year after the death of her husband, Peter Goelet Gerry. Her funeral was held at Grace Episcopal Church.

Edith left art to her family and to the National Gallery (where Whistler's painting of George still resides), as well as an annuity to her younger sister, Pauline. Her grandson William received Frith House in Biltmore Forest, and grandson George Buck Spring Lodge. The rest of her estate was divided between her grandsons, George and William, and would be fully theirs once William—the youngest—reached thirty-five years of age.

Edith's legacy is difficult to quantify, though her impact on the lives of those less fortunate than her—from literacy students at the Moonlight School she established at the dairy, to young students at the School of Domestic Science—likely affected generations in the community. George's dream—perhaps a wildly misguided one, but a masterpiece nonetheless—had faced demise countless times. Edith had been there to protect not just the structure and its entire contents, but a truly irreplaceable icon of an era of American history. She now left her grandsons with big shoes to fill, as there were few examples in America of how to make this kind of preservation—that of a private home—a successful venture. She may not have realized it at the time, but all of her efforts to keep Biltmore House intact while selling off the village and other investments achieved something she likely never predicted. She changed the course of her family's future not through what she had sold, but rather what she bought in the process: time. Over the years, what had once been the epitome of Gilded Age extravagance had become obsolete but then, surprisingly, relevant once more as an anachronistic novelty. When all the castles of her and George's childhood had met the wrecking ball or the hotel developers, Biltmore House would still be dressed in the tapestries of their youth.

Taking over this responsibility was not an easy road for her grandsons, and in the beginning they did a lot of work themselves, including starting their own advertising agency to handle promotions, and often taking the photographs themselves to keep costs in check. The house, as well as its interior, was constantly in need of upkeep and restoration.

By 1960 Biltmore House had welcomed its one millionth visitor and William had left his job at Chase National Bank in New York to join his older brother George in Asheville. Despite increased tourism, the house was losing around $250,000 a year. A year earlier, William had run into Chase president David Rockefeller, whose family had provided the funding to help establish Colonial Williamsburg in Virginia. Rockefeller asked William what the family planned to do with Biltmore House. When William said they intended to make the estate profitable, Rockefeller was incredulous. "Can't be done," he said. "I've tried it at Williamsburg."

The young men, for better or worse, remained undeterred. When Judge Junius Adams passed away in 1962, George became president of Biltmore Dairy Farms. Adams had been instrumental in keeping Biltmore House intact and as a privately held home. The structure that many had viewed as an irrelevant if opulent burden, was now a curious relic of a bygone era—one that people would pay to see. Yet even with tens of thousands of visitors a year, they were hemorrhaging money. Finally, in 1968, 96,000 people walked through the doors of Biltmore House doors and George and William's estate saw its first profit:

$16.32.

It was a start.

■ ■ ■

Cornelia and her second husband, Vi, led a quiet life at the Mount. During their time together, Cornelia ("Mary") and Vi had amassed a vast collection of art and furniture, including Italian Renaissance masterpieces, Chinese ceramics, English furniture, and sporting pictures. Among the treasures were *Christ Carrying the Cross* by Marco d'Oggiono, an Italian who died in the sixteenth century, William Blake's *The Magdalene at the Sepulchre*, *The Madonna and Child*, by Sano di Pietro, dating to the mid-1400s, and a Chinese verte baluster vase dating from the Kangxi period. Cornelia herself possessed valuable jewelry as well, including a star sapphire bracelet. But these items would eventually serve as more than mere décor. Just prior to the start of the Second World War, Cornelia had contacted solicitors in London saying she wanted to spend her remaining years in England and establish a fund for those in need. After the close of the war, she added a significant amount of capital to her original donation. The eventual sale of some of these valuable objets d'art would increase that amount even more. Above all, she told her London representatives, she wished to remain anonymous. And so The Mrs. Smith Fund had been born.

Cornelia developed a friendship with Edward Adamson, an artist who was known in the field of art therapy, and who had pioneered the use of art as a means of treating mental illness. Adamson visited Cornelia and Vi at their home, and Cornelia and Adamson participated in art fairs in Oxfordshire. Cornelia would write her friend about "frantically making children's patchwork quilts," or asking Adamson for prizes for a raffle. But talk of exhibit stalls and May fairs were secondary to their growing friendship. "Don't forget to make Easter a really long rest with us with much sleep, eat, drink and talk and only a lazy minimum of Xmas fair," she wrote him in 1965. Adamson advised Cornelia on pricing for art and pottery and she advised him on working with wealthier private patients, saying, "Those sort of customers will not think you are any good unless you cost them a lot."

Cornelia, through her Mrs. Smith Fund, had sought to support

Adamson's work over the years and get his wages increased. It was a natural fit for Cornelia, a combination of her love of art and her desire to do something for those less fortunate.

"It positively makes me boil under the collar to see you wasting at your age and with your ability as a Civil Servant," she wrote her friend in 1963, regarding his work at the Netherne Hospital and the pushback she was receiving in seeking to augment his salary. She was not going to give the hospital any grants unless he was being paid what she considered to be an appropriate stipend. "Mrs. Smith's Trust was originally conceived—as I conceived it, to help individuals and not state controlled bodies."

In 1968, Vi died. The Mount Trust collection of Chinese Art he worked to assemble was placed on exhibit later at London's Victoria and Albert Museum in 1970. Cornelia's friendship with Adamson endured, and one evening, several years after Vi's death, Cornelia was dining with Adamson and another acquaintance in London when a young waiter caught Cornelia's eye. Cornelia was smitten. "I want to marry him," she reportedly announced. The fellow's name was William "Bill" Goodsir, and he had already been married, but that proved to be temporary. Bill and Cornelia were wed in 1972 and Bill and Cornelia spent much of their time at her home, The Mount. She was 72, he was 46.

Cornelia's cousin Natalie—one of Edith's sister Pauline's children—visited England in 1975 and later wrote John Nicholas Brown II to update him on their cousin. Natalie had seen Cornelia's home before. It was outside Oxford, near Kingham, where dons could come from the university and find some peace and quiet to do research if they liked. Natalie remembered that Cornelia preferred river punts for travel, and "detested motor cars." Natalie went again to call on Cornelia, and asked her neighbors for any news. "Cornelia is now called 'Mary,'" cousin Natalie wrote John, before updating him on the death of Bulkeley-Johnson and Cornelia's present life with Bill. According to Cornelia's nosy and chatty neighbors, Cornelia had taught Bill to ride and "fancified him."

As the years passed, Cornelia had continued actively divesting herself of her possessions and further funding her charity. Then, on February 7, 1976, four years after her marriage to Bill, Cornelia Mary Goodsir of the Mount, Churchill, Oxon, died at seventy-five years of age. Bill was at her side. Besides her husband, William Robert Goodsir, she was survived by her two grown sons, George and William, in North Carolina. The value of her personal assets at the time of her death was 1.1 million pounds, or about $2.2 million.

As it was for her father, there would eventually be one last crossing for Cornelia, this one to the Orkney Islands, where a small chapel stood near an unmarked grave: perhaps her one last attempt at anonymity.

Like her mother, she shared her fortune with those who had none. Like her father, she had been born to incredible wealth and a name synonymous with privilege, yet sought a life quite different from that which others might have prescribed for her.

On the day she died, in a land an ocean away, a cucumber magnolia devoted to her birth and her memory still grew in the heart of southern Appalachia. It was as hardy as any child of Buncombe, its blooms as fragile and fleeting as any fairy tale, its roots deep in the red clay that surrounded the last castle.

EPILOGUE

Riding in a shuttle full of tourists from one of the estate's parking lots to Biltmore House is a short yet instructive journey.

Frederick Law Olmsted's deftly executed vision for his Approach Road offers visitors a taste of the master's caprice. His belief in the element of landscape surprise is validated here daily as the shuttle passes through grand iron gates and turns right to face the house and the mountains beyond. As the shuttle makes its way along the esplanade, that first glimpse of the house on the horizon elicits audible gasps. Biltmore House is still an awe-inspiring sight.

Though it may be necessary to look past a sea of Bermuda shorts and ball caps and navigate legions of audio-tour zombies, a walk through the house today can transport you. Stroll past the lions and into the main entrance hall where the family welcomed many a guest; step into the room where Cornelia and her two sons were born, or out onto the loggia where George held his newborn in his lap. Gaze up at the painting on the library ceiling, marvel at the books lining the walls. Touch the Indiana limestone, breathe the mountain air as you amble through manicured gardens whose plants have a history all their own. Some things have changed since that Christmas in 1895 when George first welcomed family and friends to his new home. The Music Room was "completed" and opened in 1976, for example—though much has stayed the same or been expertly refurbished or restaged. Walking the halls of Biltmore House for a day is a journey back in time.

Biltmore House and its gardens remain privately owned by

George and Edith's descendants, the Cecil family. The current CEO, William—"Bill"—Amherst Vanderbilt Cecil, Jr., is George and Edith's great-grandson. Private ownership means that the estate receives no government grants, nor is it eligible for any associated not-for-profit tax breaks. Property and inheritance taxes remain a financial hurdle to be cleared, as they were for Vanderbilts and their gilded brethren in the early twentieth century. However, George and Edith's descendants have managed to make the home, gardens, and more modern additions like the winery profitable in a way that likely seemed impossible that March day in 1930 when paying guests first stepped through Biltmore's doors.

There is something to be said for "for profit." Tickets for a look inside the house that went for $2 in 1930 are, as of fall 2016, $65 to $85, depending on whether you make a regular daytime visit or wish to see the house's halls festively decked in all their holiday splendor. The family makes the most of the roughly 8,000 acres available, and visitors can traipse through the gardens, eat in any one of several restaurants, and shop stores housed in the refurbished horse stables. Day-trippers can rent bikes to ride along the French Broad River, or paddle down it with a guide. They can zip along paths on a Segway, learn to drive off-road in a Range Rover, or stay on foot and poke their heads into the blacksmith's shop or pet the farm animals.

In the spring of 1890, when the newspaper reader called "Anti-Biltmore" wrote a letter about George's plans to rename the train station and village of Best, ranting about the potential Biltmore-i-zation of town, imagining such additions to the area as "Biltmore hotel, Biltmore park, Biltmore street, Biltmore block, Biltmore sheep, cows, ducks, cloth . . . Biltmore bustle," this was actually a gross underestimation of the impact that the Vanderbilt family would have on the region.

All of Anti-Biltmore's predictions and many more have come to pass. Biltmore Avenue is one of downtown Asheville's main drags and, as predicted, is full of "bustle." More than a hundred businesses in this city carry the name "Biltmore": Biltmore dental and medical groups, Biltmore Oil, Biltmore barber and body shops, catering, and coffee traders. In every direction, the name graces the signage of stores offering services and wares ranging from house paint to prom rentals, churches to childcare, computers to consultants, massage treatments to Masonic temples.

Perhaps more remarkably, the name "Biltmore" is found far beyond North Carolina, too. While one is hard-pressed to find any reference to that word prior to 1890 when George named his new home, the word now connotes glamour and wealth. High-end condos, hotels, and resorts bearing that name can be found in Arizona; Palm Beach; Palm Springs; Miami; Los Angeles; and Providence, Rhode Island. New York's legendary Biltmore Hotel opened alongside the new Grand Central Terminal in 1913, linking the name of George's estate to the railroad industry long dominated by his family.

Much of New York's Gilded Age is no more, though memories and legacies of Biltmore characters can be found if you know where to look. One of the two homes constructed by Richard Morris Hunt's sons for George still stands at 647 Fifth Avenue. It is a Versace store. The 1849 iron fencing still fronts the former Pinchot family home at 2 Gramercy Park—once rented to the Dresser children and their grandmother—and is now a fashionable apartment building. The brownstone where a young Edith Wharton peered out her windows at the New York life that she would one day illuminate for readers everywhere is a Starbuck's.

The genius of Biltmore artisans Richard Morris Hunt, Frederick Law Olmsted, and Rafael Guastavino is evident throughout the city. Guastavino tiles can be spotted in the Boathouse of Brooklyn's Prospect Park and the Elephant House of the Bronx Zoo. They grace St. John the Divine, Grand Central Terminal's "whispering corridor" and Oyster Bar, and countless other structures including Manhattan's Municipal Building and Ellis Island's Registry Room. The vaulted space Guastavino and his son created beneath the Queensboro Bridge is available today for events, and is aptly called "Guastavino's."

Richard Morris Hunt's work is one with the Guastavino firm's at that historic immigrant gateway, and his architectural influence abounds in places like the Metropolitan Museum of Art. A monument to Hunt stands on Fifth Avenue at Seventy-First Street, alongside Frederick Law Olmsted's Central Park, which remains one of the great public outdoor spaces of our time.

But it is in Asheville that perhaps their legacies best shine. The town has grown into a mecca for foodies, outdoor enthusiasts, and artists—those seeking to reinvent themselves far from urban centers—without forgoing access to theater, film, excellent restaurants, beautiful surroundings, and *lots* of beer. Ironically, the town that adopted prohibition more than a decade before the Volstead Act became law, has repeatedly earned the title of "Beer City." At this writing, the mountain town of fewer than 100,000 boasts one of the largest number of craft breweries per capita of any city in the United States.

In the Montford Area Historic District, many homes designed by Richard Sharp Smith still stand, some past their century mark (and many with "breathing porches"). The Grove Park Inn is still there, boasting an astonishing collection of Roycroft and Arts and Crafts furniture, and guests can visit the former grounds of Biltmore Industries, which were given a helping hand by Edith more than a hundred years ago. Riverside Cemetery is the eternal home to the town's native son Thomas Wolfe and its dear adopted O. Henry. "The Gift of the Magi" inspires visitors to leave pennies on O. Henry's grave. Guastavino's now Basilica of St. Lawrence anchors the north end of downtown, and still boasts the largest freestanding elliptical dome in the country. All Souls in Biltmore Village is architect Richard Morris Hunt's only existing church. You will find a plaque there in George's honor, but no stained-glass window.

The struggles that Cornelia's sons faced when they returned to Biltmore House would now seem to any observer's eyes to have been handily overcome. Here and abroad, many country homes and estates have been opened to tourism to generate income, but Biltmore's is an astonishing enterprise. Visitors come in droves in spring to view the azaleas—credit due to Chauncey Beadle's tireless efforts. There is a pub named for Cedric, one of the Vanderbilts' many pets, which offers a specially brewed beer named in honor of the St. Bernard. Biltmore's winery is the most visited winery in the United States—but likely holds that title for all of North America.

There are two hotels on the estate. The exclusive Inn on Biltmore Estate features suites named for Biltmore House's more notable guests, such as Edith Wharton, Henry James, and John Singer Sargent. Family and friends are represented as well in the Dresser, Sloan, Webb, Burghley, and Pinchot suites. The *Chariot of Aurora* painting that adorns the ceiling of George's library has inspired the Pellegrini Bedding Collection, which is available for purchase along with a host of other items featured in the Biltmore line of home furnishings, linens, and accessories. Biltmore House has been featured in films such as *Being There* and *Hannibal*. Waterfalls that were once part of George's massive tract of land can be seen in the film *The Hunger Games*. Biltmore navigates the intersection of then and now, surviving in modern times by selling the glamour of the past.

Yet in many ways our curiosity about George, Edith, and Cornelia is difficult to sate. George Vanderbilt remains "the biggest mystery of Biltmore House," Biltmore's director of museum services told the Associated Press in 2005. In the past, many people did not keep copies of the letters they wrote, so much of what we know of their thoughts and activities must be gleaned from missives scattered among the archives of others. Edith and her sisters made no qualms about burning their own family papers in the backyard of their grandmother's home after her death. What insights were among them we'll never know. It appears Cornelia left few of her words behind, though the legacy of her charitable trust remains intact today, continuing to serve those whose lives are much less fortunate than was hers. Yet the mystique of the family and the home has only increased. "George Vanderbilt never imagined 700,000 people a year flushing his toilets," William Cecil—Cornelia's son—told the

New York Times back in 1992 while he was still involved with the house's daily operation.

George Vanderbilt could have simply spent his life as a wealthy man in a fancy house, and Edith as the wife of such a man, spending her time hosting celebrities of the day, making the social rounds, and giving to charities via her solicitors. Instead, these two people invested in the community with time as well as money, giving openly to the less fortunate, and in the process made an impact on the land and surrounding area that exists to this day, and raised a daughter whose charitable contributions continue to help those in need. As of 2016, the assets of what is now known as the Mrs Smith & Mount Trust totaled 7.5 million pounds, or about $9.3 million.

If his name were George Washington—rather than George Washington Vanderbilt—we would, without hesitation, talk about the design of his house, his impact on the forests, his family, and the legacy he left behind. And though George Vanderbilt was not a statesman, his contributions to history, culture, and forestry cannot be denied as he employed some of the greatest minds behind America's civic, private, and untamed spaces. Though Edith was not the wife of a president, her tireless efforts in the community changed many a life; ensured the education of those with limited access to school, books and teachers; and fostered craftsmanship and self-sufficiency.

One would like to think Edith would approve of the museums dedicated to mountain crafts, including one dedicated to Biltmore Industries. George would likely thrill at the agricultural and financial success of the winery and the estate's commitment to solar energy and canola biofuel. That forest that once seemed overlumbered and undervalued has rebounded heartily. These investments in the land are finally bringing the estate a level of self-sufficiency that George Vanderbilt envisioned, while tens of thousands of acres remain largely untouched. Protected, as George and Edith wished.

I kayak the French Broad often, the current carrying me through the Biltmore Estate. It feels peaceful and protected there, though as I head north the city springs much larger on the shores than it did even when I first arrived here little more than eleven years ago. As I move downstream, hop-infused industry looms on a horizon of renovated factories-cum-galleries; a red fox tears along the banks past sunning box turtles.

A great blue heron catches me off-guard, gliding low and sleek over the waters once called the Tahkeyostee. Peering down through its mountain waters I spy shells on the riverbed, bivalve visitors from perhaps far away shores.

My paddle slices the water's surface. Sun pierces a canopy of locust and oak. Time and the river roll ever on.

ACKNOWLEDGMENTS

Writing a book can feel a lot like constructing a house: Ideas are sketched, a structure emerges, finishing touches are added, and some dearly held ideas eventually go the way of George Vanderbilt's arboretum—well intentioned, but unrealized. Much like Biltmore House, this book would not exist without the expertise and support of many individuals and institutions. Without them, the floor would have fallen out from beneath me.

My agent of many years, Yfat Reiss Gendell, is part sounding board, part truth-telling voice of reason, and full-time advocate. She is a dedicated student of a constantly changing and often volatile industry, making her insights of invaluable importance to me. She and her team at Foundry Literary + Media—especially Jessica Felleman—are a unique and brilliant bunch, and I feel very fortunate to be on their roster.

I am grateful to editor Michelle Howry for believing in the potential of this story, and to Trish Todd for picking up where Michelle left off, as sometimes happens in this business. Trish dove in with enthusiasm, blue pencil at the ready, and treated this project as if it had always been on her docket. She was ably assisted by Kaitlin Olson. Tara Parsons, David Falk, and Susan Moldow guide an incredible team at Touchstone/Simon & Schuster—many of whom I was fortunate to work with on *The Girls of Atomic City*—and never wavered in their support of my book. The production team headed by Linda Sawicki, including copy editor Josh Karpf and proofreader W. Anne

Jones, asked all the right questions and, more important, cleaned up my mistakes when I could not see them anymore. The publicity and marketing crew—including Brian Belfiglio, Meredith Villarello, and publicist Jessica Roth—helped ensure my work found the right audience. Erich Hobbing gave my words a happy home on the page, and cover designer Cherlynne Li wrapped my work up in the prettiest package I could ever want.

This book would not have been possible without the countless manuscripts, letters, and other archives that provided a peek into the past. While much is digitized today, the vast majority of paper archives is not. Most notably, I would like to acknowledge the work and assistance of the librarians and archivists at Brown University's John Hay Library, the New York Public Library's Manuscript and Archives Division, Vanderbilt University's Jean and Alexander Heard Library, Yale's Beinecke Rare Book & Manuscript Library, the archives of the National Gallery of Art, the Manuscript Division of the Library of Congress, the Manuscripts Collections at Indiana University's Lilly Library, the Archives of Grolier Club, and the Archives and Manuscripts Division at the Wellcome Library in the UK. Closer to home, I must thank the librarians of the wonderful North Carolina Room at Pack Memorial Library.

I made many trips around the country to hunt down papers and photographs, but on occasion needed an extra pair of boots on the ground when I could not be everywhere at once. I thank the intrepid Deirdre Cossman in New York, my west coast arm, Drake Witham, and DC researcher Jessica Kaplan.

I wish to thank George Vanderbilt for his dedication to his dream and, even more so, Edith Vanderbilt for her tenacity in seeing that the remarkable historical treasure that is Biltmore House continues to exist. Today, her descendants and countless employees devote time and energy to ensure that the estate remains an inviting, year-round oasis for visitors. I know it is for me.

My North Carolina support system is vast, and there are too many friends and family to thank for getting me out of the house when

ACKNOWLEDGMENTS

I needed it, for a shot of perspective or a glass of wine. However, I must call out Lauren Harr and Caroline Green, my always-available, go-to-gals publicity team at Gold Leaf Literary, and Brenda Lilly, Asheville native and storyteller extraordinaire. Abbott Kahler's talent as a writer and generous spirit as a friend helped keep me moderately sane. I am joyfully indebted to my sister, Christine Fisher, and her husband, Todd, for their understanding, patience, and kindness, as this book intersected with our lives in unexpected and trying ways.

And finally, I can never thank my husband, Joseph D'Agnese, enough, for serving as in-house editor, expert anxiety-reliever, and all around exceptional human being.

Thank you all for seeing this through with me.

NOTES AND SOURCES

Throughout the research and writing of this book I consulted many historical archives and books, and numerous newspaper, magazine, and scholarly articles. I have walked the hallways, gardens, and grounds of Biltmore House countless times over the last eleven years. While I wish I had decades' worth of George, Edith, and Cornelia Vanderbilt's diaries, sometimes authors don't get that lucky. I was fortunate, however, that their lives impacted so many others, and some of their family members and friends kept extensive records which provided a more personal look into their lives at the time at which these events were occurring.

In these notes, I elaborate on any issues of importance or curiosity that I feel are worth sharing, but which would have detracted from the flow of the story were I to have mentioned them in the course of the narrative.

The following citations are substantial, but they are by no means exhaustive.

People

ESV: Edith Stuyvesant Dresser; Edith Vanderbilt; Edith Gerry
GWV: George Washington Vanderbilt
FLO: Frederick Law Olmsted
RMH: Richard Morris Hunt
WBOF: William B. Osgood Field
GP: Gifford Pinchot
CAS: Carl Alwin Schenck
NBB: Natalie Bayard Brown
JNBII: John Nicholas Brown II
CSV: Cornelia Vanderbilt

Principal Archives and Collections

JNBII papers: John Nicholas Brown II papers, Ms. 2007.012, Brown University Library.
NBB papers: Natalie Bayard Brown papers, Ms. 2007.011, Brown University Library.

NOTES AND SOURCES

WBOF papers: William B. Osgood Field Papers, Manuscripts and Archives Division, New York Public Library.

PLFNY: Paul Leicester Ford Papers, Manuscripts and Archives Division, New York Public Library.

FFNY: Ford Family Papers, Manuscripts and Archives Division, New York Public Library.

PLFB: Paul Leicester Ford Papers, Beinecke Rare Book & Manuscript Library, Yale University.

VAC: Verley Archer Collection, Jean and Alexander Heard Library, Vanderbilt University.

FLO vols. 9 and 10: Olmsted Papers and Records, Manuscript Division, Library of Congress, Washington, DC.

Olmsted Associates Records, Manuscript Division, Library of Congress, Washington, DC.

Theodore Roosevelt Papers. Library of Congress Manuscript Division. Theodore Roosevelt Digital Library. Dickinson State University.

UGW: *The Correspondence of James McNeill Whistler, 1855–1903*, ed. Margaret F. MacDonald, Patricia de Montfort, and Nigel Thorp; including *The Correspondence of Anna McNeill Whistler, 1855–1880*, ed. Georgia Toutziari, online edition, University of Glasgow, whistler.arts.gla.ac.uk /correspondence.

Gertrude Vanderbilt Whitney papers, 1851–1975, bulk, 1888–1942. Archives of American Art, Smithsonian Institution. Whitney Museum of American Art, Gertrude Vanderbilt Whitney papers. Gift of Flora Miller Irving.

Biltmore Industries Collection (1901–1980), D.H. Ramsey Library, Special Collections, University of North Carolina at Asheville.

Grolier Club Archives, New York, New York.

Correspondence of Edward Adamson, Wellcome Library; Great Britain.

Gallery Archives, National Gallery of Art, Washington, DC.

1. A Winter's Tale

Information regarding the personal life of Edith Dresser (ESV) and her family, including her childhood, housing, parents' courtship, and the deaths of George Warren Dresser and Susan LeRoy Dresser are taken from the unpublished manuscript *Reminiscence*, Pauline Merrill. John Nicholas Brown II papers, Ms. 2007.012, Brown University Library.

Pinchot family and residences at Gramercy Square from *Reminiscence* (previously cited) and other sources, including:

All Around the Town: Amazing Manhattan Facts and Curiosities, Patrick Bunyan (New York: Fordham University Press, 1999).

Shapers of the Great Debate on Conservation: A Biographical Dictionary, Rachel White Scheuering (Westport, CT: Greenwood Press, 2004).

Information regarding the history of Gramercy Square and its occupants, including

Dr. Valentine Mott, the Pinchot family, Edwin Booth, and the Players Club from sources including:

Exploring Gramercy Park and Union Square, Alfred Pommer and Joyce Pommer (Charleston, SC: History Press, 2015).

"East 17th Street/Irving Place Historic District Designation report," Gale Harris and Jay Shockley, N.Y.C. Landmarks Preservation Commission, 1998.

"Letter to Edwin Booth and His Reply," *New York Times*, Apr. 19, 1865; "Players," Leslie Stainton, *Common-Place*, April 2008, vol. 8, no. 3.

"Honors to Edwin Booth," *New York Times*, Jan. 1, 1893; untitled news clippings, page 1, *Pittsburgh Post*, Dec. 15, 1888; "The Amusement World," *Chicago Daily Tribune*, Oct. 14, 1888; "Bill Nye and Caesar," *St. Louis Post-Dispatch*, Jan. 1, 1888.

"Eulogium on Valentine Mott, M.D., L.L.D.," Gunning S. Bedford, *Transactions of the New York State Medical Society*, article XXVI, read before the Medical Society of the County of New York, Feb. 1, 1866.

"Death of Dr. Valentine Mott," *New York Times*, Apr. 27, 1865.

"Valentine Mott. American Surgeon Pioneer," Luis H. Toledo-Pereyra, *Journal of Investigative Surgery*, 2006, vol. 19, no. 2.

"The 1849 Dr. Valentine Mott Mansion," Tom Miller, *Daytonian in Manhattan*, Jan. 25, 2012, daytoninmanhattan.blogspot.com/2012/01/1849-dr-valentine-mott-mansion-no-1.html.

Body Snatching: The Robbing of Graves for the Education of Physicians in Early Nineteenth Century America, Suzanne M. Shultz (Jefferson, NC, and London: McFarland & Co., 1992).

Additional information regarding Pinchot family and Grey Towers from multiple sources, including:

"About Grey Towers: History," Grey Towers National Historic Site, USDA Forest Service, www.fs.usda.gov/main/greytowers/aboutgreytowers/history.

"U.S. Forest Service History: Gifford Pinchot (1865–1946)," Forest History Society, foresthistory.org/ASPNET/People/Pinchot/Pinchot.aspx.

"Nettie" Pinchot and dancing class from *Reminiscence*, previously cited.

"The Pinchot Family and the Battle to Establish American Forestry," James G. Lewis, *Pennsylvania History*, Spring 1999, vol. 66, no. 2.

NYC transportation and University Place: "History of Public Transportation in New York City," New York Transit Museum, transitmuseumeducation.org/trc/background.

Around Washington Square: An Illustrated History of Greenwich Village, Luther S. Harris, Baltimore: Johns Hopkins University Press, 2003. Union Square neighborhood and maps: *The "New Woman" Revised: Painting and Gender Politics on Fourteenth Street*, Ellen Wiley Todd, Berkeley: University of California Press, 1993

1883 fire at Hazelton Brothers piano manufactory from *Reminiscence*, previously cited. Also Jan. 20, 1889, New York periodical advertisement: "Hazelton Pianos, Established 1850" and "The Fire Record," *Detroit Free Press*, Jan. 30, 1883.

George Warren Dresser career details, military history, and family background;

additional information regarding Susan LeRoy Dresser and George Warren Dresser lives and deaths from: "Miscellaneous News: The Late Major G. W. Dresser," *The Journal of Gas Lighting, Water Supply, & Sanitary Improvement*, Jul. 8, 1883; *Reminiscence* and collected newspaper clippings in the Natalie Bayard Brown papers, Ms.2007.011, Brown University Library (NBB papers), including: "The Late Major Dresser," dated 1883, and "Obituary— George Warren Dresser," *American Gas Light Journal*, June 16, 1883; "Four Men Whose Work in Fraternizing the Gas Fraternity was of the Pioneer Type," Arthur. E. Boardman, *American Gas Light Journal*, July 19, 1909; *The Class of 1861: Custer, Ames and Their Classmates After West Point*, Ralph Kirshner (Carbondale, IL: Southern Illinois University Press, 1999).

Two-story addition onto LeRoy home in Newport reported in *Newport Mercury*, May 17, 1884.

Death of Daniel LeRoy taken from newspaper clippings in NBB papers, dated 1885.

Details regarding the Vanderbilt genealogy, the life of Cornelius "Commodore" Vanderbilt, origin of the name Vanderbilt, development of the New York Central railroad, and Vanderbilt roles in that venture, the life and death of William Henry Vanderbilt, and details of the Vanderbilt inheritances and bequeathments are highly documented. Sources include:

Commodore Cornelius Vanderbilt, Sophia Johnson Vanderbilt, and Their Descendants, Verley Archer (Nashville, TN: Vanderbilt University Press, 1973). This extensive genealogy was compiled by Archer for the university in preparation for its hundredth anniversary. Additional personal notes regarding the history of the Vanderbilt family were consulted in Verley Archer Collection, Jean and Alexander Heard Library, Vanderbilt University (VAC).

"Tales of the Commodore: Cornelius Vanderbilt at 200," Gaynelle Doll, *Vanderbilt Magazine*, Summer 1994, vol. 77, no. 3.

"Cornelius Vanderbilt. A Long and Useful Life Ended," *New York Times*, Jan. 5, 1877.

The First Tycoon: The Epic Life of Cornelius Vanderbilt, T. J. Stiles (New York: Vintage, 2009). In this book, Stiles posits that the perry auger story is most likely legend, and that his parents let him keep a portion of earnings from his initial ferry service.

The Last Will and Testament of the Late William H. Vanderbilt, With Portrait (New York: Taggart & Miller, 1886).

The Vanderbilt Legend: The Story of the Vanderbilt Family, Wayne Andrews (New York: Harcourt, Brace and Company, 1941).

Fortune's Children: The Fall of the House of Vanderbilt, Arthur T. Vanderbilt II (New York: William Morrow, 1989).

The Vanderbilt Era: Profiles of a Gilded Age, Louis Auchincloss (New York: Collier Books, 1989).

The New Netherland Institute, newnetherlandinstitute.org.

"The House of Vanderbilt," Frank Crowninshield, *Vogue*, Nov. 15, 1941.

"The House of Vanderbilt: A Railroad Prince's Fortune," *New York Times*, Nov. 13, 1877.

Regarding St. John's Freight Terminal: The history is well documented, including "Tribeca North Historic District: Designation Report," NYC Landmarks Preservation Commission, December 1992. Architect John Butler Snook: *Grove Encyclopedia of America Art*, vol. 1, ed. Joan Marter (New York: Oxford University Press, 2011).

Details regarding bronze frieze of Cornelius Vanderbilt also from "Tribeca North Historic District: Designation Report," as well as "The Curious Travels of the Commodore," Christopher Gray, *New York Times*, Mar. 19, 2006.

The Cruise of the Steam Yacht North Star; *a Narrative of the Excursion of Mr. Vanderbilt's Party to England, Russia, Denmark, France, Spain, Italy, Malta, Turkey, Madeira, Etc.*, Rev. John Overton Choules, D.D. (Boston: Gould & Lincoln; New York: Evans and Dickerson, 1854).

Grand Central Depot (later incarnations were Grand Central Station and Grand Central Terminal) from sources including: Author visits to "The History of Grand Central Terminal," on display at Grand Central Terminal, New York, NY, last visited Oct. 7, 2016. Also "100 Years of Grandeur: The Birth of Grand Central Terminal," Sam Roberts, *New York Times*, Jan. 18, 2013. "The Lost 1871 Grand Central Depot," Tom Miller, *Daytonian in Manhattan*, Feb. 4, 2013, daytoninmanhattan.blogspot.com/2013/02/the-lost-1871-grand-central-depot-42nd.html.

Details regarding Vanderbilt homes in New York and Newport, including the Triple Palace at 640 Fifth Avenue, are widely available. Sources include:

Auchincloss, previously cited.

Crowninshield, previously cited.

The Vanderbilts, Jerry E. Patterson (New York: Harry N. Abrams, 1989).

Gilded Mansions: Grand Architecture and High Society, Wayne Craven (New York, London: W.W. Norton, 2009).

The Vanderbilt Homes, Robert B. King with Charles O. McLean (New York: Rizzoli, 1989).

The Vanderbilts and the Gilded Age: Architectural Aspirations 1879–1901, John Foreman and Robbe Pierce Stimson (New York: St. Martin's Press, 1991).

"The Battle Money Couldn't Win: The Vanderbilts and Their Battle over Fifth Avenue," Christopher Gray, *New York Times*, June 12, 2004.

Regarding GWV inheritances and bequeathments, sources include: *The Last Will and Testament of William Henry Vanderbilt* (previously cited).

George W. Vanderbilt's Biltmore Estate: The Most Distinguished Private Place, John M. Bryan (New York: Rizzoli, 1994).

Letter from James T. Maher to Mr. and Mrs. John Nicholas Brown, dated June 21, 1965. John Nicholas Brown II papers, Ms. 2007.012, Brown University Library (JNBII papers).

"The Celebrated Trotting Mares Maud S. and Aldine, as They Appeared June 15th 1883: At the Gentlemen's Driving Park, Morrisania, N.Y. Driven by Their

Owner, William H. Vanderbilt, Esq." New York: Currier & Ives, 1883. Image, Library of Congress, loc.gov/item/90715687/.

GWV interest in the priesthood from Foreman and Stimson, previously cited; diary quotes and habit of recording expenses from Auchincloss, previously cited. GWV invitation to be a founding member of the Grolier Club from: Grolier Club. Records, 1884–1984, Archives, Letters & Manuscripts, the Grolier Club, 47 East Sixtieth Street, New York, NY. GWV's language proficiency in many sources, including: "Dusting Off the Pages of a Bookish Vanderbilt's Passion," Peter Applebome, *New York Times*, Mar. 11, 1999. Also GWV biography in *Dictionary of North Carolina Biography*, 6 vols., ed. William S. Powell (Chapel Hill, NC: University of North Carolina Press, 1979–1996).

GWV "Books I Have Read" cited in "The 1888 Jackson Square Library: No. 251 W. 13th Street," Tom Miller, Aug. 27, 2013, daytoninmanhattan.blogspot.com/2013/08/the-1888-jackson-square-library-no-251.html.

Best, North Carolina; and W. J. Best, railroad magnate, drawn from: "The W. North Carolina Railroad Syndicate," *Semi-Weekly Citizen* (Asheville, NC), Apr. 29, 1880; "The Western Railroad," *The Observer* (Raleigh, NC), Feb. 11, 1880; "The Western N.C. Railroad. Mr. Best in Possession and at Work," *Semi-Weekly Citizen*, June 3, 1880.

GWV and Maria Vanderbilt decisive visit to North Carolina in 1888 from many sources, including:

Correspondence of Frederick Law Olmsted. Author originally consulted Olmsted Associates Records, Manuscript Division, Library of Congress, Washington, DC; and Olmsted Papers and Records, Manuscript Division, Library of Congress, Washington, DC. This latter collection of FLO correspondence is now available in book form. Those volumes are cited here:

The Last Great Projects, 1890–1895, vol. 9 of *The Papers of Frederick Law Olmsted*, ed. David Schuyler and Gregory Kaliss (Baltimore: Johns Hopkins University Press, 2015) (FLO vol. 9).

The Early Boston Years, 1882–1890, vol. 8 of *The Papers of Frederick Law Olmsted*, ed. Ethan Carr, Amanda Gagel, and Michael Shapiro (Baltimore: Johns Hopkins University Press, 2013) (FLO vol. 8).

Richard Morris Hunt, Paul R. Baker (Cambridge, MA: MIT Press, 1980).

National Historic Landmark Nomination, NPS Form 10-900, Biltmore Estate, US Department of the Interior, National Park Service, prepared by Davyd Foard Hood, September 2003 (NHL nomination).

"Vanderbilt's View," *Asheville Citizen*, July 29, 1888.

"News Items," *Alamance Gleaner* (Graham, NC), May 10, 1888.

"Scenes in New York on the Lazy Summer Days," *Indianapolis News*, July 14, 1888.

"Great Smoky Mountains National Park: Threatened by Air Pollution," *Air Quality in the National Parks*, 2nd ed., chapter 4 (Washington, DC: US Department of the Interior, National Park Service, Air Resources Division, 2002), www.nature.nps.gov/air/Pubs/pdf/aqNps/aqnpsFour.pdf.

"Volatile Trees," Laura Naranjo, Earthdata, Earth Observing System Data and

Information System, NASA, earthdata.nasa.gov/user-resources/sensing-our
-planet/volatile-trees.

"Great Smoky Mountains National Park," previously cited.

Asheville's reputation as a "sanitarium destination" is well documented, including
advertisements throughout newspapers from the mid-1800s.

Cherokee "shaconage" or "place of the blue smoke" from sources including: "Great
Smoky Mountains National Park: Tennessee and North Carolina," National
Park Service, US Department of the Interior, nps.gov/nr/travel/cultural
_diversity/great_smoky_mountains_national_park.html. Also "The 'Place of
Blue Smoke,'" Jan. 22, 2017, Earth Observatory, NASA, earthobservatory
.nasa.gov/IOTD/view.php?id=89485.

Legend of Judaculla from author visits to Nantahala National Forest. Also "Judaculla Rock Jackson County," US Department of Agriculture, Forest
Service, www.fs.usda.gov/detail/nfsnc/learning/history-culture/?cid=stel
prdb5209548.

"Judaculla Rock," William L. Anderson, *Encyclopedia of North Carolina*, ed. William S. Powell (Chapel Hill: University of North Carolina Press, 2006).

Dr. Samuel Westray Battle cared for Maria Vanderbilt: NHL nomination, previously cited. Also "Dr. S. Westray Battle a Christian Scientist?" Dr. Irby Stephens, *Asheville Citizen-Times*, July 5, 1999.

Quote regarding Pisgah from Deuteronomy 34:1 (King James Bible).

GWV buying his first 661 parcels: Vertical files, Biltmore Estate Archives, as cited
in Bryan, previously cited.

Purchasing agents Burnett and McNamee from sources including: NHL nomination, previously cited. Untitled news clippings, page 1, *Asheville Citizen*, June
28, 1888; "Vanderbilt's Purchase," *Charlotte News*, Jan. 4, 1889; also, FLO
vol. 9, previously cited.

Newspaper quote citing "young Croesus" from "Vanderbilt's Lands. What the *New
York Herald* Says About It," *Asheville Citizen*, Jan. 9, 1889.

2. A Lady of the Long Man Rising

FLO biographical background, including work with Calvert Vaux and other proj-
ects is widely cited, including: *A Clearing in the Distance: Frederick Law
Olmsted and America in the 19th Century*, Witold Rybczynski (New York:
Scribner, 1999).

A Journey in the Seaboard Slave States: With Remarks on Their Economy, Frederick
Law Olmsted (London: Sampson Low, Son, & Co.; New York: Dix and
Edwards, 1856).

Information and quotes contained in this section regarding FLO initial meeting
with GWV and his overall impressions are drawn from FLO correspondence.

FLO letter to Frederick Kingsbury, dated Jan. 20, 1891, from FLO vol. 9, previously cited, and includes:

FLO initial visit to home site with GWV; FLO disappointed with initial impression; "vagabondish region," and "potentialities" quote; description of GWV visit to area with his mother, the "mild and invigorating" climate, GWV wandering; "miserable" woods; GWV concern about neighbors and sending McNamee to purchase; 2,000 acres purchased so far, GWV concern he had made a mistake; "good, distant outlook"; GWV desiring a park, FLO suggestion for game preserve, "pleasure ground and garden," and "forestry made on a large scale."

FLO also wrote RMH on Mar. 2, 1889: "local scenery not attractive" "exceedingly bleak place" and stated concern about northwest winds hitting carriages as they would approach the house. FLO vol. 8.

Letter dated Apr. 18, 1889, from FLO to Robert Douglas, then seventy-five-year-old horticulturist from England who worked often with FLO and helped plan plantings at Biltmore, from FLO vol. 8, and includes:

Reference to land "skinned by poor white farmers," and "occupied at present by negroes"; GWV desire for a park and FLO advising GWV instead on managed forestry; FLO desire for an arboretum.

Information regarding wagon arrival at Tribune Building: "A New Vanderbilt Home. All in the Land of the Sky," *Sun* (NY), June 29, 1890. Also from Patterson, previously cited.

Additional information regarding Tribune Building:

"Black and White and Red All Over," Christopher Gray, *New York Times*, May 6, 2012.

Richard Morris Hunt biographical information drawn from: Baker, previously cited.

The Architecture of Richard Morris Hunt, ed. Susan R. Stein (Chicago and London: University of Chicago Press, 1986).

"The Man Who Gilded the Gilded Age," David Garrard Lowe, *City Journal*, Autumn 1996.

Alva Vanderbilt ball: "All Society in Costume: Mrs. W. K. Vanderbilt's Great Fancy Dress Ball," *New York Times*, Mar. 27, 1883; also Patterson, Craven, and Lowe, all previously cited.

Mark Twain and the Gilded Age: *The Gilded Age: A Tale of Today*, Mark Twain and Charles Dudley Warner (Hartford: American Publishing Co., 1873).

"The Gilded Age," T. Jackson Lears, Gilder Lehman Institute of American History, gilderlehrman.org/history-by-era/gilded-age/essays/gilded-age (subscription required).

Ward McAllister, Caroline Astor. "The Father of the Four Hundred," William Bryk, *Sun* (NY), Aug. 9, 2005.

Hunt's work with Alva and the Petit Chateau drawn from Patterson, Baker, Foreman and Stimson, and Stein and Lowe, all previously cited.

Acorns as part of the Vanderbilt crest drawn from: Foreman and Stimson, previously cited. Also *Edith Wharton as Spatial Activist and Analyst*, Renee Somers (New York: Routledge, 2005).

Tenement life and pay scales from "Rent, Wages and the Cost of Living," 2005, Lower East Side Tenement Museum, web.archive.org/web/20160824221927/; www.tenement.org/encyclopedia/housing_rent.htm.

RMH quote regarding Vanderbilt "plantation" also from the *Sun*'s "A New Vanderbilt Home," previously cited.

Jackson Square Library: "The New Vanderbilt Library Opened," *New-York Tribune*, July 6, 1888. Estimation of Vanderbilt family wealth at $274 million and GWV share in it from "The Wealth of the Vanderbilts," *Tobacco Plant* (Durham, NC), Jan. 9, 1889. Similarly: "The Vanderbilt Wealth. No Other Single Family in the World Is so Enormously Rich," *Salina Daily Republican*, Apr. 9, 1889.

GWV, RMH, and Catharine Hunt 1889 trip to Europe, including itinerary, houses, and impressions, drawn from: Patterson, Craven, Baker, Stein, Foreman and Stimson, and NHL nomination, all previously cited. Additional details, itinerary, and quotes from Catharine Hunt, from *Unpublished Biography of Richard Morris Hunt: Written by His Widow Catherine Clinton Howland Hunt, Between 1895 and 1909*, Library of Congress Prints and Photographs Division, Washington, DC.

GWV sending tapestry measurements back to RMH offices, drawn from: "A Flemish Set of Venus and Vulcan Tapestries. I.-Their Origin and Design," Ella S. Siple, *Burlington Magazine for Connoisseurs*, Nov. 1938, vol. 73, no. 428.

Regarding GWV Napoleon chess set: Repeated author visits to Biltmore House and Estate between 2006 and 2017. C. Hunt, previously cited. Also, "Of Kingdoms, Principalities and Carolina Castles," Sarah Booth Conroy, *Washington Post*, Jan. 1, 1978.

News and Comments section, *Furniture Gazette*, Jan.–June 1884, vol. 21.

"A Home for Napoleon's Chess Set," Mike Welton, *Architects + Artisans*, Sept. 16, 2010. "Biltmore's Most Important Manuscript," Mike Welton, *Architects + Artisans*, Feb. 23, 2012.

Brooklyn Chess Chronicle, Oct. 1883–Sept. 1884, vol. 2.

FLO wrote GWV an extensive report on July 12, 1889, FLO vol. 8, previously cited. This letter addresses numerous issues, including: concern for water supply, comments regarding "campers, squatters and transient settlers," tree specifics, FLO desire for nursery, comments regarding Approach Road. "Wild and secluded," as though visitors were in the "remote depths of a natural forest," FLO comments and quotes regarding naming estate (Broadwood, etc.):

FLO quotes about "capabilities of the estate" and "people crossing the Atlantic to see it" from FLO letter to GWV of July 12, 1889, previously cited.

Site possessing a good outlook, concern about northwest winds hitting carriages as they would approach the house: FLO to RMH, Mar. 2, 1889, FLO vol. 8.

Old Colonial House for G. W. Vanderbilt: from Bryan, previously cited.

Cherokee name(s) regarding French Broad River from various sources, including: *The French Broad*, Wilma Dykeman (Knoxville: University of Tennessee Press, 1955) and "History of French Broad River," RiverLink, riverlink.org/learn

/about-riverlink/history-of-french-broad-river/. Spellings of "Tahkeyostee" vary. Author chose Dykeman usage.

GWV ancestors and history of name Vanderbilt drawn from Archer genealogy, previously cited; *Commodore: The Life of Cornelius Vanderbilt*, Edward J. Renehan Jr. (New York: Basic Books, 2007); Doll, previously cited.

Bilton issue from Foreman and Stimson, previously cited, also: "He Has Named the Baby," *Daily Citizen* (Asheville, NC), Feb. 16, 1890; "Biltmore is the Name," *Semi-Weekly Citizen* (Asheville, NC), Mar. 6, 1890.

Anti-Biltmore Van-ity and W. J. Best letters: "Asheville Junction's New Name," *Semi-Weekly Citizen*, (Asheville, NC), Mar. 20, 1890; "Mr. Vanderbilt's Estate," *Charlotte Observer*, (Charlotte, NC), Mar. 21, 1890; "Sic Transit Gloria Mundi," *Hickory Press* (Hickory, NC), Mar. 13, 1890.

Rail spur arrival and cost: NHL nomination, previously cited. *The State Chronicle* (Raleigh, NC), Mar. 29, 1890; "At Biltmore: Progress of the Work on the Vanderbilt Estate," *Semi-Weekly Citizen* (Asheville, NC), May 29, 1890; news clips of *Semi-Weekly Citizen* (Asheville, NC), Mar. 27, 1890; *The Quest for Progress: The Way We Lived in North Carolina, 1870–1920*, Sydney Nathans (Chapel Hill: University of North Carolina Press, 1983).

Trains jumping tracks: Bryan, previously cited.

Visiting *Sun* reporter and article, including discussion of population growth, property assessment, schools, fishing stream, "booms of the west," etc.: From "A New Vanderbilt Home. All in the Land of the Sky," *Sun* (NY), June 29, 1890.

Asheville as gilt-edged health resort from ' "Booming' Buncombe: A Gilt-Edged Health Resort," *Asheville Democrat*, July 17, 1890. Rockefeller stay also noted in news clips of *Semi-Weekly Citizen* (Asheville, NC), Mar. 27, 1890.

Kenilworth Inn information, view, and GWV investment drawn from: "The Kenilworth Inn," *Asheville Daily Citizen*, Sept. 17, 1890; *Around Biltmore Village*, Bill Alexander (Charleston, SC: Arcadia Publishing, 2008); "Kenilworth Inn Burned To-Day the Loss $310,000," *Evening Chronicle* (Charlotte, NC), Apr. 14, 1909.

FLO hoping GWV could move forward with land purchase at "market rather than Vanderbilt prices," from FLO letter to Douglas, Apr. 18, 1889, previously cited.

Hilliard and Brookshire Farm purchases, quote regarding "wealthiest land-owner": "Vanderbilt's Acres: The Millionaire Adding to His Already Large Domain," *Daily Citizen* (Asheville, NC), Oct. 9, 1889.

Sale of Patton farm from *Reidsville Review* (Reidsville, NC), June 26, 1889.

Sale information also from Buncombe County Register of Deeds, Buncombe County, NC.

GWV "may even yet own the famous mountain peaks" from *Charlotte News* (Charlotte, NC), June 21, 1890.

Charles Collins holding out from selling, postcards: "Vanderbilt Buys Log Cabin: Negro Who Had Spurned Millionaire's Offer for Years Relents," *Washington Post*, Jan. 27, 1907; "Collins Willing to Sell, George Vanderbilt's Negro Neighbor Wants to Dispose of Farm," *Boston Post*, Aug. 18, 1901; "Mr. Vanderbilt Buys Collins' Famous Hut," *Madison County Record* (Marshall, NC), Feb. 15, 1907.

T. H. Lindsey, photographer, documenting the construction of the estate: "Vanderbilt's View," *Asheville Citizen*, July 29, 1888.

Descriptions of early Biltmore Village from numerous author visits to the Biltmore Estate and village; and Alexander, previously cited. New AME church and quote of thanks from congregation from Alexander.

Water arriving on esplanade: NHL nomination, previously cited.

Biltmore Brick and Tile Works: Quote from ad in *Asheville Daily Citizen*, Mar. 3, 1893. Additional information from: "Biltmore Is Thriving, Its Brick and Tile Manufactory," *Asheville Daily Citizen*, Feb. 24, 1891.

25,000 to 30,000 or more bricks per day: "At Biltmore. Progress of Work on the Vanderbilt Estate," *Semi-Weekly Citizen*, May 29, 1890; "In Ninety Years, Family Has Learned to Make Profit from Experience," Louise Lione, *Charlotte Observer*, Dec. 22, 1985; Patterson, previously cited.

Asheville Woodworking Company starting business: *Asheville Daily Citizen*, May 16, 1893. "Notice of Incorporation of Asheville Woodworking Company," *Asheville Daily Citizen*, Apr. 10, 1893.

Worker wages from Bryan, previously cited.

Gouverneur Morris Ogden house in Bar Harbor $200,000: from NHL nomination, previously cited. "Vanderbilts Under the Pines," Brad Emerson, *New York Social Diary*, Feb. 24, 2011.

1893 World's Columbian Exposition and its organization, including FLO and RMH roles in it from Rybczynski, Baker, FLO vol. 9, all previously cited.

Chain of command at Biltmore, titles, roles here and in future chapters: from NHL nomination and Bryan, previously cited.

FLO letter to James Gall offering work, GWV being delicate, description of area: Letter from FLO to James Gall of Oct. 30, 1888, Olmsted Associates Records, Manuscript Division, Library of Congress, Washington, DC (FLO Assoc.).

Chauncey Beadle background drawn from: NHL nomination, previously cited; *The Silva of North America: A Description of the Trees which Grow Naturally in North America Exclusive of Mexico,* Charles Sprague Sargent (Boston and New York: Houghton, Mifflin and Company, 1894).

FLO sick in 1890, quotes about "jar of the cars" and "Southern doctor": FLO to Kingsbury, Jan. 20 1891, previously cited.

Station Inn opening in Biltmore: "Vanderbilt's Hotel: The 'Station Inn' to be Opened at Biltmore," *Semi-Weekly Citizen* (Asheville, NC), Nov. 20, 1890; Station Inn advertisement from *Asheville Daily Citizen*, Dec. 11, 1890.

3. Rhapsody in Mauve

1890 Christmas poem sent to Dresser sisters from NBB papers.

Information regarding Dresser family movements, houses, descriptions, schooling, and polo matches from JNBII papers, *Reminiscence*; also "The Closing of Mrs. Gilliat's School" from newspaper clippings in NBB papers, dated 1888.

Daniel Dresser–Emma Burnham wedding: newspaper clippings in NBB papers, previously cited.

Newport Casino history and scene setting from *Reminiscence*, previously cited, also including men's singles tennis championship, from "Historic Grounds: Newport Casino," International Tennis Hall of Fame, tennisfame.com /museum-and-grounds/historic-grounds/.

Information on The Breakers and Marble House from Patterson, King, and Craven, previously cited.

Mauve Decade: "The Color of Money," Marcia Bartusiak, *New York Times*, Apr. 12, 2001, review of *Mauve: How One Man Invented a Color That Changed the World*, Simon Garfield (New York: W.W. Norton, 2001); *The Mauve Decade: American Life at the End of the Nineteenth Century*, Thomas Beer (New York: A.A. Knopf, 1926).

Queen Victoria, Empress Eugénie use: "How Mauve Was Her Garment," Priscilla Long, *American Scholar*, June 19, 2013, theamericanscholar.org/how-mauve -was-her-garment/.

William H. Perkin dye and patent information from "How Was Mauve Made?," Assessment for Learning: Chemistry, Royal Society of Chemistry, rsc .org/Education/Teachers/Resources/Aflchem/resources/72/72%20 Resources/72%20How%20was%20mauve%20made.pdf.

"Raid on the Low Cuts," Cholly Knickerbocker, *Argus*, Dec. 31, 1894.

Vanderbilts buying up Adirondacks: "What Will They Do With It? The Vanderbilts, Who Are Not Sportsmen, Buying Up the Adirondacks," Cholly Knickerbocker, *The Hutchinson News* (Hutchinson, KS), Jan. 23, 1894.

Irving satire of early New York: *A History of New-York: From the Beginning of the World to the End of the Dutch Dynasty: Containing, Among Many Surprising and Curious Matters, the Unutterable Ponderings of Walter the Doubter, the Disastrous Projects of William the Testy, and the Chivalric Achievements of Peter the Headstrong, the Three Dutch Governors of New Amsterdam: Being the Only Authentic History of the Times That Ever Hath Been, or Ever Will be Published, by Diedrich Knickerbocker*, Washington Irving (New York: Inskeep & Bradford, 2 vols., 1809).

GWV construction rumors, including schools: "Personals" column, *Chicago Daily Tribune*, Nov. 6, 1888; also "Vanderbilt's Purchase," *Charlotte News*, Jan. 4, 1889; "Vanderbilt's Lands. What the *New York Herald* Says About It," *Asheville Citizen*, Jan. 9, 1889; "Go find the brains," regarding Teachers College, "Nicholas Murray Butler and the Teaching Profession," Richard Whittemore, *History of Education Quarterly* 1, no. 3 (1961): 22-37. doi:10.2307/366924; also "A Tribute to TC's Founding Families," Teachers College, Columbia University, March 7, 2013, tc.columbia.edu/articles/2013/march/a-tribute -to-tcs-founding-families/, and "TC Timeline," Teachers College, Columbia University, tc.columbia.edu/articles/2013/march/a-tribute-to-tcs-founding -families/, and Andrews, previously cited.

NOTES AND SOURCES

FLO finding GWV "refined and bookish" from FLO to Kingsbury, Jan. 20, 1891, previously cited.

GWV as "trustful," "cordially friendly": FLO letter to engineer W. A. Thompson, Nov. 6, 1889, FLO Assoc.

Queen Victoria has gout: "Personals" column, *Chicago Daily Tribune*, Nov. 6, 1888.

GP diary entries and quotes taken from *The Conservation Diaries of Gifford Pinchot*, Gifford Pinchot, ed. Harold K. Steen (Durham, NC: Forest History Society, 2001).

GP history and schooling, James Pinchot friendship with FLO: from Foreman and Stimson, previously cited.

Grey Towers information: Grey Towers National Historic Cite, previously cited.

"James Wallace Pinchot (1831–1908): One Man's Evolution toward Conservation in the Nineteenth Century," Nancy P. Pittman, *Yale F&ES Centennial News*, Fall 1999.

Dietrich Brandis, Bernhard Fernow background from: *Cradle of Forestry in America: The Biltmore Forest School, 1898–1913*, Carl Alwin Schenck, ed. Ovid Butler (Durham, NC: Forest History Society, 1955, 1983) and GP *Diaries*, previously cited; Lewis, *Pennsylvania History*, previously cited.

GP impressions of FLO from *Diaries*, previously cited.

Pinchot quote about Biltmore House not belonging and GWV being sheltered by female relatives, concept of wasting timber, from his autobiography, *Breaking New Ground*, Gifford Pinchot (New York: Harcourt, Brace, and Co., 1947).

Fernow disappointment in Pinchot declining invite: Lewis, *Pennsylvania History*, previously cited.

Brick House information and use, *The Standard* (Concord, NC), Oct. 23, 1890. Also, NHL nomination, previously cited.

Pinchot's Working Plan: *Biltmore Forest: The Property of Mr. George W. Vanderbilt: An Account of Its Treatment, and the Results of the First Year's Work*, Gifford Pinchot (Chicago: R. R. Donnelly & Sons).

Adele Sloane quotes and comments from her diaries, as cited in *Maverick in Mauve: The Diary of a Romantic Age*, Florence Adele Sloane, with commentary by Louis Auchincloss (Garden City, NY: Doubleday, 1983).

Laura Houghteling information drawn from *Maverick*, GP *Diaries*; Houghteling family living across from estate: Asheville as gilt-edged health resort from ' "Booming' Buncombe: A Gilt-Edged Health Resort," *Asheville Democrat*, July 17, 1890. "The Mystery of Gifford Pinchot and Laura Houghteling," James G. Bradley, Grey Towers, USDA Forest Service, Milford, PA.

Death of Edith Dresser's grandmother: Various news clippings, NBB papers; "Memorial of Susan E. Leroy," *New York Times*, June 29, 1899.

History, St. Mark's Church: "St. Mark's Historic District, Borough of Manhattan," Landmarks Preservation Commission, Jan. 14, 1969.

Letter from Edith's grandmother to family members: NBB papers, previously cited. Additional information regarding vacating the house, Thanksgiving, from *Reminiscence*. Additional Edith Wharton information from *Backwards*

Glance, previously cited; "Mrs. Wharton in New York," Elizabeth Hardwick, *New York Review of Books,* Jan. 21, 1988; *The Letters of Edith Wharton,* ed. R. W. B. Lewis and Nancy Lewis (New York: Collier Books, 1988).

Panic/Depression of 1893: "The Depression of 1893," David O. Whitten, *EH.Net Encyclopedia,* ed. Robert Whaples, Aug. 14, 2001, eh.net/encyclopedia /the-depression-of-1893/.

ESV trip to South America from *Reminiscence,* previously cited, Ship registry of the S.S. *Seguranca,* dated April 4, 1893.

History of equator crossing: "Behind the Strange and Controversial Ritual When You Cross the Equator at Sea," Cale Weissman, *Atlas Obscura,* Oct. 23, 2015, atlasobscura.com/articles/behind-the-strange-and-controversial-ritual -when-you-cross-the-equator-at-sea.

Quotes from William B. Osgood Field (WBOF) regarding return to Hoboken: WBOF letter to his mother, dated Apr. 11, 1893; also Field biographical information, from: William B. Osgood Field Papers, Manuscripts and Archives Division, The New York Public Library (WBOF papers).

Chauncey Beadle plantings and numbers: "Beadle's Report of Nurseryman for Week Ending December 28, 1893 and January 4, 1894," Biltmore Estate Archives, as cited in *The Biltmore Nursery: A Botanical Legacy,* Bill Alexander (Charleston, SC: Natural History Press, 2007); "Where Nothing Succeeds Like Excess," Benjamin Forgey, *Washington Post,* Nov. 12, 1994.

Planned acquisition of Pink Beds and larger tracts from GP *Diaries.*

World's Columbian Exposition of 1893: Rybczynski, Baker, FLO vol. 9, previously cited.

Biltmore Forest, Gifford Pinchot, previously cited.

Adele comments, Courtlandt Palmer information from her *Maverick,* previously cited. Additional Courtlandt Palmer information from "Courtlandt Palmer, Composer, Pianist, 79," *New York Times,* Dec. 16, 1951.

Construction challenges (mortar not setting, flooded clay pits): Bryan, previously cited.

Powder explosion from "Powder Exploded: Two Men Seriously Injured at Biltmore," *Semi-Weekly Citizen* (Asheville, NC), May 15, 1890.

FLO increasing frustration with Gall: "he blunders": from FLO letter to John Charles Olmsted, Oct. 27, 1890, FLO vol. 9.

GP impressions of FLO from GP *Diaries.*

FLO detailed instructions, "purling sound": FLO letter to James G. Gall Jr., Mar. 12, 1891, FLO vol. 9.

GWV travels to Gibraltar from *Mauve.*

Gardener's, shepherd's cottages first ones finished: NHL nomination, previously cited.

RMH to Catharine regarding scale, approach road, "professional joy" GWV devotion to mother: *Unpublished Biography of Richard Morris Hunt,* previously cited.

FLO regarding "first great private work": FLO letter to his nephew and later stepson, John Charles Olmsted, Oct. 27, 1890, FLO vol. 9.

Palmer engagement rumor: "Cholly's Chimes," *Daily Republican* (Monongahela, PA), Nov. 15, 1894.

4. Collaborations and Consecrations

Dresser family life in Paris from *Reminiscence*.

Paris in 1890s, Jules Chéret, and Henri Toulouse-Lautrec: "The Life and Art of French Painter Jules Cheret," 2012, cheret.info; "Posters of Paris: Toulouse-Lautrec & His Contemporaries," Milwaukee Art Museum, mam .org/posters-of-paris/biographies.php.

La Touraine menu: UNLV Libraries Digital Collections: *La Touraine* steamship, menu, Oct. 7, 1893, digital.library.unlv.edu/u?/menus,6031.

Catharine Hunt taking in Dresser family dog from *Reminiscence*.

FLO beliefs about/conflict with Hunt regarding the village, and related quotes from FLO: letter to Charles Eliot dated Apr. 29, 1895, FLO vol. 9, previously cited.

The circumstances surrounding John Singer Sargent's painting of the portraits of FLO and RMH are widely documented, and are drawn from: Patterson, Baker, and Rybczynski, previously cited. Sargent quote from his May–June 1895 letter to Sarah Choate Sears, as cited in *John Singer Sargent: His Portrait*, Stanley Olson (New York: St. Martin's Press, 1986). Catharine Hunt disappointment with paintings from *Unpublished Biography of Richard Morris Hunt*, previously cited.

Desire for FLO to come home after sitting: letter from John Olmsted to FLO Jr. dated May 1895 (as cited in Bryan).

GP departure and consultancy pay: "Gifford Pinchot, Consulting Forester," Harold T. Pinkett, *New York History* 39, no. 1 (January 1958); *Gifford Pinchot: Forester-Politician*, M. Nelson McGeary (Princeton, NJ: Princeton University Press, 1960).

Carl Alwin Schenck (CAS) biographical information drawn from: *Cradle of Forestry*, previously cited.

GP comments on CAS from Pinchot *Diaries*.

Adele marriage to Jay Burden: "Burden-Sloane Wedding," *New York Times*, June 7, 1895.

Adele to Biltmore after wedding: "Mr. and Mrs. Burden at Biltmore," *New York Times*, June 9, 1895.

RMH death, GWV stopping work: "Death of Richard M. Hunt," *New York Times*, Aug. 1, 1895; "Richard Morris Hunt Dead," *Asheville Daily Citizen*, Aug. 1, 1895.

Description of exterior of house, tiles, ornamentation from repeated author visits to Biltmore House; Patterson and Craven, previously cited.

Indiana limestone, Hallowell from Patterson, previously cited, and "Etched in Stone: The Façade of Biltmore House," Joanne O'Sullivan, *Open House: The Official Blog of Biltmore*, Mar. 18, 2015, biltmore.com/blog/article/etched-in -stone-the-facade-of-biltmore-house.

NOTES AND SOURCES

Rosso di Verona lions: "Caring for Our Outdoor Sculptures," Biltmore *Ambassador*, Fall 2014; 1,700-pound chandelier: "A Behind-the-Scenes Visit to Biltmore," Leigh Ann Henion, *Our State Magazine*, March 2011.

Background and information on Guastavino: *Guastavino Vaulting: The Art of Structural Tile*, John Ochsendorf (New York: Princeton Architectural Press, 2010); "The American Dream of Rafael Guastavino (1842–1908), Mercè Piqueras, *Contributions to Science* (Barcelona) issue 9, 2013; "Guastavino National Historic Home Site," christmount.com.

Letter from John Olmsted to FLO Jr., that GWV did not intend to finish the house before opening, cited in Bryan.

House unfinished aspects: from Bryan, Covington, previously cited; "Vanderbilt's New Palace," *Salt Lake Herald* (UT), May 19, 1895.

On GWV expenses and outlays: Baedeker, *The United States*, published in 1904, describes GWV home as costing $4 million to build.

Karl Bitter: "Karl Theodore Francis Bitter," *Paintings and Sculpture in the Collection of the National Academy of Design*, ed. David B. Dearinger, vol. 1 (New York and Manchester: Hudson Hills Press, 2004).

House statistics (square footage, rooms) are widely available, including from repeated author visits to Biltmore House; 11 million bricks from "George W. Vanderbilt Lived, Built on a Grand Scale," Doug Reed, *Asheville Citizen*, July 17, 1960. The citing of number of bedrooms, etc., varies over the years. Numbers here based on current tour publications from the Biltmore Estate.

Arrival of Vanderbilt party at Christmas from WBOF papers; *Swannanoa* railcar description from "Vanderbilt Ahead of 'Downton Abbey' in Cars and Trains," Bruce C. Steele, *Citizen-Times* (Asheville, NC), Mar. 2, 2015; McNamee preparations, fish orders: *Christmas at Biltmore: Celebrating at America's Largest Home* (Asheville, NC: Biltmore Company, 2014).

Western Union line, arrival of guests: "Christmas at Biltmore House," *Asheville Daily Citizen*, Dec. 19, 1895.

Seating arrangement and Gertrude Vanderbilt Whitney diary from "Dinner book, vol. II, 1895 Nov. 9 through 1896 Mar. 5," Gertrude Vanderbilt Whitney papers, 1851–1975, bulk, 1888–1942, Archives of American Art, Smithsonian Institution.

The Breakers rebuilding details: "The Breakers," Preservation Society of Newport County, newportmansions.org/explore/the-breakers; Foreman and Stimson, previously cited.

Consuelo marriage to duke, a non-American match: *Maverick*, previously cited.

Alva–Willie K. divorce: "W. K. Vanderbilt Loses: His Wife Gets an Absolute Divorce and Custody of Children," *New York Times*, Mar. 6, 1895.

WBOF descriptions of house, weather, hunting trips, New Year's Eve: from letters to his mother, undated, from Dec. 31, 1895 and Jan. 1, 1896. Travel back to New York City from WBOF diary entries, WBOF papers.

Alice Twombly death and funeral service drawn from: WBOF papers, and "Miss Alice Twombly," *Chicago Daily Tribune*, Jan. 5, 1896.

Marguerite Shepard death from Sloane-Auchincloss, previously cited, and "Death of Miss Marguerite Shepard," *Democrat and Chronicle* (Rochester, NY), Feb. 1, 1895.

Clarence Barker death: Telegram from GWV to WBOF dated Feb, 12, 189; WBOF papers; "North Carolina News" (brief), *Charlotte Democrat*, Mar. 6, 1896; "Death of Clarence Barker," *Wilmington Messenger*, Feb. 15, 1896; "A Memorial Concert. Mr. Clarence Barker's Fantasia heard in Public after His Death," *New York Times*, Feb. 28, 1897.

Adele Burden loss of baby, from *Maverick*, previously cited.

GP comments on GWV OK with GP directing business at Biltmore from Pinchot *Diaries*, previously cited.

Opening of All Souls from book, deeding of church, description of interior, opening day, drawn from repeated author visits to site, and *The Story of a Church: All Souls in Biltmore: Book One, The First Sixty Years, 1896–1956* (Asheville, NC: All Souls Church, 1979).

St. Bartholomew's information from author visit and "A Brief History of St. Bart's" (pamphlet), St. Bartholomew's (New York, n.d.).

Helen and Maitland Armstrong: "Maitland Armstrong, Artist, Dies at 82," *New York Times*, May 27, 1918; "Opalescent Decades, Part 2," from "Style, Status, and Religion: America's Pictorial Windows, 1840–1950," Virginia Chieffo Raguin, college.holycross.edu/RaguinStainedGlassInAmerica/Home/index.html.

Death of Maria Louisa Kissam Vanderbilt from book and news reports, including: "Mrs. W. H. Vanderbilt Dead: Stricken with Heart Failure at Scarborough," *New York Times*, Nov. 7, 1896; "Mrs. Vanderbilt's Will," *New York Times*, Nov. 14, 1896.

5. A Crossing of Some Consequence

Rue Vernet recital: newspaper clipping in Natalie Bayard Brown papers, Ms.2007.011, Brown University Library (NBB papers).

Description of life in Paris from *Reminiscence*, previously cited.

Veuve Poulard and La Mère Poulard referred to in *Reminiscence*, and remains legendary in France. Additional detail provided by "La Mere Poulard," E. Couillard, parish priest of Mont-St-Michel (1932), full text online at le-mont-saint-michel.org/mere-poulard-01.htm; Mont St-Michel description from author visit.

Brittany tradition of mistletoe/cider from *Reminiscence* and "The Contributor's Club: A Breton Survival," *Atlantic Monthly*, June 1901.

Jacut-de-la Mer letter from ESV to NBB dated Aug. 8, 1896, NBB papers, previously cited.

President McKinley at Biltmore: "M'Kinley Visits Biltmore: Refuses to Enter George Vanderbilt's House Unless His Newspaper Guests Can Go Along," *New York Times*, June 15, 1897. Harding's response: "The Visit to Biltmore House," *Asheville Daily Citizen*, June 14, 1897.

"Queen Victoria's Diamond Jubilee," Christopher Klein, June 5, 2012, history.com
/news/queen-victorias-diamond-jubilee.

GWV, family, and friends in London for Jubilee (PLF–Beinecke papers, newspapers) GWV time in London and dinners: PLF Norway.

Regarding yacht to Norway: Newspaper clippings, *Logansport Pharos*, Aug. 5, 1897.

Details of WBOF's travel to India, description of GWV's meetings with ESV,
GWV's personality while abroad, and GWV's subsequent courtship of
ESV are drawn from two sources: WBOF's travel letters to his mother,
1897–1898; and WBOF's later typescript of these same 1897–1898 letters,
WBOF papers, previously cited.

Natalie Dresser marriage to John Nicholas Brown: Newspaper clippings, including those in NBB papers and *Reminiscence*; description of coming out at
Kingscote from *Reminiscence* and newspaper.

Pauline Dresser marriage to George Merrill: "Miss Pauline Dresser to be Married,"
New York Times, Oct. 16, 1897. "Merrill-Dresser," *Sun* (NY), Dec. 2, 1897.

Royal Blue Book: Fashionable Directory and Parliamentary Guide (London: Kelly &
Co. Limited, 1897).

James McNeill Whistler (JMW) biographical information and correspondence:
The Correspondence of James McNeill Whistler, 1855–1903, ed. Margaret F.
MacDonald, Patricia de Montfort, and Nigel Thorp; including *The Correspondence of Anna McNeill Whistler, 1855–1880*, ed. Georgia Toutziari, online edition, University of Glasgow, whistler.arts.gla.ac.uk/correspondence
(UGW). GWV engaging JMW to do portrait: letter from GWV to JMW
dated May 18, 1897.

Paris itinerary, dinner, and theater descriptions, Christmas celebration all from
WBOF letters.

Quo Vadis: A Narrative of the Time of Nero, Henryk Sienkiewicz (New York: Gros-
sett & Dunlap, 1897).

India travels from WBOF letters and autobiography.

GWV $1 million life insurance policy cited in letter from E. G. Kennedy to JMW
dated Dec. 9, 1897, UGW. Also "New York without a Vanderbilt," *World*
(New York), May 29, 1898; "The Richest Two Bachelors in America to Wed
within a Month Two of America's Most Beautiful Girls," *New York Herald*,
May 8, 1898.

GWV letters to WBOF detailing his activities in Paris, dated and to PLF.

And telegrams from WBOF papers, previously cited.

6. New Mistress

It is challenging to quantify the amount of attention this engagement and marriage commanded, on par with any celebrity wedding of the modern age, especially when considering the limited communications technology. Quotes
and other information regarding the wedding, engagement, and honeymoon
are drawn from:

"Counting Up the Eligible Males that Remain in the Vanderbilt Family," *New York Journal*, May 8, 1898.

ESV-GWV wedding invitation from NBB papers, previously cited.

"Palace for a Bride: George Vanderbilt's Beautiful Home in Biltmore, N.C.," *The Inter Ocean* (Chicago), June 5, 1898. Also discusses the physical appearance of GWV and ESV, especially ESV height and height of her brother, Daniel: "A woman of stalwart proportions," "handsome as the typical venus," "bold irregular features."

"A Vanderbilt Wedding: Owner of Biltmore House to be Married Thursday," *Asheville Daily Citizen*, May 30, 1898. Details include, dress, attendants, ushers, breakfast.

"A Daughter of the Gods: Miss Edith Dresser Is Six Feet Tall and Divinely Fair," *Washington Times* (Washington, DC), May 29, 1898.

"Captured a Millionaire," *Evening Wisconsin* (Milwaukee), Apr. 28, 1898.

"A Multi-Millionaire in Cupid's Clutches," *Lima News* (Lima, Ohio), June 10, 1898 (calls GWV "impossible catch").

"A Wealthy Benedict Who Surrenders at Last," *Morning Telegram* (New York), May 8, 1898. Also includes: "supposed to have been a confirmed bachelor," "capitulated only after he had fallen in love."

"America's richest bachelor is going to wed. Even in the midst of war we must pay some attention to this stupendous fact," *New York Journal*, date unknown.

Noting the Spanish-American War: *Courier* (Syracuse, NY), Apr. 30, 1898.

Met while at Queen Victoria Jubilee theory posited by "The Vanderbilt Wedding," *Asheville Daily Gazette*, Apr. 30, 1898; and "G.W. Vanderbilt to Marry: His Engagement to Miss Edith Dresser Announced," *New York Times*, Apr. 29, 1898. "New York without a Vanderbilt," *The World* (New York, NY), May 29, 1898.

"Three American Graces," *New York Herald*, May 8, 1898: "All the Dresser Girls are finely educated and are considered particularly brilliant."

Utica Press, May 3, 1898: "Biltmore . . . suitable retreat for a prince or a monarch."

"Society: New York," *Form: The Monthly Magazine of Society*, 1898, vols. 3 and 4.

"A Daughter of the Gods: Miss Edith Dresser is Six Feet Tall and Divinely Fair," *Washington Times*, May 29, 1898.

GWV "decidedly foreign of aspect," ESV "handsome" from *Times Democrat* (New Orleans, LA), April 28, 1898:

GWV "delicate" nature was commented on widely, not just during his engagement and wedding, including a previously cited letter from FLO to James Gall, and his overall fragility is referenced in Foreman and Stimson. Also: "Scenes in New York on the Lazy Summer Days," *Indianapolis News*, July 14, 1888.

New York Times, May 8, 1898, commented on ESV height.

"For him to strike out for himself in the matrimonial field amazes" from "The Vanderbilt Wedding: New York Papers Do Not Agree as to the Place," *Asheville Daily Citizen*, Apr. 30, 1898. Also refers to ESV height, referred to her as "handsome."

GWV promise not to marry while his mother alive, surprised that he is engaged: "Betrothal of a Vanderbilt: George W. to Wed Miss Edith Dresser," *San Francisco Chronicle*, Apr. 29, 1898; also *Chicago Tribune*, Apr. 29, 1898, "Vanderbilt Wedding June 1."

New York Press, May 8, 1898: "he was looked on as almost unattainable."

"A Vanderbilt to Wed," *St. Louis Star*, Apr. 28, 1898. Item includes: "members of the smart set . . . George would always live a bachelor's life," and "modest means."

The American (Nashville, TN), May 1, 1898, addressed rumors of GWV past engagements.

Item (New Orleans, LA), May 3, 1898, "thoroughly American match," quoting Cornelius Vanderbilt as not wanting his sons or grandsons to marry women "whose interests are not thoroughly American." Also *Times-Democrat* (New Orleans), May 3, 1898.

"New York without a Vanderbilt," *World* (New York, NY), May 29, 1898. Item includes: "Extraordinary Tribute to the Talents and Personal Charm"; photo of army post housing; "We mean all our marriage arrangements to be simple and quiet"; "it is a fairy tale"; "when they open their mouths, people like to listen"; "Those Dresser girls . . . haven't any money to speak of"; jubilee rumor; discussion of the Dresser girls and their figures, description of dress, ushers (at that moment, best man was still believed to be Jonathan Sturges), honeymoon, breakfast.

"The Richest Two Bachelors in America to Wed within a Month Two of America's Most Beautiful Girls," *New York Herald*, May 8, 1898. Item includes: "Mr. Vanderbilt has . . . Miss Dresser has"; "most cultivated multi-millionaire in America"; "handsome girl," of "splendid physique"; GWV "remarkably swarthy," "very delicate."

Letter from Catharine Hunt to PLF regarding GWV-ESV engagement, undated, from PLFNY. PLF to Catharine Hunt in response, letter dated Apr. 30, 1898, PLFNY.

PLF background drawn from: *Paul Leicester Ford: An American Man of Letters, 1865–1902*, Paul Z. Dubois (New York: Burt Franklin, 1977); *The Lives of Dwarfs: Their Journey from Public Curiosity toward Social Liberation*, Betty M. Adelson (NJ: Rutgers University Press, 2005). Also PLFNY, previously cited.

GWV letter to PLF about engagement from letter dated Apr. 19, 1898, PLFNY.

WBOF frustration with role in wedding, "thank god," and details of ESV/GWV's wedding and WBOF's increasing frustration about money and his expected duties are drawn in part from WBOF's letters to his mother from London and Paris during the months of May and June, 1898, WBOF coll., NYPL.

Sturges as original best man: Letter from GWV to WBOF dated May 27, 1898, WBOF papers; also "Are Wedded in Paris: Miss Edith Dresser Becomes Mrs. George Vanderbilt," *Chicago Daily Tribune*, June 2, 1898.

Letter from GWV to WBOF "absolute trust and confidence": dated May 11, 1898, WBOF papers.

Speculation that the Duchess of Marlborough might attend, and other attendees, from *New York Journal*, May 8, 1898.

Cornelius Vanderbilt hosting dinner: "Paris Letter," *Brooklyn Life*, June 25, 1898.

Rue d'Anjou ceremony and donation from letter WBOF papers, previously cited. Also "Are Wedded in Paris: Miss Edith Dresser Becomes Mrs. George Vanderbilt," *Chicago Daily Tribune*, June 2, 1898; "French Civil Marriage: George Vanderbilt Yielded to the Custom of Land—The Big Event To-day," *Democrat and Chronicle* (Rochester, NY), June 2, 1898.

Wedding ceremony description, including dress, attendants, music, decoration, drawn from:

Various editions of the *New York Herald* covered the affair. "Mr. Vanderbilt Weds Miss Dresser," *New York Herald*, June 2, 1898 (including "simple, tasteful affair"); "Mr. Vanderbilt's Church Wedding," *New York Herald* (cable from European edition), June 2, 1898, also refers to Italian honeymoon; "Mr. Vanderbilt Wedded in Paris," *New York Herald*, June 2, 1898.

Aunty Mary King's dress, family seating in church, from *Amelia Gayle Gorgas: A Biography*, Mary Tabb Johnston with Elizabeth Johnston Lipscomb (Tuscaloosa, AL: University of Alabama Press, 1978).

Telegram "Sailed Germanic Happy" dated June 9, 1898, WBOF papers.

Honeymoon information: Letter from GWV to WBOF dated Apr. 22 and Apr. 25, 1898, WBOF papers.

Karl Baedeker regarding Villa Vignolo taken from *Italy Handbook for Travellers: First Part: Northern Italy*, K. Baedeker (London, Leipsic: Karl Baedeker, 1892).

Letter GWV to PLF, "tantalizing," dated July 31, 1898, PLFNY.

August 1898 travel, ship register of the *Augusta Victoria* from Southampton to New York.

Letter from, ESV to WBOF thanking for gift dated May 29, 1898, WBOF papers.

7. Forest for the Trees

Description of ESV arrival at Biltmore House drawn from newspaper reports and CAS *Cradle*.

"Mr. and Mrs. Vanderbilt: Arrival at Biltmore House on Saturday," *Asheville Daily Citizen*, Oct. 3, 1898; "Are at Biltmore: George Vanderbilt and His Bride Now at Their Mansion," *Asheville Daily Gazette*, Oct. 2, 1898.

Description of house, artistic treasures, and room decor from repeated author visits, and description of decor being "fait accompli" from letter, Maher to Brown, JNBII papers, previously cited.

Unfinished aspects of the house are widely cited, drawn from author visits to Biltmore House; "Vanderbilt's 'house' is castle in every way," Martin Plessinger, *The Baltimore Sun*, Mar. 1, 1979; NHL nomination, previously cited.

NBB and husband to visit, from "Around Town," *Asheville Daily Citizen*, Oct. 31, 1898.

Thirty dozen eggs per week: "Poultry in Motion: Biltmore's Feathered Friends," *Open House: The Official Blog of Biltmore*, Feb. 29, 2016.

Biltmore Dairy ad from *Asheville Daily Gazette*, June 16, 1898.

Bulletin of the Torrey Botanical Club, vol. 23, New York, 1896. The New Era Printing House, Lancaster, PA.

Biltmore Herbarium, Chauncey Beadle (Biltmore, NC: 1896).

CAS comments on ESV from CAS *Cradle*.

Squatters on game preserve: "Vanderbilt vs. Squatters," *Allentown Leader*, Oct. 20, 1898.

CAS in favor of a feudal style: Letter from CAS to Charles McNamee, Biltmore Estate Archives, Mar. 24, 1896, as cited in Bryan.

Biltmore Forest School history drawn from CAS *Cradle*, previously cited; author visits to Cradle of Forestry, Pisgah Forest, NC; Biltmore Forest School images, Forest History Society, Durham, NC: http://www.foresthistory .org/ead/biltmore_forest_school_images.html. Letter from John Muir to Louie Wanda Muir dated Sept. 30, 1898, University of the Pacific Library Holt-Atherton Special Collections.

Brandis letter described in CAS *Cradle*, previously cited.

Richard Sharp Smith background from NHL nomination, previously cited; "Smith, Richard Sharp (1852–1924)," *North Carolina Architects & Builders: A Biographical Dictionary*, Clay Griffith, 2009, ncarchitects.lib.ncsu.edu/peo ple/P000100.

Reverend Dr. Rodney Rush Swope background, pay, and establishment of schools and programs from *The Story of a Church*, previously cited.

Young Men's Institute (YMI) history, including kindergarten, Dr. Edward Stephens, Issac Dickson, GWV support, drawn from: "More Than Biltmore," Mark Derewicz, *Endeavors* (UNC Research), Fall 2009; "Leaders Debate YMI Survival," Joel Burgess, *Asheville Citizen-Times*, Apr. 9, 2012; "A History of Pride," Milton Ready, *Asheville Citizen*, Feb. 13, 1983; "In Search of Edward Stephens," *Asheville Citizen-Times*, Feb. 20, 2011; *The Black Heritage of Western North Carolina*, Lenwood Davis (Asheville, NC: Grateful Steps Foundation, 1983).

Kindergarten, McNamee involvement: "Our Little Children," *Asheville Daily Citizen*, Apr. 2, 1895.

Ad for McNamee lecture: "The Water We Drink," *Asheville Daily Citizen*, Mar. 10, 1894.

Concert with seats reserved for "white people" from *Asheville Daily Citizen*, June 19, 1895.

Caryl Florio, choirmaster: "For All Souls' Church. Caryl Florio Selected as Choirmaster and Organist," *Asheville Daily Citizen*, Mar. 30, 1896.

Organ information, George Hutchings background, E. M. Skinner, drawn from *Story of a Church*, previously cited; "The Cathedral of All Souls: Our History," allsoulscathedral.org/Who-We-Are/About; *The History of the Organ in the United States*, Orpha Ochse (Bloomington & Indianapolis: Indiana University Press, 1975).

Swope comments on congregation (newspaper and congregant quoting him) from *Story of a Church*, previously cited.

Armstrong stained-glass windows and description for GWV mother, Clarence Barker, RMH: "Vanderbilt Memorial Windows," *New York Times*, Dec. 18, 1898. "Memorial Windows. George Vanderbilt's Tribute to His Mother and Two Friends," *Harper's Bazaar* cited in *Virginia Enterprise*, Jan. 13, 1899. Also author visits to All Souls Cathedral.

Quote from Helen Maitland ("present both the Old and New Testament . . . good and lovely woman"): National Register of Historic Places Nomination Form for "Biltmore Village Historic Resources," as submitted by the North Carolina Division of Archives & History, Survey & Planning Branch, Raleigh, NC, Deputy State Historic Preservation Officer, Aug. 20, 1979.

FLO to McLean Hospital in fall of 1898: Rybczynski, previously cited.

ESV letter to WBOF mother, inviting to bring maid at Christmas: dated Dec. 3, 1898, WBOF papers.

CAS letter to WBOF regarding going on a hunt dated Dec. 19, 1898, WBOF papers.

ESV childhood Christmas in New York from *Reminiscence*.

Christmas background, 1898 Salvation Army Christmas at Madison Square Garden and "The Rich Saw Them Feast" drawn from: "Salvation Army's Bounty," *New York Times*, Dec. 26, 1899; *The Battle for Christmas*, Stephen Nissenbaum (New York: Vintage, 1996).

MSG history: "Madison Square Garden's Many Incarnations—and Locations," Lois Weiss, *New York Post*, Oct. 24, 2013; "Mad. Sq. History: Madison Square Garden," Madison Square Park Conservancy, Aug. 1, 2014, madisonsquarepark.org/news/mad-sq-history-madison-square-garden.

GWV and ESV travels to Paris, Cannes, Rome, and Florence from ESV letter to WBOF mother dated Feb. 5, 1899; WBOF papers, also ship registers; ESV and GWV listed in the "Court Circular," *Times* (London), on Jan. 5, 1899, June 28, 1906.

GWV letter to PLF regarding "short stays" at Biltmore dated Aug. 2, 1899, PLFB.

Susan Dresser wife of the Viscount d'Osmoy, from untitled news clipping, *News and Observer*, October 17, 1899.

Death of Cornelius Vanderbilt II: "Mr. Cornelius Vanderbilt Dead," *New York Times*, Sept. 13, 1899; "Cornelius Vanderbilt," *New York Times*, Sept. 13, 1899; "Mr. Vanderbilt's Memory," *New York Times*, Sept. 15, 1899.

ESV to WBOF mother "cloudless sky . . ." dated Sept. 23, 1899, WBOF papers.

GWV letter to PLF inviting him to stay ("on account of mourning") dated Dec. 10, 1899, PLFNY papers.

WBOF's observation of ESV's pregnancy ("up slump"), from WBOF letter to his mother, Mar. 2, 1900, WBOF coll., NYPL.

8. Births of the Century

CAS comments on ESV pregnancy, forest fires, forest school enrollment from *Cradle*.

"All honor to" quotation: "Farmer Vanderbilt," *Charlotte News*, Dec. 28, 1900.

Carnegie Steel the largest steel producer in the world as of 1890, from *Famous Firsts of Scottish-Americans*, June Skinner Sawyers (Gretna, LA: Pelican, 1997).

Standard Oil's dominance: "May 15, 1911: Supreme Court Orders Standard Oil to Be Broken Up," The Learning Network, *New York Times*, May 15, 2012, learning.blogs.nytimes.com/author/the-learning-network.

Benz-Duryea cars: Duryea Brothers, from "Duryea Bros. Build 1st US Motorcar, Despite Themselves," New England Historical Society, newenglandhistorical society.com/duryea-brothers-build-1st-us-motorcar-despite; also "America on the Move," Smithsonian Institution, amhistory.si.edu/onthemove; "History of Carl Benz," Carl Benz School of Engineering, carlbenzschool.kit .edu/history_of_carl_benz.php.

Construction beginning on New York City subway, from "Rapid Transit Tunnel Begun—Ground Officially Broken," *New York Times*, March 25, 1900.

Suffrage history details from the National Women's History Museum, "Reforming Their World: Women in the Progressive Era," nwhm.org/online-exhibits /progressiveera/introprogressive.html.

GWV's stopping new work at Biltmore from Rybczynski, previously cited. Also, reduction of expenditures at Biltmore is widely discussed in NHL nomination; Covington, Bryan, Patterson, Foreman & Stimson, Craven, King, and Vanderbilt II, all previously cited. Warnings from Twombly mentioned in: "Reasons Why George Vanderbilt Abandoned Biltmore," *San Francisco Call*, Jan. 2, 1898; "Vanderbilt's Costly Fad," *Evening Times* (Washington, DC), Dec. 27, 1897. Twombly and FLO Jr. cited in: *FLO: A Biography of Frederick Law Olmsted*, Laura Wood Roper (Baltimore: Johns Hopkins University Press, 1973).

GWV purchase of lands at 645 and 647 Fifth Avenue, Marble Twins, Hunt & Hunt as architects: "G.W. Vanderbilt to Build in Town," *New York Times*, Sept. 7, 1902; "A Versace Restoration for a Vanderbilt Town House," Christopher Gray, *New York Times*, Apr. 9, 1995; *Guide to New York City Landmarks*, 4th ed., ed. Matthew A. Postal, New York City Landmarks Preservation Commission (Hoboken, NJ: John Wiley & Sons, 2009).

Description of Biltmore House library and books therein drawn from: repeated author visits to Biltmore House; Craven, Foreman and Stimson, Patterson, all previously cited; "George Vanderbilt's Library: A Dream Realized," Craig Stark, July 10, 2006, BookThink, bookthink.com/0072/72gwv1.htm; "Dusting off the Pages of a Bookish Vanderbilt's Passion," Peter Applebome, *New York Times*, Mar. 11, 1999.

Paderewski concert from letter of GWV to PLF dated Apr. 14, 1900, PLFNY papers; also "Mr. Paderewski's Last Recital: A Chopin Performance at Carnegie Hall Yesterday Afternoon," *New York Times*, May 13, 1900.

Edwin Davis French and Biltmore House bookplate: "Autobiography of Edwin Davis French," *Catalog of the Engravings Issued by the Society of Iconophiles of the City of New York* (New York: 1908).

Riviere & Sons bindery: "Riviere & Sons (Biographical Details)," British Museum, britishmuseum.org/research/search_the_collection_database/term_details. aspx?bioId=188547; also "George Vanderbilt's Library: A Dream Realized," previously cited.

On impossibility of fooling GWV and his knowledge of book bindings: "Bogus Historic Bindings," *Publishers Weekly*, citing a *Daily News* article, Feb. 7, 1891, vol. 39, no. 993.

Secluded passages in Biltmore House from repeated author visits to house, also "Unlocking the Hidden Doors Inside the Biltmore Estate," Eliza Murphy, Nov. 6, 2015, *Good Morning America*, ABC News.

Chariot of Aurora and Pellegrini background from repeated author visits to house; also Craven, Patterson, NHL nomination, previously cited; also "The History: The Pisani Family 1500–1900," Villa Pisani, villapisani.it/ing/storia .php?a=2; "History," Palazzo Pisani Moretta, www.pisanimoretta.com /frame_ing.html; "Giovanni Antonio Pellegrini: Artworks," *The Athenaeum*, the-athenaeum.org/art/list.php?m=a&s=tu&aid=6148.

Janice Meredith and dedication: *Janice Meredith: A Story of the American Revolution*, Paul Leicester Ford (New York: Grosset & Dunlap, 1899); ESV as inspiration: "Summer Amusements," *Milwaukee Journal*, Aug. 6, 1902; News brief, *Asheville Citizen*, Oct. 3, 1902.

GWV letter to PLF thanking him for dedication dated Oct. 16, 1899, PLFNY papers.

GWV congratulating PLF on engagement from letter to PLF dated Mar. 6, 1900, PLFB.

Dedication of Cornelius Vanderbilt II window at All Souls: "In Memory of Cornelius Vanderbilt: A Handsome Stained Glass Window for the Church at Biltmore," *New-York Tribune*, July 22, 1900.

ESV letter to WBOF mother (pregnant, thanks, radiantly happy) dated July 31, 1900, WBOF papers.

JNB death and death of brother: "John Nicholas Brown," *New York Times*, May 2, 1900; Death of Harold Brown," *New York Times*, May 11, 1900.

JNBII birth, estimates of inheritance: "Richest Baby in the World," *Sun* (KS), June 24, 1900; "Richest Baby in the World Worth $10,000,000," *St. Louis Post-Dispatch*, Aug. 24, 1900; "Richest Baby in the World," *St. Louis Post-Dispatch*, June 3, 1900.

GWV letter to WBOF regarding Cornelia birth dated Aug. 23, 1900, WBOF papers.

Information regarding the birth, christening gifts, etc. drawn from: *Democrat and Chronicle* (Rochester, NY), Dec. 2, 1900; "Biltmore's New Star," *Asheville Daily Citizen*, Sept. 21, 1900; "Child Born at Biltmore," *New York Times*, Aug. 23, 1900 (includes Edith supposed distaste for NC); "A Daughter of Buncombe," *Burke County News* (NC), Aug. 31, 1900; "Stork Comes to Biltmore," *Asheville Citizen*, Aug. 23, 1900; "Biltmore Baby" poem, Howard A. Banks, *Charlotte Observer* as cited in *Asheville Daily Citizen*, Aug. 27, 1900.

Tar heel meaning: The meaning of "tar heel" had its roots in two possible camps—
both of them war torn. During the Revolutionary War, British soldiers were
said to have complained that when they crossed North Carolina rivers they
emerged with tar on their heels, citing one of the state's most valuable pine
products. Years later, during the Civil War, North Carolina soldiers reportedly threatened to tar the heels of any comrades attempting to retreat during
battle: "Tar Heel Meaning Evolved from Derogatory to Proud," Madeline
Fraley, *Daily Tar Heel*, Nov. 3, 2016, dailytarheel.com/article/2016/11/tar
-heel-meaning-evolved-from-derogatory-to-proud; "Tar Heel," Michael W.
Taylor, *Encyclopedia of North Carolina*, ed. William S. Powell (Chapel Hill:
University of North Carolina Press, 2006).

NBB photo of GWV and Cornelia on Biltmore House loggia from NBB papers.

CAS comments about birth from *Cradle*.

Christening ring: "Another Fad Started: George Vanderbilt Responsible for 'Christening Rings,'" *Sunday Oregonian*, Oct. 7, 1900.

Clarence Barker Memorial Hospital: "Clarence Barker Memorial Hospital (Biltmore Hospital)," National Park Service, nps.gov/nr/travel/asheville/cla.htm;
"New Hospital at Biltmore," *Asheville Citizen*, Sept. 1, 1900.

"Her very presence is sunshine" from "New Star," previously cited.

Planting of cucumber magnolia: "Cornelia's Tree on Great Estate," *Asheville Citizen*, Oct. 20, 1900.

Thomas Wolfe birth: "Thomas Wolfe Memorial: Biography of Thomas Wolfe,"
North Carolina Historic Sites, nchistoricsites.org/wolfe/bio.htm; "February
1968—redevelopment and Thomas Wolfe's birthplace," Rob Neufeld, *The
Read on WNC*, thereadonwnc.ning.com/special/february-1968redvelopment
-and.

9. Trials and Toymakers

Stories of ESV interacting with local and estate families, sewing school in Horse
Barn: "Mrs. G. W. Vanderbilt, Who Presides So Gracefully at Biltmore,"
Irma Dooly, *Atlanta Constitution*, Aug. 26, 1900; "Edith Vanderbilt's Relationship with Estate Families," Sue Clark McKendree, *Learn NC*, learnnc.
org/lp/pages/1834.

GWV and ESV involvement with parish school and drills on the green, from:
"Mr. Vanderbilt's Model School at Biltmore," *Asheville Citizen*, Apr. 10,
1902; *Story of a Church*, previously cited.

History and early days of Vance and Yale arrival in Biltmore, Boys/Girls Club,
Swope involvement, constitution notes, Vance and Yale history and back-
ground drawn from: *Story of a Church*, previously cited; "Eleanor Vance,
Charlotte Yale, and the Origins of Biltmore Estate Industries," Bruce John-
son, in *May We All Remember Well, Volume II: A Journal of the History &
Cultures of Western North Carolina*, ed. by Robert S. Brunk (Asheville, NC:
Robert S. Brunk Auction Services Inc., 2001); "We Came as Tourists,"

Bruce Johnson, May 15, 2016, *Arts and Crafts Collector*, artsandcraftscollec
tor.com/we-came-as-tourists/; "Uplifting the Southern Highlander: Handcrafts at Biltmore Estate Industries," Kelly H. L'Ecuyer, *Winterthur Portfolio*,
Summer/Autumn 2002, vol. 37, no. 2/3; "Biltmore Estate Industries, Com-
mon Things, Done Uncommonly Well," Melinda B. Willms, *Style 1900*,
Summer 2008; "A Brief History of Biltmore Industries," Bruce Johnson,
Pebbledash, December 2002; "Biltmore Estate Industries: Charlotte L.
Yale & Eleanor Vance Years," and other documentation and related images
at: The Biltmore Industries Collection (1901–1980), D. H. Ramsey Library,
Special Collections, University of North Carolina at Asheville.

Jane Addams, Ellen Gates Starr, and Hull-House information: "About Jane Addams
and Hull-House," Jane Addams Hull-House Museum, hullhousemuseum
.org/about-jane-addams; "Jane Addams: Biographical," Nobelprize.org, nobel
prize.org/nobel_prizes/peace/laureates/1931/addams-bio.html; The Chicago Arts and Crafts Society Constitution, adopted Oct. 31, 1897.

Roycroft movement, Elbert Hubbard, *Fra* magazine, The Webpage of the Roycrofters, roycrofter.com; "Elbert Hubbard," Arts & Crafts Society, arts-crafts.
com/archive/ehubbard.shtml; "The Roycroft Community, 1894–1938," Hil-
ary Davis, Arts & Crafts Society, arts-crafts.com/archive/hdavis.shtml;
Roycroft-Hubbard Papers, 1887–1965, D.77, River Campus Libraries, University of Rochester; *Elbert Hubbard of East Aurora*, Felix Shay (New York:
Wm. H. Wise & Co., 1926); author visits to Grovewood Gallery, Grove Park
Inn, Asheville, NC.

School of Domestic Science, details, Mary Isabella McNear as principal: "Biltmore
School of Domestic Science for Colored People" (application notice), *Ashe-
ville Citizen*, Oct. 3, 1901; "Biltmore School of Domestic Science," *Home
Science Magazine*, Oct. 1903–Mar. 1904, vol. 20; school ad: *Asheville Daily
Citizen*, October 3, 1901; "The School of Domestic Science for Colored
Girls," *Asheville Daily Gazette*, Sept. 12, 1902; "Lake Placid Conference on
Home Economics, Proceedings of the First Second and Third Conferences,"
Lake Placid, NY, 1901; *Boston Cook Book* used at school, Biltmore referred to
in: *Boston Cooking School Cook Book: A Reprint of the 1884 Classic*, Mrs. D. A.
Lincoln (Dover Publications, 1996).

Work of Vance-Yale students at parish school closing ceremonies: "Closing Exer-
cises of Biltmore Parish School," *Asheville Citizen*, June 5, 1902.

Annie Mae Nipson: Black Women Oral History Project, Interviews, 1976–1981,
Annie Mae Nipson, OH-31, Schlesinger Library, Radcliffe Institute, Harvard University, Cambridge, MA, guides.library.harvard.edu/schlesinger
_bwohp.

The United States, published in 1904 by Karl Baedeker, mentions the School of Domestic Science in his Asheville section.

The murder of PLF, and the suicide of Malcolm Ford, was widely covered at the
time. Information about that event, PLF life, career, and family, Malcolm
Ford, and Ford family background drawn from: "Brother Slays Paul L. Ford:

Malcolm W. The Athlete, Shoots the Author, In His Home, and Then Kills Himself," *New-York Tribune*, May 9, 1902. "Paul Leicester Ford, the Author, Killed by His Brother; the Slayer, in Frenzy, Then Turns the Weapon Upon Himself," *Evening World* (New York), May 8, 1902; "Beats the Standing Long Jump Record," *San Francisco Chronicle*, Sept. 2, 1902; "The Celebrated Novelist and Malcolm Ford Had Been at Odds Over their Father's Estate: Murderer's Attempt at Suicide Successful: Victim but Recently Married," *Evening World*, May 8, 1902; "Ford Brothers Lie at Father's Side" (includes first wife's letter to editor), clipping from PLFNY, undated; "Paul Ford Shot," *Evening Sun*, May 8, 1902; "One Grave for Ford Brothers; Double Funeral To-Morrow," *Evening Telegram*, May 2, 1902; "Two Brothers," *Saturday Review of Books and Art*, May 10, 1902; "Ford Brothers to Lie in the Same Grave," *New York Times*, May 10, 1902; "Paul L. Ford's Estate," *New York Times*, Nov. 21, 1902; "Ford Brothers Will Be Buried Today," *Boston Post*, May 10, 1902; "Ford's Many Books," *Charlotte News*, May 13, 1902; "Paul L. Ford's Career," *New York Times*, May 9, 1902; DuBois, previously cited.

Value of Gordon Lester Ford's collection, from "Ford, Gordon Lester, 1823–1891," Social Networks and Archival Context database, University of Virginia, socialarchive.iath.virginia.edu/ark:/99166/w6h13cn1.

PLF requests to write from *Saturday Evening Post*, telegrams from GWV and Theodore Roosevelt, in PLFNY, previously cited.

PLF window at All Souls: "Architects' and Builder's Magazine," September 1903, vol. 4, no. 12.

Caravaggio's style, use of tenebrism: *Caravaggio: A Life Sacred and Profane*, Andrew Graham-Dixon (New York: W.W. Norton, 2011).

WBOF at Biltmore writing mother about Lila and her acceptance of engagement: Letters dated Mar. 17, 1902, and Mar. 19, 1902, WBOF papers; GWV and ESV to Cherbourg from WBOF letter dated Mar. 17, 1902, WBOF papers.

Otis Mygatt and Kellogg and Holophane Glass Company and association with WBOF from: multiple pieces of correspondence between Mygatt and WBOF, WBOF papers; also Historical/Biographical Information, WBOF papers at NYPL, previously cited.

Field-Lila wedding, guarding of presents, honeymoon: "The Sloane-Field Wedding," *New York Times*, July 8, 1902; "Field-Sloane wedding," *Brooklyn Daily Eagle*, July 8, 1902; "Special Guard for Presents," *Baltimore Sun*, June 24, 1902; "Vanderbilt Wedding without Objection," *St. Paul Globe*, July 6, 1902 (includes lingerie, "good angel," "fairy land"); "Mr. and Mrs. Field Have Arrived at Biltmore," *Asheville Citizen*, July 11, 1902.

Descriptions of Biltmore House technology (dumbwaiters, washing machines, lighting, etc.) from repeated author visits to Biltmore House, including the "Butler Tour"; also "A Technological Tour of the Biltmore Estate," Sue Clark McKendree, *Learn NC*, learnnc.org/lp/editions/biltmore-techtour/.

Additional information about Otis Brothers & Co. from "Otis: A Visual Timeline," otisworldwide.com/d31-timeline.html.

Tribune Building elevator: *From Ascending Rooms to Express Elevators: A History of the Passenger Elevator in the 19th Century*, Lee E. Gray (Mobile, AL: Elevator World, 2002).

Wolf's Domelre details: *How the Refrigerator Changed History*, Lydia Bjornlund (Minneapolis, MN: Abdo Publishing, 2016). Twenty-five tons of coal burned winter 1900, from "Technological Tour," previously cited.

Hatzel and Buehler electricians for Edison, wiring Biltmore: "The Electrification of America: The First 100 Years," Hatzel & Buehler, hatzelandbuehler.com /history/.

Victoria death: Queen Victoria details from *The Last Days of Glory: The Death of Queen Victoria*, Tony Rennell (New York: St. Martin's Press, 2000).

10. The More Things Change

Theodore Roosevelt as youngest U.S. president yet from "Theodore Roosevelt," History and Grounds, The White House, whitehouse.gov/1600/presidents /theodoreroosevelt; History of the Teddy Bear, Roosevelt visit to Asheville and Daniel LeRoy Dresser's role in Mississippi hunting trip from: "In North Carolina: Day Spent by the President in the 'Tar Heel' State," *The Indianapolis Journal*, September 10, 1902; "That Black Bear Hunt," *The Asheville Weekly Citizen*, June 10, 1902; "The Cuddly Teddy Bear is Fifty Years Old Today," *The Brooklyn Daily Eagle*, November 16, 1952; "The Story of the Teddy Bear," Theodore Roosevelt Birthplace, The National Park Service, nps.gov/thrb/learn/historyculture/storyofteddybear.htm; "Real Teddy Bear Story," Theodore Roosevelt Association, theodoreroosevelt.org/site/c .elKSIdOWIiJ8H/b.8684621/k.6632/Real_Teddy_Bear_Story.htm; Letter from D. LeRoy Dresser to Theodore Roosevelt, theodoreroosevelt center.org/Research/Digital-Library/Record?libID=o37081; Letter from Theodore Roosevelt to Daniel LeRoy Dresser, theodorerooseveltcenter.org /Research/Digital-Library/Record?libID=o183058; Letter from Theodore Roosevelt to Daniel LeRoy Dresser, theodorerooseveltcenter.org/Research /Digital-Library/Record?libID=o183078; all from Theodore Roosevelt Papers. Library of Congress Manuscript Division. Theodore Roosevelt Digital Library. Dickinson State University.

Alice Roosevelt visit and 1903 Charity Bazaar drawn from: "Miss Roosevelt's Visit," *Tennessean*, Apr. 21, 1903; "Miss Alice at Biltmore: President's Daughter Guest at Vanderbilt's Chateau," *Atlanta Constitution*, Apr. 15, 1903; news brief, *Tennessean*, Apr. 19, 1903; "Miss Roosevelt the Central Figure: The Biltmore Charity Bazaar Has Active Cooperation of Mrs. George Vanderbilt," *News and Observer* (Raleigh, NC), Apr. 18, 1903. Alice Roosevelt Longworth's colorful life and feistiness from Keyes, previously cited; and *Alice: Alice Roosevelt Longworth, from White House Princess to Washington Power Broker*, Stacey A. Cordery (New York: Penguin Books, 2007); also "A Presidential Daughter You Could Pick On," Carol Felsenthal, Decem-

ber 3, 2014, politico.com/magazine/story/2014/12/first-daughters-alice
-roosevelt-113302.

Daniel LeRoy Dresser difficulties, Dresser & Co., Trust Company of the Republic, involvement of J.P. Morgan, Bethlehem Steel role, etc., drawn from: "The United States Shipbuilding Company," *San Francisco Chronicle*, June 15, 1902.

Shipbuilding loan $4,750,000, Daniel loss of $570,000, involvement of J. P. Morgan, Bethlehem Steel, Schwab, Daniel hearing in front of special examiner in NYC. Dummy investing:

"Says He'll Expose Trust Fraud," *New York Times*, Mar. 6, 1907,

"Digging for Facts in Dresser Failure," *Evening World*, Nov. 11, 1903; "Reorganization Committee of Shipbuilding Company Will Make Revelations Today," *Chicago Daily Tribune*, June 17, 1902 (Vanderbilt hold bonds); "Deposit Proves Short in Value: Affairs of Dresser & Co. Are Aired Before Referee," *San Francisco Call*, Oct. 17, 1903; *Steel Titan: The Life of Charles M. Schwab*, Robert Hessen (Pittsburgh: University of Pittsburgh Press, 1975).

"The fall in reputations in the Wall Street district lately has been quite as marked as the fall in stocks," the *Financier*, as quoted in *The Literary Digest* 27, no. 17, Oct. 24, 1903 (New York: Funk & Wagnalls, 1903).

"My sisters . . . had nothing whatever to do with my business": "How Dresser Came to Grief," *Herald Democrat* (CO), Oct. 28, 1903; "Names of Sisters Were Not Used to Aid His Credit," *Los Angeles Herald*, October 28, 1903; "Saved Brother From Ruin," *The Barton County Democrat* (Great Bend, KS), June 26, 1903.

CAS description of D. Dresser telegram and shares, time spent at Three Day Camp, from CAS *Cradle*.

Biltmore Forest School history, tuition, schedule, description of CAS summer residence, cabin descriptions, and life in the Pink Beds from author visits to site at Cradle of Forestry; also CAS *Cradle*, previously cited; Biltmore Forest School collection, previously cited.

School songs by Douglas Sayre Rodman: "Down Under the Hill," Ramsey Library, University of North Carolina at Asheville, toto.lib.unca.edu/finding aids/mss/hanlon/down_under_the_hill_song.htm.

CAS lectures: "Lectures on Forest Policy, Second Part: 'Forestry Conditions in the United States,'" C. A. Schenck (Biltmore, NC: Biltmore Forest School, 1904).

CAS budget denied by GWV from CAS *Cradle*.

US Forest Service (previously the Bureau of Forestry and Division of Forestry) and forest service history: *The USDA Forest Service: The First Century*, Gerald W. Williams (Washington, DC: USDA Forest Service Office of Communication, 2005).

GP hiring CAS and subsequent disagreements thereafter, firing Schenck as consultant in 1902, GP asking GWV to shut school, from *Cradle*, previously cited.

Whistler death, funeral: "Artist Whistler's Remains," *Tennessean*, July 23, 1903; "Funeral of Mr. Whistler," *New York Times*, July 23, 1903.

Ivoire et or: Portrait de Madame Vanderbilt (YMSM 515), by James McNeill Whistler, completed in 1902, was displayed at the 12th Exhibition of the Société National des Beaux-Arts, Paris, a/k/a Le Salon du Champ-de-Mars, which opened Apr. 21, 1902. UGW, previously cited, whistler.arts.gla.ac.uk /correspondence/exhibit/display/?rs=8&exhibid=PaSNat-1902; "The *Nation* was impressed," *Nation*, June 12, 1902, vol. 74, page 463.

The *Portrait of George W. Vanderbilt* remained in Whistler's studio at the time of his death: *George W. Vanderbilt*, 1897/1903, National Gallery of Art, Washington, DC, nga.gov/content/ngaweb/Collection/art-object-page.45880.html.

Olmsted quote regarding institutionalization ("You cannot think . . . Anything but that"): FLO to Charles Eliot, Sept. 26, 1895, FLO Papers, vol. 9.

Christmas at Biltmore "with Hamlet left out": "Christmas Tree Celebrated at Biltmore," *Morning Post* (NC), Dec. 26, 1903.

McNamee resigns; "a curtailment of expenses in every department," from "To Cut Biltmore Expenses [Asheville, NC, telegram to the *Chicago Record-Herald*], *Courier-Journal* (Louisville, KY), June 19, 1904.

GWV and ESV with Duchess of Marlborough for leap New Year: "Court Circular," *Times* (London), Apr. 25, 1904.

Five-hundred-ton coal order in 1904: "Vanderbilt to Be Own Overseer," *Charlotte News*, Aug. 18, 1904.

Natalie and Pauline visiting in 1905. Untitled news clipping in *The Evening Star* (Washington, DC), March 10, 1905.

"Nonsense Book" description, quote from: Foreman and Stimson, previously cited; *Images of America: Biltmore Estate*, Ellen Erwin Rickman (Charleston, SC: Arcadia Publishing, 2005).

May 1905 Floral Parade: "Floral Parade at Biltmore. About Fifty Vehicles in Line—Mrs. Vanderbilt Wins First Prize," *New-York Tribune*, May 26, 1905.

FLO window description: "Awesome Archives! Memorial Window to F. L. Olmstead [sic] Unveiled," ed. Martha Fullington, *Cathedral Connection: Cathedral of All Souls*, July 2014.

Henry Frick leasing GWV home: News clipping, *Washington Post*, Aug. 19, 1905. Also "Frick to Live in New York," *Washington Post*, Mar. 23, 1905; "Mr. Frick to Leave City," *Pittsburgh Daily Post*, Mar. 22, 1905.

Edith Wharton "lords of Pittsburgh" and "conformity" quotes: *A Backward Glance*, Edith Wharton (New York: D. Appleton–Century Company Incorporated, 1934).

Edith Wharton's known visits to Biltmore in November 1902 and December 1905, from Biltmore author visits and *The Letters of Edith Wharton*, ed. R. W. B. Lewis and Nancy Lewis (New York: Collier, 1988), also "The Architecture of Manners: Henry James, Edith Wharton, and the Mount," Sarah Luria, *American Quarterly*, June 1997, vol. 49, no. 2.

Wharton gift of two-volume set of Dante Gabriel Rossetti, from Lila Vanderbilt
Sloane Field's list of "Wedding Presents," WBOF papers, NYPL.

Details of Henry James's gout-filled visit to Biltmore in February 1905, from
Henry James to Henry James III (his nephew Harry), Feb. 4, 1905, and from
Henry James to Edith Wharton, Feb. 8, 1905, *1895–1916*, vol. 4 of *Letters
of Henry James*, ed. Leon Edel (Cambridge, MA: Harvard University Press,
1984), also Luria, previously cited.

Wharton's Books: *The Decoration of Houses,* Edith Wharton and Ogden Codman
Jr. (London: B.T. Batsford, 1898); and *Italian Villas and Their Gardens,* Edith
Wharton, illustrations by Maxfield Parrish (London: The Century Co.,
1904).

"Mrs. Wharton in New York," Elizabeth Hardwick, *New York Review of Books*,
Jan. 21, 1988.

Wharton's "Ruling passions" most popularly cited from R. W. B. Lewis's *Edith
Wharton: A Biography* (New York: HarperCollins, 1975), from an unpub-
lished manuscript fragment by Edith Wharton, Edith Wharton Collection,
Lilly Library, Indiana University, Bloomington.

Dining table and details, oysters, and chef Ellen Davis: "Biltmore inspires a gilded
Thanksgiving," David Hagendorn, *Washington Post*, Nov. 21, 2014.

The Gift of the Magi, O. Henry (William Sydney Porter), first published in *New
York Sunday World*, Dec. 10, 1905; later published in book form in O. Henry's
anthology *The Four Million* (New York: Doubleday, 1906).

1906 YMI buys out GWV loan, from "Leaders debate YMI survival," Joel Burgess,
Asheville Citizen-Times, Apr. 9, 2012; "More Than Biltmore," Mark Derewicz, *Endeavors* (UNC Research), Fall 2009.

Richard Sharp Smith description and engagement to Isabella Cameron from
"Smith, Richard Sharp (1852–1924)," *North Carolina Architects & Builders,
A Biographical Dictionary,* Clay Griffith, 2009, http://ncarchitects.lib.ncsu
.edu/people/P000100

Guastavino firm commissions, St. Lawrence Basilica in Asheville: drawn from
Ochsendorf and Piqueras, previously cited.

The Panic of 1907, or Knickerbocker Crisis, from: "The Panic of 1907," Jon R.
Moen and Ellis W. Tallman, federalreservehistory.org/Events/Detail
View/97; "The Financial Panic of 1907: Running from History," Abigail
Tucker, Oct. 9, 2008, smithsonianmag.com/history/the-financial-panic-of
-1907-running-from-history-82176328/; and "The 1907 Crisis in Historical Perspective," Center for History and Economics, Harvard University, fas
.harvard.edu/~histecon/crisis-next/1907/index.html.

Happy financial end to 1906: "Stock Exchange Turned into Fairyland," *Pittsburgh
Daily Post*, Jan. 1, 1907.

Closing of poultry operations, from NHL nomination and "No More Biltmore Poultry: George Vanderbilt to Abolish His Famous Farms," *New York Times*, Nov. 9,
1906. Falling timber prices in 1907 from NHL nomination, previously cited.

Collins selling land to GWV for $2,000: "Vanderbilt Buys Log Cabin: Negro Who

Had Spurned Millionaire's Offer for Years Relents," *Washington Post*, Jan. 27, 1907. "Collins Willing to Sell, George Vanderbilt's Negro Neighbor Wants to Dispose of Farm," *Boston Post*, Aug. 18, 1901; "Mr. Vanderbilt Buys Collins' Famous Hut," *Madison County Record* (Marshall, NC), Feb. 15, 1907.

Roosevelt expected to hunt: "Will Hunt in North Carolina," *Washington Post*, Oct. 21, 1907.

Burglar hunt on estate: "Search Vanderbilt Grounds: Trail of Burglars at Biltmore Led Straight to House," *New York Times*, Oct. 10, 1907; "Burglars Use Chloroform," *Washington Post*, Oct. 10, 1907.

Correspondence from Eleanor P. Vance, Jan. 8, 1904, CAS selling lumber to the Boy's Club through her; Oct. 25, 1904, received CAS's pictures of Roycroft furniture, from Series V, 1896–1909, Finding Aid, Biltmore Estate Forestry Department Manager's Records, The Biltmore Company, Museum Services Department, Archives Division, North Carolina State University, lib.ncsu .edu/specialcollections/forestry/biltmore/tbc2_v.html.

Jamestown Exposition of 1907: "North Carolina Week at Jamestown Exposition," *The Enterprise* (Albemarle, NC), Aug. 15, 1907; "Mrs. Vanderbilt Sends Exhibit to Jamestown," *Lincoln County News* (Lincolnton, NC). May 21, 1907; Cornelia participation in: "Liquor Election Oct. 8th. Asheville to Vote for Prohibition—Celebration on a Large Scale for Monday—Doings of the Biltmore Industry Club," *Charlotte Observer*, Aug. 31, 1907.

"Mrs. Vanderbilt in Homespun," *Chicago Tribune*, May 18, 1907.

CSV relationship and interaction with children of village and employees is well documented. Sources include repeated author visits to Biltmore House; McKendree, previously cited; "Biltmore Estate Industries, Common Things, Done Uncommonly Well," Melinda B. Willms, *Style 1900*, Summer, 2008.

11. High and Dry

Christmas 1907: "Happy Day at Biltmore," *New York Times*, Dec. 26, 1907.

Vanderbilt ditty as related to author by Brenda Lunsford Lilly.

Asheville and North Carolina prohibition background: "Liquor Election Oct. 8th. Asheville to Vote for Prohibition—Celebration on a Large Scale for Monday—Doings of the Biltmore Industry Club," *Charlotte Observer*, Aug. 31, 1907; "No More Saloons for Asheville," *Farmer and Mechanic* (NC), May 19, 1908.

Eureka Saloon ad from *Asheville Daily Gazette*, Feb. 22, 1902.

W. O. Wolfe former patron of Eureka: "Of Time and the City: Issues Facing Asheville in Wolfe's Youth Mirror Today's Concerns," Max Hunt, *Mountain XPress* (NC), Nov. 20, 2015.

CAS view of GWV "hobby" and finances, ESV crying, instruction of GWV to CAS sell Pisgah, from CAS *Cradle*, previously cited.

Information about Biltmore Forestry Fair of 1908 drawn from: CAS *Cradle*; see more below.

GWV and ESV in Paris from CAS *Cradle*.

Grey family visit from Canada from CAS *Cradle*, previously cited, and untitled news clipping from *French Broad Hustler* (Hendersonville, NC), Apr. 23, 1908.

Death of Guastavino and burial, including musical compositions: "Body of Raphael Guastavino May Lie in New Catholic Church," *Asheville Citizen*, Feb. 4, 1908; "R. Guastavino the Architect Dies at B'K Mtn," *Asheville Citizen*, Feb. 3, 1908; "Raphael Guastavino Dead," *New York Times*, Feb. 3, 1908; "Funeral of R. Guastavino Yesterday," *Asheville Citizen*, Feb. 7, 1908; "History," The Cathedral Church of St. John the Divine, stjohndivine.org; also Piqueras and Ochsendorf, both previously cited.

GWV threat to burn Biltmore: "Threat for G. W. Vanderbilt," *New York Times*, June 28, 1908.

NBB advancing monies to brother from "Memo of Mrs. Brown's advances a/d D. L. R. Dresser," NBB papers.

D. LeRoy and Emma Dresser divorce, Emma experience in Sioux Falls, SD, and final ruling: "Mrs. LeRoy Dresser in Divorce Colony," *New York Times*, June 8, 1908; "Award to Mrs. Dresser," *New-York Tribune*, Aug. 11, 1908;

"Divorce, the Vanderbilt Curse," *Chicago Daily Tribune*, Oct. 24, 1909.

Lila and Field living at Marble Twins: "A Versace Restoration," previously cited; "High Lawn Estate," collection description at Avery Architectural & Fine Arts Library, Columbia University Libraries, library.columbia.edu /locations/avery/da/collections/high_lawn.html.

Time spent at Westfield, farm in Mohegan Lake, from biographical and historical information of William B. Osgood Field Papers, Manuscripts and Archives Division, New York Public Library.

Description of, invitation to Biltmore Forestry Fair, days' events, student roles: "The Biltmore Rangers," *Sun* (NY) June 13, 1909; CAS *Cradle*, previously cited.

Biltmore Stick description and use: Author visits to Cradle of Forestry, NC; also "Using a Biltmore Stick," Justin Black, Utah State University Department of Forestry, forestry.usu.edu/htm/rural-forests/forest-management/forest-timber -management/measuring-tree-volume-with-a-biltmore-stick/.

1909 Wright flight over Statue of Liberty, *Lusitania*: "Wilbur Wright and the Statue of Liberty," Dean Mosher, *Air & Space Magazine*, December 2013.

"1909 Wright Military Flyer," Smithsonian National Air and Space Museum, airandspace.si.edu/collection-objects/1909-wright-military-flyer.

Steamships "from small shells to floating cities," and building of new ships: "Development of Steamships," *Scientific American*, reprinted in the *Washington Post* on June 27, 1909; construction on White Star Line: "Information Bureau Notes," *Brooklyn Daily Eagle*, Mar. 28, 1909; "The Biggest Ships in the World," *Inter Ocean* (Chicago), Jan. 25, 1909.

ESV, Schenck and muskrats: Series V, 1896–1909, Finding Aid, Biltmore Estate Forestry Department Manager's Records, The Biltmore Company, Museum

Services Department, Archives Division, North Carolina State University, lib.ncsu.edu/specialcollections/forestry/biltmore/tbc2_v.html.

GWV, ESV unpaid tax while in Paris: "Biltmore Tax Unpaid, Neglect of Vanderbilt Estate Causes Teachers to Go without Their Salaries," *Harrisburg Telegraph* (PA), Jan. 5, 1909; "Mr. Vanderbilt's Taxes," *Greensboro Daily News*, Jan. 14, 1909; "Waiting on Vanderbilt," *Washington Herald*, Jan. 6, 1909.

GWV-ESV return Biltmore after Easter: "Cholly Knickerbocker's Society Gossip," Cholly Knickerbocker, Mar. 6, 1909.

CAS dismissal in 1909, repudiated hunting and fishing lease, $5,000 per year: "Hunt in Biltmore Forest," *Tennessean*, June 6, 1909; "Schenck Has Resigned," *Wilmington Morning Star*, June 3, 1909; CAS *Cradle*, previously cited.

April forest fires, suspicion of arson: "Vanderbilt Forest Razed by Firebugs," *Pittston Gazette* (PA), Apr. 7, 1909; "Early Morning Fire on Biltmore Estate," *Asheville Citizen*, Apr. 9, 1917; "Stubborn Forest Fire on Biltmore Estate," *Asheville Citizen*, Apr. 5, 1909; "Blaze at Biltmore," *Washington Post*, Apr. 7, 1909; "Fire on Biltmore Estate," *New York Times*, Apr. 7, 1909; "Enmity to Vanderbilt," *Allentown Leader*, Aug. 11, 1909; also CAS *Cradle*, previously cited.

Fire at Kenilworth Inn and estimated losses: "Kenilworth Inn Burned To-Day the Loss $310,000," *Evening Chronicle* (Charlotte, NC), Apr. 14, 1909; "Kenilworth Inn Is Destroyed," *Wilmington Morning Star* (NC), Apr. 15, 1909.

Taft praise of GWV: "President Near Journey's End," *Coshocton Daily Age* (OH), Nov. 10, 1909.

Beadle, CAS relationship, fight, and subsequent fine: described in CAS *Cradle*, previously cited, also: "Had Scrap at the Biltmore Estate," *News and Observer* (NC), June 6, 1909; "Dinner Party," *Asheville Citizen*, Nov. 16, 1904; "Warrants Issued for Biltmore Scrappers," *Asheville Citizen*, Apr. 30, 1909.

Moonshiners and CAS: "Held for Blockading," *Concord Daily Tribune* (NC), Apr. 27, 1909; "Distillery Near Biltmore," *Daily Arkansas Gazette*, Apr. 25, 1909; "Illicit Still Near Biltmore," *Washington Post*, Apr. 25, 1909; and CAS *Cradle*, previously cited.

GWV and CAS settlement of suit from: "Vanderbilt Settles Suits: Owner of Biltmore Agrees to Pay Claims of His Ex-Forester," *New York Times*, Aug. 9, 1910; "Mr. Schenck Resigns," *News and Observer* (NC), June 3, 1909; CAS *Cradle*, previously cited.

Edison sending CAS on radium hunts from *Cradle*, previously cited. CAS quotes about end of Biltmore School of Forestry, "It is better to die too early than too late," from *Cradle*.

GP-Ballinger controversy and resulting rift in Republican Party drawn from: "Pinchot Defends Glavis against Taft," *New York Times*, Jan. 7, 1910; "Ballinger to Face Full Senate Inquiry," *New York Times*, Dec. 21, 1909; "Taft Fears No Harm from Pinchot Row," *New York Times*, Jan. 9, 1910; "Ehistory: Aftermath of the Controversy," Ohio State University, ehistory.osu.edu/exhibitions

/1912/conservation/aftermath_of_the_controversy; "Pinchot Ousted; Party War On," *New York Times*, Jan. 8, 1910; GP dismissal letter widely cited, including: "Taft Ousts Pinchot for Insubordination; Washington Aroused," Jan. 8, 1910.

Sale of Berkshire hogs by Dr. Wheeler (William Cocke, Loyal Lee, Loyal Highclere): "Vanderbilt Sells His Hogs," *Washington Post*, Feb. 11, 1909.

Selling of water rights: "Vanderbilt Sells Water," *Washington Post*, Aug. 23, 1909.

Selling of electric plant: "Sold His Plant," *Alexandria Gazette* (VA), Jan. 5, 1909; "Quits Lighting Biltmore," *Washington Post*, Jan. 3, 1909.

Closing of parish school: "Parish School Not Needed: Vanderbilt Will Discontinue One Run by Him at Biltmore," *Charlotte Observer*, Feb. 3, 1909; "Biltmore School Closes: Public School Competes with Place Maintained by Mr. Vanderbilt," *Washington Post*, Feb. 3, 1909.

Purchase of Stoddard-Dayton in 1907: Steele, previously cited.

Chalmers-Detroit car purchase, locals hopeful roads would opened: "May Open Biltmore Estate for Automobiles One Day in Week," *Salisbury Evening Post* (NC), May. 14, 1909; "Vanderbilt Has 'Reformed,'" *St. Louis Post-Dispatch*, May 30, 1909.

George Logan loan from GSV: "Vanderbilt Lends to Negro," *Salisbury Post*, Aug. 19, 1909; "George Vanderbilt Loans Negro $500," *Allentown Democrat*, Aug. 18, 1909; "Vanderbilt Lends $500 to Fireman," *Washington Times*, Aug. 16, 1909.

Financial allotments to Biltmore Estate Industries drawn from "Uplifting the Southern Highlander: Handcrafts at Biltmore Estate Industries," Kelly H. L'Ecuyer, *Winterthur Portfolio*, Summer/Autumn 2002, vol. 37, no. 2/3.

ESV and industries, current fashion, including "preferred running a hand loom to playing bridge," from: "What Women Are Doing," *Tennessean*, Aug. 29, 1909.

O. Henry, Sara Coleman: "Mrs. Porter, 91, O. Henry's Widow," *New York Times*, Aug. 15, 1959

O. Henry's *The Four Million*, and jobs described therein, previously cited.

Mark Twain death, Halley: "Mark Twain and Halley's Comet," R. Friderici letter to the editor, *New York Times*, Apr. 22, 1910; "Mark Twain Is Dead at 74," *New York Times*, Apr. 22, 1910.

Comet Halley panic: "Miner Crucifies Himself, Thinks Visit of Halley's Comet Portends End of World," *New York Times*, May 10, 1910.

Cyanogen gas, Camille Flammarion: "Fantastically Wrong: That Time People Thought a Comet Would Gas Us All to Death," Matt Simon, *Wired*, Jan. 7, 2015.

TB leading cause of death: TB leading cause of death: "Thomas Wolfe: Chapel Hill Days and Death from Tuberculosis," S. Robert Lathan, *Proceedings of Baylor University Medical Center*, 2012, vol. 25, no. 4, 334–37; "Mortality and Cause of Death, 1900 v. 2010," Rebecca Tippett, June 16, 2014, UNC Carolina Population Center, Carolina Demography, demography.cpc.unc.edu/2014/06/16/mortality-and-cause-of-death-1900-v-2010.

The Old Kentucky Home: Ownership conveyed to Julia E. Wolfe as of Aug. 30, 1906, NC Historic Sites, nchistoricsites.org/wolfe/OldKyHome.htm.

Boldini info: "In Impressionist Paris, the Face of the Belle Epoque," Roderick Conway Morris, *New York Times*, Nov. 13, 2009.

Description of ESV painting: "Boldini's Latest Portraits," *American Art News*, May 13, 1911, vol. 9, no. 31; "Repose of a Statue," from "Paris Letter," *American Art News*, Feb. 11, 1911, vol. 9, no. 18.

Positioning of ESV portrait in Paris Salon: Auction listing, Lot 38: Giovanni Boldini, Sotheby's, "Property from the Estate of Giancarlo Baroni," New York, Jan. 29, 2013.

House at 1707 New Hampshire Avenue in DC: News brief, *Washington Post*, June 13, 1909.

Biltmore Industries ad/sale in DC featured in *Washington Post*, Dec. 7, 1908.

Purchase of 1612 K Street from Matthew Quay and $65,000 mortgage from: "Matter of the Estate of George W. Vanderbilt," Surrogate's Court, New York County, October 1918.

12. Final Crossings

Titanic information and details (ship structure, passengers, soaps, plates, menus) drawn from: author visit to Titanic Museum, Pigeon Forge, TN; *Titanic: Minute by Minute*, Jonathan Mayo (London: Short Books, 2016); *Titanic: Building the World's Most Famous Ship*, Anton Gill (Guilford, CT: Lyons Press/Globe Pequot, 2011); "Noted Men on the Lost Titanic," *New York Times*, Apr. 16, 1912; "The Appalling Disaster," *New York Times*, Apr. 16, 1912.

Beadle letter to GWV regarding "floating city," and Adele letter regarding GWV not sailing on *Titanic*: "A Titanic Mystery," Eric Sauder and Brian Hawley, Feb. 16, 2014, luxurylinerrow.com/titanic-mystery-eric-sauder-brian-hawley/.

Decision not to sail on *Titanic*: ESV letter to Emily Ford Steel dated Nov. 21, 1912, FFNY.

A "link to the past": Letter from GWV to Emily Ford Steel dated July 23, 1913, Ford Family Papers, Manuscripts and Archives Division, New York Public Library (FFNY).

Entertaining on K Street, tea dance at Shoreham: News brief, *Washington Post*, Jan. 23, 1914; News brief, *Washington Times*, Jan. 25, 1914; News brief, *Washington Post*, Jan. 14, 1914.

Diet Kitchen information, fundraiser, venue, attendees, and ESV role in the event drawn from: "Society Out in Force to Help Charity and Enjoy 'Columbia,'" Jean Elliot, *Washington Times*, Feb. 4, 1914; "Health Officer Tells How to Save Lives," *Washington Post*, Apr. 30, 1914; "Where's My Milk," *Washington Post*, Nov. 7, 1914; News brief, *Washington Times*, Feb. 26, 1914; News brief, *Washington Post*, Feb. 25, 1914; "Beauties of Washington Society Dancing Like Woodland Fairies to Aid Children of the Needy," *Washington Post*, Feb. 27, 1914; "Dazzle in 'Variety,'" *Washington Post*, Feb. 27, 1914.

GWV illness, surgery, and death were widely reported, drawn from: "George Vanderbilt Better: He is Getting Along Nicely Following Recent Serious Operation," *Greensboro Daily News* (NC), Mar. 4, 1914; "Blood Clot Clogged Vanderbilt's Heart, Multi-Millionaire Talking to Wife When the End Came: Biltmore Wants Body," *Atlanta Constitution*, Mar. 8, 1914 (also describes art collection). "G. W. Vanderbilt Dies Suddenly," *New York Times*, Mar. 7, 1914. "Sorrow at Biltmore: How Mr. Vanderbilt Lived at His Great North Carolina Estate," *New York Times*, Mar. 7, 1914; "G. W. Vanderbilt Dead, Expires Suddenly After Reading Newspapers," *Washington Post*, Mar. 7, 1914; "George W. Vanderbilt," *Asheville Citizen*, Mar. 7, 1914; "G. W. Vanderbilt Buried," *New York Times*, Mar. 11, 1914.

NBB in DC with ESV: two letters from JNBII to NBB, dated Feb. 14, 1914 and Mar. 9, 1914, both from NBB papers.

"A very direct and heavy blow to North Carolina": "Death of Mr. Vanderbilt a Blow to Our State," *State Journal* (Raleigh, NC), Mar. 13, 1914; and the *Asheville Citizen* wrote that "no individual death . . . greater loss" from *Asheville Citizen* March 7, 1914.

Quote from All Souls memorial service from VAC, also "In Memoriam: George W. Vanderbilt," *The Churchman*, The Churchman Co., 1914, vol. 109.

GWV will details, art collection: Will Records (Buncombe County, North Carolina), 1831–1964; Index, 1831–1964; Author: North Carolina. Superior Court (Buncombe County); Probate Place: Buncombe, North Carolina; "Vanderbilt Estate to Widow and Child: Biltmore and $5,000,000 Trust Fund in Daughter's Share of $50,000,000 Fortune," *New York Times*, Mar. 13, 1914; additional information regarding art collection also from: Patterson and Craven, previously cited.

Provisions for All Souls: "Church Not Provided For," *Chatham Record* (Pittsboro, NC), May 6, 1914.

Emily King: departure, marriage, Biltmore Inn: "Apopka News Notes," *Morning Sentinel* (FL), December 1914; "Downton Servants Take Heart: Biltmore's Found Success," Bruce C. Steele, *Asheville Citizen-Times*, Feb. 16, 2016.

Edith paying organist and rector, total $5,000 year: *The Story of a Church*, previously cited.

13. Washed Away

Revised detailing of GWV financial holdings drawn from:

Will Records (Buncombe County, North Carolina), 1831–1964; Index, 1831–1964; Author: North Carolina. Superior Court (Buncombe County); Probate Place: Buncombe, North Carolina.

Letter from Maher to JNBII, JNBII papers, previously cited; "Must Cut Bequests of G. W. Vanderbilt," *New York Times*, June 20, 1918; Covington, previously cited; Andrews, previously cited; Vanderbilt, previously cited; NHL nomination, previously cited; $65,000 mortgage on DC home from: "Matter of the Estate of George W. Vanderbilt," Surrogate's Court, New York County, October 1918.

Revision of tax laws and the Sixteenth Amendment: House Resolution 54, 37th Congress, 1st Session. First read before Congress July 19, 1861. Courtesy of the National Archives and Records Administration, Washington, DC.

General knowledge of the Weeks Act from US Forest Service online history exhibit, foresthistory.org/ASPNET/Policy/WeeksAct/index.aspx.

GWV wants $690,000 for 90,000-acre tract after Schenck left: The price requested ranged from $630,000 to $690,000, depending on the source: GWV wants $630,500 for 86,000 acres, from *Asheville Gazette-News*, June 27, 1913; GWV wants $690,000 for 90,000 acres, from Report to National Forest Reservation Commission, Pisgah Forest, May 1913, Department of the Interior, National Archives, Washington, DC, as quoted in Covington.

National Forest Commission visiting Asheville, and passing on purchase of Pisgah Forest, drawn from "New National Park a Beautiful Playground," *French Broad Hustler* (Hendersonville, NC), June 29, 1916. Also, "History on the Road: Asheville, North Carolina, and the Cradle of Forestry," Bill Alexander, *Forest History Today*, Spring/Fall 2011.

Louis Carr 1912 sale rights: Buncombe County Register of Deeds, Book 161, page 518, filed Jan. 17, 1913.

Regarding sale of forest, ESV letter to Secretary of Agriculture, and related history drawn from: NHL nomination and *Cradle*, previously cited; "Buys Pisgah Forest," *New York Times*, May 22, 1914; "Government Buys Pisgah Forest; Will Become Great National Park," George H. Manning, *Asheville Citizen*, May 22, 1914; "Pisgah Forest," *Scranton Truth*, May 29, 1914; "Name of 'Pisgah' Will Be Retained," *Asheville Gazette-News*, May 27, 1914; "Vanderbilt Forest Now National Park," *New York Times*, June 25, 1916.

Miss Madeira's School: Ad from the *Washington Post* dated Oct. 4, 1913; Madeira, madeira.org.

Beadle writing CSV: "A Special Bond," Jean Sexton, *Open House: The Official Blog of Biltmore*, Mar. 6, 2015, biltmore.com/blog/article/a-special-bond.

1915 visit with Pauline: News brief, *Farmer and Mechanic* (Raleigh, NC), Jan. 5, 1915.

ESV leasing Bar Harbor: *Asheville Gazette-News*, Feb. 16, 1915.

Germany threats, sinking of *Lusitania*: "Sinking the *Lusitania*, Part 2: Death and Blame, May 7, 1915," Dan Schlenoff, *Scientific American*, blogs .scientificamerican.com/anecdotes-from-the-archive/sinking-the -lusitania-part-2-death-and-blame-may-7-1915/, May 7, 2015; "Germany Warns Against Travel in Allies' Ships," *New-York Tribune*, May 1, 1915; "Mr. Alfred Gwynne Vanderbilt," *The Lusitania Resource*, rmslusitania .info/people/saloon/alfred-vanderbilt/; "Vanderbilt Lost on the *Lusitania* and Also Frohman," *Atlanta Constitution*, May 8, 1915. Details of Alfred

Vanderbilt's death on the *Lusitania*, his family's $5,000 reward, his wife's denial and self-imposed seclusion from *The Lusitania Resource*, previously cited; *Dead Wake*, Erik Larson (New York: Broadway Books, 2015); "Alfred Gwynne Vanderbilt," Dorking Museum & Heritage Center, dorking museum.org.uk/alfred-gwynne-vanderbilt/; "The 1912 Vanderbilt Hotel—Park Avenue and 34th Street," Tom Miller, *Daytonian in Manhattan*, November 10, 2012.

Suicide of Daniel Dresser, Trust Company failings, drawn from: "D. Leroy Dresser, once Rich Banker, Commits Suicide, Brother of Mrs. G. W. Vanderbilt and Mrs. John Nicholas Brown Shoots Himself," *New York Times*, July 11, 1915; "No Dresser Funeral Plans," *New York Times*, July 12, 1915; "Daniel LeRoy Dresser Ends Life by Shooting," *Times Dispatch*, (Richmond, VA), July 11, 1915; "Dresser, Ex-Banker Suicide; His Bride a Brooklyn Girl," *Brooklyn Daily Eagle*, July 11, 1915; "Funeral of D. L. Dresser," *Brooklyn Daily Eagle*, July 12, 1915; "D. LeRoy Dresser Kept Wedding Quiet," *New York Times*, Mar. 5, 1915; "Dresser a Brother of Mrs. Vanderbilt," *Greensboro Daily News* (Greensboro, NC), July 12, 1915.

Christmas at Biltmore, JNBII and NBB visiting. NBB notes from her diary, NBB papers.

Description of Flood of 1916, convergence of Gulf and Atlantic storms, drama surrounding Mabel Foister, Charlotte Walker, Marion Walker, Captain James Lipe, Kathleen Lipe, ESV role in aftermath, drawn from: Dykeman, previously cited; "Marooned in Asheville: A Story of the Great Flood," Col. Fred A. Olds, *Wilmington Morning Star*, Aug. 2, 1916; "Death List Increases," *Asheville Citizen*, July 18, 1916; "The Great Flood: The Loss is Appalling," *Union Republican* (NC), July 27, 1916; "Hell and High Water," Heidi Coryell Williams, *Our State Magazine*, Jan. 10, 2013; "Earlier Estimates of Property Loss Reduced in Only a Few Instances: Relief for Flood Sufferers and Repair Work Being Rushed as Rapidly as Possible: Weeks Will Elapse Before Railroad Traffic is Normal," *Twin-City Daily Sentinel* (NC), July 20, 1916; "The Great Flood," *State Journal* (NC), July 21, 1916; "Toll of Flood in West," *The Robesonian* (NC), July 20, 1916; "Biltmore Village Under Water," *Concord Daily Tribune*, July 17, 1916; "Reaper Claims More," *Asheville Citizen*, July 19, 1916; "Death List Increases," "Trail of Devastation Revealed as the Flood Waters Recede," "Marshall Hard Hit By the Flood," "Passengers Marooned on Carolina Special Will be Brought Here," Five States Are Flood Stricken," all from *Asheville Citizen*, July 18, 1916; "Asheville Victims Claimed by Flood," *Asheville Citizen*, July 17, 1916; *Mount Holly*, Lee Beatty, Jim Love, Charles A. Rhyne Jr. (Charleston: Arcadia Publishing, 2011); *Year Book 1916: City of Charleston* (Charleston: JNO J. Furlong, 1917). Beadle quote regarding losses cited in *Biltmore Nursery*, Alexander, previously cited.

14. Homespun and a Great War

Information regarding founding of Grove Park Inn, Edwin Wiley Grove, Paris
Medicine Company, and Fred Seely widely available and here drawn from:
Repeated author visits to Grove Park Inn and associated Grovewood Gal-
lery and Biltmore Industries exhibits located therein, Asheville, NC; *Built
for the Ages: A History of the Grove Park Inn*, Bruce E. Johnson (Asheville,
NC: Grove Park Inn/Archetype Press, 2004); additional Seely background,
Parke-Davis, marriage to Evelyn, role in *Atlanta Georgian* from: "Fred L.
Seely Dies; Medicine Firm Aide," *New York Times*, Mar. 15, 1942.

GPI hotel size (fireplace, "Big Room," floor plans, boulders, GPI logos, Roycroft
furnishings, etc.) from author visits to Grove Park Inn, Asheville, NC; (seven
hundred fixtures, French rugs) from F. L. Seely letter to Mr. Kenney dated
Aug. 8, 1913, *The Biltmore Industries Collection (1901–1980)*, D. H. Ramsey
Library, Special Collections, University of North Carolina at Asheville (Industries coll.); Grove Park Inn New York Booking Office brochure.

Bryan speech and opening events: "Most Unique Hotel in the World," *State Journal*
(NC), July 18, 1913; "Friendship and Faith Mr. Bryan's Theme at Banquet,"
News and Observer, July 15, 1913.

GPI use of Biltmore Dairy products: Ad for GPI in *Charlotte Observer*, June 2,
1916; Grove Park Inn booking office brochure, Industries coll., UNCA, previously cited.

Ads for various elixirs and cures of the times from numerous newspaper ads across
the country. One such testimonial for Lydia E. Pinkham: "Positive Proof of
Pinkham Cures," *Brooklyn Daily Eagle*, Feb. 27, 1903.

Junius Adams, adviser to Edith: National Historic Landmark Nomination, NPS
Form 10-900, Judge Junius G. Adams House, US Department of the Inte-
rior, National Park Service, National Register of Historic Places Registration
Form, prepared by Daniel J. Vivian, 2001. (Adams Nomination); "Junius G.
Adams," *Legendary Locals of Asheville*, Kevin D. Frazier (Charleston, SC: Ar-
cadia Publishing, 2014).

Southern Railway purchase of lands: "Purchase by Southern of $175,000 Van-
derbilt Lands Part of Company's New Million Dollar Terminals Here,"
Asheville Citizen, Mar. 21, 1917; "Southern Railway Purchases Land from
Biltmore Estate," *Wilmington Morning Star* (NC), Mar. 23, 1917.

Gold Medal 1915 Panama Pacific Expo, *Harper's*, *Vogue*, Reems Creek Woolen Mills,
list of noted wearers of homespun from author visits to exhibits at Grovewood
Gallery, Grove Park Inn, as well as Industries coll., UNCA, previously cited.

Additional information regarding Biltmore Industries: "Old-Time Arts Revived
in Carolina Mountains," *Asheville Gazette-News*, Feb. 1, 1915; Melinda B.
Willms, *Style 1900*, previously cited, Johnson, *Pebbledash*, previously cited.

Vance and Yale move to Tryon and founding Tryon Toy-Makers drawn from Industries coll. at UNCA; Willms, *Style 1900*; Johnson, *Pebbledash*, all previously cited, tryontoymakers.org; and author visits to Grovewood Gallery,

Grove Park Inn, Asheville, NC; "Regenerating Handicrafts in the Carolinas," Lila Rose McCabe, *Art World*, November 1917.

Initial purchase offer and price from L'Ecuyer, *Winterthur Portfolio*, previously cited. Seely letter to paper: "Why I Purchased the Biltmore Estate Industries," *Asheville Citizen*, Apr. 14, 1917.

Seely ads from: Listing, weavers, *Asheville Citizen*, May 7, 1917; "Wool Wanted for Cash," *Tennessean*, May 15, 1917.

"The Genius of Mountain Youth Developed by Biltmore Industries," Louise Dooly, *Atlanta Constitution*, Aug. 19, 1917. Item includes references to "mountain girl," George Arthur, eagle carved of cherrywood, Pan American San Francisco Expo and medal, wool from sheep in NC, dyes from vegetation. Looms brought from Scotland. Work found in home of Senator Clark on Fifth Avenue.

Regarding the Four Vagabonds: Repeated author visits to Grove Park Inn; "The Adventure of the 'Four Vagabonds,'" Bachmann, *The Shelf: Preserving Harvard's Library Collections*, July 24, 2013; *Our Vacation Days of 1918*, John Burroughs, unpublished, iiif.lib.harvard.edu/manifests/view/drs:46429194$1i.

The closeness between Seely, Vance, and Yale is clear from both the volume and affectionate quality of their correspondence. These, as well as the letter from Charlotte Yale and Eleanor Vance to F. L. Seely regarding ESV ("direct, sincere . . .") dated Oct. 2, 1920, are from Industries coll. at UNCA, previously cited. GPI orders from Vance Yale from numerous receipts and bills in the Industries coll., previously cited.

Wilson as friend of Seely, from author visits to Grove Park Inn, Asheville, NC, and exhibits therein; also *The Road to the White House*, vol. 1 of *Wilson*, Arthur S. Link (Princeton, NJ: Princeton University Press, 1947).

US and WWI: "U.S. Entry into World War I, 1917," Office of the Historian, US Department of State, history.state.gov/milestones/1914-1920/wwi.

Complete text of President Wilson's Joint Address to Congress Leading to a Declaration of War against Germany in 1917 via National Archives database, ourdocuments.gov/doc.php?doc=61#.

Alfred Vanderbilt son William in Naval Reserve: "William H. Vanderbilt, 79, Dead; Former Governor of Rhode Island," William G. Blair, *New York Times*, Apr. 16, 1981.

Edith activities during the war, early enrollment in NC Red Cross, drawn from: Correspondence with Jean Shulman, RN, Volunteer, Historical Programs and Collections, American Red Cross, Washington, DC; (sending nurse overseas) *Red Cross Magazine*, 1915; "A Message from the American Red Cross to the Women of America," Mrs. Belmont Tiffany, *Harper's Bazaar*, Aug. 1917; "Benefit: American Red Cross Society," *Asheville Citizen*, Apr. 15, 1917; "Mrs. Vanderbilt to Ask Aid for U.S. Soldiers," *Charlotte Observer*, July 5, 1917; "Relief Branch Formed," *Chatham Record*, Feb. 2, 1916; "Mrs. Vanderbilt Sells Flowers in Streets," *Charlotte Observer*, Mar. 19, 1918; "From Russia, With Love," *Asheville Scene/Asheville Citizen-Times*, Jan. 23, 2015.

NOTES AND SOURCES

Biltmore as potential site of military camp: "Biltmore Estate Offered as Mobilization Camp," *Concord Times*, Apr. 6, 1917; "Biltmore Likely to Get Government training Camp," *Asheville Citizen*, Apr. 21, 1917; "Col. H. J. Slocum Inspects Biltmore," *Asheville Citizen*, Apr. 20, 1917; "Biltmore Is Offered to War Department," *Atlanta Constitution*, Apr. 4, 1917; "Government Will Accept Offer of Site Made by Mrs. Vanderbilt," *Asheville Citizen*, Apr. 21, 1917; *Around Biltmore Village*, Alexander, previously cited; *The United States in the Great War*, Willis J. Abbot (New York: Doubleday, Page & Company, 1919).

Soldier parade and games on Biltmore green: "Mrs. Vanderbilt Entertains U.S. Soldiers at Asheville," *Atlanta Constitution*, Aug. 12, 1917; Mrs. Vanderbilt Hostess to the Soldiers of Local Guard Units," *Asheville Citizen*, Aug. 9, 1917.

Swope death: *Story of a Church*, previously cited; "In Memoriam," *Asheville Citizen*, Dec. 7, 1917; "Dr. R. R. Swope Dies at Biltmore Hospital," *Asheville Citizen*, Dec. 1, 1917.

15. Freedoms and Flappers

ESV "soldier boy" letter to WBOF, dated Feb. 11, 1918, WBOF papers.

WBOF assignments in WWI from preferred citation is: Field-Osgood Family Papers, Manuscript Division, Library of Congress, Washington, DC.

ESV leasing building to US government, from *Around Biltmore Village*, Alexander, previously cited; and "Village Stories," Historic Biltmore Village, historic biltmorevillage.com/historytour/village-stories.

ESV leasing Staten Island property to army: "Cecil vs. United States," cases decided in the Court of Claims of the United States at the . . . with the rules of practice and the acts of Congress relating to the court. Washington: W.H. & O.H. Morrison.

ESV bringing soup to family of sick workers: "Estate Families," McKendree, previously cited; Red Cross home for girls during flu: "Smart Washington Women Drop Frills for Uniforms," *Delaware County Daily Times*, Nov. 13, 1918.

Details of banquet hall service flag from "Thank You to Those Who Serve and Have Served," Leeann Donnelly, Nov. 12, 2012, biltmore.com/blog/article/thank-you-to-those-who-serve-and-have-served; and "Biltmore House Contains Antiques, Treasures from All Over the World," Fred Michaelove, *Asheville Citizen-Times*, June 12, 1938.

Alice Roosevelt "weaned on a pickle" quote: In an interview late in life, Alice Roosevelt Longworth admitted she swiped her famous "weaned on a pickle" comment from her physician, who heard it from a patient. *The Quote Verifier: Who Said What, Where, and When*, Ralph Keyes (New York: St. Martin's Griffin, 2006).

"19th Amendment to the US Constitution: Women's Right to Vote (1920)," Our Documents, National Archives, ourdocuments.gov/doc.php?doc=63.

In 1920 election, the Harding-Coolidge ticket won 404 electoral votes to Cox-FDR's 127. Harding took slightly more than 60 percent of the popular vote, and Cox 34 percent, resulting in a popular-vote presidential margin of 26.17% that still ranks as highest in US history. See *1920: The Year of Six Presidents*, David Pietrusza (New York: Basic Books, 2009).

Belmont's crusade for women's rights from *Alva Vanderbilt Belmont: Unlikely Champion of Women's Rights*, Sylvia D. Hoffert (Bloomington: Indiana University Press, 2012).

The North Carolina Equal Suffrage Association (aka League) formed in November 1894, though less active until 1913. See "North Carolina Suffragettes' Crusade to Cast a Ballot," Lisa Sorg, Our State: Celebrating North Carolina, Oct. 26, 2016, ourstate.com/north-carolina-suffragettes-crusade-to-cast-a-ballot.

Lillian Exum Clement, first female legislator, "you have to start a thing": "Reception to Be Tendered First Woman Legislator," *Twin-City Sentinel* (NC), Dec. 31, 1920; "130 Democrats Begin Next Assembly," Max Abernathy, *Fayetteville Observer*, Nov. 26, 1920; "First Step," Staff, *Our State*, Apr. 28, 2011.

ESV first woman president of the NC Agricultural Society: "Mrs. Vanderbilt Is Named President," *Winston-Salem Journal*, Oct. 22, 1920; "A Good Selection," *Durham Morning Herald*, Oct. 24, 1920; "Mrs. Vanderbilt Fair President," *News and Observer*, Oct. 22, 1920; "Mrs. Vanderbilt Elected President State Fair," Oct. 25, 1920.

Pisgah marker in forest: "Bronze Tablet to Vanderbilt to be Erected in Pisgah Forest," *Sunday Citizen* (NC), Aug. 22, 1920; "Geo. Vanderbilt Tablet Will Be Dedicated at Pisgah Forest Today," *Asheville Citizen*, Oct. 28, 1920.

George Stephens purchase of Biltmore Village: "Vanderbilt's Village of Biltmore is Sold," *Greensboro Daily News* (NC), Mar. 19, 1920; "Large Real Estate Deal in Asheville," *Winston-Salem Journal*, Mar. 21, 1920; "Biltmore Deal Has Now Been Closed," *Asheville Citizen*, Mar. 24, 1920.

Ad for lots and homes in Biltmore: *Asheville Citizen*, Mar. 25, 1920 and Mar. 26, 1920.

ESV to Paris for funeral, visiting Rambaud, Myron Herrick on board: News clipping of death of Viscount d'Osmoy in *Asheville Citizen*, June 27, 1920; dated photographs of traveling party on ship and with Mlle. Rambaud, NBB papers; Herrick rumor: "Mrs. Vanderbilt Denies It," *Charlotte News*, Sept. 15, 1920.

Kansas City Star ("He is dead; the dream is dust and ashes") cited in "George Vanderbilt's Dream Vanishes with the Sale of the Model Town of Biltmore," *Edgefield Advertiser* (SC), Apr. 21, 1920.

Wharton *Innocence* Pulitzer, Pulitzer history, Sinclair Lewis Main Street, "Pulsifer" prize (from which later book), Wharton letter to Lewis for "uplifting American morals":

ESV speech before NC General Assembly: "Forward North Carolina, Urges Mrs. Vanderbilt Before Solons," R. E. Powell, *Asheville Citizen*, Feb. 3, 1921;

NOTES AND SOURCES

"A Packed House," Jule B. Warren, *Durham Morning Herald*, Feb. 3, 1921; "Mrs. Vanderbilt in Address Makes Plea for Good Roads," Mrs. W. T. Bost, *Greensboro Daily News*, Feb. 3, 1921; "Woman Makes First Address to Legislature," R. E. Powell, *Charlotte Observer*, Feb. 3, 1921.

ESV driving record: "Mrs. Edith Vanderbilt Claims Trip Record," *Atlanta Constitution*, Oct. 9, 1921.

ESV/CSV living in bachelor quarters, author visits to Biltmore House, Covington, previously cited.

Details of CSV twenty-first birthday party: "Miss Vanderbilt's Majority Celebrated at Biltmore," *Tennessean* (TN), Aug. 28, 1921; "Miss Vanderbilt is Accorded Honors on Reaching Majority," *Asheville Citizen*, Aug. 24, 1921; "Ladies of Biltmore," Marla Hardee Milling, *Smoky Mountain Living*, June 1, 2012; "Biltmore vs. Downtown Abbey: Which Had the Best Party?" Bruce C. Steele, *Asheville Citizen-Times*, Feb. 24, 2014; also Rickman, previously cited.

Edison phonograph quote from ad in *Popular Mechanics*, December 1910.

Quote from Willa Cather's speech first reported in "State Laws Are Cramping," *Lincoln Evening State Journal*, Oct. 31, 1921.

Formation of Biltmore Estate Company, Biltmore Forest Country Club, CSV and ESV roles therein, Donald Ross, opening day drawn from: "A Brief History of Biltmore Forest Country Club," biltmoreforestcc.com/history; "Biltmore Forest Country Club Opens Today," *Asheville Citizen*, July 4, 1922; "Are to Develop Tourist Resort," *Charlotte News*, June 20, 1920.

Biltmore Forest history, funding, charter, ESV and CSV involvement, ESV unable to smoke, and other country club details from "Biltmore Forest: Our History, Our Lives," ed. David Schulman (1998, updated 2010), via biltmore forest.org/Data/Sites/1/media/documents/history-of-bf.pdf; and "From Vanderbilts to a U.S. Championship," Keith Jarrett, *Asheville Citizen-Times*, July 3, 1999.

John Francis Amherst Cecil peerage, ancestry, job history from "Miss Vanderbilt Reported Engaged," *New York Times*, Mar. 6, 1924; and "John Cecil, Ex-Aide of British Embassy," obituary, *New York Times*, Oct. 23, 1954; and The Peerage, thepeerage.com/p6476.htm#i64755.

Cornelia marriage announcement, ceremony, details: "Miss Vanderbilt Reported Engaged," ("She does not deny rumor . . ."), *New York Times*, Mar. 6, 1924; "Engagement of Miss Cornelia Vanderbilt Announced Saturday," *Asheville Citizen*, Mar. 9, 1924; "Miss Vanderbilt's Troth Announced," *New York Times*, Mar. 9, 1924; "Miss Vanderbilt to Wed April 29," *New York Times*, Mar. 16, 1924; "Miss Vanderbilt Weds Hon. J. F. Cecil," *New York Times*, Apr. 30, 1924; "Cornelia Vanderbilt's Wedding: It's All in the Details," Judy Ross, *Open House: The Official Blog of Biltmore*, Apr. 28, 2014, biltmore.com /blog/article/cornelia-vanderbilts-wedding-its-all-in-the-details; (engravers Adolph and Dungan, Inland Press Asheville, five hundred invited to ceremony): "A Legendary Southern Wedding," CJ Lots, *Garden & Gun*, Feb. 12,

2016; "Married at Biltmore House," Mar. 31, 1934; young cupid, Polly Ann Fowler, per Rickman, previously cited.

Description of CSV wedding portrait, reception from repeated author visits to exhibits at Biltmore House, photos of the NBB papers, JNBII papers, previously cited; Harris & Ewing photos and firm information from The Harris & Ewing Collection, Library of Congress Prints and Photographs Division, Washington, DC; (Chauncey orange blossom) from "A Special bond," previously cited; (tar on heels) *Garden & Gun*, previously cited; (time at lodge): "Honeymoon at Vanderbilt Lodge," *New York Times*, May 1, 1924.

Details of Old Frank, Biltmore's gatekeeper, from "Faithful Retainer Overcome by Joy at Happy Occasion," *Asheville Citizen*, Apr. 30, 1924.

ESV preferring farm life, dairy comments: "Mrs. G. Vanderbilt Happy at Farming," *New York Times*, Aug. 26, 1924.

Birth of George Henry Vanderbilt Cecil: "Vanderbilt Heir Born at Biltmore House," *New York Times*, Feb. 27, 1925;

ESV marriage to Gerry; gerrymandering: *Signing Their Lives Away: The Fame and Misfortune of the Men Who Signed the Declaration of Independence*, Denise Kiernan and Joseph D'Agnese (Philadelphia: Quirk Books, 2009); "Senator Gerry, Vanderbilt Widow to Wed, Is Report: London Paper Says Two Prominent Social Figures Plan Marriage," Oct. 22, 1925, *Times-Picayune* (New Orleans); "The Senator and Mrs. Gerry," Ray Hill, *Knoxville Focus*, Apr. 28, 2013.

ESV romantic rumors: "Dame Rumor, Seeking Romance, Couples Name of War Chief and Wealthy Widow," *Bisbee Daily Review* (AZ), Aug. 28, 1921; "Rumored That Mrs. Vanderbilt Engaged to Gen. J. J. Pershing," *Asheville Citizen*, Mar. 14, 1921; "Will General Pershing Win the Much-Wooed Widow Vanderbilt?" *The Pittsburgh Press*, Sept. 18, 1921; "Governor a Suitor for Hand of Mrs. Vanderbilt," *The Review* (High Point, NC), Sept. 8, 1921.

ESV having home built in forest: "Mrs. Vanderbilt Returns Tomorrow: Will Supervise Construction of New Residence in Forest: House to Be of Moderate Size," *Asheville Citizen*, Aug. 27, 1924; NHL nomination, previously cited.

Cornelia's twenty-fifth birthday and vesting in estate personal estate drawn from: "Mrs. Cecil Gives 25th Birthday Ball," *New York Times*, Aug. 23, 1925; "Vast Estate Turned Over to Mrs. Cecil," *Atlanta Constitution*, Aug. 23, 1925;

Dairy/cake: "I Scream, You Scream, We All Scream for Ice Cream!" Sue Clark McKendree, *Learn NC*, learnnc.org/lp/pages/1842.

The Great Gatsby, F. Scott Fitzgerald (New York: Charles Scribner's Sons, 1925).

16. Glimpse of a Castle

Coolidge State of the Union, Dec. 8, 1928, from John T. Woolley and Gerhard Peters, The American Presidency Project online, Santa Barbara, CA: University of California, presidency.ucsb.edu/ws/?pid=29569#axzz1vd78MB7K.

Details of the great (or long) bull market of the 1920s from *Crash! How the Eco-*

nomic Boom and Bust of the 1920s Worked, Philip G. Payne (Baltimore: John Hopkins University Press, 2015); and *The Great Bull Market: Wall Street in the 1920s*, Robert Sobel (New York: W.W. Norton, 1968).

Cornelia, Jack in DC: Covington, previously cited.

Architect biography from "Ellington, Douglas D. (1886–1960)," Clay Griffith, 2009, *North Carolina Architects and Builders: A Biographical Dictionary*, Copyright & Digital Scholarship Center, North Carolina State University Libraries, Raleigh, NC.

Coolidge Red, Hoover Gray, and Hollywood distribution from brochures and exhibits at Grovewood Gallery, Asheville, NC, as well as the Industries coll. at UNCA, both previously cited.

Asheville population growth between 1920 and 1930: the population went from 28,504 to 50,193—about a 76% increase, via population.us/nc/Asheville

Battery Park Hotel torn down, Grove Arcade going up, drawn from: "Visiting Our Past: 1st Battery Park Hotel Opens in 1886," Rob Neufeld, *Asheville Citizen-Times*, Jul. 6, 2014; "E. W. Grove & Grove Arcade: A Brief History," grovearcade.com/wp-content/uploads/2010/06/GA_BriefHistory. pdf; "History of the Grove Arcade in Asheville," Grove Arcade Public Market Foundation Inc., grovearcade.com/history/; Providence Arcade: "The Arcade Providence: A National Historic Landmark," arcadeprovidence .com/history/.

$25 billion lost, ticker-tape consumption, and other details about the Crash of 1929 from "Brief History of the Crash of 1929," *Time*, Claire Suddath, Oct. 29, 2008; and *America in the Thirties*, John Olszowka, Marnie M. Sullivan, Brian R. Sheridan, Dennis Hickey (Syracuse, NY: Syracuse University Press, 2014).

Thomas Wolfe biographical details from Thomas Wolfe Memorial: "The Biography of Thomas Wolfe," North Carolina Historic Sites, hnchistoricsites.org /wolfe/bio.htm.

Details of the length and editing of Wolfe's *Look Homeward Angel* from *O Lost: A Story of a Buried Life*, The original version of *Look Homeward Angel*, by Thomas Wolfe, ed. Arlyn and Matthew J. Bruccoli (Columbia, SC: University of South Carolina Press, 2000).

Local reception to Thomas Wolfe's *Look Homeward, Angel* from "Asheville and Thomas Wolfe: The Story of a Famous Battle," George W. McCoy, *Asheville Citizen-Times*, Apr. 19, 1953; "Amazing New Novel Is Realistic Story of Asheville People," Walter S. Adams, *Asheville Times*, Oct. 20, 1929, as reproduced at *Learn NC*, learnnc.org/lp/editions/nchist-newcentury/6052; "Stirring First Novel by Local Man Making Big Hit in Literary World," *Asheville Citizen*, Lola M. Love, Oct. 20, 1929.

Delay title going to CSV until 1929: Covington, previously cited.

Cecil Inquiring with JNBII about valuation of Biltmore House assets from correspondence dated Nov. 15, 19, and 25, 1929; Dec. 13, 14, and 21, 1929; Jan. 10, 16, and 23, 1930; JNBII papers, previously cited.

Ella Siple regarding GWV tapestries and mystery solved from Siple in *Burlington Magazine*, previously cited; related tapestry purchase at Hôtel Drouot from Bryan, previously cited.

Details of Biltmore House opening, $2 for adults, $1 for children under 12, drawn from "Biltmore House Will Open to Public Today: Famous Mansion Will Be Viewed for First Time by Crowds," *Asheville Citizen*, Mar. 15, 1930; "Mr. Cecil and I hope . . . all the benefit they deserve . . ." from "Biltmore House is Thrown Open for the First Time," *Sunday Citizen* (Asheville), Mar. 16, 1930.

Taxes $50,000 year: *Amazing Asheville: Guide to Asheville and the Beautiful North Carolina Mountains*, Lan Sluder (Asheville, NC: Equator, 2013); Covington, previously cited.

Photo of family from Verley Archer papers, previously cited.

Nearly 40,000 visitors in the first year, drawn from NHL document and Covington, previously cited.

Demolition of 660 Fifth Avenue in 1926 from King, previously cited.

Challenges felt in England and death tax, drawn from: "Time and Taxes Uproot Oldest England," Clair Price, *New York Times*, Mar. 27, 1932; "Death Tax Wrecks British Estates," *New York Times*, Feb. 10, 1929.

Banks closing in Asheville area: "Four Banks in N. Carolina Close Doors," *Cumberland Evening Times*, Nov. 20, 1930.

Roberts suicide, Rankin suicide, Bradford attempt: "Former Asheville Mayor Kills Himself," *Burlington Daily Times* (Burlington, NC), Feb. 25, 1931.

CSV, Jack Cecil to Florida Keys, New York, CSV seeking publisher from Covington, previously cited.

ESV home in Providence from author visits to site, also "The Senator and Mrs. Gerry," previously cited, also includes reference to farm in Lake Delaware.

ESV involvement in DC scene, president of Congressional Club: "Mrs. Peter Goelet Gerry, wife of the United States Senator and President of the Congressional Club, delivering the address of welcome to the American War Mothers and the Gold Star Mothers when they gathered at Arlington National Cemetery today, Mother's Day, to pay homage to America's Unknown Soldier, just back of Mrs. Gerry is Maj. Gen. and Mrs. Charles P. Summerall," Harris & Ewing, photographer, Arlington Virginia, 1928, Library of Congress, loc.gov/item /hec2013004919/, last accessed March 21, 2017; "Dawn to dusk" radio address: Oldtime Rally Of Democrats to Greet Ham Lewis," *The Tennessean* (Nashville), Sep. 30, 1928; "Democrats Give First 'Dawn-Dusk' Air Program," *The Evening News* (Harrisburg, PA), Oct. 1, 1928.

ESV and NBB speaking at Young Women's Democratic League of Rhode Island, from *Providence News*, Oct. 25, 1928. "Edith Gerry Club" referred to in undated letter to JNBII following NBB death in 1950. JNBII papers.

Gerry as Wilsonian moralist, biography, political views: "Wilsonian Moralist: Sen-

ator Peter G. Gerry and the Crusade for the League of Nations," Leonard
Schlup, *Rhode Island History*, February 2000, vol. 58, no. 1.

ESV as first lady of fashion from: "Capital Wonders Who'll Be New First Lady of
Fashion," *Times-Herald* (Olean, NY), Mar. 14, 1929; "Post of First Lady of
Fashion Is Awaiting Some Senator's Wife," *St. Louis Star and Times*, Mar. 15,
1929; "Washington's Social Set Is Wondering Who Will Be Its New First
Lady of Fashion," Hortense Saunders, *Enquirer and Evening News* (MI),
Mar. 22, 1929.

Bergdorf Goodman ready-to-wear department launched: *From Main Street to Mall:
The Rise and Fall of the American Department Store*, Vicki Howard (Philadelphia: University of Pennsylvania Press, 2015).

ESV wardrobe details: "New RISD Exhibit Reveals R.I. Socialite's Glamorous
Wardrobe," Jenna Pelletier, *Providence Journal*, Mar. 22, 2015; "Golden
Glamour: The Edith Stuyvesant Vanderbilt Gerry Collection: Costume
and Textiles: March 13–July 5, 2015," RISD Museum, risdmuseum.org/art
_design/exhibitions/57_golden_glamour_the_edith_stuyvesant_vanderbilt
_gerry_collection.

1932 Adams, CSV, creation of new Biltmore Company (from old) and details of
1932 formation of Biltmore Co. from Covington, Sluder, previously cited.

Cutbacks of staff and butler quotes from Covington and Foreman and Stimson,
all previously cited.

Adams residing at Farmcote from "Biltmore Estate Fire Alarm System," Gallery
Archives, National Gallery of Art.

CSV-Jack Cecil split, subsequent divorce, CSV as "Nilcha": (Cholly comments)
"Notes from New York," Cholly Knickerbocker, *Cincinnati Enquirer*, Nov. 1,
1931; "Cecils Will Seek Divorce in Paris," *New York Times*, Mar. 31, 1934;
"Left Husband Two Years Ago," *New York Times*, Mar. 31, 1934; "The Hill-
Billy Heiress Finds Romance," John Cahill, Albuquerque Journal, Jul. 10,
1938; "The Strange Matrimonial Disaster of Cornelia Vanderbilt," *The Milwaukee Sentinel*, Jul. 29, 1934; "Romantic Rebels: Cornelia The Unconven-
tional Vanderbilt," *American Weekly*, Jan. 1, 1950.

17. You Might Go Home Again

ESV campaigning for Gerry, Gerry reelection: "Vanderbilt Kin Goes on Stump for
Her Husband," *Reading Times* (PA), Oct. 17, 1930.

$64,000 earned first year at BH from Covington, previously cited.

Fitzgerald in Asheville at Tryon and at GPI, Zelda at Highland, Scott room numbers, Wolfe mother thought him drunk:

*Critical Companion to F. Scott Fitzgerald: A Literary Reference to His Life to His Life
and Work*, Mary Jo Tate (New York: Facts on File, 2007).

F. Scott Fitzgerald's beer consumption—fifty ponies of beer a day—as well as
knowledge of rooms 441 and 443, where Fitzgerald stayed at the Grove Park

Inn, are drawn from conversations with Professor Brian Railsback of Western Carolina University, during author visits to Grove Park Inn during annual September celebrations of Fitzgerald's birth. In that era, a "pony" of beer was a 7 US fluid ounce (207 ml) bottle. To avoid "strong" alcohol, Fitzgerald was consuming 2.7 gallons of beer a day.

Michel Mok article "The Other Side of Paradise, Scott Fitzgerald, 40, Engulfed in Despair," appeared in the *New York Post*, Sept. 25, 1936. Edited version available at theguardian.com/books/2007/sep/18/classics.fscottfitzgerald.

Fitzgerald's September 1936 suicide attempt via morphine—from which he vomited and survived—is recounted widely in biographies and critical assessments of his work, including: *F. Scott Fitzgerald in the Twenty-First Century*, ed. Jackson R. Bryer, Ruth Prigozy, Milton R. Stern (Tuscaloosa: University of Alabama Press, 2003).

Marjorie Kinnan Rawlings and letters from Perkins and meeting of F. Scott from: "Marjorie Kinnan Rawlings Meets F. Scott Fitzgerald: The Unpublished Accounts," Rodger L. Tarr, *Journal of Modern Literature*, Bloomington: Fall 1998, vol. 22, no. 1, 165.

Fitzgerald's discharging of a firearm at the Grove Park Inn is recounted widely. See "For F. Scott and Zelda Fitzgerald, A Dark Chapter in Asheville, N.C.," Susan Stamberg, Sept. 3, 2013, National Public Radio, npr.org/2013/09/03/216164420/for-f-scott-and-zelda-fitzgerald-a-dark-chapter-in-asheville-n-c.

F. Scott letter to daughter Scottina from ' "Nothing Any Good Isn't Hard': F. Scott Fitzgerald's Secret to Great Writing," Maria Popova, *Atlantic*, Jan. 9, 2013. Deaths of both Scott and Zelda are widely reported, including "Dark Chapter," previously cited.

Editing of Wolfe's million-word count *Of Time and the River* by Perkins: ' "Of Time and the River': The Final Editing," Francis E. Skipp, *Papers of the Bibliographical Society of America*, Third Quarter, 1970, vol. 64, no. 3, pp. 313–22.

Wolfe writing about Nazism from his novella, "I Have a Thing to Tell You," ran in three installments in the *New Republic*, on Mar. 10, 17, and 24, 1937.

Wolfe's 1937 stay at college friend's cabin in the Asheville neighborhood of Oteen is detailed in "Oteen Cabin in Disrepair Boasts Literary Past," Carol Motsinger, *Asheville Citizen-Times*, Nov. 14, 2014. More details ongoing preservation efforts may be found at: thomaswolfecabin.com.

Wolfe death: "Rites in Asheville for Thomas Wolfe," *New York Times*, Sept. 19, 1938; "Thomas C. Wolfe, Novelist, 37, Dead," *New York Times*, Sept. 16, 1938; "Author Wolfe Buried Near O. Henry's Grave," *Albuquerque Journal* (New Mexico), Sept. 19, 1938.

CSV affair with Baer, trial, and aftermath drawn from: "The 'Hill-Billy' Heiress Finds Romance," John Cahill, *Albuquerque Journal* (New Mexico), July 10, 1938; "Swiss Suit Names a Rich American," *New York Times*, June 4, 1938; "Guy Baer's Wife Wins Case in Swiss Court," *New York Times*, June 7, 1938.

CSV 1939 attempt to get secure money from Biltmore Company for her stake, from Covington, previously cited. NHL nomination, previously cited.

Six hundred people still working at estate, dairy operation first-time profit in 1936, $200,000 to CSV for family stake in Staten Island property from Covington, previously cited.

Axis diplomats, Germans, and Japanese at GPI, then recuperation for navy from Johnson, previously cited.

Jack Cecil to England: "Cecil to Sail to Join War," *New York Times*, Nov. 8, 1939.

George 14, William 11, when fighting began in Europe. 1941 from Switzerland to London. 1943 George in navy, from Covington, previously cited.

National Gallery letters to donors regarding art storage from Finley letters to various donors including Finley to Mr. Kress, dated Oct. 31, 1941. Shipping, storage of Whistler's painting from letter to ESV from C. Powell Minnigerode, dated Nov. 6, 1939, and Finley to ESV dated Nov. 16, 1939; Walker meeting with Adams and Beadle at BH, ban on pleasure driving affecting closure of Biltmore House from Junius Adams letter to David Finley, dated Jan. 14, 1943; caravan date cited in letter from H. A. McBride to David Finley dated Jan. 7, 1942; contents and valuation from "Installation Record" dated Jan. 13, 1942, Time to return paintings, letter from Finley to ESV dated Oct. 14, 1944, Finley thanks to Biltmore from letter to Junius Adams dated Oct. 14, 1944; National Gallery press release regarding return of art to Washington, DC, dated Oct. 21, 1944; Edith letter to Finley, "great privilege to be of service," dated 10-28-1944; All items here from holdings of the Gallery Archives, National Gallery of Art, Washington, DC.

ESV in DC volunteering, surgical dressings, during WWI: "Your Capitol Commentator," Jane Eads, Associated Press, Jan. 27, 1947; "Senate Ladies Meet Weekly," *Ironwood Daily Globe* (Michigan), Feb. 1, 1947.

1945: Best & Co. Purchases, 645 Fifth Avenue: "A Versace Restoration for a Vanderbilt Town House," Christopher Gray, *New York Times*, Apr. 9, 1995.

1947 640 torn down drawn from: *The Opulent Interiors of the Gilded Age*, Arnold Lewis, James Turner and Steven McQuillin (Mineola, NY: Dover Publications, Inc., 1987); and "Vanderbilt Home Being Torn Down: 5th Avenue Mansion Will Be Replaced With 19-story Business Structure," *New York Times*, Sep. 18, 1947.

American Express renovation of 647 Fifth Avenue in 1930 from "Versace Restoration," previously cited.

1947 George William drive to NC, Covington, previously cited.

1947 Cornelia wants to settle finances: The settlement of Cornelia's interest in the estate, the $2 million figure, and the disposition of it in two installments, the last coming in 1950, comes from two sources: NHL nomination, and Covington, previously cited.

Cornelia marriage to Vivian Bulkeley Johnson: "Cornelia Vanderbilt Married Second Time," *Kentucky New Era*, Oct. 13, 1949. "Cornelia Vanderbilt Secretly Marries British Banker," *Daily Times-News* (Burlington, NC), Oct. 13, 1949; Untitled newspaper clipping, *Star Tribune* (Minneapolis), Sept. 22, 1949.

GP, eugenics, death from: Pinchot listed on letterhead of the "American Eugenics Society Inc." in a letter regarding the planning of a public education fair.

"Culling the Herd: Eugenics and the Conservation Movement in the United States, 1900–1940," Garland E. Allen, Biology Faculty Publications & Presentations of Washington University in St. Louis, 2013; "Conservation and Eugenics," *New York Times*, June 30, 2010. Citing Charles Wohlforth in *Orion Magazine*; Death: Grey Towers National Historic Site (previously cited) and "The Life of Gifford Pinchot," Pennsylvania Department of Conservation and Natural Resources, dcnr.state.pa.us/stateparks/thingstoknow /history/lifeofgiffordpinchot/index.htm.

WBOF death, additional marriages, Lila death, children: "W. B. O. Field Weds Miss Erika Segnitz," *New York Times*, Jan. 1, 1936; also Biographical/ Historical Information, WBOF papers at NYPL, previously cited.

1950 George working at dairy and CSV receiving final payment from Biltmore Company, NHL nomination, previously cited.

ESV coronary attack, in March 1950 from NHL nomination, previously cited.

NBB death: "Mrs. Nicholas Brown Funeral Conducted," *Newport Daily News*, Mar. 30, 1950; "Mrs. Nicholas Brown Dies, Was Long Ill," *Newport Mercury* (RI), Mar. 31, 1950. Condolence telegrams to JNBII from NBB papers, previously cited.

Adams's letter regarding Beadle's death from NHL nomination, previously cited.

1951 Schenck to Redwood Grove, Pisgah: Schenck Redwood Grove Dedicated," *Oakland Tribune*, July 5, 1951; author visits to Cradle of Forestry.

Pinchot/GWV markers in California: The Prairie Creek Redwoods State Park in Humboldt County, CA, dedicates a redwood grove to the memory of Carl A. Schenck. The Schenck grove features markers dedicated to other prominent figures in US forestry, among them Frederick Law Olmsted and George W. Vanderbilt. From "History on the Road: Carl Alwin Schenck Grove, Prairie Creek Redwoods State Park, California," James G. Lewis, *Forest History Today*, Spring/Fall 2014, foresthistory.org/publications/FHT/FHTSpring Fall2014/SchenckGrove.pdf; also "Prairie Creed Redwoods State Park," Save The Redwoods League, savetheredwoods.org.

George Cecil's 1955 wedding as ESV's last visit to Biltmore, NHL nomination, previously cited.

Jack Cecil's death: "J. F. A. Cecil Dies at 64 in Hospital," *Asheville Citizen*, Oct. 23, 1954; "John Cecil, Ex-Aide of British Embassy," *New York Times*, Oct. 23, 1954.

ESV death: "Mrs. Peter G. Gerry, 83, Dies; Wealthy Widow of R.I. Senator," *Bridgeport Post* (Bridgeport, CT), Dec. 22, 1958.

The Frith deeded to William, Buck Spring Lodge to George, from the will and testament of ESV, probated Jan. 13, 1959, State of Rhode Island Probate Court of the City of Providence; Biltmore bequeathed to each grandson upon William's thirty-fifth birthday, from Covington, previously cited.

Biltmore Estate's first profit in 1967 or 1968, variously cited as $16.32 ("In 90

Years, Family Has Learned to Make Profit From Experience," Louise Lione, *Charlotte Observer*, Dec. 22, 1985), $16.34 ("The Baron of Biltmore," Jonathan Walters, *Historic Preservation*, May/June 1988; and Covington, previously cited), and $16.37 ("William A. V. Cecil: The Baron of Biltmore," Ralph Roberts, *Carolina Senior Citizen*, April 1990).

1968 attendance 96,000 visitors from Covington, previously cited.

Junius Adams death in 1962, Frazier and NHL Nomination, previously cited.

George president Biltmore Dairy Farms: NHL Nomination, previously cited.

CSV artworks: *Christ Carrying the Cross*, provenance from The J. Paul Getty Museum, getty.edu/art/collection/objects/780/attributed-to-marco-d'-oggiono-christ-carrying-the-cross-italian-about-1495-1500/; *The Magdalene at the Sepulchre*, provenance from The William Blake Archive, blakearchive.org/copy/biblicalwc?descId=but504.1.wc.01; *The Madonna and Child*, provenance from Christie's, christies.com/lotfinder/Lot/sano-di-pietro-siena-1405-1481-the-madonna-5916237-details.aspx; Chinese ceramics included Verte Baluster Vase dating from the Kangxi reign of Qing dynasty, provenance from Alain R. Truong, alaintruong2014.wordpress.com/tag/kangxi-period/page/7/; star sapphire bracelet provenance from Bonham's, bonhams.com/auctions/19753/lot/296/.

Mount Trust Collection and Mrs. Smith Fund/Mrs. Smith & Mount Trust: from "The Mrs Smith Fund," mrssmithandmounttrust.org/the-mrs-smith-fund/, also "History of the Trust," The Mrs Smith & Mount Trust, mrssmithandmounttrust.org/history/.

CSV life at Mount, Edward Adamson and friendship with CSV, quotes from letters, CSV advice to Adamson on business, CSV vision for Mrs. Smith Trust, drawn from letters from CSV to Adamson dated Jul. 16, 1963, Mar. 6, 1965, Mar. 26, 1965, and Nov. 11, 1966, All from Correspondence of Edward Adamson, Wellcome Library Archives, Great Britain.

Adamson background drawn from above and: "Edward Adamson, 84, Therapist Who Used Art to Aid Mentally Ill," Henry Fountain, *New York Times*, Feb. 10, 1996; obituary "Art As a Panacea: Edward Adamson," John Timlin, *Guardian* (Manchester, UK), Feb. 12, 1996.

JNBII and CSV cousin, Natalie, letter to JNBII dated July 11, 1975, JNBII papers.

Vivian Bulkeley-Johnson death 1968 from England & Wales, Civil registration Death index, 1916-2007, 1968, Q1, Jan-Feb-Mar. Exhibit: *The Mount Trust Collection of Chinese Art* (London: Victoria and Albert Museum, 1970).

CSV meeting William Goodsir at restaurant and wedding to Goodsir from in 1972 from letter of CSV cousin Natalie to JNBII, previously cited, also NHL doc, previously cited. Additional details about CSV death from "A Remarkable Life: Cornelia Stuyvesant Vanderbilt," Susan McKendree, posted on a Biltmore Facebook fan page that no longer exists. I copied the story and created the file Feb. 14, 2014.

Value of CSV estate at death from Last Will and Testament of Cornelia Mary Goodsir.

CSV ashes in Orkney Islands from Find A Grave, findagrave.com/cgi-bin /fg.cgi?page=gr&GRid=119723523; and McKendree.

Cucumber magnolia planted in 1900 to celebrate the birth of CSV was removed in 2008 due to age and decay, its timber used to build furnishings on the estate: from plaque on display at Biltmore Estate and author visits there; Alexander, previously cited; and "55" Cucumber Magnolia," Treebuzz, treebuzz.com /forum/threads/55-cucumber-magnolia.10442.

Epilogue

Description of the house today from repeated author visits over the last eleven years.

Music Room's opening in 1976: "Vanderbilt's 'house' is castle in every way," Martin Plessinger, *The Baltimore Sun*, Mar. 1, 1979; also Covington, previously cited.

Information about the modern company, ticket prices, etc., from Biltmore.com.

Challenges of being private rather than nonprofit, from Lione, Covington, and Walters, previously cited.

Anti-Biltmore comments from "Asheville Junction's New Name," previously cited.

Biltmore "named" companies from search of local phone listings in the Asheville area.

Use of the Biltmore name prior to 1890, based on extensive searches on newspaper database (newspapers.com) and books of the period.

Biltmore Hotel, New York City, from "A Rendezvous with 1,000 Rooms," Christopher Gray, *New York Times*, Mar. 21, 2013, nytimes.com/2013/03/24 /realestate/a-long-gone-rendezvous-with-1000-rooms.html.

Versace store "Versace Restoration," previously cited.

2 Gramercy Square info from *Exploring Gramercy Park and Union Square*, Alfred Pommer & Joyce Pommer (Charleston, SC: The History Press, 2015), and "The James Pinchot House—No. 2 Gramercy Park," Tom Miller, Aug. 1, 2014, *A Daytonian in Manhattan*, daytoninmanhattan.blogspot .com/2014/08/the-james-pinchot-house-no-2-gramercy.html.

Wharton's home at 14 West Twenty-Third Street, New York, NY, now a Starbucks, from "From Wharton's Window, the Ghosts of a Scandalous New Year's," Mark Lewis, Dec. 26, 2008, *New York Times*, nytimes.com/2008/12/28 /nyregion/thecity/28whar.html.

Guastavino works in New York City, from Ochsendorf, previously cited; Guastavino's event space beneath Queensboro Bridge from guastavinos.com; Hunt works in New York City from Baker, previously cited; Olmsted's works in New York City from Rybczynski, previously cited; and author visits. Basilica of St. Lawrence, largest freestanding elliptical dome in North America, from author visits to basilica, also "National Register of Historic Places Travel Itinerary, Asheville, NC, National Park Service, US Department of the Interior, nps.gov/nr/travel/asheville/stl.htm.

Beer City title is derived from an online poll in which the city tied with Portland, Oregon, in 2009; won outright in 2010 and 2011; and tied with Grand Rapids, MI in 2012, from "Asheville Tops Portland as Best City for Beer Drinkers," Mackensy Lunsford, Dec. 28, 2016, *Asheville Citizen-Times*, citizen-times.com/story/entertainment/dining/2016/12/28/asheville-tops-portland-best-city-beer-drinkers/95915690/.

More breweries per capita, from "Which U.S. Cities Have the Most Microbreweries Per Capita?" Niall McCarthy, Nov. 1, 2016, *Forbes*, forbes.com/sites/niallmccarthy/2016/11/01/which-u-s-cities-have-the-most-microbreweries-per-capita-infographic/.

Biltmore Winery visitation, from "Biltmore Winery, Nation's Most-Visited Wine Maker, Turns 30," Tony Kiss, May 13, 2015, *Greenville Online*, greenville online.com/story/entertainment/2015/05/13/biltmore-winery-asheville/70892612/.

Pellegrini bed setting from Biltmore.com, biltmore.com/blog/article/pellegrini-bedding-collection.

Hunger Games, other movies, from "Top Movie Film Locations in Asheville and North Carolina Mountains," Mar. 13, 2012, PRNewswire.com, prnewswire.com/news-releases/top-movie-film-locations-in-asheville-and-north-carolina-mountains-142459425.html.

The assertion that George W. Vanderbilt remains a "mystery" from "In Time for 75th Birthday, Biltmore Adds a Look at Life Backstairs," Tim Whitmire/Associated Press, as seen in *USA Today*, July 18, 2005, usatoday30.usatoday.com/travel/hotels/2005-07-18-biltmore_x.htm.

CSV's continued philanthropy from website of The Mrs. Smith and Mount Trust, mrssmithandmounttrust.org, previously cited. Total assets of charities, from "The Mrs Smith & Mount Trust, Annual Report and Financial Statements for the Year Ended 31 January 2016, Registered Charity No: 1009718," Charity Commission for England and Wales. Phone conversations and email correspondence with the trust's solicitors reveal that they remain strictly private to this day, divulging little information about the identity and past of its benefactress. The Trust offers grants in areas such as mental health, learning disabilities, and homelessness, among others, designed to "assist disadvantage people towards greater independence or a better quality of life." In the financial year ending Jan. 31, 2016, the trust as a whole distributed £244,278 to various organizations.

"700,000 . . . toilets," from "Profile: William Amherst Vanderbilt Cecil: Opening His Door to 700,000 Visitors," Allen R. Myerson, *New York Times*, Dec. 13, 1992.

Canola oil, etc., from "Clean Energy Tour" of the Biltmore Estate, showcasing the estate's 6-acre, 1.2 megawatt solar array and 60-acre canola field, conducted Mar. 15, 2014, under the auspices of the Western North Carolina Alliance.

INDEX

INDEX

ABOUT THE AUTHOR

Denise Kiernan is a journalist and author whose work has appeared in *The New York Times, The Wall Street Journal,* the *Village Voice, Ms., Reader's Digest, Discover,* and other publications. Her previous book, *The Girls of Atomic City,* was a *New York Times, Los Angeles Times,* and NPR bestseller. She lives in North Carolina. Visit the author at www.denisekiernan.com.

THE LAST CASTLE

DENISE KIERNAN

This reading group guide for The Last Castle *includes discussion questions and ideas for enhancing your book club. The suggested questions are intended to help your reading group find new and interesting angles and topics for your discussion. We hope that these ideas will enrich your conversation and increase your enjoyment of the book.*

TOPICS & QUESTIONS
FOR DISCUSSION

1. Why do you think Denise Kiernan chose to title her book *The Last Castle*? In what ways does Biltmore function like a castle for George Vanderbilt and his family? How does it differ?

2. Edith Vanderbilt's mother hailed from the Fish-LeRoy and Stuyvesant families. These families were "exceptionally well known in New York circles where names carried the weight of history and bore the shackles of expected romantic pairings" (p. 3). What expectations do Edith; her mother, Susan Fish LeRoy; and their peers face with regard to marriage? Do you think these expectations lead to some disastrous marital pairings among Edith's peers? If so, give some examples.

3. Describe the origins of the name that George chooses for his Asheville estate. What does "Biltmore" signify? Why do you think it's important for George to choose a name for his estate? The citizens of Asheville have mixed reactions to the name "Biltmore." Discuss them.

4. Kiernan describes William B. Osgood Field as being "like the Nick Carraway to George's Gatsby: playing matchmaker, yet unable to keep up with his friend financially" (p. 99). Describe George's friendship with Field. Do you think Kiernan's comparison is apt? Why or why not? What other friendships are particularly important to George?

5. When Field accompanies George Vanderbilt to Europe, George's sisters inform Field that "he should be more than George's companion on this trip. He should seek to help George land his life's companion" (p. 81). Why do George's sisters think that Edith is a good match for him? Do you agree? What considerations must someone of George's social class take into account when looking for a spouse?

6. During the Gilded Age, being "a son of the Vanderbilt dynasty was to have your every move, dalliance, chance encounter, and passing venture watched and analyzed" (pp. 7–8). Why do you think the public is so interested in the lives of the Vanderbilt family? Discuss the impact the constant public scrutiny has on the behavior of its members. Can you think of any modern equivalents that are scrutinized in the same way the Vanderbilt family was in their time? Who are they?

7. In letters, George's niece, Adele, describes herself as "Biltmore homesick" (p. 46). What does she mean by this expression? Why does Adele enjoy herself so much during her visits to Biltmore? How is life better for women of Adele's social class on country estates? What freedoms are afforded to them that they do not have while they are in cities?

8. One of Edith's great strengths was that she "strode deftly between . . . two worlds, one of Victorian elegance, the other of rugged mountain simplicity" (p. 156). How is Edith able to move between these two vastly different realms? What about her upbringing may have prepared her for this balance? In what ways is Edith able to make herself an integral part of the greater community in Asheville?

9. When Cornelia is born, the locals honor her by "conferring the 'tar heel' moniker upon [her]" (p. 134). How does Cornelia's birth connect George and Edith with the community in Ashe-

ville? Why do the residents feel a sense of ownership over her? Describe Cornelia's connection to her birthplace as an adult. Were you surprised by it?

10. In 1873, Mark Twain and coauthor Charles Dudley Warner wrote a book about the age of excess in which they lived titled *The Gilded Age: A Tale of Today*. Do you think "Gilded Age" is an appropriate title for the time? If so, why? Would you have liked to live during the Gilded Age? Why or why not?

11. Why does George Vanderbilt elect to build Biltmore in Asheville, North Carolina? What is the effect that Biltmore has on the region socially, economically, and in terms of infrastructure? If you could build an estate anywhere, where would you do so? Explain your answer.

12. Kiernan writes that Biltmore "may not have been in New York or Newport, but if this house didn't make an impression on the Four Hundred, nothing would, acorns or no" (p. 66). Explain this statement. What kind of impression did Biltmore make on visitors? Was there anything you found particularly impressive about the house?

13. When President McKinley expresses a desire to visit Biltmore, E. J. Harding, the auditor of Biltmore Estate, specifies that McKinley, his wife, and any cabinet members are welcome to the estate, but the media is not. Why does Harding object to the presence of the press? Is he right in doing so? How does the press interact with members of the Four Hundred and with the president? Why do you think McKinley might want to have press during his visit?

14. Lillian Exum Clement, who became the first female legislator in North Carolina, said, "I know that years from now there will be many other women in politics, but you have to start a thing"

(p. 245). Discuss the role that women played in politics prior to the ratification of the Nineteenth Amendment. In what ways were women active before they were granted the right to vote?

15. As a young man, George Vanderbilt tells Field that he wants to see the world before getting married, and that when he does get married, "he imagined she would perhaps be ten years his junior" (p. 85). Contrast George's philosophy for finding a life partner with Field's. Do you agree with either of the men? Which one and why? Given the men's philosophies, were you surprised by the choices they made in choosing their spouses?

ENHANCE YOUR BOOK CLUB

1. At a young age, George Vanderbilt began to keep a series of notebooks titled "Books I Have Read" in which he recorded all the literary and academic texts that he consumed. Create your own list and share it with your book club. Do any of your book club members have titles on their lists that intrigue you? Pick a selection from your shared lists for your next book club meeting.

2. Kiernan writes that "walking the halls of Biltmore House for a day is a journey back in time" (p. 297). Visit Biltmore's official website at Biltmore.com and take a virtual tour of the estate through the site's photo gallery. Was there anything about the house and the grounds that you found particularly striking? If so, what?

3. Edith Wharton became the first woman to receive the Pulitzer Prize for her novel, *The Age of Innocence*. Read the novel with your book club. Discuss the ways in which it depicts upper-class society. Would you have liked to live during this time? Why or why not?

4. To learn more about Denise Kiernan and find out if she will be in a city near you, visit her official website at denisekiernan.com. You can also connect with Denise at facebook.com/DeniseKiernan Author, Twitter.com/DeniseKiernan, and Instagram.com/iamde nisekiernan for updates about her writing and tour schedule.

A CONVERSATION WITH
DENISE KIERNAN

The story behind Biltmore Estate and its influence on the Asheville, North Carolina, community is fascinating. What attracted you to it?
A combination of factors played into it. I visited Biltmore for the first time while I was still in high school and loved the grounds in particular. I never anticipated, at that time, that I would ever live in Asheville. When my husband and I moved here more than eleven years ago now, I had the opportunity to visit as an adult and fell in love with the place. I was also stunned at how many people I knew—especially in other parts of the country—who had no idea about the rich history of Biltmore, let alone the fact that no other house in the United States has ever come close to equaling it in size. I kept collecting information over the years, the way I do with lots of ideas, but this one wouldn't leave me alone. Then I just felt that it was time to write about it.

***The Last Castle* is meticulously detailed. Can you tell us how you conducted your research?**
I spent many, many hours buried in old documents, letters, newspaper clippings, and photographs. I traveled to New York; Washington, DC; Providence, Rhode Island; and elsewhere to dig into archives. I read books, researched academic journals, and also spoke to longtime residents of Asheville whose family members would tell stories of the house and the family. And of course, I have visited the house countless times over the years.

Your previous book, *The Girls of Atomic City*, was a *New York Times*, *Los Angeles Times*, and NPR bestseller and was named one of Amazon's Top 100 Best Books of 2013. As a result of all this acclaim, did you feel any added pressure when you were writing *The Last Castle*? How did you combat it?

I absolutely do feel more pressure, but I think that's unavoidable. To combat it, I speak to other writer friends who have been in the same situation. I also look to the experiences of extremely well-known authors whom I admire greatly from afar who have endured ups and downs in their careers. Overall, I feel incredibly fortunate that *Girls* did so well and that I have been given the opportunity to share another story I find fascinating with readers.

Your descriptions of Biltmore in *The Last Castle* make the estate come alive. Do you have any favorite parts of the estate? Which parts would you advise visitors not to miss and why?

As a writer, I am absolutely in love with the library. It is a spectacular sight. I really enjoy the view from the loggia and like to stand out there and try to spot wild turkeys. The view is astounding. The basement is remarkable. It is fantastic to get into the bowels of the house and marvel at what a massive undertaking Biltmore House was on a technological level and try to envision the space buzzing during the holidays in the early 1900s or when famous visitors came to call. So much has been preserved in the house that you really can let your imagination take you back a hundred or so years.

For both your *Signers* and *Stuff* series, you worked with a coauthor. How did that experience differ from that of writing *The Last Castle*? Does your writing process change when you're collaborating versus working independently? If so, how?

That's kind of a loaded question, because in that situation the coauthor was my husband, Joseph D'Agnese (josephdagnese.com). Collaboration can be challenging for writers, because most of us are used to spending hours alone inside of our own heads. For Joe and me, the general approach is that what one of us writes, the other edits. In the beginning, we write and swap smaller sections until we're fairly confident that we have arrived at the same voice. Even when we are working on our own titles, we are each other's first reader, and it is very helpful to have an in-house editor. We disagree at times, but so far the marriage has survived it.

As a *New York Times* bestselling author, do you have any advice for aspiring writers? Is there anything that you wish you had known before beginning your career?

The advice I will give is the advice I still work to follow: 1) Write every day. It's a muscle. It's a skill. You need to work out to stay in shape. 2) Also incredibly important—and this one can be difficult to follow—is to give yourself permission to write really, really badly. Write a horrible first draft, but get it out of your system. If you're obsessing about things being perfect along the way . . . they won't be. Also, you are a better editor once you have the whole thing down. Books are often best edited with the entire text in mind, no matter how drastically you end up changing it. 3) Be careful who you share your work with and when. Outside readers are very important, and you want ones who will be both astoundingly blunt *and* considerate of how unnerving feedback can be. You want someone who is critiquing you from a frank yet compassionate place. You don't want people telling you everything is great—that's a red flag—but you also don't want creative saboteurs, either. 4) TURN OFF THE INTERNET. You don't have to do it all day, but you need large stretches of quiet for things to rumble around a bit.

In addition to your career as a *New York Times* bestselling author, you are a professional producer. Has your background as a producer helped you in your writing career? If so, how?

I think perhaps it helps me visualize scenes. I like to think visually when I write and keep lots of images around. It certainly helps with project management as well. There can be a lot of moving parts when you're promoting one book, traveling for research for another, and still needing time to write. I like visual storytelling, and sometimes thinking of how a story might be told on film or television gives me structural ideas when I write.

What would you like readers to take away from *The Last Castle*?
Honestly, whatever they want. Over the years, I have heard so many different reactions to and perspectives on books I've written—I can never anticipate what they are going to be. I also would never want to tell anyone what to think about anything I've written. Everyone brings a little bit of themselves to stories they read, and I sincerely hope the story of *The Last Castle* is relatable enough that readers will be able to engage with it in their own unique way. I, personally, find the philanthropic activities—not just check writing—that Edith, especially, engaged in rather inspiring. I also find that no matter how much money you have, there is no protection from harrowing tragedy and personal loss. What is impressive to me is how people handle those kinds of situations.

Is there anything you have found particularly rewarding about publishing *The Last Castle*? Can you tell us about it?
More of my friends are interested in actually reading *The Last Castle*—as opposed to just buying it to support me—than *The Girls of Atomic City*. I know a lot of folks who don't want to read about science or war, so it has been nice to hear from people who have been genuinely excited about the book. It's fun to dive into a different time and place for a while.

Are you working on anything now? Can you tell us about it?
Yes, I am, and no . . . I won't. Nonfiction can be tricky, because history belongs to all of us. No one has "dibs" on anything. In the early stages of a book, I am very protective of my material, in part because if I've come across a way of discussing a certain moment in history, I want to make sure I hang on to that. Also, and this is probably more important, I am HORRIBLE at discussing things in the early stages, and I don't want to turn off anyone unnecessarily.

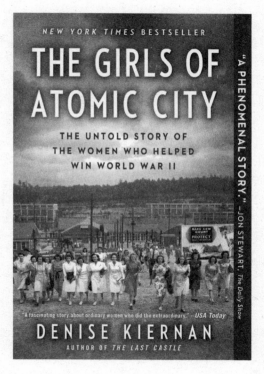